THE CHARITABLE ARBITRATOR

THE CHARITABLE ARBITRATOR

How to Mediate and Arbitrate in Louis XIV's France

DEREK ROEBUCK

HOLO BOOKS
THE ARBITRATION PRESS
2002

First published 2002 by
HOLO Books: The Arbitration Press
Clarendon House
52 Cornmarket
Oxford OX1 3HJ
email: holobooks@yahoo.co.uk
www.umbrellabooks.com

ISBN 0 9537730 2 7

10   9   8   7   6   5   4   3   2   1

Designed and produced for HOLO Books: The Arbitration Press by
Chase Publishing Services, Fortescue, Sidmouth EX10 9QG
Printed in the European Union

for

St John's School Dukinfield
The Manchester Grammar School
Hertford College Oxford

who taught me more than I know

and now to the memory of
Judy Hoe

who died 2 February 2002
la belle-mère la meilleure du monde

SPONSORS

The author expresses his deepest gratitude to the sponsors, those individuals and organisations whose names are listed here. They made publication possible. Michael Shone organised that sponsorship. The book is offered as a small token of what can be achieved by French and English cooperation in the avoidance, management and resolution of disputes.

En beuvant, il s'y fait bien des accords
[Alexandre de la Roche] *L'Arbitre Charitable* XXIII, 7

Les Caves de Landiras

Caves des Vignerons de Rasteau, Vaucluse

Gabriel et Andreu Cognac Ferrand, Bordeaux

M Jean-David Guedj, Paris

M Guy Lepage, COFACE, Paris

Me Jean-Étienne Leva, Cabinet Leva et Associées, Paris

Michael Shone, Commercial Intelligence, Singapore

Yvon Mau SA, La Reole

Unicognac SA, Jonzac

Vinival SRL, La Sablette de Mouzillon, Vallet

William Pitters Guilde du Vin, Lormont

THE CHARITABLE ARBITRATOR

TO
PREVENT SUITS
AND DISPUTES,
Or, at least to finish them quickly,
without trouble and cost.

This will be easily done

If the Bishops and Parish Priests,
Provincial Governors, and Lords of Great Fiefs,
Are Pleased to be Mediators,
As they formerly were and are obliged to be,
by the Gospel, the Fathers, the Canons, the Councils,
and the Ordinances of our Kings.

*Monsieur le Prince de Conty appropriately did so during his life
in his own lands and in his public offices*

And Our Monarch, in the midst of all his cares, takes great pains
to give public audiences even to the least of his Subjects,
to bring their suits and differences to a prompt conclusion.

*After such an illustrious example, who can refuse to approve
the good intentions of our Prince?*

Presented to the KING in the year 1668

By the Prior of S. PIERRE

PARIS
LAURENS RAVENEAU
In the Street and at the Door of Saint Victor

MDCLXVIII
WITH THE APPROBATION AND PRIVILEGE OF THE KING

CONTENTS

LIST OF ILLUSTRATIONS

PREFACE

In July 1998[1] I found in the British Library catalogue an item in French called *To Avoid Litigation*.... Its full title showed it to be a book on mediation and arbitration from Paris in the time of Louis XIV. Once in my hands it revealed itself to be a call for reform by an author, apparently a clergyman called Alexandre de la Roche, who was not only knowledgeable about but experienced in the practice of mediation and arbitration in Paris, in other parts of France and even in other countries. Moreover, he was clearly committed to extending their use as a cure for the evils of the chicanery which he saw was a blight on the body politic.

Being no expert in French, let alone that of the time of Louis XIV, and knowing little of French society or its legal system, I determined to read the book as an important contribution to a general history of arbitration, based on primary sources.[2] But to find its meaning I had to understand its context. I became convinced that it had such relevance that a translation into English should be published with such introductory material as would help to make it understood. There is always a danger that those who today work so hard for the improvement of systems to resolve disputes without litigation will be handicapped by their assumption that ideas are new which have already been thought and tested. That is my excuse for not heeding the proverb: *'chacun à son métier, les vaches seront bien gardées'*.[3]

The introductory chapters, which make up Part One, cannot hope to give more than a sketch of the context. The first three describe what was happening in France at the time, the elements of the legal system which produced the problems La Roche was

---

1 Just too late for inclusion in 'Sources for the History of Arbitration' 1998.
2 The first volume has recently been published: *Arbitration in Ancient Greece* 2001; the second, *Roman Arbitration*, (with Bruno de Loynes de Fumichon) is due in 2003.
3 'Each to their trade, the cows will be well watched'.

eager to solve, and other contemporary attempts to reform the law. Chapter 4 provides some biographical information about the people he introduces. I have not found out as much as I would have liked about the author. He may be what he seems, Alexandre de la Roche, Sieur de la Rivière, Prior of St Pierre. I call him La Roche for convenience. My doubts and difficulties are set out in Chapter 5. Because of its comparative interest, and inaccessibility, Champlair's pamphlet *L'Ami de la Concorde* is quoted at length in Chapter 3, with Voltaire's earlier comments, which Champlair quotes.

Part Two is my translation of La Roche's text, as it appears in the second edition. I have shown where it varies from the first or fourth but have not been able to find a copy of the third, which I suspect to be an almost identical reprint of the second, as the fourth is. Chapter numbers have arabic numerals for the Introduction, roman numerals for the Text in Translation. For the sake of consistency, accents are used according to modern conventions, though they did not appear uniformly in the earlier material.

Part Three is the whole of the French text of the first edition in facsimile. Five of the eight plates illustrate arbitrations. They come from the second edition, inserted, as La Roche said, for those who cannot read or are too lazy to bother. The others are the title page of Champlair, a facsimile of the elusive *arrest* of Henri IV and an etching by Bosse, showing a lawyer's office of the same period.

I thank all those who have helped to produce this book. Ray Addicott is much more than the production manager. He has helped at all stages, with advice on every technical aspect of the book. Michael Shone has encouraged me with enthusiasm and organised the support of the sponsors, who have made the publication possible. Their names are set out on p. vi.

None of the research on which this work is based would have been possible without the help of libraries, in particular the Taylorian, the Athenaeum and the Bibliothèque Nationale. The British Library provided copies of the five La Roche plates from the second edition, the Sackler library for the Bosse. Their permissions to reproduce them are acknowledged with thanks. The Beinecke Library of Yale University and the University of Iowa Library supplied copies of other editions. I gratefully acknowledge the generosity of the Centre d'Accueil et de Recherche des Archives Nationales (CARAN) in allowing the reproduction of the plates of the *arrest* of Henri IV.

I have also been greatly encouraged by the support of Professor Charles Jarrosson.

My untutored work on La Roche's text made submission of the results to an expert as anxious as it was necessary. I could not have wished for a more careful, prompt and scholarly response than that of David Sturdy, who read the proofs and saved me from errors of form and substance. It is specially pleasing to have his evidence to confirm my lifelong belief that generosity is one mark of the true scholar.

My wife, Susanna Hoe, my partner in this as in all my endeavours, has watched over every step in the work and read every draft.

I am happy to be able to dedicate this book to those places of learning which tried so hard to make a scholar of me.

Derek Roebuck
Oxford
January 2002

PART ONE

INTRODUCTION

1 BACKGROUND, SCHEME AND STYLE

Philinte Against your opponent rant on a bit less
And lend to the lawsuit a bit of your mind.
Alceste I'll not give a second – it's open and shut.
Philinte But who do you want, then, to take up your case?
Alceste Reason! The merits! And equity, too!
Philinte And no-one to call on the judge with a bribe?[1]

THE BACKGROUND

The period is 1665 to 1668. It starts with England at war with Holland and ends with them both in alliance against France. Charles II is on the throne of England and Louis XIV, king since 1643 (at the age of five), has been settled into his personal rule for five years.[2]

In France Molière, Corneille, Racine and La Fontaine are at the height of their powers and in England Milton, Dryden, Bunyan and Hobbes. It is the time of Rembrandt and Vermeer and Bernini. In Paris the great east front of the Louvre is being finished in the new French style and the first plans for Versailles begun. London is suffering from the plague and the Great Fire gives birth to Wren's rebuilding. Descartes has just published his pioneering work on physiology and geometry and is becoming influential and Newton would soon start working on gravity and calculus.

---

1 Molière *Le Misanthrope* (1666).
Philinte *Contre votre partie éclatez un peu moins*
Et donnez au procès une part de vos soins.
Alceste *Je n'en donnerai point, c'est une chose dite.*
Philinte *Mais que voulez-vous donc qui pour vous sollicite?*
Alceste *Qui je veux? La raison, mon bon droit, l'équité.*
Philinte *Aucun juge par vous ne sera visité?*
2 Roger Mettam *Government and Society in Louis XIV's France* 1977; David J Sturdy *Louis XIV* 1998.

La Roche has a bee in his bonnet. He is determined to do something about what he considers France's worst failing: chicanery. Litigation is everywhere, passionate and never-ending. It has nothing to do with the merits. It ruins rich and poor alike. It keeps peasants from their farms, lords from their estates, priests from their parishes and nuns from their convents. It leads to duels which in some families have killed off grandfather, father and son. It keeps good Christians away from the sacraments by the animosities it arouses. Neither the King nor the Church has been able to stop these evils. La Roche knows the answer: arbitration.[3]

THE SCHEME OF THE MANUAL

La Roche's primary purpose is to persuade. He wants to get rid of chicanery, as he calls the evils of litigation, by persuading his readers to seek an amicable settlement of all their disputes by mediation and, if necessary, arbitration instead of lawsuits. He takes pains to stress that it is arbitration that is the answer, not the amelioration of litigation.[4] For him, 'arbitration is a holy and a sacred thing, and something more venerable than mere judging. Because, as well as judging, you are trying to reconcile their hearts.'[5]

In the France of the middle of the seventeenth century arbitration was not only a desirable substitute for litigation. As it had

3   At this period, as has been usual in most times and places, mediation towards a mutually acceptable compromise was naturally a part of the arbitration process. Each party chose one arbitrator, who together chose a third unless the parties could agree on one, or some other system applied, as the author recommends in Chapter XXI, paragraph 3. A decade before, Cromwell had asked William Sheppard for his advice on law reform. In his *England's Balme*, published in London in 1656, Sheppard recommended arbitration, see NL Matthews *William Sheppard, Cromwell's Law Reformer* 1984 pp144–52, 151: 'The initial effort to avoid litigation called upon the assistance of local arbitrators, or daysmen, chosen by the adversaries as their representatives in mediation ... In Sheppard's generation, arbitration was still widely used ... Sheppard's innovation was simply to elevate this familiar process to the status of a required pre-litigation procedure.' Also Donald Veall *The Popular Movement for Law Reform 1640–1660* 1970 170–71. See footnote 7 on English legislation in Chapter 2 below and the first line of Chapter XXXIV. A century later, some of La Roche's indignation is repeated in Champlair's *L'Ami de la Concorde* 1779, discussed in Chapter 3.

4   Nor the use of charitable lawyers in litigation, see for example Chapter III, section 2: 'this is an arbitration and a settlement, which is something better than judgments and sentences'.

5   Chapter XXIII, para 7.

been elsewhere since at least the time of Homer, it was an alternative to private as well as international[6] war, to the duelling which still bedevilled France, though one monarch after another had legislated to prohibit it.[7]

La Roche's first weapon is authority. His highest but most general is Christ's injunction and blessing – peace be unto you! But most of all he hammers home, with conscious repetition, the clear religious authority of the Gospel (in which he includes the Epistles), Fathers, Canons and Councils and the temporal authority of the capitularies, *édits* and *ordonnances* of the rulers of France from Charlemagne to the present Louis XIV.[8]

Secondly he cites precedents.[9] What he is recommending is nothing new, speculative or radical. It has already been put into practice – without trouble or expense – by a host of practitioners

6 War between feudal chiefs was still an option in the thirteenth century if one of them found an arbitral award unacceptable, François Olivier-Martin *Histoire du Droit Français des Origines à la Révolution* 1948 s166.

7 Chapter XXVIII. This legislation is too voluminous even to cite here. Louis XIV was active in the suppression of duels at this time. An *édit* of his grandfather Henry IV stated the objective: 'We enjoin all our said subjects, of whatever quality and condition they may be, to live in future one with another in peace, union and concord, without insulting, harming, despising or provoking to hatred or enmity, on pain of incurring our displeasure and exemplary punishment.' *Édit* against Duels, Fontainebleau June 1609 s1, in Jourdan, Decrusy and Isambert eds *Recueil Général des Anciennes Lois* 1822–33 XV pp351, 353, cited hereafter as *Anciennes Lois*. See Sully in Chapter 2 below and on duels, Francois Billacois *The Duel* 156ff and 184n65.

8 The authorities are reiterated: Jesus Christ (2); Saints Paul (10+), Augustine (3), Ambrose, Yves (2) and the eight canonised French bishops mentioned in Chapter III; Solomon (3) and Job; Aristotle and Plato; kings Charlemagne (9), St Louis IX (2), Louis Auguste (4), Henry IV (7), Louis XII and Louis XIV (10+). He also cites legal authority both secular and spiritual: capitularies, *édits*, *ordonnances* and letters circular, and even the law of nations and mercantile custom; the Gospel, Fathers, Canons and many individual Councils. He seems to have discovered these legal authorities between the first and second editions.

9 He ranges widely: religious communities including the primitive Church, the contemporary Eastern Church and even the Huguenots; from Paris the Archbishop, the President of the *Parlement*, the nobility's convention, the parish of St Sulpice, the judge of the *faubourg*, the *Procureur-Général*'s work with prisoners; from elsewhere in France Henry IV's scheme in Provence, and other initiatives in Brittany and in Lyons, Nantes and Clermont; and the activities of the Ducs de Sully, de Liancourt and de Luynes, the Duchesse de Longueville, the Marquis de Sillery, *Chancelier de France*, and various named persons of importance, including regular arbitrators; and of course the estimable republic of Venice.

religious and lay, in France and abroad. They do it in Venice, giving that republic the reputation of being the most advanced in Europe – to France's shame, it is implied.[10] Even the Huguenots do it, to the shame of the Catholics.[11] The Eastern Church as well – just like the primitive Church did. In France, bishops, abbots, priests and the religious orders, as well as the highest temporal authorities, including not only the saintly Prince de Conti but the King himself, already go some way towards it.

Thirdly, there are the examples of individual settlements. The behaviour of the ingrate son who left his aged father with 'only a handful of straw' is held up as an example of the worst of chicanery; and contrasted with that of the bishop who sat in the pouring rain outside the door of the recalcitrant litigious lord. And there are the disputes whose settlement has been accomplished to the joy of all. They have included quarrels in which the parties have been bishops, abbots, chapters, priests and convents, as well as the great lords whose disputes so readily produce duels.

Fourthly, there are the handy tips – the holy artifices as La Roche calls them – whereby disputing parties can be brought to agree to submit to arbitration: 'to make them do good in spite of themselves'. The great lord is well advised to pay his stewards according to the litigation they avoid; it is a good idea to keep a stock of forms so that they are on hand when you need them to incorporate a compromise; it is better for the arbitrators to sit in a religious house than in a tavern; get the parties to write just four lines setting out on one side how much they think the litigation is going to cost them in money, time and trouble and, on the other, the most they could hope to gain if all went well. Most important, make them start by identifying the issue.

The characteristics of a good mediator, and of a good arbitrator, are discussed in depth. Probity and patience are the

---

10 La Roche may well have relied here on what he had read in Antoine de Laujorrois *Advis pour l'Institution Charitable des Advocats et Procureurs &c* 1610 p104, who similarly praised Venice's Order of the Procureurs of St Mark, who (he says) gave their services free but were rewarded on their retirement by membership of the Senate, see Chapter 2 below.

11 La Roche is no bigot. He speaks respectfully of the Huguenots in general and makes no secret of his regard for individuals such as the Duc de Sully, who remained a Huguenot, and the Jansenist Duc de Liancourt.

first requirements, all supported by *charité*, by which he means goodwill. These recommendations are supported by practice and procedure hints and by forms and precedents of the documents likely to be needed in practice.

There are statistics, too. The Church in France has more than 30,000 parishes. If the curé could only bring about the settlement of twenty lawsuits in each, that would be 600,000 less every year.[12]

Underlying all this persuasion and instruction are the threats. The Councils impose excommunication on those who fail to respond to the appeal the celebrant always makes to them before they partake of the sacrament of communion. The priest calls on all communicants to make up their differences, to avoid that hatred which disqualifies the Christian from the grace of God.[13] Nor is La Roche afraid to remind Louis XIV[14] that the crown is reserved for those kings who persevere until they have successfully accomplished that justice, especially for the poor, which the Gospels demand.

The good curé knows how to deal with a member of his flock who will not heed the shepherd. He goes to the wife of the man determined to litigate and asks her to persuade him towards arbitration. If that does not work, he reminds her that God is not mocked. A heavy hint that evil befalls the stubborn is appropriate at that stage. Then wait a while. To every family in the space of a year comes a satisfactory share of grief. A member dies or falls sick; business is bad. Only the gentlest of reminders is then necessary. 'Vexation produces understanding', as the good Prior says; 'When you are smitten you return to the faith.'[15]

STYLE

La Roche denies any claim to rhetorical skill – perhaps the oldest rhetorical device – and admits his boring repetition is intended

---

12 At the end of Chapter XX. That would help bring about the reduction in the waste of human resources which Colbert deplored, see Chapter 3.
13 La Roche mentions this risk of excommunication at least nine times.
14 Directly, in the prefatory Epistle to the King, p23.
15 At the end of Chapter IV. In similar forms, such as 'suffering is learning', this saying has been well known at least since Aeschylus's *Agamemnon*, and may even underpin all tragic drama, H Dörrie 'Leid und Erfahrung' 1956; Albin Lecky *A History of Greek Literature* 1996.

for the parish priest who takes a while to understand:[16] 'Even the least efficient and the least intelligent of preachers, monks and nuns, whom one does not want to discourage, can manage it if you tell them often and carefully enough.'[17] And for anyone who cannot read there are pictures – 'persuasive for the common people' – to show them what has been and can be done.[18] And, as he repeats endlessly, he can show that all he is asking for can be done 'without trouble or expense'.

Repetition, though, is by no means the only or the most effective element of the author's style. He speaks most effectively from his own experience. He is not averse to exaggeration or afraid to push his arguments beyond what his evidence or authority can support. In Louis XIV's opposition to duels and in his granting of regular audiences for the resolution of disputes he finds sufficient authority for his statements about the King's support of mediation and arbitration generally. He interprets an *arrest* of Henry IV's, which would have set up a legal aid scheme by which *avocats* and *procureurs* would have provided gratuitous services to the poor, as if it had set up a system of charitable arbitrators. Moreover, to prove it, one of the pictures in the second edition, withdrawn in the fourth, shows the arbitrators in session.[19]

He is also blessed with a command of metaphor and allusion which often add life to his arguments. He conjures up images of the unfortunate litigant, whether pauper or great lord or bishop, burdened with worry and forced to bustle about the courts, like a messenger who leaves before he arrives, a law court rat with paws full of waste paper, or a desk caterpillar, engulfed in the

16 In the first lines of Chapter I. He repeats his formulas 'Gospel, Fathers, Canons and Councils and the *Ordonnances* of the Kings' in much the same words at least ten times. Duels usually arise from 'passionate and never-ending' quarrels. Litigation is repeatedly compared with war.
17 Chapter XX.
18 Though he points out that it is cheaper to print the book without them, p66. The five which appear in the second edition are not in the first edition, which calls for a different picture 'of the misfortunes of the litigant' – 'to persuade the common people', though it is missing in the only copy I have found, as discussed in Chapter 5.
19 This picture (see p. 210) is not in the first or fourth edition. No copy of the third seems to have survived in any of the major libraries. A translation of the *arrest* is given in Chapter 2 below.

wars of the desk.[20] And the cost! To get justice you must eat an ox to save an egg.[21]

And he knows what lawyers are like. The lawyer's gown is 'the feather of the eagle ... their neighbourliness is that of the wolf, their companionship that of the lion, who wants the lot'. Litigants who will only act through a lawyer may find they have asked the wolf to save the sheep. Judges are no better. There is not a meadow or a vineyard close to their house which is safe from them. You would never litigate against them – that would be to gamble with a cheat in his own den. They all hold hands throughout the whole country. But all those with lawsuits, like the bishops who complain that the judges are biased against them, have the answer in their own hands. A healthy man needs no doctor. Get rid of the litigation and fear no judge![22]

The medical profession provides good analogies. Like lawyers they are corrupted by greed. A charitable doctor who works for nothing would like to cure his patient on the first visit. Not so the doctor or lawyer who can build up the fees.[23]

He knows a proverb and a story or two from other lands. There is the wise Dutchman who makes his future son-in-law renounce his only patrimony because it is involved in litigation.[24] There is a good old German saying that drinking produces good settlements but good quarrels too.[25] And he ends by giving the Turks credit for the wise old saw: 'better to lose early than win late'.[26]

TRANSLATION

All translations are mine except where I have declared otherwise, as in Charlotte Lennox's version of Sully's memoirs, interesting in itself. I believe my translation needs the colloquialisms and even anachronisms of style, if it is to retain the salty flavour of

---

20 Chapter XI, para 5.
21 Epistle to the King, para 1.
22 Chapter XVIII.
23 At the end of Chapter XVI.
24 Chapter XXXVI.
25 Chapter XXIII, para 7.
26 Chapter XXXVI.

the original and to maximise the modern reader's chances of fully comprehending it.[27]

I have translated into English all quotations in the text but that seemed unnecessary in the footnotes. Where La Roche quotes a passage in a language other than French, I have translated it and put the original in a footnote.

La Roche calls his book a *livret*. After hesitating and changing my mind throughout the work of translating, I have come to the conclusion that he intended to write a manual and that is what he meant by *livret* rather than a self-deprecatory 'little book', but he must have been aware of the ambiguity and wanted something of both meanings. Though it is primarily a reformist tract, it is intended for use by practitioners, not only in the promotion but also in the practice of resolving disputes. That is obvious from the inclusion of forms and precedents and the many insights and handy tips, clearly based on experience. Therefore I have consistently translated *livret* as manual.

I have not preserved La Roche's system of capitals – which sometimes appears to have depended on available type – or his punctuation. I have also replaced his system of numbering which is not at all consistent. He starts his whole text with a paragraph numbered 2 and calls the next one 2 as well. Often he prefaces the number with the abbreviation 'Art.' but he frequently loses interest after a few numbers and drops it.

I have kept to certain stock translations. *Procez et querelles* are always 'suits and disputes'. They tend to have their recurrent epithet: *animés et immortels*, which I have translated as 'passionate and never-ending'. I have translated both *accommoder* and *accorder* as 'settle', except where it seemed necessary to translate *accommoder* as conciliate.

I have retained French terms (in italics) when any attempt to translate into one word in English may give the wrong impression or just seems odd: the offices and professions of

---

27 I have preferred modern English to that of the 1660s for reasons I hope are obvious but have been argued for in Derek Roebuck and KK Sin 'The Ego and I and Ngo: Theoretical Problems in the Translation of the Common Law into Chinese' 1993; KK Sin and Derek Roebuck 'Language Engineering for Legal Transplantation: Conceptual Problems in Creating Common Law Chinese' 1996; and most recently in Chapter 3 'Language and Translation' in *Ancient Greek Arbitration*. See now Lorna Hardwick *Translating Words, Translating Cultures* 2000.

avocat, greffier, huissier, intendant, officier, procureur, sergent and *solliciteur*, technical terms such as *arrondissement* and *département* and *Parlement*, and explained them in the Glossary Index. Curé has been treated as an English word. I preferred to keep *arrest*, in La Roche's spelling, rather than translating it as judgment or order or changing it to its modern form *arrêt* with a potentially different meaning, however slight. For similar reasons I have kept *ordonnance* and *édit* in French. I have translated *justice* as 'legal system' or left it as 'justice' particularly in quotations, except where it represents the legal profession and the most idiomatic translation is 'the law'.[28] Proper names have been given the form in which they are most likely to be recognised.

Charité and *charitable* caused problems because they contain two elements, unpaid and well-intentioned. I have translated the adjective as charitable in phrases describing arbitrators or *avocats* and *procureurs*, because both elements of meaning are usually present, but translated *charité* as goodwill, because there is rarely any element of unpaid in it.

I am not satisfied with my translation of *gouvernemens*. They are the administrative responsibilities placed by the King on such men as the Prince de Conti.[29] They include provincial governorships but are not restricted to them. I have translated them as public offices, for want of inspiration.

I began by trying to put all the biblical quotations into the English King James version, trusting that was the one with which most readers of English would be familiar. But the originals are in the Vulgate, or in the Apocrypha, and in any case I eventually felt more comfortable with my own translation. Where I can find it I have given the reference to chapter and verse in the King James version.

I have tried to avoid anachronism in substance, particularly when it arises from the temptation to force a parallel with modern dispute resolution to enable comparative conclusions to be drawn. I have therefore preferred consistency in translating

---

28 As in Colbert's memorandum, when he criticises the professions of 'finance and *justice*', in Chapter 3 below.

29 See Chapters IX and XV of the text. De Conti was a provincial governor but he carried out other administrative duties which the author no doubt included when he wrote of De Conti's *gouvernemens*, see the section devoted to him below in Chapter 4. La Roche usually spells him De Conty.

arbitres as arbitrators (even when they are clearly mediating at the time), *arbitrage* as arbitration, *médiateurs* as mediators and *entremetteurs* as intermediaries, though the author has no such scruples.[30] He was untroubled by the modern concern to distinguish mediation, where a third party brings disputants together to help them to settle their differences themselves, from arbitration, where the third party adjudicates the dispute and that decision is imposed on them. Commentators on the Roman law devoted considerable scholarship to the distinction between *arbiter*, *arbitrator* and *amicabilis compositor* but there is no justification for rehearsing it here. The French word for arbitrator is *arbitre*. *Arbitrateurs* are only found when that Latin trio is translated, as in the ordinances of Jean II (1363) and François II (1560), discussed in the next chapter.

---

30 Compare the terminology of the heading of Chapter III of the text with its description in the Contents pages.

2 THE LEGAL SYSTEM

'In every period the French have been mistrustful of their legal system.'[1]

THE BACKGROUND

The role of arbiter was one of the first attributes claimed by French kings.[2] At first it was more natural for the king to mediate and arbitrate than to judge:[3]

> In relation to the legal system, royal interventions were mediations or arbitrations rather than judgments; legislation and decrees were most often mere privileges or exemptions: the king made serfs free, bestowed favours on religious houses and, in the twelfth century, granted several charters to towns.

Even in matters of religion, the *Parlement* of Paris five hundred years later acknowledged that the king was still the natural arbitrator. In the controversies over Jansenism which led to strife in the early years of Louis XIV, Denis Talon, *Avocat-Général*, declared in the *Parlement* in 1657: 'the bulls against Jansen should be administered through the authority of the king, who is the arbiter in these matters'.[4]

The *Parlement* of Paris itself, acting as the most important part of the king's machinery of justice, arbitrated in disputes between municipal officials, between guilds, between workers and employers, and in disputes with foreign merchants.[5]

Before the reforms of Louis XIV, France was bedevilled by an unorganised proliferation of legal systems, local, seigneurial and

1   *De tout temps les Français se sont méfiés de leur justice.* Arlette Lebigre *La Justice du Roi* 1988 p230.
2   Lebigre *La Justice du Roi* 'Le Chêne de Vincennes: du roi arbitre au roi justicier'; Olivier-Martin *Histoire du Droit* s148.
3   Paul Ourliac and Jean-Louis Gazzaniga *Histoire du Droit Privé Français de l'An Mil au Code Civil* 1985 p141.
4   JH Shennan *The Parlement of Paris* 1998 pxxxi.
5   Shennan *The Parlement of Paris* pp89, 91.

ecclesiastical as well as royal at many levels.[6] The country was divided into the *pays de droit écrit*, which had a system loosely based on Roman law writings, and the *pays de coutumes*, all the rest of the country, each bit with its local customs. Arbitration was subject to this patchwork of laws[7] but French kings passed legislation relating to arbitration centuries before their counterparts in England did, and even attempted to enforce it in place of litigation.[8]

LEGISLATION

By the middle of the twelfth century, the kings of France used various forms to communicate their more serious and general instructions, in French *ordonnances* or (in the earliest times) *établissements*, or sometimes *édits* and *arrests*.[9] *Ordonnance* is the most general term, often used to include not only the *ordonnances sans adresse ni sceau*, without address or seal, which were authenticated by the king's signature and addressed to the whole realm, but other forms, including letters patent and *arrests* of the Council. Though the king usually chose the *ordonnance* as his preferred form for matters of general import, he frequently made use of the *arrest du Conseil*, which usually was made in his presence at first, less often in later times. The *arrest* was not sealed and did not have

6   Shennan *The Parlement of Paris*, particularly Chapter 2 pp50–85, is an accessible and attractive general account of the development of French law for the English reader.

7   Lebigre *La Justice du Roi* p29; Olivier-Martin *Histoire du Droit* s148.

8   The first English legislation to deal directly with arbitration was 9 & 10 Will III c15 1697, usually called the first Arbitration Act, though legislation of 1504, 19 Henry VII c7, had attempted to inhibit arbitration by declaring ineffective those rules of the guilds which required their members to arbitrate rather than litigate. And Art 10 of the Laws of Hlothere and Eadric, from some time between 673 and 688, refers to arbitration, see Derek Roebuck 'A Short History of Arbitration' 1994 ppxliii, liii–liv, lvii–lxi. Arbitration had been well-known as an institution to both French and English kings for centuries; *Anciennes Lois* p297 contains the award of Louis IX in January 1263 in an arbitration between Henry III of England and the barons. In 1340 the Pope was appointed arbitrator between Philip de Valois and Edward III of England in the matter of the French throne. The Hundred Years War was the result of Edward III's refusal to accept the award.

9   Olivier-Martin *Histoire du Droit* ss270, 271 describes the distinctions; François Olivier-Martin *Les Lois du Roi* 1945–46. These *arrests* are to be distinguished from the *arrêts de règlement* passed by the *Parlement* of Paris, Shennan *The Parlement of Paris* pp86–7.

to be registered with the *Parlement* of Paris. It was addressed to those officers who were responsible for carrying it out.

It was usual for new kings to pass legislation confirming that of their predecessors, if they wished to ensure that it was enforced. Repetition of the same measures by one king after another may be evidence that all were having difficulty in enforcing the law. On the other hand, while an ambitious attempt to create a scheme of arbitration may fail, so that the legislation is better evidence for intention than implementation, interstitial modifications presupposing an existing system are good evidence of the ordinariness of practice.

From the fourteenth century there are many examples of French kings legislating to give their support to arbitration, sometimes even making it compulsory for certain kinds of dispute.

Ordonnance *of Jean II 1363*

An *ordonnance* of Jean II in December 1363 was concerned to restrict access to the royal courts in cases of first instance to those who had been granted that privilege or had acquired it by custom. Everybody else should go first to the court whose jurisdiction was appropriate for them, seigneurial, religious or whatever. The *ordonnance* also provided that, if anyone appealed to a good man (*bonus vir*)[10] against the award of an *arbitre, arbitrateur* or *amiable compositeur*, none of the parties should be allowed to bypass that process by an appeal to the royal court.[11]

The trio '*arbitres, arbitrateurs et amiables compositeurs*', though well-known to scholars, appears only in the books and the legislation. It does not seem to have been used in practice in France:[12]

---

10 The institution of *boni vires*, or more usually *boni homines*, has been the subject of much learning, e.g. Camilo Giardina 'I *Boni Homines* in Italia' (1932) 28–98, 313–94 and the *gens de bien* of Laujorrois discussed later in this chapter.

11 *Anciennes Lois* V pp160–2 Ordonnances ou Établissements du Roi sur l'Ordre Judiciaire etc s2: 'si quis autem a dicto aut pronunciatione arbitrorum, arbitratorum aut amicabilium compositorum, ad arbitrium boni viri duxerit appellandum, non liceat appellanti dictam curiam nostram pro viro bono eligere; nisi partes aut ipsarum altera de jure inibi debeant litigare'.

12 PB Boucher *Manuel des Arbitres* 1807: 'La loi actuelle ne reconnoît pas que deux espèces d'arbitres: les arbitres proprement dit, et les amiables compositeurs. Elle ne reconnoît pas les arbitrateurs ...'; KS Bader 'Arbiter, Arbitrator seu Amicabilis Compositor' (1960) 239–76.

The law in practice recognises only two kinds of arbitrators: arbitrators (*arbitres*) properly so called and *amiables compositeurs*. It does not recognise *arbitrateurs*.

Yet an early writer on arbitration, writing a commentary on the *Édits* of August 1560 considered below, attempted to differentiate the *arbitrateur* by function. The *arbitrateur* is a *mediateur* (though with the functions of an expert or valuer and with power to adjudicate):[13]

> As, for example, to fix the price of building works or to make a distribution between those who have entered into a contract for the community of goods.

And a dispute, which began in 1730 and lasted just into the nineteenth century, was submitted to Brochon Snr, Linars and Jaubert ... as *arbitres, arbitrateurs et amiables compositeurs*.[14]

Ordonnance *of Louis XII 1510*

An *ordonnance* of Louis XII of 12 June 1510[15] introduced technical reforms to civil procedure; s34 provided:

> in the case of arbitration there shall be recourse to the *juge ordinaire*, but implementation of the award is not postponed.

Édits *of François II 1560*

Two more substantial pieces of legislation were passed in 1560, in the reign of François II: the *Édit* on the Execution of Arbitral Awards and the *Édit* on Merchants' Disputes.[16]

---

13 Jean Pierres *Commentaire sur l'Édit des Arbitres* 1564 pp38, 39: 'comme, par exemple, pour arrester le prix de l'oeuvre d'un bâtiment, ou, pour faire les partages entre ceux qui ont contracté communité des biens.'
14 See the matter described at the end of this chapter.
15 Ordonnance sur la Réformation de la Justice etc, *Anciennes Lois* XI pp575–7 s34: 'En cas d'arbitrage, il y aura recours au juge ordinaire, mais l'exécution sera préalable.'
16 Édit sur l'Exécution des Sentences Arbitrales et sur la Juridiction qui doit Connaître de l'Appel de ces Sentences; and Édit Portant que Tous Différens entre Marchands pour Fait de Leur Commerce, les Demandes de Partage et les Comptes de Tutelle et Administration Seront Renvoyés à des Arbitres. Both were passed in August 1560, *Anciennes Lois* XIV pp49–52. Pierres *Commentaire sur l'Édit des Arbitres* 1564.

The *Édit* on the Execution of Arbitral Awards 1560 stated its purpose unequivocally: 'our particular concern is to shorten and get rid of litigation' and to promote 'negotiation and settlement between the parties themselves, or by arbiters, arbitrators or *amiables compositeurs*, chosen by the mutual agreement of the said parties'. Its method was to cut down appeals, always a temptation to a party who feels disgruntled once the relief of a settlement has worn off.

The distribution of estates on death requires the taking of accounts, matters of fact not law, and members of the same family ought not to get involved in litigation. So mediation and arbitration would be better and would be forced on the parties if they did not sort out their differences themselves. Moreover, a better outcome is likely if needs as well as legal rights are borne in mind by all concerned – equity rather than the strict law, which since Aristotle had been acknowledged a characteristic of arbitration.[17]

This legislation gave general application to the practice the kings had often adopted of submitting to arbitrators matters of delicacy, for example disputes in the great families about succession and questions of family settlements, dowry and dower.[18] Appeals were restricted:

Édit on the Execution of Arbitral Awards and on the Jurisdiction which ought to be Recognised for an Appeal against these Awards

As the true way to shorten these proceedings ought to come first, and to prevent them being brought before the judges, and so that they may be decided without a judgment by negotiation and settlement between the parties themselves, or by arbiters, arbitrators and *amiables compositeurs*, chosen by the mutual agreement of the said parties.

---

17 Aristotle *The Art of Rhetoric* I 13 17–19: '... the arbitrator looks to the equity but the *dikast* to the legal rule. It was for this reason that an arbitrator was chosen, so that equity should prevail'. and Cicero *Pro Roscio Comoedo* 4 5; discussed in Derek Roebuck *Ancient Greek Arbitration* 2001 Chapter 9. This 'equity', though grounded in the same concepts, does not have the same range of meanings as those included when 'equity' is used in the Common Law, where it became a term of art as early as the beginning of the sixteenth century, JH Baker *An Introduction to English Legal History* 3rd edn 1990 pp126–8.

18 Olivier-Martin *Histoire du Droit* s390. The arbitrations of D'Ormesson are good examples, see Chapter 4 below.

Sometimes people's minds are so full of contentiousness that that which they have just a little while before approved and settled soon afterwards they disagree about and deny, resiling from the compromises and settlements they have agreed on and concluded. Upon which we have by our *édit* of this very day provided and ordered concerning these transactions.

In respect of compromises and arbitrations, our right honoured lord and great-grandfather, King Louis XII, would have ordained that all parties who would have made a compromise to go to arbitration, with a penalty bond, should have the right to appeal against their awards to a *juge ordinaire*. And where the awards were confirmed, no appeal should be allowed without as a precondition the penalty fixed by the arbitration having been paid, except that it could be recovered by the party to whom it was granted at the end of the action. That *ordonnance* was passed to shorten proceedings. Always, by human ill-will, the effect has been totally contrary to the intention of the said *ordonnance*, which has only brought about greater delay in proceedings and in the place of one appeal has caused two.

Because our particular concern is to get rid of and shorten litigation, the length of which ruins and destroys our subjects, having by our *édit* confirmed and authorised, we confirm and authorise that all judgments upon compromises should not have any penalty attached, preferring that they should have whatever force and strength our judges give to them by their judgments, and that there should be no appeal against those judgments and that as a precondition the penalty should be entirely executed, both principal and costs, if a penalty was attached, without any hope of recovering that penalty, unless the award has been set aside in whole or in part. And the said appeal from the said arbiters or arbitrators shall be brought in our sovereign courts unless it was a question of matters which the presiding judges could judge as a question of last resort, in which case the said appeal shall be brought before them.

Fontainebleau, August 1560

The *Édit* on Merchants' Disputes 1560, made at the same time, had two quite separate objects. The first was an attempt by legislation to foster trade by reducing the harmful effects of litigating commercial disputes, in some ways a precursor of the *tribunaux de commerce*. Its purpose was stated to be to force merchants, who broke their commercial agreements and then tried to take advantage of chicanery, to go instead to arbitration. If they would not agree to nominate arbitrators, then the court would appoint them. And the royal judges were instructed to enforce the award without further proceedings, as if it were one of their own judgments.

The second part was an attempt to take family quarrels out of the courts and force the parties to mediation and arbitration:

Édit Requiring that All Differences between Merchants
Arising from their Business, and Requests for Distribution and
Accounts in Trusts or Administrations shall be Sent to Arbitrators

The desire we have to ensure that our subjects live in peace and quiet makes us think all the time of new ways to prevent as much as we can the start of new litigation or stopping it as soon as it starts; and inasmuch as there is nothing which brings more prosperity to towns, lands and kingdoms than traffic in merchandise, which rests and depends entirely on the trust of merchants, who most often work hard together in good faith without written evidence or notaries and without taking care to observe the subtleties of the law: from which it follows that if any of them are wily and mischievous and, instead of paying or doing what they have promised, worry with litigation those with whom they have done business and distract them from their commerce, to such an extent that the trust and confidence of the one for the other is in this way removed, and the course of commerce diminished and destroyed.

So to obviate and remedy this, with the advice of the Princes of the Blood and those of our Council here with us, we have declared and ordained and do declare and ordain:

1. Henceforth no merchants shall summon one another before our judges or others on a matter of commerce but they shall choose and agree on three persons, or a greater unequal number if the matter so requires, merchants or of some other calling, and shall lay before them their differences, and whatever shall be adjudged or arbitrated between them shall be held to be a settlement or sovereign judgment; otherwise it is permissible to object by way of *approximation* or *appellation* or otherwise. And our judges shall be required at the request of the parties to grant or have awarded summary execution of the

award in full, without further proceedings, as if it had been made by themselves.

When the said parties are unable or unwilling to agree on the said persons, in that case the *juge ordinaire* of that place requires them to do so and if they refuse or delay to nominate them, he will choose and nominate them and the parties will not be heard to appeal against that nomination.

2. Because in the case of distribution and divisions it is necessary to appoint arbitrators to divide and distribute inheritances properly and to balance income and expenses, which is a question of fact rather than of law, and also to maintain peace and friendship between near relatives, we ordain by these presents, that in division and distribution of inheritances and the common goods of father or mother, grandparents and grandchildren, brothers, sisters, uncles and children of brothers and sisters, and accounts of guardianships, and other administrations, restitutions of dowry and dower between the said persons, the relatives of full age are bound to choose and nominate some good and respectable persons, up to three relatives, friends or neighbours, on whose advice the said divisions and distribution, rendering of accounts and restitution of dowries or delivery of the said dower, shall be made. And whatever they shall do shall have the force of a judgment and shall be executed by the judges of the place, notwithstanding any objections or appeals whatever, and without detriment to them.

And no appeal shall be allowed before the said distributions shall have been executed completely, which appeal shall be brought directly and immediately to the *Cour de Parlement* where the parties reside. And if one of the parties should be dilatory, or refuse to agree to the arbitrators, in that case that party shall be constrained to do so by the judges, as provided above.

Fontainebleau, August 1560.

When La Roche refers to 'the *Ordonnance*' he must mean one or other, or most likely both,[19] of these two *édits* of François II. This is clear from Chapter XXI paragraph 8, where he says:[20]

---

19 Pierres' *Commentaire sur l'Édit* covers both, though its title refers to a singular.

20 He makes no changes in later editions to avoid the confusion that he should have realised would be created by the recent enactment of the *Ordonnance Civile* 1667.

The mediator will require the parties to deposit in his hands the penalty on forfeiture, which will not be reported in the compromise, for fear that what often happens will happen here, that the judges decide to award the sum fixed by this penalty, even though the *Ordonnance* prohibits that.

Ordonnance *of Charles IX 1566*

Six years later, in an *ordonnance* which set out to reform the legal system generally and confirm his predecessor's legislation,[21] Charles IX ordained that: 'The *ordonnance* on arbitrators for the judgment of causes between near relatives in matters of distributions and other differences shall be preserved and observed without any impediment.' That can only refer to the second part of François II's second *ordonnance* of 1560.

At just that time in England, Elizabeth I's Court of Chancery was taking the same approach:[22]

Joye v Joye 5 May 1580 The Lord Chancellor declared, that he had been written to by some of honour, being good friends unto the said defendant, that the matter might be rather referred to some friends, to be chosen, to hear and end the cause between the said plaintiff (being the natural son to the defendant), which the said Lord Chancellor moved the defendant, by earnest persuasions, that it might be done accordingly. But the defendant standing long upon the request to this Court, that the cause might be openly heard, the plaintiff himself, upon his knees, weeping tears, besought his said father that it might be referred even to his own counsel, which this Court thought very reasonable. And therefore, at the persuasion of this Court, and by consent of the defendant, the whole cause is referred to Mr Solicitor General and Mr Amersham, they being of the said defendant's counsel, to hear all the matters in this Court depending between the said parties, and to end and compound the same, according to their wisdoms and

---

21 *Ordonnance* on the Reform of Justice 1566 s83, *Anciennes Lois* XIV p211.
22 Cecil Monro *Acta Cancellaria* 1847 pp492–3; also *Fysh v Fysh* 30 October 1598 (father and son) at p721 and *Masterson v Masterson* 4 November 1598 (brothers) at p722. The rules were similar in Renaissance Italy, Thomas Kuehn *Law, Family and Women* 1991 p27: 'the 1355 statutes of the Podestà ... A smorgasbord of relatives in male and female lines, including bastards, within about four degrees of relationship ... were judicially enjoined "at the request of the other party" to elect *arbitros et arbitratores*'.

discretions; or else to report to the said Lord Chancellor the cause, why they can make no end between them.

It is noteworthy that the mediator-arbitrators were required to act 'according to their wisdoms and discretions', or, in the vocabulary of the civil law, as *amiables compositeurs* rather than *arbitres*.

Ordonnance *of Henri III 1579*

This *ordonnance* was passed in response to the requests of the Estates-General and dealt generally with many disparate problems.[23] In a chapter which listed articles rescinded by order of the king, it provided:

> We wish that the *ordonnance* on arbitrators of the late King François, our very dear lord and brother, for the judgment of causes between near relatives, in matters of distribution and other differences, shall be preserved and observed according to its form and tenor.

Arrest *of Henri IV 1610*

Ordonnances and *édits* can be classified with confidence as legislation. They lay down rules to be applied generally, rather than dispose of disputes between parties. *Arrests* can do both or either. That is one reason for keeping the word in French, in its older form. *Arrests* can perform the same function as case law does in Common Law jurisdictions. Even if they purport only to dispose of a private dispute, they may contain the application of law which can be detected and applied to later cases, a *ratio decidendi*.

La Roche often refers to Henry IV's[24] intention to institute a system of charitable arbitrators and mediators, and of charitable *avocats* and *procureurs*, to be set up in all the courts and jurisdictions of the realm. In the first edition, in the epistle to the bishops (p5), he asks them to persuade Louis XIV:

23 *Ordonnance* in Response to the Complaints and Grievances of the Estates-General Assembled at Blois in November 1576, relating to the General Criminal Justice System [*Police*] of the Realm, Paris, May 1579 s181.
24 14 December 1553–14 May 1610; baptised a Catholic, became leader of the Huguenots, and reconverted on his accession to the throne of France in 1589, 'Paris is worth a Mass'.

to carry out the good intentions and the *ordonnances* of his grand-father Henry IV, that Prince of everlasting memory, who ordained on 6 March 1610 that in all the towns, courts and jurisdictions of the Kingdom there should be charitable consultants and arbitrators, who would take care of the litigation of the poor for nothing. That was established in Provence but was not possible in the rest of France because of his sad and sudden death, which checked the course of that Monarch's grand designs.

But no such *ordonnance* was ever enacted. Neither *ordonnance* nor *édit* appears in any collection of French legislation.[25] In later editions La Roche changed this passage to refer to a system of charitable *avocats* and *procureurs* only, with no mention there of arbitrators. But he still insisted in the epistle to the bishops that such a limited scheme was in action: 'They take charge of the litigation of the poor for nothing, and settle nearly all of it amicably.' And he forthrightly challenged Louis XIV to finish off his grandfather's scheme – reminding him that the crown is deserved only by kings who accomplish what they intend.

It was said that Henry IV's biography by Hardouin de Péréfixe[26] was Louis XIV's favourite reading as a child, so La Roche knew what he was doing when he repeatedly presented Henry IV to Louis XIV as a model. Péréfixe stressed Henry IV's concern with the evils of litigation (p525):

One of the projects he wanted to work on with greater vigour was to get rid of the delays and chicaneries of litigation. Nearly every time his chancellor and Achille de Harlay, the *Premier Président*, came to see him, he begged them to find ways to do so, so that his people would no longer be tormented by that war of the desk, sometimes more ruinous than that of arms.

But there is no mention of arbitration, let alone of any legislation in 1610, in Péréfixe, or even in the journal of Henry IV, in which the most trivial gossip is recorded day by day.[27]

---

25 Not in *Anciennes Lois* nor in *Recueil d'Édits et d'Ordonnances Royaux sur le Fait de la Justice et Autres Matières les Plus Importantes...* 1720.
26 Hardouin de Péréfixe *Histoire du Roi Henri-le-Grand* 1822.
27 P de L'Estoile *Journal de Henri III, de Henri IV et de Louis XIII* new edn 1826 vol IV. Nor does the *Arrest* or *Édit* or its scheme seem to be mentioned in the other monumental histories, eg Auguste Poirson *Histoire du Règne de Henri IV* 2nd edn 1862.

In his second edition, La Roche drives his point home with a splendid illustration of the charitable *avocats* and *procureurs* appearing before the charitable arbitrators in Provence, but it may be significant that that is the one picture which has been removed from the fourth edition.

The mystery is resolved once it is revealed that Henry IV had made an order on 6 March 1610, but in the form not of an *ordonnance* but an *arrest*, though in a collection headed '*Édit*'. Having found that this had survived in manuscript, of which there was one version in the Bibliothèque Nationale and another in the Centre des Archives, and having studied the latter, it became clear that it had nothing to do with charitable arbitrators at all. It was concerned to establish a system of legal aid, by means of charitable *avocats* and *procureurs*.

Arrest on Charitable *Avocats* and *Procureurs*[28]

Paris 6 March 1610

Whereas it has been demonstrated to the King in Council that a great number of widows, orphans, poor gentlefolk, merchants, workers and other unhappy people, for lack of assistance and support, some of advice, some of a little money and some of both, every day allow themselves to lose their property and their rights, whether as plaintiff or defendant, and have no way of starting proceedings or the necessary costs in their litigation and actions brought or to be brought, civil or criminal, before the courts of the kingdom, whether sovereign, ordinary or subordinate, because of the great costs which the legal system demands; and that it is not reasonable on the excuse that a bit of charity is lacking today, that his subjects for lack of advice or of a little money or of both of them should be abandoned to the mercy, wrong, oppression and calumny of those more powerful than them and unhappily lose their property and their honour, and in this way often fall, or might fall if it were not remedied, into unusual misfortunes, disadvantages and calamities.

28 This is a translation of a manuscript, E 25b, fol 77r in CARAN (Centre d'Accueil et de Recherche des Archives Nationales, Paris). There is another copy, cited as Ms Fr. 18177, fol 288r in the Bibliothèque Nationale, but I have been unable to obtain access or a photocopy. Because it is not accessible in print in any of the collections of French laws, despite its interest not least in the history of legal aid, it is reproduced here in facsimile with a transcription.

The King in Council, moved by a charitable and paternal affection towards his poor people, Desiring to provide in future that justice should be rendered in full open-heartedness to the widows, orphans, poor gentlefolk, merchants, workers and generally to those persons who are reduced to such poverty and necessity that they have not the means to pursue their litigation, rights and actions, brought or to be brought, civil or criminal,

Has Ordered and Orders that in all the said courts, whether sovereign, ordinary or subordinate, there shall be commissioned and deputed *avocats* and *procureurs* for the poor, in such number as he shall be advised in his Council, according to the size and need of each Court or tribunal, to assist with their advice, industry, labour and attendance, all those of the aforesaid quality, without however taking from them anything, however small it may be, on whatever pretext, on the penalty of extortion, contenting themselves with their simple wages, salary and pre-rogatives which it pleases his Majesty to allot to the said *avocats* and *procureurs* who shall have been commissioned and chosen as the more capable men of good will and those retained on the said duties insofar as they have done that which will be their duty. And to this effect there shall be admitted and received the advice which shall be found just and reasonable in his Council for them to take and collect the wages and emoluments belonging to the said *avocats* and *procureurs* of the poor.

[signature]   [signature]

On the 6th day of March 1610 at Paris

Transcription

Paris 6 mars 1610

Sur ce qui a esté remonstré au Roy en son Conseil q'un grand nombre de vesfes, orfelins, pauvres gentilshommes, marchans, laboureurs et autres personnes miserables, faute d'estre assistez et secouruz les uns de conseil, aucuns de quelque peu d'argent, les autres de tous les deux ensemble, laissent journellement perdre leur biens et leurs droitz soit endemandant ou defendant et n'ont moyen de faire les poursuites et frais necessaires en leurs instances et actions intentées ou a intenter civiles ou criminelles és courts

...urs qui a esté remonstré au roy en son conseil qu'un grand nombre
de veufues, orfelins, pauures gentilz hommes, marchans laboureurs
et autres personnes miserables, faulte d'estre assistez et secouruz soit
vngz de conseil, aucuns de quelque peu d'argent, soit autres de
tous les deux ensemble, laissent iournellement perdre leurs
biens et leurs droictz soit en demandant ou defendant de
n'ont moyen de fer les poursuites et frais necessaires es leurs
instances et actions intentées ou a intenter ciuilles ou criminelles
es cours tant souueraines, ordinaires que subalternes de son royaume
a cause des grands frais qui se font en iustice, & qu'il n'est
pas raisonnable que soubz pretexte du peu d'esgard qui se
voit auiourd'huy soit subiectz faulte de conseil ou d'un genre
peu d'argent, ou de tous les deux soient abandonnez a la mercy
iniure, oppression et calomnie de plus puissans qu'eux perdent
miserablement leurs biens & honneur, depuis ce moyen semblent
soient en bourreau s'il n'y est remedié tombez es d'estranges
malheurs, incommoditez et calamités. Le roy en son conseil
meu d'une affection charitable et paternelle enuers son pauure
peuple desirant pouuoir a l'aduenir que la iustice soit
rendue en toute sincerité aux veufues, orfelins, pauures gentilzhommes
marchans, laboureurs et generallement aux personnes reduites
a telle misere et necessité qu'ilz n'ont pas le moyen de poursuivre
leurs instances, droictz et actions intentées ou a intenter ciuilles
ou criminelles. A ordonné et ordonne qu'ilz soient leur
cours tant souueraines ordinaires que subalternes, soient

commis et députés des Aduocats et procureurs de les
pauvres en tel nombre quil sera aduisé en son conseil
selon la grandeur et necessité de chacune Cour ou siege
lesquelz seront tenus d'assister de leur conseil Industrie
labeur et vacations tous ceux de ladite qualité, sans
neanmoins prendre d'eux aucune chose tam petite soit elle
desoubz quelque pretexte que ce soit sur peine de concussion
se contentans de leurs simples gages, salles et prerogatives
quil plaira a sa Majesté atribuer ausd aduocats et procureurs
qui seront commis et choisis comme plus capables et gens de
bien et leurs entretenus ausd chargés tam quils y seront et
qui sera de leur auoir, et aue effect seront admis et
receus les aduis qui seront trouvés Justes et raisonnables en son
conseil pour leur faire prendre et percevoir les gages et apointemens
qui seront atribuez ausd aduocats et procureurs des pauvres.

Du Gd seur de mon tres humble affaire

tant souverains, ordinaires que subalternes de son royaume, a cause des grands frais qui se font en Justice et qu'il n'est pas raisonable que sous pretexte du peu de charité qui se void aujourdhuy, ses subjectz faute de conseil ou de quelque peu d'argent ou de tous les deux soient abandonnez ala mercy, injure, opression et calomnie de plus puissans qu'eux perdent miserablement leurs biens et honneur, et par ce moyen tombent souvent, ou pourroient (s'il n'y est remedié) tomber en d'estranges malheurs, inconveniens et calamités.

Le roy en son conseil, meu d'une affection charitable et paternelle en vers son pauvre peuple, Desirant pourvoir al' advenir que la justice soit rendue en toute sincerité aux vesfes, orfelins, pauvres gentilshommes, marchans, laboureurs et generallement aux personnes reduites a telle misere et nécessité qu'ils n'ont pas moyen de poursuivre leurs instances, droitz et actions intentées ou a intenter civilles ou criminelles,

A ordonné et ordonne qu'en toutes lesdites cours tant souverains, ordinaires que subalternes seront commis et deputés des Advocats et procureurs pour les pauvres en tel nombre quil sera advisé en son conseil selon la grandeur et necessité de chacun Cour ou siège lesquels seront tenus d'assister de leur conseil industrie labeur et vacation tous ceux de la susdite qualité sans neanmoins prendre d'eux aucune chose tant petite soit elle, et sous quelque pretexte que ce soit sur peine de concussion se contentants de leurs simples gages, sallaires et prerogatives quil plaira à sa Majesté attribuer ausdits advocats et procureurs qui seront commis et choisis comme plus capables gens de biens et iceux entretenus et au dites charges tant quils y feront ce qui sera de leur devoir. Et à cest effect seront admis et receuz les advis qui seront trouvez justes et raisonnables en son Conseil pour sur iceux prendre et percevoir les gages et apointements qui seront attribuez ausdits advocats et procureurs des pauvres.

[signature]   [signature]

Du 6e jour de mars 1610 a Paris

It is noteworthy that the manuscript itself classifies the order as an *édit*, not an *arrest*. This may well have been the only source which La Roche or his informant read, which may explain his description of it as an *édit*. What may be more likely is that neither the writer nor La Roche gave great importance to the classification.[29]

There is no record of this *arrest* ever having been printed but it appears as an appendix to Laujorrois *Advis pour l'Institution Charitable*, with no substantial variation but with the heading:[30]

> *Arrest* of the Council of State, bearing the Institution of *Avocats* and *Procureurs* of the Poor
> Extract from the Registers of the Counsel of State

and the ending:

> Made at the Council of State held at Paris, the 6th day of March 1610, signed thus:
>
> Malier

SULLY'S SCHEMES FOR ARBITRATION LAW REFORM

Perhaps La Roche can be forgiven his enthusiastic anticipation, as he had it directly from Henry IV's 'great confidant and minister', the Duc de Sully,[31] that Sully 'already had everything drafted, and that the King himself had corrected it and added a recommendatory postscript (*apostillée*) in his own hand.' Sully, he says, confirmed that Henry IV intended to proclaim this by *ordonnance* on his return from Germany but his assassination prevented it.

In his voluminous memoirs,[32] Sully does not mention any relevant legislative act in 1610, though he does refer to one of

---

29 See the discussion earlier in this chapter. There is a note on the manuscript which reveals its provenance: 'ex Bibliotheca mss Coisliniana, olim Seguerina, quam Illust. Henricus du Cambout, dux de COISLIN, Par Franciae, Episcopus Metensis, &c Monasterio S. Germani a Pratis legavit An MDCCXXXII' [from the manuscript library of Coislin, formerly of Seguer, which the Illust. Henry of Cambout, Duke of Coislin, Peer of France, Bishop of Metz, &c left to the Monastery of St Germain des Prés Year 1732].

30 'Arrest du Conseil d'Estat, portant l'Institution des Advocats et Procureurs des Pauvres Extraict des Registres du Conseil d'Estat.'

31 Maximilien de Béthune, Baron de Rosny, Duc de Sully 1560–1641. One of the leading Huguenots, he was Henry IV's valued link with them after the King's reconversion. On the King's assassination he was forced out of office and lived in retirement for thirty years.

32 *Mémoires de Sully, Principal Ministre de Henri le Grand, Nouvelle Édition, plus Exacte et Correcte que les Précédents* 1788, cited hereafter as *Mémoires de Sully*. I have quoted from the translation of Charlotte Lennox *Memoirs of Maximilian de Bethune, Duke of Sully, Prime Minister to Henry the Great etc* 1756, cited as Lennox *Sully*.

about the same time on duels. Moreover, after discussing measures to suppress luxury, he describes the King's great eagerness and impatience to reform the legal system through legislation. Sully worked day and night to draft it, constantly prodded and encouraged by the King. On one occasion in 1609, Sully chased after the King on his way to church. The King told the priests to postpone the service until he had talked to Sully about the law reform drafts, commenting that Sully was not much of a one for the Mass. They then spent the next two hours discussing the drafts.[33] Sully wrote that Henry's plan was first to communicate with all the presidents of the various courts and the King's men in the various *Parlements*:[34]

> not to be argued against but to get their criticisms and advice, to see if they had any better ideas for shortening litigation and putting an end to the despicable art of chicanery. When the last draft of these regulations had been finished, the King was determined to lay them before the *Parlement*, written in his own hand, for them to record.

Sully described that part of the intended legislation which dealt with arbitration:[35]

> In all suits between relations, counted nearly according to the canonical degrees of consanguinity and affinity, as well temporal as spiritual, the plaintiff was obliged in the first place to make an offer, from which he was not to depart, of referring all the differences to the arbitration of four persons, two chosen by each party, among their friends or relations; to name these two arbitrators on the spot, and to set down in distinct articles, signed by his own hand, all his pretensions and demands, to which he was not allowed to make any additions.
>
> The same thing was to be done by the defendant, who had only a month allowed him to name his arbitrators. In another month the arbitrators were to be in possession of all the proofs and writings of both parties; another month was allowed the arbitrators to pronounce judgment; and a month after that was allowed to a superior arbitrator to determine those points on which the voices had been equally divided. For all other points were to be

33 *Mémoires de Sully* IV p588.
34 *Mémoires de Sully* IV p583.
35 Lennox *Sully* III pp138ff.

considered as determined and came not under the cognisance of
the superior arbitrator.

The same regulation took place with the judges. They could not
recall the main cause back before them nor make enquiry into the
fundamental question; but only give sentence according to the
judgment, good or bad, of the arbitrators on the pieces laid before
them. The sovereign courts had, in this respect, no higher
privileges than ordinary jurisdictions. They could neither appoint
a new enquiry nor receive new proofs; and they were allowed only
a month or six weeks to make a decree, which, if they exceeded
that time, became void and the judges themselves were
condemned to pay the losses and damages of both parties.

But this compulsory arbitration scheme was restricted to family
disputes.[36] There is no hint of an intention to create any general
system of charitable arbitrators, or of the legal aid scheme of
charitable *avocats* and *procureurs*.[37]

A footnote which appears quite early in the French editions of
Sully's memoirs reads:[38]

I leave it to the examination of men of a discerning and extensive
genius, how far it would be practicable to accustom the people of
this kingdom to refer their differences and disputes to the decision
of a small number of grave and reverend old men, chosen on
account of their abilities, and the reputation of their integrity, to
perform the office of arbitrators in all the cities, towns and other
considerable places; and who would execute that office in such a
manner that honour, distinction, veneration, the public respect
and at the most such advantages as the sovereign could, without
expense to anyone, add to these, should be to them in lieu of all
profit and recompense. Examples are not wanting! Nay, it is even

36 Similar cases in England and Florence are discussed above.
37 Charlotte Lennox's translation is interesting in itself. She was a woman of
    many parts. She was the darling of Dr Johnson and the husband of
    Alexander Lennox, clerk to William Strahan, later MP, the publisher not
    only of Johnson's *Dictionary* and Gibbon, Hume and Adam Smith but also
    of Blackstone's *Commentaries*. Her famous admirers, who liked to read her
    drafts and offer her advice, may therefore have known of this arbitration
    scheme across the Channel. The entry in the *Dictionary of National Biography*
    has been superseded by fuller and more accurate notices, particularly in
    Virginia Blain, Patricia Clements and Isobel Grundy eds *The Feminist
    Companion to English Literature* 1990; Janet Todd ed *British Women Writers:
    a Critical Reference Guide* 1989 and the fullest biography in Janet Todd ed *A
    Dictionary of British and American Women Writers 1600–1800* 1987.
38 Lennox *Sully* III pp138ff.

common to see persons whom the sole consideration of the interest of poor men, sinking under the weight of the ruinous proceedings of law, induces to take on them this charitable office[39] and to exercise it without fee or reward. Happy are those who have such a mediator among them! The respect and love attendant on this employment cause many to embrace it with joy and amply repay them for the labour they undergo in executing it.

DE LAUJORROIS' *RECOMMENDATION*

To further the King's plans, Sully enlisted the cooperation of Antoine de Laujorrois,[40] a trusted legal adviser of the king, to write *Reformation de la Justice*, showing how the sale of judicial offices caused corruption and injustice.[41] Though he wrote it in 1608, it was not published until 1615, perhaps because of Henry IV's death in 1610.[42] La Roche tells us that Laujorrois also wrote a treatise in favour of the institution of charitable *avocats* and *procureurs* who would act for the indigent, not in arbitrations but in the ordinary courts,[43] and that it was De Laujorrois who suggested that France should follow the example of Venice and reward the charitable arbitrators and lawyers with honours rather than fees.[44]

That book's title is:

Recommendation for the charitable institution of *avocats* and *procureurs* in favour of widows, orphans, poor gentlemen, the middle class, merchants, labourers and other unhappy peoples, who, lacking advice or help and financial support lose their rights ... with the *arrest* of the *Conseil d'Estat*, relating to the Institution of the said *avocats* and *procureurs* of the poor.

Though the work is anonymous, the name of the author is revealed in the dedication to Sillery by Antoine de Laujorroys and in the privilege to publish, granted to Anthoine de Laujorois.

---

39 Is it fanciful to hear this echoing in many similar statements in the manual, eg Chapter XXV, paras 12ff?

40 Born near Langres about 1550 of humble family, died in 1617, classical scholar and editor of Juvenal, Martial and Horace.

41 Antoine de Laujorroys *Reformation de la Justice* 1615.

42 See M Prevost and Roman d'Amat *Dictionnaire de Biographie Française* Paris Librairie Letouzey et Ané Vol 4 1948 p578.

43 Antoine de Laujorroys *Advis pour l'institution charitable des advocats et procureurs* ... 1610.

44 Chapter XXV, section 12, p122.

The work contains 105 folios (210 pages) of which the first 168 pages are taken up by a call to charity and the care of the poor, with many examples including non-Christians such as Cimon of Athens and the Muslims, by which Laujorrois means Turks. His rubrics include (102) 'One must give counsel to those who need it'; (103) 'There needs to be set up a perpetual *conseil*, made up of good and capable people, for and on behalf of the poor.'

He begins to get to the point at p170, when he asks:

> What is it which today causes so much beggary of all sorts of people in this kingdom and which disturbs it? We know that the costs of Justice are insupportable mainly because of the venality of offices of judicature, (i.e. the *venalité des charges*).

By p184 he reaches his proposal:

> It is time to come to the Practice, and to describe a prompt, easy, very profitable and infallible way to alleviate, relieve and sustain an infinite number of poor creatures of all kinds, who for lack of Charity and of a little bit of support have today fallen prey to audacious men ... *chicaneurs*.

And on p186:

> And so I say that to carry out this very commendable design, it is absolutely necessary to do two things. The first is to establish a permanent advice bureau (*conseil*) for all those poor people who would like to seek Justice. The second is to have a fixed revenue and an assured fund for the proper appointment and payment of all those who make up this advice bureau ... With regard to this *conseil*, it should be composed of people of substance (*gens de bien*), mature, wise, enemies of avarice, not timid, but decent and brave, steady and hardworking; and yet accessible and courteous, so that all those poor people who go to them to get advice and counsel to put right the wrongs, injuries, grievances, extortions, assaults and activities against them, their wives and their children ...

The *avocats* and *procureurs* to do the job would be available. They would act like the jurisconsults in ancient Rome. Of course, they would cost most in Paris, next Toulouse, third Rouen, fourth Bordeaux, and fifth Brittany where their salaries would be likely to be less. The most senior would distribute the work among them so that no one would be overburdened and none get off too lightly. And on p200:

Whenever any doubt or difficulty shall arise in any matter, they shall discuss it among themselves and, if they get nowhere, then as a last resort they shall review it with the *avocat* for the other side, so that they can advise what is for the best; so that they will not trouble the Judges with actions which are frivolous or not reasonable or without Justice.

The charitable *avocats* and *procureurs* should be given privileged access to registries, which should be open to them even in vacation.

Laujorrois points out (p208) that the Procureurs of St Mark in Venice perform these functions, thanks to the wisdom of the Venetians. Like them, the French *avocats* and *procureurs* should be rewarded by membership of the Senate on retirement.

The scheme, if it was ever put into practice, does not appear to have survived even in Provence. A comprehensive description of the legal systems in Provence nearly a century later, while including such detail as the judicial role of the elected arbitrators of the fishermen of Marseilles, makes no mention of charitable arbitrators, *avocats* or *procureurs*.[45]

ORDONNANCE OF LOUIS XIII 1629 (CODE MICHAUD)

The *arrest* of 1610 can have had little impact or permanence because, less than a generation later, again in response to complaints presumably that the law was not being observed, Louis XIII in the Code Michaud of 1629 provided:[46]

The *ordonnance* of August 1560 on the subject of arbitrations shall be followed; and to it must conform the execution of arbitral awards referred to *juges ordinaires*, and the appeals from such arbitral awards to *juges présidiaux*, which are in their jurisdiction and not within that of the *Parlements*, unless the parties have agreed to submit the appeal to our *Parlements*; and the said appeals cannot be allowed unless the award has first been completely executed and any penalty stipulated has been paid; on pain of nullity of any judgment given contrary to this section.

45 François-Xavier Emmanuelli *L'Intendance de Provence à la Fin du XVIIe Siècle* 1980 p342.
46 *Ordonnance* on the Complaints of the Estates Assembled in Paris in 1614 and of the Assembly of Notables Meeting at Rouen and Paris in 1617 and 1626, Paris 1629 s152, *Anciennes Lois* XVI pp223, 268.

THE *RÉPERTOIRE UNIVERSEL ET RAISONNÉ DE JURISPRUDENCE*

The remainder of the law which governed arbitration in La Roche's Paris is neatly extracted from the *arrests* and set out in an admirable encyclopedia of which there is no English equivalent, the *Répertoire Universel et Raisonné de Jurisprudence*.[47] Rather than attempt to paraphrase it, I have translated the most relevant parts, though lengthy:

> ARBITRATION, ARBITRATORS One calls arbitrators those who are chosen by the parties to decide a dispute or conflict.
>
> In general, one may choose as arbitrator whomever one wishes, even a son in his father's dispute. One must exclude from this disposition, however, the mad, the deaf and dumb, the *infames*, slaves and members of religious orders.
>
> Women can no longer be arbitrators, that having been forbidden them by the Emperor Justinian. But canon law did not want this disposition to extend to women of eminent rank, which is why Pope Alexander III confirmed an arbitral award made by a queen of France. Even in this case, it was a temporal matter, rather than one for the Church. Jeanne de Bourbon, wife of Charles V, sat at his side when, in 1369, he took his seat on the bench at the Palais in the case against the Prince of Wales. Mathilde, Countess of Artois, having been created a peer of France, attended in person the *Parlement* of 1314. She had a seat and a deliberative voice, the same as the other peers of France, in the criminal prosecution of Robert, Count of Flanders. Jeanne, daughter of Baudouin, took the oath of allegiance of a peer of France, and her sister Marguerite, once she had inherited, took part as a peer in the famous judgment of the peers of France, on the earldom of Clermont en Beauvoisis. At the *Parlement* held on 9 December 1378 for the Duke de Bretagne, the Duchess of Orleans sent a written excuse for her absence.
>
> These examples and others similar[48] have persuaded several authors to lay down a principle that queens, princesses, duchesses

47 M Merlin *Répertoire Universel et Raisonné de Jurisprudence* 1807. I have used the 3rd edn, *sub* 'Arbitrage, Arbitres' pp292–307. I thank M Jean Magis, *libraire-savant* of Paris, for the knowledge which directed me to this source and the generosity which provided me with a copy.
48 For example in Theodore Evergates ed *Aristocratic Women in Medieval France* 1999, particularly his 'Aristocratic Women in the County of Champagne' pp74–110 at 100 and p216 n128. In the thirteenth century, the powers of

and other women of distinguished rank may be chosen as arbitrators and make legal awards. However, an *arrêt* of 29 August 1602, cited by Brillon, rejected an arbitral award rendered by the Maréchale of Lavardin, with another lady and a gentleman, even though the award was just and reasonable, and then the court made a similar judgment. Another *arrêt* of 14 January 1603 declared null an arbitral award made by the Marquise of Nesle and two other ladies chosen to be arbitrators with her, but this no doubt was because it was a matter of the rights of the registrar (*greffier*) of the Marquise of Nesle's own court, so that she would have had an interest in the case.

As far as other women are concerned, there is no doubt of their incapacity to be arbitrators in Rome. Devolant, A, cap 9, reports an *arrêt* of the *Parlement* of Brittany, of 6 September 1610, which so decided.

Mornac believes that a minor of less than twenty-five years cannot be chosen as arbitrator. He bases his opinion on the fact that arbitrations have been established following the example of the judgments of the ordinary courts (*juges ordinaires*). But other writers say, quite rightly, that if a minor of recognised capacity has been chosen as arbitrator and in that capacity has made an award, the appeal courts will not declare it void on account of the incapacity of the arbitrator. In fact, one sees *avocats* everywhere who have not yet attained the age of twenty-five, but who have acquired the understanding necessary to be able to bring a dispute to an end judiciously. Indeed, some of those arbitrators are preferable to most of those one could appoint from the older members of a rank or profession.

Article 17 of the *coutume* of Brittany says expressly that the judge of the parties may not become arbitrator of their differences. The *Parlement* of Rennes has made an *arrêt* of 20 March 1576 in

---

women to arbitrate were differently defined by Philippe de Beaumanoir *Coutumes de Beauvaisis* ed Amédée Salmon 1899–1900 tr FRP Akehurst 1992. De Beaumanoir dealt with arbitration in Beauvaisis, extensively in Chapter 41 and *passim*. In Akehurst's translation: '1287. It is certain that women subordinated to others, such as in marriage or in religion, cannot and should not agree to be arbitrators. But those who are independent [*en delivre poesté*] certainly can, and give the report, even though the law says that women cannot give a judgment; but this means judgments given in court in a judicial proceeding [*plet ordené*]; for judgments given by arbitrators are given by the will and consent of the parties, and by their consent parties can make judges out of those who are not judges [*pueent fere de leur non juges leur juges*].'

conformity with that law. An *ordonnance* of October 1535 forbids presidents and counsellors of the *Parlement* of Provence accepting appointment as arbitrators in matters before the court or the *justices du ressort*. An *ordonnance* of Abbeville, of 23 February 1539 extends the same prohibition to all judges in general, but these laws have never been accepted by the *Parlement* of Grenoble. The reason Guy-Pape gives is that the Dauphin Humbert II, when he established the Council of the Dauphin, allowed the officers of that tribunal to be arbitrators between the parties; and that Louis XI, when later he converted that Council into a *Parlement*, preserved all its rights and privileges.

There are rules of the *Parlement* of Toulouse, which provide that the presidents, counsellors and King's men (*gens du roi*) who serve there may not accept any appointment as arbitrator without the permission of the court. The *Parlement* of Dijon has decided by an *arrêt* of 29 November 1571 that a counsellor of that court, who is a *juge nécessaire*, may not be an arbitrator, at least if he is related or is challenged.

The *Parlement* of Paris permits any of its officers to be appointed arbitrator in any matter in which he may be judge. This practice is based on public policy, which gains its authority from the preference for settlements.

It should always be borne in mind that if we are concerned with the settlement of a matter which is already before the court, that anyone who acts as *rapporteur* may not sit as one of the arbitrators. It should also be noted that, by article 17 of the Letters Patent on the *arrêt* of 13 December 1728, officers of the Council of Artois are forbidden to accept appointment or make awards in arbitrations *en corps* (in banco, as a body). This prohibition clearly assumes that every officer of the court may be appointed arbitrator as an individual; its intention is to prevent the Council of Artois from accepting arbitrations *en corps* and thereby depriving the lower provincial courts of jurisdiction over cases which may not be brought before the Council at first instance.

[Article 5 of the Imperial Decree of 20 Prairial Year 13, concerning the administration of justice in the former states of Parma and Piacenza, and Article 5 of that of the following 15 Messidor for the *départemens* de Genoa, Montenotte, the Apennines and Marengo, provide:

No *juge de paix* or magistrate may ask for or take any pay or present on the pretext of the time they would have spent or the work they would have done in getting the parties to settle, or when they were appointed arbitrators for them.

This clearly supposes that judges today may accept appointment as arbitrators.]

The powers of arbitrators extend only to those matters set out in the arbitration agreement (*compromis*). Anything they do beyond that remains of no effect. That is why, if a new conflict arises between the parties, neither has the right to insist, without the other party's assent, that it be judged by the arbitrators at the hearing to which they both agreed to put their original dispute. That was also decided by an *arrêt* of 19 June 1617. But to avoid the inconvenience of having hearings at the same time before arbitrators and before the *juges ordinaires*, it is customary to include in the arbitration agreement the general clause, that the arbitrators have power to decide, not only the disputes referred to in the arbitration agreement, but also those which may arise between the parties in the course of the arbitration.

If the arbitration agreement fixes a certain time for the commencement of proceedings in the matter for the decision of the arbitrators, they may not make an award before that period has expired.

The functions of arbitrators are the same as those exercised by judges in litigation. They may, when necessary, make interlocutory decisions, require evidence of disputed fact, hear the testimony produced by the parties, and even accept their oath. But they cannot compel witnesses to appear and give evidence because they do not exercise any public power; nor even to issue a subpoena to appear before them, because they have no right of jurisdiction over the witnesses. That was decided by an *arrêt* of the *Parlement* of Dijon of 28 March 1714. So, when a witness refuses to appear before arbitrators, one must resort to the authority of the *juges ordinaires* to make the witness give evidence. Article 10 of Title 26 of the *Ordonnance Civile* of Duke Leopold of November 1707, made for Lorraine, provides that, if the arbitrators have any enquiry (*enquête*) to make, they should obtain a *pareatis* from the judges to put their rulings into effect.

However, arbitrators may call before them a party to the arbitration agreement to be questioned about the relevant facts and points of law, etc.

Arbitrators may decide those matters which arise in the course of the hearing of the matter submitted to their decision, and which are relevant to the matter in dispute. But if one of the parties attempts to lodge a challenge against an item of evidence which has been produced, and of which the other party declares a wish to take the benefit, the arbitrators must order the parties to resort in respect of the disputed matter to the appropriate judge; and the item must be deposited in the office of that judge, after having been initialled by the arbitrators. The matter is then stayed until the judgment of the civil court and the period set by the arbitration agreement does not run until after the hearing and the decision on the challenge [Code of Civil Procedure article 1015].

[Can arbitrators give permission to obtain and publish a *monitoire*? This question was presented to the *Parlement* of Dijon in 1694. After two litigants had made an arbitration agreement, one of them asked the arbitrators for permission to obtain a *monitoire*. The arbitrators allowed it and started proceedings. Appeal on the ground that the *monitoire* was wrongly obtained. The respondent acknowledged that to be so and offered damages and costs; but he maintained that the evidence from the proceedings should be admissible, according to the accepted case law on the subject. The appellant replied that this case law was fine when the proceedings had been heard by a judge who had legal standing to do so; but that the arbitrators had the power neither to start a prosecution nor to grant a *monitoire*. By an *arrêt* of 9 August 1694, the court quashed the whole procedure and issued prohibitions both against the arbitrators granting permission to obtain a *monitoire* and against the officials or *grand-vicaires* agreeing with that permission.

The purpose of this *arrêt*, says Raviot on Périer, Question 328, is 'That *monitoires* should only be issued for weighty reasons, usually in criminal prosecutions, which arbitrators have no jurisdiction over. Punishment of crimes is a matter of public law. To exercise such a jurisdiction, therefore, it is necessary to be invested with public authority, arising *de jure* and not by agreement of the parties.

The use of *monitoires* has been abolished throughout France.]

Arbitrators may order that inheritances or other places in contention be visited by experts chosen by the parties or appointed *ex officio*. But if it is a matter of subpoenaing such experts to appear before arbitrators, or to make their report to them, it is necessary to have recourse to a *juge ordinaire*, as we have said must be done with regard to the summoning of witnesses.

Arbitrators may themselves visit places in contention and make their own examination; but if it is necessary to order an on-site inspection, a *pareatis* from a *juge ordinaire* is needed for the execution of their orders. [For that, as for the summoning of witnesses and experts before arbitrators, see Code of Civil Procedure articles 1009 and 1021.]

If the parties give the arbitrators power to decide 'by one and the same award' all the disputed matters set out in the arbitration agreement, can they make final decisions on some of the matters in issue and postpone judgment on the others (*interloquer les autres*)?

Here follow the facts of a dispute which began in 1730 on the death of the father of twelve children and seventy years later was submitted to arbitrators, 'Brochon Snr, Linars and Jaubert ... as *arbitres, arbitrateurs et amiables compositeurs* ... to decide on all their rights by one and the same award (*par un seul et même jugement*).' They then made a partial award, leaving important issues undecided, and attempted to delegate some issues to assessors. The award was challenged in a court of first instance, though the arbitration agreement purported to take away the parties' rights to resort to the courts. The plaintiff was nonsuited. An appeal was brought before the *cour d'appel* in Agen and dismissed. The author of the *Répertoire*, Merlin himself, argued against the validity of the award, before the *section des requêtes* when the case came up for *cassation*, not only on the ground that the arbitrators had failed to decide all issues in one and the same award but had exceeded their powers by delegating some of them to assessors. Once again the appeal was dismissed.

CONCLUSION

The law which governed arbitration at the time of La Roche can be extracted from the materials translated in this chapter, though there has been no attempt to provide a comprehensive description, let alone an analysis. On the one hand:[49]

The King does not seem to have claimed any monopoly for the public legal system. He always allowed recourse to arbitration, that is to say to the decision of one or more private persons, chosen by agreement of the parties in dispute. Arbitration often took place

---

49   Olivier-Martin *Histoire du Droit* s383.

between members of the same group. And it is currently practised, not only in commercial matters but in civil as well, and above all in matters of delicacy which it is better not to expose to public gaze. The parties thus have great latitude to resolve their differences; very often public approval finally determines whether this kind of justice is successful.

On the other hand, despite the legislation which was apparently still in force in the time of Louis XIV, there was probably no effective requirement that parties to any dispute should arbitrate, nor any comprehensive and effectual scheme for the supervision of arbitrators and arbitrations or the enforcement of awards. That was true at the time La Roche wrote and for a long time afterwards. Yet La Roche gives plenty of evidence of the prevalence of mediation and arbitration.

It is likely that La Roche found out that his first enthusiastic espousal of Henry IV's scheme of charitable arbitrators was premature and that nothing of the sort had ever been established. Not even the charitable *avocats* and *procureurs* had taken root, not even in Provence. From the first to the fourth editions La Roche trimmed the range of his authorities. Whatever else is clear from his manual, nothing could be more certain than that all attempts at reform through legislation had failed. Though arbitration, following unsuccessful attempts at mediation, was available and La Roche gives examples of its use, particularly in family matters,[50] 'passionate and never-ending' litigation continued to take its toll of time and money and goodwill. Yet, though from time to time there may be detected a note of desperation, there is no sign of despair or slackening of enthusiastic effort in La Roche's campaign for reform, which he kept up for at least five years and four editions.

50 Chapter IV.

3 LOUIS XIV AND LAW REFORM

There remained yet one great undertaking to be performed, one more beneficial change to be effected, which – after the hand of Louis and his great minister had raised up agriculture and commerce from the state of depression into which they had been thrown, had introduced various new sorts of manufactures, had brought back old ones which had been lost, and had bestowed splendid encouragement upon literature, science and the elegant arts, – called for even deeper and more searching attention than the great objects which had gone before. This was the reform of the civil and criminal law of the country; and it was immediately undertaken.[1]

LOUIS XIV

La Roche begins with an Epistle to the King and a splendid illustration of him granting an audience, with the caption: 'Behold the Great King Louis XIV!' The King is portrayed as a model for all, because he regularly settles disputes – giving priority to the poor. But he is also reprimanded by implication for not yet carrying out his grandfather Henry IV's plans for charitable arbitration, after five years of personal rule. Moreover, La Roche reminds him that the crown belongs only to those who persevere in their good intentions for the implementation of justice.

By the time of the manual's first publication in 1666, Louis XIV had made a good start. Determined to rule as an absolute monarch, he was concerned first to ensure that there could be no further challenge to his personal exercise of royal power.[2] For that he needed an efficient bureaucracy which he could control

---

1   GPR James *The Life and Times of Louis the Fourteenth* 1851 Vol 2 119–20.
2   The Wars of Religion had been followed by the insurrections of the *Frondes*, Sturdy *Louis XIV* pp25–34; for another view Orest Ranum *The Fronde: a French Revolution 1648–1652* 1993.

from the centre.[3] His own developing ideology made justice an important and necessary element of kingship and he took a personal interest in the reform of the legal system.[4]

Fortunately we have his own account of how he approached the problems:[5]

> Justice, whose function was to reform everything else, seemed to me to be itself the most difficult thing to reform. An infinite number of reasons contributed to this: posts filled haphazardly and for money, rather than by selection and merit; little experience in some judges, and even less wisdom; ordinances about minimum age and conditions of service evaded almost everywhere; chicanery established by usage of several centuries, fertile in inventing ways of getting round the best laws, and finally the chief cause – I mean those people who love litigation too much and nurture lawsuits as if they were their own inheritance, with no purpose other than to increase their length and number. My own Council, instead of controlling the other jurisdictions, too often created greater disorder by the extraordinary number of contradictory *arrests* it made, all published in my name, of course, as if they came from me personally, which made their contradictions all the more shameful.

The King took care to point out that it was the poor who suffered most. In an *édit* of 1667 he had attempted to protect them from the overweening, declaring his 'paternal love for all his subjects'.[6] Though his efforts to stop duelling were being jeopardised, the

---

3 Mettam *Government and Society* pp129–32. Michelet makes the point in his chocolate fudge-cake style: 'Puissance créatrice! un monde, une France nouvelle naissait de la pensée du roi. Le roi voulait, et Colbert écrivait ... une construction énorme, inouïe, de fantastique grandeur. En cette création multiple, tout se trouve à la fois. Les lois, les instruments des lois, les choses avec les hommes, administration, industrie, commerce, enfin, par-dessus, la machine à faire marcher tout (bien ou mal?) – la bureaucratie. – *Les lois* (1667, 1670) – Des travaux immenses du XVIe siècle qui a tout préparé, les commissions de Colbert tirent l'Ordonnance civile et l'Ordonnance criminelle.' Jules Michelet *Histoire de France* 1874 XIII p101.

4 We have Louis XIV's own memoirs for just this period: Jean Longnon ed *Mémoires pour les Années 1661 et 1666* 1923 pp59–60; (in English) Paul Sonnino ed *Louis XIV King of France and Navarre: Mémoires for the Instruction of the Dauphin by Louis XIV* 1970. Sturdy *Louis XIV* pp7–13.

5 Longnon *Mémoires* pp25–6 and p239 fn: 'Louis XIV recevait les placets en des audiences publiques qu'il donnait à certains jours. C'était la une survivance de l'ancienne justice directe et patriarcale comme alle que rendait St Louis sous le chêne de Vincennes.'

6 Olivier-Martin *Histoire du Droit* s267 fn2.

success they had achieved was proof that good legislation firmly and consistently applied could avert social evils. He was taking the lead:

> I made myself subject to a law: I would work twice a day, two or three hours at a time, with various officials, not counting the hours I spent alone or on any unexpected business that might arise ... I allocated to the secretaries of state two days of my time each week for petitions ... I ordered them to sign nothing whatsoever without consulting me ... I instructed the Chancellor similarly not to seal anything except when I told him to ... I let them know that there were some kinds of business where my advice should be sought directly and that I would give all my subjects, without distinction, the right to address me at any time, both orally and by way of written *placets*.

There was a long tradition of the ordinary people having a right of audience. The women of Les Halles, the great Paris market, 'had such a privilege, at their request, of haranging him (*haranguer* – surely no pun on *hareng* is intended) in their fishwife's tongue, with their proverbial straightforwardness'.[7]

Louis XIV became increasingly concerned with his religious duties and the support he could give to the Catholic Church. Being a Bourbon he was only partly French and, moreover, from a Protestant family, only some of whose members had converted with his grandfather Henri IV. For whatever reason, he felt the need to display how devout he was and how much he championed the Gallican Church. Though the Huguenots had played no recent part in opposition to the Crown, and at this time were still protected by the Edict of Nantes 1598, he ensured that they were physically coerced into conversion if he could when prejudicial discrimination failed. The Jansenists, too, discovered the lengths to which he was prepared to go in persecuting what he believed to be heresy. He wanted absolute control but he could live with the moderate demands of the Gallican Church, which allowed him political independence from the Pope.

In supporting arbitration as a means of settling disruptive quarrels, Louis XIV would have been in a natural alliance with

7   Olivier-Martin *Histoire du Droit* s267.

the Church.[8] The Church, too, was involved with the administration of law and order. La Roche was not only worried that disputes would turn into hatred, which could and should prevent the ones who felt it from partaking of the sacraments. Litigation kept priests from their parishes and all other clergy were tempted away from their duties. Even monks and nuns took the opportunities which lawsuits offered them to escape from their convents and the discipline of their rule. From the evidence he provides, La Roche shows that there were some ecclesiastical authorities at all levels who made a practice of mediating disputes. Similar initiatives on the part of the civil authorities, such as those of the Prince de Conti, show that in this matter there was a coincidence of interest and practice of Church and State. And Denis Talon, *Avocat-Général*, quoted in the last chapter, confirmed the opinion of the *Parlement* of Paris that the King was the appropriate arbitrator of such doctrinal disputes.

Once he had established his personal rule, Louis XIV determined to provide a better and more systematic legal system not only through reform of the judiciary and reduction of the multiplicity of courts and jurisdictions but by national codification of the rules of civil procedure. By an instruction of September 1663 he had already attempted to curb the powers of the courts outside his direct control from which no appeal to the King had previously been possible. The question of 'sovereignty', of these courts and in other contexts, remained for a while politically volatile. It was a matter of difference between the King and the *Parlement* of Paris. The question was whether there were courts, and the *Parlement* of Paris claimed to be one, which had an authority separate from the King's to deliver final judgments unappealable to him.[9]

---

8   Lebigre *Justice du Roi* p30: 'L'Église, tôt alarmée par la violence ambiante, a tenté d'imposer des institutions de paix ... Éviter la guerre en proposant l'arbitrage est donc, pour le roi, un moyen de s'associer aux efforts de l'Église ...' 'Seules quelques seigneurs écclesiastiques acceptèrent l'offre d'arbitrage ... Mais religion oblige les plus douces s'inclinèrent.' Lebigre quotes Charles Loyseau *Discours de l'Abus des Justices des Villages* 1660: 'Mais voici le comble du mal, c'est que non seulement la Justice est longue et de grand coûte aux Villages mais surtout elle est très mauvaise ... 1st parce qu'elle est rendue par gens de peu, accoutumés à vivre en débauche aux tavernes.' Later he tells us that they learned their chicanery as litigants.

9   Mettam *Government and Society* p132: 'The sovereign courts were those which gave judgment without the right of appeal: the *parlements, cours des*

Even more dangerous to his control was the *Parlement* of Paris's claim to the right to scrutinise legislation before it could come into effect. The King would have none of that.[10] When Louis XIV spoke of sovereign courts, he merely meant those which carried out his wishes directly.

Such jealous concern for retention of power to himself may have been a factor in Louis XIV's failure to support La Roche's arbitration schemes more wholeheartedly – if he had ever heard of them.

JEAN-BAPTISTE COLBERT

Louis XIV's chief minister from 1661 was Jean-Baptiste Colbert (1619–1683).[11] His concern was primarily good management and he could see that what La Roche always calls *chicane* was above all else wasteful. On 22 October 1664, at a time no doubt when La Roche was formulating his arguments against the same evil, Colbert wrote to the King:[12]

> My zeal for Your Majesty's glory will, if it please you, serve as my apology, should I sometimes seem to speak my mind rather freely ... Your Majesty must limit the ways in which your subjects make

---

aides, *chambres des comptes*, and *cours des monnaies*. In a slightly different category but of a similar prestige was the Grand Council.' By far the most important court was the *Parlement* of Paris. A close study of its personnel and activities, political and judicial, at just this period, is AN Hamscher *The Parlement of Paris after the Fronde 1653–1673* 1976, with a full and helpful bibliography. Hamscher never mentions La Roche, or indeed arbitration, which may be some evidence that the vast manuscript sources he has used do not make much reference to it. Also JH Shennan *The Parlement of Paris* 2nd edn 1998 Chapter 8.

10   'M de Verthamont said ... that it had been established that it was the sovereignty of the king alone which could issue laws in the kingdom, and that the sovereign courts and others were ... simply to obey ... The verification of edicts was not some kind of confirmation which the ordinances and the wishes of kings had to receive before they could be carried out ... the word "sovereign" signified not independence but only superiority [ie over lower courts].' Quoted by Mettam, *Government and Society* p135 and see Sturdy *Louis XIV* p13; and see Shennan *Parlement of Paris* Chapter 2.

11   La Roche mentions him only once and then tangentially when praising his brother, the Bishop of Luçon, p25.

12   From Paris; Pierre Clément ed *Lettres, Instructions et Mémoires de Colbert* 7 vols 1861–82 VI pp3–4, translated Mettam *Government and Society* pp132–3. He had written to Mazarin in 1659, criticising his administration's failure to deal with the cost to the country of the inefficient legal system, Hamscher *Parlement of Paris* pp156ff.

their living, in so far as this is possible, to those callings which further your grand designs. These are agriculture, commerce, war on land and war at sea ... The two professions which consume the talents of one hundred thousand of your subjects, aimlessly and without adding to your glory, are finance and the law ...

The law has this fault above all, which is that, apart from using up the energies of more than seventy thousand men, it imposes a tyrannical and burdensome yoke, in your name, upon all the rest of your peoples; by its chicanery it occupies a million men and gnaws away at a million others,[13] reducing them to such misery that they can think about no other profession for the rest of their lives.

If Your Majesty were to consider, should it please him, how much his glory would increase, were so many men to contribute to it, this could indeed be brought about; not in one year of course, nor in two, but perhaps in ten, fifteen, or twenty. To reach such a goal it is necessary to start at once, and to follow a sure and steady path, without letting anyone see Your Majesty's plans. Secrecy is vital to the success of grand designs, not only in order to avoid obstacles which would be great and even insurmountable if such intentions were made public, but also to foster the reputation which Your Majesty will acquire as not just the most powerful but also the most virtuous prince in the world, when one will read in the history books not just that you had formulated these plans at a time when usage and custom would have prompted no man to think of them, but that you brought them to fruition unbeknown to the whole population.

The King must have accepted Colbert's suggested policy because he felt encouraged to write to the King again with more detailed plans on 15 May the following year:[14]

As His Majesty has informed us that he wishes to reduce to a single corpus of ordinances all those things which are necessary for the establishment of a stable and unquestioned jurisprudence, and to diminish the number of judges – the only methods which have not been tried until now as ways of shortening law suits – it remains for us, following the instructions which it has pleased His

13 Though this is no doubt a figure intended to make a general impression and unlikely to be based on calculation, it chimes well with La Roche's estimate of how many lawsuits would be prevented by each parish priest arranging settlement of twenty a year.
14 From Saint-German-en-Laye, Clément *Lettres de Colbert* VI pp5–11.

Majesty to give us, to expound our views on the means which could be used in an attempt to attain these two great goals.

It seems that His Majesty's first step must be to select subjects who are capable of undertaking work of such profound importance; and he appears to have decided to resolve this by ordering all members of his council to send him their opinions, so that he might decide in the fullest knowledge the number of men he wished to employ for this grand design.

At the same time ... he should choose eight *maîtres des requêtes* who are men of both ability and honour, and send them to serve at this moment in all the *parlements* of the realm, bearing instructions to the *Premier Président*, the royal *avocats* and one or two of the most skilful men of goodwill that they should assemble twice weekly at the house of the *Premier Président*, to examine the abuses which have slipped into the workings of the courts and suggest remedies for them, sending their views without delay to His Majesty's Council. It will be necessary to draw up a full set of instructions for these said *maîtres des requêtes*.

Having chosen the people who are to form the special council which His Majesty is creating for the reform of the legal system, it is important that a regular day be chosen for its meetings, either weekly or fortnightly, and that the topics for investigation be divided up among the members as follows:

The scrutiny of every *ordonnance*, in order to decide on the changes which should be proposed. For this task, which is the most crucial and extensive of all, it will be necessary to choose four or six of the ablest councillors of state, who should take with them four or six of the most skilful *avocats* from the *Parlement*, thus forming themselves into a special commission which will meet at the house of the senior councillor of state.

The legal system will have to be divided up into civil law, criminal law and the criminal justice system (*police*). Two councillors and two *avocats* will investigate each of these fields, discussing in the council of twelve what has been decided by each group of four, and finally reporting their conclusions, clearly tabulated, to the royal council ...

The six councillors and the *avocats* who have been chosen to reduce all these *ordonnances* into a single corpus shall examine every ordinance, old and new, article by article, distinguishing those which have been enforced from those which have not, weighing carefully those which need change or correction; and they shall note all the variations which are encountered in the jurisprudence of the different courts ... Consider the discipline of the courts, both internally, between their various chambers, and between one court and another, in order to make them as uniform as possible ...

Having promoted these reforms, perhaps His Majesty will decide to extend this enquiry to cover the whole range of his *ordonnances* ... in order to produce a body of laws as complete as that of Justinian for Roman law.

The second part of His Majesty's design concerns the diminution of the excessive number of officers of justice in the realm, on which depends the realisation of the first part of the plan, granted that it is impossible to dispense pure justice if one does not reduce the ranks of those men who corrupt it daily ...

On 30 May 1665, Louis XIV set up a special law reform commission, the *Conseil de Justice*, as Colbert had suggested.[15] It

15 Pierre Adolphe Chéruel ed *Journal d'Olivier Lefèvre d'Ormesson et Extraits des Mémoires d'André Lefèvre d'Ormesson publié par de Chéruel* 1860–61. D'Ormesson was not a member but he knew what was going on; II p363: 'Sunday 31 May 1665; the King announces his intention of working towards the reform of the legal system and asks the commissioners for memoranda on the reforms to be made.' Olivier was the son of one André and the father of another, both *maîtres des requêtes*, which office Olivier bought on 16 February 1643. He seems to have been a judge with some principles, which naturally brought him to grief. He was in charge of the prosecution of Colbert's predecessor, the former Finance Minister Nicolas Fouquet. His refusal to follow Colbert's instructions to vote for the death penalty thwarted Louis XIV, and allowed Colbert to block his many applications for promotion to the *Conseil d'État*. His father André's place was given instead to Poncet, who had voted for Fouquet's death. He tried many times to win back the King's patronage. Pierre Adolphe Chéruel *De l'Administra-tion de Louis XIV (1661–1672) d'Après les Mémoires Inédits d'Olivier D'Ormesson* 1850 p33 tells of an audience in 1665, when Olivier's father André was ill and the King expressed his concern for his health. Olivier took advantage of the apparent opening to push his ambitions but suffered the King's reproof: 'When you deserve it I will willingly grant it.' No better came from an audience arranged by the Duc d'Aumont on 16 June 1670, Chéruel *Administration de Louis XIV* pp209–12, one hopes not in gratitude for a favourable verdict D'Ormesson gave him as arbitrator just three months earlier, see Chapter 4. D'Ormesson sold his office of *maître des requêtes* in 1667, not out of any moral principle but on the sound financial judgment that the King would soon make it unprofitable by one of his many heavy levies, Chéruel *D'Ormesson* II. But when D'Ormesson presented his son to Louis XIV on his admission as an advocate, the King is said to have told him: 'You could have no better model than the man who prosecuted Fouquet.' The D'Ormesson family archives do not appear to contain anything about arbitration: Michel Antoine and Yvonne Lanhers *Les Archives D'Ormesson* 1960, which has a portrait of Olivier.

met every fortnight from 27 September 1665. Neither the *Parlement* of Paris nor the legal professions were represented as institutions and by the time the *Parlement* got round to making its own suggestions, the work was well advanced. Half the members were from the *Conseil d'État*,[16] the others eminent jurists chosen for their individual merits. Suggestions for criticism and reform were widely solicited, however, and *maîtres des requêtes* were appointed and sent out to *parlements* around the country to discuss the replies, to seek more opinions and to report back to the commission.[17] From 28 October 1666 to 10 February 1667 it met every week, sometimes for several days.[18] It seems likely that La Roche knew what was going on and the apparent opportunities to influence reform may have encouraged him to prepare a manuscript for publication.

Drafts of what had become a new code of civil procedure were discussed by the commission, sometimes in the presence of the King, who is said to have resolved difficult or controversial problems himself. Certainly his determination to create a comprehensive and detailed yet succinct code of civil procedure seems not only to have equalled that of his grandfather Henry IV but this time to have had some success.

THE *ORDONNANCE CIVILE* 1667

The *Ordonnance Civile* came into force on 20 April 1667, the year after La Roche's book first appeared.[19] It has been claimed to be

16 Their memoranda fill several hundred folios in the *Bibliothèque Nationale*, Hamscher *Parlement de Paris* p236 n11. It was assisted by Charles d'Aligres de la Rivière, see below Chapter 5 fn36.

17 Clément *Lettres de Colbert*. On 11 October 1665, Hotman said the criminal justice system had too few laws and regulations, its civil equivalent too many.

18 *Anciennes Lois* XVII p103 fn1 says that its members were: Chancelier Séguier, Maréchal de Villeroi, Colbert, D'Aligre, D'Ormesson, De Lézeau, De Machault, De Sève, Menardeau, De Morangis, Poncet, Boucherat, De la Marguerie, Pussort, Voisin, Hotman and Marin. But this information is not dependable, since it is clear from his *Journal* that D'Ormesson was not a member, see Chapter 4. Chéruel *Administration de Louis XIV* pp113–16 also describes the creation and operation of this commission and reports that the King himself said that it should meet every other Sunday from 10am till noon.

19 The *Ordonnance Civile* concerning the Reform of the Legal System, St-Germain-en-Laye, *Anciennes Lois* XVII p103ff. Chéruel *Administration de Louis XIV* p123 says that it was 'enregistré' by the *Parlement* of Paris on that day in the King's presence. The '*Code Louis*' remained substantially in force until the *Code Napoléon* and in part until after World War II. The *Ordonnance Criminelle* 1670 is outside our scope, though La Roche perhaps looks forward to

the 'greatest legislative monument between the Roman law and the *Code Napoléon'*.[20] Its preamble states its policy:

> As the legal system is the most solid foundation for the survival of states, which ensures peace among families and the peoples' welfare, we have put all our efforts into re-establishing it by the following laws of our kingdom, after granting it peace through the force of our arms. That is why, having learned from the reports of persons of wide experience that the *ordonnances* so wisely laid down by the kings our predecessors to end litigation have been ignored or tampered with by the passage of time and the ill-will of litigants; that they are even interpreted differently in some of our courts, which brings ruin on families by the multiplicity of proceedings, the cost of the actions and the inconsistency of judgments; and that it is necessary to provide for these matters and expedite such business more promptly, more simply and more reliably by getting rid of some of the delays and unnecessary litigation, and by establishing uniformity of procedure in all our courts and sessions. For these reasons, with the advice of our Council and of our own certain knowledge, full power and royal authority, we declare etc.

La Roche must have been disappointed that, despite the King's apparent approval of his manual and the widespread support he insists the first edition received, the new *Ordonnance Civile*, for all its size, comprehensiveness and detail, and the thoroughness of its preparation, showed no sign that the King had taken any notice of La Roche's recommendations, though it seems unlikely that Louis XIV would not have known of them if they had any influence at all. Though much is done to ameliorate the evils of chicanery, there is nothing in the *Ordonnance* which directly promotes arbitration or mediation. Perhaps La Roche's disappointment explains the impatience occasionally revealed in our edition of 1668, and the persistence with which he is determined to drive its message home.[21]

---

it in Chapter XV. It was much more controversial, both in its creation and implementation, than the *Ordonnance Civile*. A *Code Marchand* was enacted in 1673 and an *Ordonnance de la Marine* in 1681.

20 Chéruel *Administration de Louis XIV* p111; Hamscher *Parlement de Paris* pp172–81.

21 Yet there is nothing in the 1668 edition of the manual to show that the *Ordonnance Civile* was in force or that La Roche knew of its contents. When he writes of 'the *Ordonnance*', he cannot mean the *Ordonnance Civile* 1667.

Except in his last chapter, where he deals with objections raised against the reforms suggested in the previous chapter, which are restricted to partnerships and commercial contracts, La Roche says nothing of any opposition to his proposals. But there is no evidence that they found favour with the King or anyone else in authority. Indeed, there may be some indication of the negative attitudes of some contemporary lawyers in a much later letter to Colbert from the *Procureur-Général* Harlay:[22]

> The Archbishop of Paris, having ordered me on behalf of the King to forbid the continuation of an assembly which was active in the Parish of St Severin, I asked him to instruct the curé, who had informed His Majesty of it, to find out who takes part and what they are up to. He tells me that a brotherhood of St Joseph has been established in the parish for some years, by virtue of Royal Letters Patent registered with the *Parlement*.
>
> Disputes having arisen among some of the members, they resolved to meet at the home of one D'Auvergne, a royal professor, and they had brought in some members of other parishes, and together they sought to mediate for and otherwise assist poor people who were involved in litigation.
>
> That was what I was able to find out. It seemed to me that if the assembly took place in his home, with people who had no dispute with *him*, there was nothing in it to object to. In default of further clarification and having discovered that M D'Auvergne was known to M Bignon, whose late father had entrusted to him the education of his brother, the *maître des requêtes*, I asked for further information.
>
> The curé informed me that one David and a doctor of theology Courbajon met several times at the home of M D'Auvergne to

---

That is clear from his statement: 'This *Arrest* merely repeated the *Ordonnance*'. The *Ordonnance* to which he refers regularly without further description must therefore have preceded the *Arrest*. And the *Arrest* must have preceded the *Règlement* which he says reported it – to which he gives the date *1526*! Moreover, the second edition repeats exactly the words of the first, published a year before the *Ordonnance Civile*.

22 Letter from Harlay to Colbert, Paris 17 June 1699, GB Depping ed *Correspondance Administrative sous le Règne de Louis XIV* 1850–55 IV p699. Harlay was *Procureur-Général* and later *Premier Président* at the *Parlement* of Paris. He did not die until 1712, Clément *Lettres de Colbert* VI pp32–3, Mettam *Government and Society* p151. His memorandum to the law reform committee survives, Hamscher *Parlement de Paris* p157. It was Harlay's practice to ask the King what he should do when he was not sure how the King would like legislation to be interpreted, Hamscher p181.

assist in the settlement of certain litigation of poor persons who had recourse to them and that M D'Auvergne had told him that, since there was objection to them having met in this way, he would give his word that there would be no more such meetings.

The advice they should be given should be that they should resolve the dispute, with the curé of St Severin, for the benefit of the brotherhood of St Joseph. The curé has talked to D'Auvergne and Courbajon together and they have both repeated the same undertakings.

So that, sir, is the report I can give you; on which I await your orders, instructing me whether upon that evidence I ought to obtain an *arrest*. I am obliged to tell you that these people seem to me quite incompetent, from the conversations I have had with them, and there is great risk if they take on the judgment of litigation.

It is interesting, then, that La Roche cites M Harlay[23] as creator and supporter of such assemblies: 'without having been asked, he has already set up assemblies where he appears regularly, to take special care of the prisons and to deal with the affairs of prisoners.'[24] Of course, public figures may find it expedient to say one thing to a reformer and another to the Chief Minister; more than thirty years had passed between first publication of the manual and Harlay writing to Colbert. And a civil servant may be more content with arbitration schemes restricted to prisoners and under his direct control than with arbitration generally available as a more attractive alternative to the courts. But this letter should make us view with caution La Roche's presentation of other authorities as wholehearted supporters of his proposals, unless there is corroboration.

AN EIGHTEENTH-CENTURY ECHO: *L'AMI DE LA CONCORDE*

An anonymous pamphlet of 1765 contains so many parallels with the arguments against chicanery which La Roche made a century earlier that they justify the translation of some of it for

23 At the end of Chapter XXV.
24 The Duchesse de Longueville also took special care of prisoners, see Chapter 4. There is no suggestion in the manual that Harlay's prisoners were also from the *Fronde*.

L'AMI
DE LA CONCORDE,

OU

ESSAI

Sur les Motifs d'éviter les Procès , & sur
les moyens d'en tarir la source.

PAR UN AVOCAT AU PARLEMENT.

A LONDRES;

Et se trouve ,

A PARIS,

Chez MONORY, Libraire de S. A. S.
Monseigneur le Prince de CONDÉ, rue &
vis-à-vis l'ancienne Comédie Françoise.

M. DCC. LXXIX.

comparison.[25] The second edition's title page, given opposite in facsimile, reads: *The Friend of Concord, or Essay on the Reasons for Avoiding Litigation & the Ways of Drying up its Source. By an Avocat at the Parlement.* London and Paris Monory. M. DCC. LXXIX. The author's name is said to be Champlair.[26]

The work is in two parts. The first is a critical analysis and condemnation of chicanery. The second suggests that the answer is education in law, first for lawyers, who it says were getting, if anything, a totally worthless sham;[27] secondly for the general public or at least the educated classes.

The Introduction (p3) begins:

> The glory of winning lawsuits has always pleased me less than the sweet satisfaction of preventing them or mediating their settlement (*les accommoder*). I have noticed that, of all the means I have used to persuade my clients to prefer conciliation or arbitration to the so-called paths of Justice,[28] that which I have most often found successful has been to paint them a true picture of the way litigation is instituted and decided upon in the courts. That lets them see, from the large number of people for whom it

25 I have found reference to only two copies of the first edition (London 1765 102pp), one in the Harvard Law Library, the other in the British Library but shown in the catalogue as 'missing'. I have not seen a copy. There is a copy of the second edition of 1779 in the New York Public Library. I have worked from my own copy of the second edition, which lacks the plate apparently called for and present in the library copies of both editions.
26 All the bibliographies state it to be so, though they give no sources.
27 This was not a new complaint. It had been made a century earlier in memoranda to Louis XIV's law reform commission, Hamscher *Parlement de Paris* p159 and the sources cited in his endnote p212 n21.
28 Champlair's own footnote reads:

> One calls recourse to judges, to decide disputes, the path of Justice; that is not because it is more just to proceed by this path than to end them by an arbitration or settlement. For, on the contrary, it conforms infinitely better with Divine Law, and is therefore more just, and more efficient as well, to avoid that path and seek peace, even at the risk of some loss, rather than litigate and get caught up in the results to which all litigation leads, which are equally contrary to altruism and self-regard (*charité et amour-propre*).

Champlair is quoting Jean Domat, on Public Law Book IV. Domat (1625–1696) wrote *Les Loix Civiles dans leur Ordre Naturel* in 1689. An English translation by William Strahan was published in London 1722: *The Civil Law in its Natural Order together with the Publick Law* 2 vols. The passage Champlair quotes is in vol II of that translation at p652, where Domat discusses generally the advantages and procedures of arbitration. He deals with the law of arbitration in detail at pp624–6 and with arbitrators' powers in vol I pp225–6.

provides a livelihood and who enrich themselves at the expense of the litigants, that the costs almost always come to exceed the amount in issue and result in the ruin of one or other, or often both, of the parties.

Most of Champlair's arguments echo those of La Roche and none of the evils of chicanery seem to have been remedied in the century between them. He sums up:[29]

> I think I have done enough to show that the lawyers' interests are always opposed to those of the parties who are forced to go to them for help, so that anybody who uses his wits will avoid litigation ... My answer is, if there are times when litigation is necessary, they are few in number. There is scarcely any point of difference which one cannot settle by conciliation or arbitration.
>
> Everybody knows how one should behave. Offer easy terms to your debtor. Don't make him give you a garnishment without first having seen him and heard his excuses. Consent to any reasonable arrangements he proposes to you. Don't demand the impossible. If you have rights you can enforce against someone, or if someone formulates a claim against you, talk to your adversary or get him to talk to you. Suggest to him that you exercise your rights against one another in a friendly fashion.
>
> Isn't it more gracious and wiser to press your demands through the intervention of mutual friends than through the employment of a *huissier*? Is there no way to make your points except on stamped paper, ridiculous in form, barbarous in style and crude in its chicanery? And at what a cost!
>
> If you cannot settle the matter by the mediation of mutual friends, or if there are special circumstances, such as when the interests of minors are involved, or the Church, or religious buildings or communities, you may have to go to court, and get a decision for the discharge of guardians or trustees, who have no power themselves to make a settlement. But even then the parties, unless they are motivated by feelings of hate or ambition or pride or jealousy, can come to an amicable arrangement about their matter, agreeing the facts, limiting the matters in issue, and presenting a collusive judgment for the court's approval. In that way they can avoid most of the costs and even the delays and pointless procedures.

29 At p48. The reforms of Louis XIV were generally accepted in the next century to have failed, Hamscher *Parlement de Paris* pp193–4, quoting among others Isaac de Larrey in 1718: 'chicanery is no less stubborn.'

Champlair introduces criticisms[30] and suggestions of his own, which are not found in La Roche. Having rehearsed once again the shortcomings of a system which devotes its resources and its learning to fostering adversarial attitudes between the parties, he advises them to appoint an *avocat* as arbitrator (p45):

> The way to avoid this inconvenience would be for the parties, before going to see their *procureur*, to have the matter placed in the hands of an *avocat* of recognised integrity. He would see that they understood the mistake they had been led to make. He would render them a service more notable than if he were to take their case and would stop them ruining themselves.

It is important to seek arbitration before you even go to a solicitor, because once you are in his hands the costs build up so quickly that they inhibit settlement (p43):

> The costs soon become more important than the object of the litigation, and an obstacle to conciliation. The matter is transferred from court to court and the proceedings become an object of commerce.

And he quotes Boileau, *Poème du Lutrin*:[31]

> And in those hearts, hot with the thirst for pleading,
> Bubble the lust to hurt and the fear of ceding.

The reform which Champlair favoured would have appealed to La Roche (pp54–6):

> There is a way, which is fully worthy of the King's support, which would prevent at least half the litigation and abuses which ruin his poor people, particularly those who live in the country, who are the dupes of the bad faith and greed of the lawyers in whom they are forced to put their trust. While we are waiting for His Majesty to be able to carry out the obligation accepted by Louis XIV and

---

30   He was particularly incensed by the conspiracy between paper merchants and the scriveners who grossly exaggerated the number of sheets required by writing very large, with few lines to a page and few words to a line, a racket which withstood all the detailed legislation forbidding it.

31   *Et dans les coeurs brûlans de la soif de plaider,*
     Versent l'Amour de nuire & la peur de céder.

Nicolas Boileau (1636–1711), French *avocat* and, as soon as he could afford it, poet and arbiter of literary style. Satires first published 1666. *Le Lutrin* (The Lectern) was published in two parts, 1674, 1683.

all the kings who preceded him, of providing his subjects with free justice,[32] and for the state of his affairs to permit him to pay the salaries and fees of those who are employed in it, there should be a temporary measure which would do no one harm and would extend great benefits.

There ought to be established in every *généralité* one or two *jurisconsultes* whose integrity and experience are well known, to give free advice, each in his own *arrondissement*, to the country people about their affairs, and to conciliate their differences, to sort out their accounts, their apportionments, and to make all those payments and do the other business which one would like to arrange amicably, or at least to show how that can all be done with the least cost.

There would be an arbitrator, who would exercise a purely voluntary jurisdiction, a minister of peace and truth, who would dictate to this precious part of the human race the conduct which they ought to adopt, explain to them the laws which affect them, and give them his advice on litigation present and future. The parties would be at liberty to follow that advice or not. Just one such arbitrator, hard working and conscientious, would be enough for several *élections* of the same *généralité*. Their appointment would be on the King's nomination and would be open only to advocates of at least ten years' standing with honour in the profession. They would combine legal learning and practical experience with integrity and a conciliatory approach.

As for any honorarium to be allotted them, they would be expressly forbidden to receive anything, either in cash or kind, however voluntarily and on whatever pretext it might be offered. Only a complete absence of self-interest would make them trusted. The *Intendant de Justice, Police & Finances* of the *Département* would receive and take note of any complaints which might be made of their negligence or their failure to carry out their duties properly; and they would be dismissed if they were found guilty.

The responsibility for paying the salaries of these offices would either be imposed on some *Bénéfice* of the Province (what fund

---

32 Champlair's own footnote here reads:

> 'Justice should be rendered without cost. The usage of earlier centuries has, however, introduced, for the judges' benefit, some allocation on top of the pay that we have granted them, for which we intend to take responsibility in future, when the state of our affairs allows it. However, we have resolved to provide for it by a reasonable *tempérament*.' Preamble to the *Édit* of 1673, on *Épices* and Fees and the Costs of Justice.

could have more pious or more useful purposes!) or on the sum allocated in each *généralité* to support the costs of Justice and *Police* and the welfare of the people. What better purpose could they put it to? What could they do that would be of more real benefit to the people than to give them the means to undertake peace and unity and avoid the upsets, the costs and the sad consequences of litigation?

When the salaries were shared out among the different parishes of the *arrondissement*, the imposition would be negligible. For less than five sous a year, every individual would be able to have an adviser for his affairs at all times. How much would that save them in costs? Even if there are one or two well-known *avocats* in the Provinces, one dreads going into their offices. *Non licet omnibus adire Corinthum* (not everyone can get to Corinth).[33] Those who live in the country are afraid to incur the costs of a consultation, just as they are afraid to call a doctor when they are sick.

This scheme would have more prompt and certain effect than all the legislation that could be passed for the reform of the administration of justice. Wisdom is never so ready to think of new safeguards as mischief is to escape them. To cure the evils you must grasp them at the root. From the litigation that I have prevented or put an end to in the little time I have spent in the countryside, I know the good a person can do who is totally occupied with this business. He would be able to do more good than two hundred could do evil. When they came to consult him, he would not inflame the passions of the litigants, but would always tell them the truth, because he would never have any interest in concealing or dissimulating. When their demands were well-founded, he would get them, before going to court, to exhaust every avenue of pleasantness and civility, every initiative and every conciliatory overture towards the party on the other side. He would even require them to spell out their own motives. He would constantly try to get them to come to an amicable resolution. There could be no more noble task, more satisfying for a true gentleman, and of more use to the nation.

---

33 A version of 'non cuivis homini contingit adire Corinthum' Horace *Epistles* 1 XVII 36. In origin a Greek proverb, it may allude to the Corinthian Games. It could then be rendered: 'everybody can't get a gold medal' rather than some variation of 'The courts of justice are open to all ... like the Ritz Hotel.' Here it is a reminder that in litigation there is always at least one loser.

Like La Roche, though without his salty directness, Champlair can make use of a good tale (pp49–50).

> I know one example, among others, of a lawsuit between two Ecclesiastics, where they were arguing over a tree worth about 28 livres. One, My Lord *Haut-Justicier*, argued that this tree was in the road, and belonged to him. The other insisted that the tree was on his land. This simple question of fact cost the *Haut-Justicier* (who lost) 2,800 livres. The winner's unrecoverable costs were more than 300 livres. If these two Ecclesiastics had got together, before the summons was served, to find out the costly information they needed before there could be a decision; if they had begun by examining the position of the tree, asked the opinion of older neighbours and looked at their title, they could have had their agreed settlement approved by the court for 24 livres. Better still there would have been no need for any litigation. If the question seemed really in doubt, they could have shared the tree.

And he ends with the moral of the whole story: 'As in medicine, it is much more ethical to prevent sickness than it is to try to cure it.'

It is likely that Champlair knew of La Roche's projects. The best evidence, for what it is worth, is from similarities between their texts. Champlair describes the *Arrest* of 1610.

> Henry IV conceived the plan of a scheme not all that different, and had even ordained it by an *arrest* of his Council of 6 March 1610. That good king was moved by a charitable and paternal affection for his poor people, and wanted to find the means of getting justice for widows, orphans, distressed gentlefolk, merchants, workers and generally for all those who lacked advice or money, the one or the other. He therefore ordained that in all his courts, sovereign as well as inferior, some *avocats* and *procureurs* should be assigned to the poor, in such numbers as his Council should advise him, according to the size and needs of each court or bench, who should be required to help with their advice, industry, labour and attendance, all those of the above-mentioned characteristics, without taking from them anything at all, however little, under whatever pretext it might be, under the penalty for misappropriation of public funds. They would have to be satisfied with just the wages, salaries and perquisites which His Majesty was pleased to grant to the said *avocats* and *procureurs*, who would be picked and chosen as the most able and respectable. They would

hold office as long as they performed their duties. The unforeseen death of that Monarch, who died the following 14 May, prevented the execution of this praiseworthy plan, which no doubt has been reserved for LOUIS LE BIEN-AIMÉ.

Though one cannot be sure, it would not be surprising if Champlair had taken some of the information and ideas in that last paragraph from La Roche, though they could have come directly from Laujorrois.[34] It is noteworthy that Champlair does not here mention charitable arbitrators, or indeed arbitration at all. And he correctly calls the measure an *arrest* of the King's Council rather than an *édit* or *ordonnance*, the terms which La Roche uses.

VOLTAIRE

Where did Champlair get his ideas? There is a copy of *L'Arbitre Charitable* in the library of the *Avocats au Parlement* in Paris[35] to which Champlair as an *avocat* would have had access if it was there in his day. But in a footnote he quotes from the letter of Voltaire (1694–1778) which I have set out in full below, with the quoted passage in bold type. Champlair, therefore, could have taken some of La Roche's ideas indirectly from Voltaire, if they are to be found anywhere in the philosopher's voluminous works.[36] But there is telling evidence against that conclusion.

Voltaire was widely read and respected, though many of his works were banned, as was this letter.[37]

It is to be hoped that the leaders of nations follow the example of people in trade. As soon as someone in London finds out that they

---

34 There is no copy of Laujorrois in the Library of the *Avocats* of the *Parlement* of Paris.

35 See Chapter 5 below. Surprisingly, there is no copy of Champlair's *L'Ami* in the catalogue of the *Avocats*.

36 Louis Moland ed *Oeuvres Complètes de Voltaire* 1877–85. There is a more complete edition, Theodore Besterman ed *The Complete Works of Voltaire* 1953–64 and a second edn by Besterman and others *Voltaire's Correspondence* 1970–. Searching is now made more efficient by the new CDRom *Voltaire Électronique* 1996.

37 'Fragment of a Letter on a Very Useful Practice Established in Holland 1739', Moland *Voltaire* XXIII pp127–8. A note explains the date attributed to it, 1739: 'this scrap, which till now has been dated 1742, or even 1745, is part of a volume entitled *Recueil des Pièces Fugitives de M de V**** in 8vo with the date MDCCXL but condemned by an *arrêt de Conseil* of 4 December 1739'.

are making a new fabric in France, they copy it. Why should not a statesman hasten to enact in his own country a useful law from abroad? We are johnny-come-latelies in making porcelain like that from China. We manage to do things as well as our neighbours do, and they take advantage of what we do best.

There is one fellow here who grows fruit in his garden which ripens naturally only south of the equator. We have on our doorstep a thousand wise laws and customs. Those are the fruits that we ought to be cultivating at home, the trees we ought to be transplanting here. They grow in any climate and do well whatever the ground is like.

The best Law, the most excellent custom, the most useful that I have ever seen, is in Holland. When two people want to sue one another, they are first obliged to go before a tribunal of *juges-conciliateurs*, called peacemakers. If the parties arrive with an *avocat* and a *procureur*, they make them retire first, as you remove wood from a fire you want to put out. The peacemakers say to the parties: 'You are very foolish to want to consume all your money in making one another unhappy. We are going to make a settlement for you and it is going to cost you nothing.'

If the frenzy of chicanery is too strong in the litigants, they are adjourned to another day, so that time may assuage the symptoms of their illnesses. Then the judges send for them to be brought before them a second and a third time. If their madness is incurable, they are allowed to litigate, as gangrenous limbs are abandoned to the surgeon's steel. That is the practice of Justice.[38]

I do not need to go on about this, or work out the amount of benefit to the human race if this law were to be adopted. Moreover, I do not want to trespass at all on the preserves of M l'Abbé de Saint-Pierre,[39] whose projects a witty government

---

38 An editor's footnote here reads: 'This example has been followed by M le Duc de Rohan-Chabot on his estates in Brittany, where some years ago he set up a conciliation tribunal. *Juges de Paix* were established in France by the law of 24 August 1790.'

39 Charles Irénée Castel de Saint-Pierre (1658–1743), born into the minor nobility and educated by the Jesuits in Caen; took minor orders and went to Paris to study in 1686; joined opposition to Louis XIV and later the service of the regent's mother. In 1695 member of the Académie Française and 1702 commendatory (absentee) Abbé de Tiron. Secretary of the Abbé de Polignac at the peace talks in Utrecht and in 1713–17 published *Projet pour Rendre la Paix Perpetuelle en Europe*, recommending the appointment of arbitrators as a way of avoiding wars. In 1717 published *Discours de la*

minister[40] called 'dreams of a do-gooder'. I know that a private individual who dares to propose something for the public good often makes a fool of himself. They say: 'What is he interfering in that for? He is a funny fellow to want us to be happier than we are! Does he not know that an abuse is always the inheritance of a good part of the nation? Why does he want to get rid of an evil by which so many people earn their living?' To that I have no answer.

Voltaire echoes La Roche in his reference to the frenzy of chicanery and, most particularly, in his quite specific metaphor of litigation as gangrene. Moreover, he then proceeds from private disputes to the arbitration of the wars of kings. La Roche more than once says that war is to kings as litigation is to individuals. But, if Voltaire had known La Roche's book, he would have known it as the work of the Prieur de Saint Pierre. Could a writer like Voltaire have made fun of his near namesake of a later generation, the Abbé de Saint Pierre, notorious for his utopian projects for inter-state arbitration, without making something of the connection?

The reference in this letter is by no means the only one. Voltaire seems to have had ambivalent feelings about the Abbé. As a philosopher and a reformer, Voltaire tried to preserve his reputation for pragmatism. He knew that politically he could be suppressed more easily by scorn than censorship. It was therefore convenient to refer to the Abbé as the personification of utopian reform, the better to throw Voltaire into contrast as the realist.

The first reference is in a letter of 27 January 1737 to the Comte d'Argental.[41] Voltaire is complaining of the calumnies being heaped on him: 'If the Abbé de Saint-Pierre has some project for stopping slander, I will happily have it printed at my own expense.'

Polysynodie in which his proposals for a new constitution were seen as an attack on Louis XIV's appetite for glory. Scandal was followed by his expulsion from the *Académie*. Poured out projects for making the world a better place until he died: 'at the last he fulfilled the Christian duties to indulge his family – for he did not believe a word of all that', see *Diction-naire de Biographie Française* VII and Joseph Drouet ed *L'Abbé de Saint-Pierre: Annales Politiques (1658–1740)* 1912.

40 A footnote suggests that this was Cardinal Dubois.
41 From Leiden, Moland *Voltaire* VI p44 letter 1212.

In a letter of 29 December 1738 to NC Thierot[42] Voltaire mocks him more openly: 'this is my little formula for passing the hat round for the Lapplanders, following the rituals of Charity (*Bienfaisance*) of the Abbé de Saint-Pierre of Utopia'. Another letter to the same recipient of the same date:[43] 'I would like you to give it to him with a hundred and fifty *livres* for him to put in the coffers of the Lapps. M l'Abbé de Saint-Pierre can call this *bienfaisance* if he likes but it is a reparation which France owes. We are not at all *publik-spirited* (sic) in France. We have not even got a word for it.'

In a letter of 8 May 1739 to the Marquis d'Argenson,[44] Voltaire mentions the Abbé again, in an aside to his flattery of the Marquis: 'I find all my ideas in your work. They are not in any way just the dreams of a do-gooder,[45] like the chimerical projects of the good Abbé de Saint-Pierre ... this is not a project for perpetual peace.' And again in a letter to the Marquis of 18 or 19 December 1744:[46] 'You are making me into a little Abbé de Saint-Pierre. I have good intentions ...'

The most interesting exchange, though, is with Frederick the Great over a period of twenty-seven years. Could Frederick II's respect for the Abbé have made Voltaire a little jealous?

In a letter to Voltaire of 12 April 1742[47] Frederick II said that the Abbé had sent him: 'a fine work on how to reestablish peace in Europe and authenticate it for ever. It is a very practical matter. To make it succeed it only needs the consent of Europe and perhaps something else equally trivial.' This seems to share Voltaire's mockery and Voltaire replied on 26 May 1742:[48] 'I think about humanity, Sire, before I even think of you; but having had the Abbé de Saint-Pierre crying over the human race

---

42 Moland *Voltaire* VIII p121 letter 1640.
43 Moland *Voltaire* VIII p124 letter 1642.
44 Besterman *Complete Works* vol 9 1913 from Cirey. René Louis de Voyer de Paulmy, Marquis d'Argenson, had been a pupil of the Abbé, Drouet *L'Abbé de Saint-Pierre* pXII. Together with the Abbé Alary they founded the Club d'Entresol (the Mezzanine Club) after Saint-Pierre was expelled from the Académie.
45 'd'un homme de bien' – a phrase Voltaire seems to have enjoyed using in this sense at that time, compare the '*gens de bien*' of Laujorrois, above Chapter 2.
46 Moland *Voltaire* XIV p85 letter 2839.
47 Moland *Voltaire* XII p30 letter 2434 from Tribau.
48 Moland *Voltaire* XII p47 letter 2441 from Paris.

– of which you are the Terror – I abandon myself to all the joy that your glory gives me. There you are... the arbitrator of Europe. You will be its peacemaker ... .' He wrote to Frederick again on 15 July 1742:[49] 'I have always hoped for this universal peace as if I were the Abbé de Saint-Pierre's bastard ... The Abbé de Saint-Pierre will tell you, Sire, that to get to heaven you must do just as much good to the Chinese as to the Brandenburgers and the Silesians.' Frederick replied on 25 July 1742:[50] 'As for the Abbé de Saint-Pierre's Platonic Arbitrator, he is not going to happen. There are no resources left to kings to end their disputes other than to take practical steps to extract from their adversaries the fair satisfactions which they cannot get by any other expedient.'

It was not just in the privacy of his correspondence that Voltaire ridiculed the Abbé. In *Le Français* he says:[51]

This will inevitably come to pass when the perpetual peace of the Abbé de Saint-Pierre is signed by the Grand Turk and the Great Powers, and when they build the city of Arbitration, near the hole where they are trying to drill to the centre of the earth to find out exactly how they should behave on the surface.

Nearly thirty years later, in his letter to Voltaire of 25 November 1769,[52] Frederick the Great says, perhaps with gentle reproof for Voltaire's sustained mockery of a well-intentioned man: 'so I would like Europe to be at peace, and the whole world to be happy. I think I must have inherited these notions from the late Abbé de Saint-Pierre. It may well happen to me, as it did to him, that I become the only member of my sect.'

All this makes it unlikely that Voltaire knew anything of the *Prieur* de Saint Pierre. It is equally unlikely that the *Abbé* had read his namesake's book. In 1725 he published *Mémoire pour Diminuer le Nombre des Procès*. With his great hopes for arbitration as an end to war, it might be expected to offer arbitration as a means of reducing the amount of litigation. But nowhere in its more than 400 pages is there any reference to arbitration, mediation or even settlement. It uses many of the same

49 Moland *Voltaire* XII p68 letter 2456.
50 Moland *Voltaire* XII pp70–71 letter 2457.
51 Moland *Voltaire* XX 'Le Français'.
52 Besterman and others *Voltaire's Correspondence* vol 73 15018.

arguments against and cites many of the same examples of the evils of chicanery. But its recommendations totally exclude those of La Roche. Its answer is to simplify, unify and clarify the law, replacing the multiplicity of customs, the encrustations of nice points, and the artificialities of language. All would be accomplished by a well-paid permanent law reform commission and the provision of prizes for good ideas; and the establishment not of mediation or arbitration but of an Academy of French Law.

4 PATRONS, ARBITRATORS AND MEDIATORS

The parson knows enough who knows a duke.
William Cowper *Tirocinium* 1785

LA ROCHE'S CHARACTERS

For authority, precedent and example, La Roche introduces the reader to a rich variety of characters, from his real hero, the humble good curé, to the King himself. Some, like the curé, are anonymous but many are well known figures in the history of the times and may be found in the standard French biographical dictionaries. There is nothing dry about those biographies, nor dispassionate, which makes them more entertaining but even less dependable than their English equivalents. Some of the characters were themselves arbitrators or more usually mediators, some were patrons and supporters of arbitration.

THE PRINCE DE CONTI: THE EXEMPLARY GOVERNOR

Armand de Bourbon, Prince de Conti,[1] (1629–1666) was the second son of Henry II, Prince de Condé, and the brother of the Duchesse de Longueville, who is described in the next section. He married the niece of Cardinal Mazarin, godfather of Louis XIV and the chief minister in control of the government while Louis XIV's mother, Anne of Austria, was regent. De Conti joined his sister and elder brother, the Grand Condé, on the anti-Regency side in the *Fronde*. He was arrested and imprisoned with his brother and his sister's husband in January 1650 and released by Mazarin a year later.[2]

1　There may have been some family connection between Conti and the author, which I have been unable to run down; a title in the Conti family was Prince de la Roche-sur-Yon.
2　Sturdy *Louis XIV* p28.

Louis XIV forgave De Conti, appointed him Provincial Governor of Languedoc and made use of his administrative skills in many ways.[3] A letter and report of a speech in 1662 show his strong support for the King in difficult circumstances.[4] Two letters written to Colbert in December 1665 from royal officials sent to the provinces, President de Novion in the Auvergne and the royal commissioners in Languedoc, show him active in the King's service in improving the legal system.[5] In his memoirs, Louis XIV wrote: 'The unforeseen death of the Prince de Conti at the end of February created a serious problem for me',[6] but not everyone thought highly of De Conti; Cardinal de Retz wrote: 'I very nearly forgot to mention him; he was a zero, only to be multiplied because he happened to be a Prince of the Blood.'[7]

He became devout and put his religious principles into practice.[8] He was persuaded that his duty required him not to give up all worldly wealth, as he said he had first intended, but to use his great power not only to ameliorate the condition of those under his administration but also to provide an example for other great lords to follow. To this end he wrote tracts which were collected and published in 1667 after his death as *Mémoires de Monseigneur le Prince de Conty Touchant les Obligations des Gouverneurs de Province et Ceux Servans à la Conduite et Direction de sa Maison*. This was translated into English and published in 1711

---

3 One of his sons, Louis-Armand, Prince de Conti, married Marie-Anne, Louis XIV's legitimated daughter.
4 From the Bishop of St-Papoul to the King via Colbert from Béziers, 13 January 1662: 'M the Prince de Conti, accompanied by other royal commissioners, entered the assembly of estates yesterday. He spoke very well and very strongly in Your Majesty's interests. He finished his speech by saying: "Remember I speak for a King, and a King who governs".' GB Depping ed *Correspondance Administrative sous le Règne de Louis XIV* 1851 I p59; and at p61: 'I will be silent once I have reminded you that he who is asking you is a King and a King who governs.'
5 Président de Novion wrote from the Auvergne: 'The Marquis de Canillac had taken refuge in a religious house. Monseigneur the Prince de Conti sent some of his guards to arrest him.' Depping *Correspondance de Louis XIV* II pp167–8; and the *Commissaires du Roi près des Etats en Languedoc* wrote from Béziers that de Conti had been active since his arrival in the province, and had taken special notice of the violence, Depping II p170.
6 Paul Sonnino *Louis XIV King of France and Navarre* p155.
7 Vita Sackville-West *Daughter of France* 1959 p70.
8 So did his wife, who sold all her jewels and used the money to care for the poor, [Armand de Conti] *Works of Conty* London W Bray 1711 xxxix–xl. He became hostile to his old schoolmate, Molière.

as *The Works of the Most Illustrious and Pious Armand de Bourbon, Prince of Conti, with a Short Account of His Life &c.*

De Conti was well known for the zeal with which he harried the Huguenots, in accordance with Louis XIV's wishes. The *Works* put it nicely:[9]

He had many Difficulties and Obstacles to surmount, to bring those of the Reformed Religion to conform to the King's Edicts; to put an end to the Violence and Tyranny which the Powerful exercised over the weak; to abolish Duels; and to appease Quarrels and Differences.

De Conti was opposed to the sale of judicial offices. He insisted that the great lords should follow his example, stressing the need to take care to get good judges on their estates, scrupulously examining them to be sure of their ability:[10]

... and never to sell offices, because above all the exercise of justice cannot be valued in money; since the *Vénalité des Charges* was introduced, they have banished all consideration of merit and ability.

The second of the most important precepts he ordained for governors was:[11]

... to take care that Justice should be well administered; that is why he carefully investigates the lifestyle and the abilities of the royal judges, *magistrats* and *procureurs*, so that if there should be something worthy of criticism in their conduct, he is able to draw their attention to it and make them put it right, by the authority of the King or by the procedure of the *Parlement* to which they are subordinate.

In several places he recommends the settlement of disputes. The governor should 'observe what St Leo recommends in a sermon of the twelfth month: "Let us concern ourselves with the ... reconciliation of those who have disputes."'[12] And again, in that part which contains his instructions for what is to happen when he is not there, he tells his servants: 'to allow absolutely

9   In that part of the *Works* called 'Life of the Prince of Conti' i–lix, xxx–xxxi.
10 De Conti *Mémoires* p152 XXIII '*touchant la conduite de sa maison*', and XXIV.
11 De Conti *Mémoires* p2 II.
12 De Conti *Mémoires* XIII.

no animosities to arise, and to apply themselves to reconciling those who have allowed them to arise between them'.[13]

Chapter XXVIII of La Roche's manual is devoted to the problem of duelling and the benefits which arbitration can bring to French society by contributing to their suppression. He is aware of De Conti's example and writings. Because De Conti was a military leader he was in a strong position to lend his aid to the King's efforts to suppress duels. He made his opinion clear. It was the great lord's duty: 'to root out by every available means that cursed custom of duelling, carrying out the *Édits* of the King; and, to prevent and calm down the disputes of Gentlemen, to appoint persons in each of the various cantons of the Province to bring them to a settlement'.[14] He sets out in detail his instructions for gentlemen commissioned by the *Maréchaux* 'to look to his Majesty's Edicts'.[15] First, they must never take sides, lest they 'give either Party occasion to be distrustful of them and to have less confidence in their Mediation'. They should apply themselves to the task of reconciliation with 'sweetness and gentleness ... that neither Friendship nor Passion may hinder them from taking the knowledge which they ought to have of the Circumstances of the Fact, which are extremely nice in these Matters'.

Not content with laying down principles, he sets out precedents for the documents to be used: the Order of Prohibition which the person commissioned by the *Maréchaux* is to send to the parties; his Letter informing the Governor that this has been done; his Order sending the Guard to put the parties under restraint; his Letter of Notice to the Governor that this has been done; a Form of Reconciliation – 'having maturely deliberated and examined all the circumstances, I instruct each party to make up, embrace and forget'; various Orders; the final report to the *Maréchaux*.

De Conti is one of La Roche's heroes:[16]

> After dinner twice a week he gave an audience of one hour, which he treated as relaxation. Everyone was admitted, even the poor, and he settled their disputes himself.

---

13 De Conti *Mémoires* p159 IX '*pour le conseil pendant mon absence*'.
14 De Conti *Mémoires* VIII.
15 [De Conti] *Works* p15.
16 Chapter XV para 2.

He got litigants to sign a compromise, agreeing to go to arbitration, and his secretary kept a register of them. La Roche hints proudly that he was De Conti's close associate, if not friend, and so perhaps not far removed in rank:[17] 'I have often heard him say to those who had the honour of being close to him.' And he tells of plans that came to nothing on De Conti's early death, which perhaps would not have been known to anyone who was not in his confidence. He also cites one of De Conti's household officials as authority for the statement that he wanted his practice of mediating his vassals' disputes to be followed after his death.[18]

THE DUCHESSE DE LONGUEVILLE AND THE DUC DE LIANCOURT

It was not only De Conti himself who patronised arbitration, so La Roche tells us, but his elder sister: 'Madame the Duchesse de Longueville has established this holy practice on all her estates.'[19]

The biographies of the Duchesse de Longueville are so partisan that it is hard to believe that any two were written about the same person; but some facts are known and we can restrict this account to the more worthy and relevant[20] aspects of her life. Anne Geneviève Bourbon (1619–1679) was the daughter of Henry II, Prince de Condé, and therefore sister not only of his successor the Grand Condé, but of the Prince de Conti, his younger brother. In 1642 she married Henry d'Orléans, Duc de Longueville, warning him that if he ever dared express any disapproval of her behaviour she would make him the unhappiest of men.[21] The Duc de Rochefoucauld (of the *Maximes*) was one of her lovers. With her brother, her husband and romantic connections she became a leader in the *Fronde* and was responsible for much devastation and loss of life. But in 1661 she changed her ways, entered a convent and sought to use her vast wealth to compensate those she had harmed. Four thousand are said to

---

17 Chapter XV para 3.
18 Chapter XVI.
19 Chapter XVI.
20 It can hardly be relevant, for example, that the gossips said that Sully's wife took the Duchesse de Longueville's mad father as one of her lovers.
21 Sackville-West *Daughter of France* pp69–71.

have relied on her charity. She busied herself in conciliating disputes between religious factions.[22]

> The lives of the Duchesse de Longueville and her husband were spent entirely in the exercise of virtue. They talk of her singular traits of generosity. She provided money for those who brought actions against her and who lacked the support necessary to obtain their rights, which required a judgment to prove them.

Such other evidence as there is, therefore, seems to support the little La Roche tells us. But there is no such corroborative evidence to support what he writes about the Duc de Liancourt: 'The Duc de Liancourt has worked on it [mediation and arbitration] with great success.'[23] Nicolas D'Ameral, Duc de Liancourt, not a Huguenot but a Jansenist, was even more unusual among the men at court in not being enamoured of Gabrielle D'Estrées, the beautiful and clever mistress of Henry IV. So the King arranged their marriage, its non-consummation and secret annulment. Sully hints that the fair Gabrielle tried unsuccessfully to seduce him, Sully.

THE BISHOP OF LUÇON: THE GOOD BISHOP COLBERT

La Roche dedicated his manual to Nicolas Colbert, who was Bishop of Luçon from 1661 until 1671, when he was transferred to Auxerre.[24] He was the brother of Jean-Baptiste Colbert, Louis XIV's chief minister.[25] The only known surviving copy of the first edition is bound with the arms on the cover of Nicolas's nephew, son of Jean-Baptiste, who became Archbishop of Rouen.[26]

La Roche holds Nicolas Colbert out as an example to all. In 1666, when he was appointed to the General Assembly of the

---

22　Compare JCF Hoefer *Nouvelle Biographie Générale* 1852 XLVI with NT Le Moyne des Essarts *Les Siècles Littéraires de la France* 1801 VI.

23　Chapter XVI.

24　PPB Gams *Series Episcoporum Ecclesiae Catholicae Quotquot Innotuerunt a Beato Petro Apostilo* 1875.

25　He is referred to as 'your esteemed brother' at p25. Colbert's position seems to have done nothing to discourage the appointment of members of his family to episcopal office. Gams *Series Episcoporum* shows at least six bishops named Colbert in French dioceses in the second half of the seventeenth century.

26　Chapter 5 below.

Clergy, and had every excuse to linger in Paris with his noble family and his powerful and loving brother, he left in the depths of winter on his long and arduous journey back to his diocese, no better than a swamp, because Easter called him to shepherd his flock.[27]

THE PARISH PRIESTS: THE GOOD CURÉ AND ST YVES

La Roche writes of two men whom he calls '*le bon curé*'. The illustration which immediately precedes Chapter I is of a parish priest whose virtues were such that he was made a saint. There he stands in the picture, the good Saint Yves, with his saintly halo, playing the role which La Roche values most highly, that of charitable arbitrator, settling the suits and disputes of his parishioners, among whom can be seen the widow and the orphan, the lame and the poor of all kinds. The caption is: 'The good curé St Yves, by his charitable intervention, managed to bring nearly all suits and disputes in his parish to an amicable settlement.' In Chapter III La Roche explains that Yves was so enthusiastic that his bishop made him his judge so that 'he could make this charity his full time profession'. He then drove all suits and disputes out of the diocese. He was canonised and all the judges of the kingdom adopted him as their patron saint.

He is shown throughout France, La Roche tells us, in pictures which illustrate the work which 'earned him altars'. He is a judge in his formal court, but it is not litigation he is presiding over. La Roche is careful to draw the distinction:[28]

> He is shown seated in a court of justice, *settling* a dispute between a poor tramp, dressed in rags, and a rich man. He is not represented holding court and passing judgment, which shows that this is an arbitration and a settlement, which is something better than judgments and sentences. And that is what we ought to believe, since the judges themselves have chosen and brought to light this Throne of Arbitration, as the most glorious action of so holy a life. That is what has earned him the prayers and offerings of poor litigants and of all the people. So there you see sanctified Arbitration, and charitable mediators, and all those who are involved in it.

27 In the Epistle to the Bishops.
28 Chapter III, para 2.

So St Yves should be a good example for parish priests and their bishops – and also for the courts, because the judges have made him their patron, so they should refer litigants to arbitration. When in Chapter II La Roche returns to the good curé who is still alive, he links him with his saintly predecessor. The title of the chapter is: 'That a good curé in our France, by his charitable intervention, manages to bring nearly all suits and disputes to an amicable settlement.' And the first sentence of the text strengthens the link:

> In that he does nothing, as we have just said in the picture of the good curé, which is not ordained by the Gospel etc ... the good curé practises this at one of the far ends of the kingdom.

The good curé came to mediation and arbitration through his own bitter experience: 'He himself had a large and controversial case against the preachers of his parish ... which had lasted many years.' He was advised to ask for settlement. He did. The other side agreed. 'It was brought to a conclusion at once, to the satisfaction of all parties.'

Now he practises his art with success. He explains to any disputing parishioner that the Councils declare that no one should approach the sacrament unless they have put aside their disputes. Excommunication is the recommended punishment. The parishioners always say they do not want to litigate but are forced to. He shows them how to avoid lawsuits and settle their disputes. He makes them sign an agreement to appoint arbitrators. Then he goes off to the other side. Without telling them he has in his pocket the first party's signed compromise and submission, he brings them round to settlement. Then he gets them to sign. If the second party lives in another parish, he gets its priest to do the job for him. If a party is recalcitrant, he uses 'holy artifices' to frighten him into submission.

He can usually settle minor matters himself. His flock accept his leadership. He never pretends to be anything other than an ordinary man. He has their confidence. He is straight, that is the first quality necessary. He is patient. He knows that many disputants just want someone to hear them out and show some sympathy with their grievance. He speaks their language. He tells them that coming to church with a dispute on their conscience is like going to a wedding with dirty clothes. You don't need eloquence. Look at Moses! He had a stammer. 'Out of the mouth of babes', as the prophet says.

There is a third curé, the parish priest of St Sulpice, who – though not called *'bon'* – is *'illustré'*. He too sets a good example to others.[29]

THE ARBITRATORS: LEFÈVRE D'ORMESSON, DE MORANGIS, DE BOUCHERAT AND LE NAIN

It cannot be said that the King or the judges on his law reform commission were unaware of the advantages of arbitration. La Roche himself tells us the names of some of the arbitrators who were busy in Paris at the time: De Morangis, De Boucherat and Le Nain.[30] This is confirmed by the independent testimony of one of their colleagues, Olivier Lefèvre d'Ormesson.[31] In his journal for Wednesday 21 April 1666 D'Ormesson reports: 'tonight after dinner I completed the settlement between M the Président de Pommereu and his sister and said she was entitled to 40,000 livres'.

On Monday 3 March 1670, he writes:

We completed the arbitration between Mme the Mareschale d'Aumont[32] and M the Duc d'Aumont we began on 10 December last. The arbitrators were MM De Morangis, Le Nain and I. Champion was advocate for the Mareschale and Caillart for the Duc. We worked all the last day from 8am till the evening and dined at M De Morangis's to decide all the questions together and to sign the award. MM De Morangis and Le Nain agreed with me on all the issues and Mme the Mareschale lost pretty well all of them. Somebody had put her up to making extraordinary demands. We had been appointed arbitrators by order of the *Conseil d'en Haut* and the King had listened in a few times.[33]

29 Chapter XXVI para 5.
30 Chapter XXIII para 21.
31 *Maître des Requêtes*, but not a member of Louis XIV's law reform commission. A short biography is in a footnote in Chapter 2 above.
32 Friend of Sully; her husband was *Mareschale de France*.
33 Within three months the successful party, the Duc d'Aumont, was putting in a good word with the King on D'Ormesson's behalf but to no avail. As we know that the King had attended some of the arbitral hearings, there may be relevance in his dismissal of D'Ormesson's solicitations with the response that they would be considered *on merit*, see Chapter 3 above.

I have also been appointed arbitrator with M De Morangis and M Pussort,[34] by order of the *Conseil d'en Haut*, in a matter between M the Duc de Tresmes and his brother-in-law, M de Tavanne, about the distribution of the estate of M the Duc de Tresmes who has just died.

On Sunday 18 May 1670, D'Ormesson writes in his journal:

I was at M De Morangis's with M Le Nain and we judged as arbitrators the matter of Mme De Broglio against Mme the Mareschale d'Aumont and M the Duc d'Aumont to find out whether the said lady should have a supplement of certain income given to Mme De Broglio ... My advice was followed.

De Morangis, De Boucherat and Pussort appear to have been on Louis XIV's law reform commission, if the list in *Anciennes Lois*[35] can be relied on. But that list wrongly included D'Ormesson. Better evidence may be found in De Morangis's memoir to the commission:[36]

The greatest evil that has been introduced and that supports and nourishes chicanery and litigation is the petty and sordid gain of *épices*, which grow daily. They are a poison which spreads insensibly in the most notable individuals, and in the end they smother what remains of the spirit of justice.

That appears to be from a non-member.

Le Nain, De Morangis, De Boucherat and Pussort were full-time professional judges in the *Parlement* of Paris. That is perhaps why they sat as arbitrators on Sundays. If they did not include any recourse to arbitration in their proposals to reform the legal system, it cannot have been out of ignorance or antipathy. It is worth noting that the subject matter of the arbitrations was restricted to the family matters required by earlier legislation to be heard by arbitrators.

---

34 Brother of Colbert's mother and, according to Cheruel (D'Ormesson's editor), arbiter of the clan Colbert's disputes. A bachelor notorious for his wealth, miserliness, misanthropy and honesty, as a judge in Fouquet's trial he argued passionately for the death sentence. But see also E Paringault 'Le Conseiller d'État Henri Pussort, Réhabilitation Historique' (1870) and Hamscher *Parlement de Paris* pp175–6 and 241 n92.

35 *Anciennes Lois* XVII p103 fn1.

36 Hamscher *Parlement de Paris* pp158ff.

AND OTHERS

La Roche names others who were involved in arbitration[37] but for whose activities I have not been able to find independent evidence: for example the bishops listed in Chapter III and M de Sale. And he describes others without naming them: the town officials of Lyons, Nantes and Clermont en Auvergne,[38] and the dukes, peers, *cordons bleus*, *présidents*, counsellors and *maîtres des requêtes* in the parish of St Sulpice.[39]

In the first edition, though, he names the curé of St Sulpice as M Poussé, and his right hand men as MM de Couder and D'Acol. There, too, he names others 'who acquit themselves worthily, the Duc de Longueville, the Duc de Vandosme in Provence, the Maréchal de la Meilleraye in Brittany, and his son the Duc de Mazarin'. He does not say directly that they acted as mediators or encouraged arbitration, just that they tried to establish peace and put an end to lawsuits and disputes.

37 He also includes Job, Solomon, Charlemagne and St Louis, Chapter XXIII paras 19 and 20.
38 Chapter XXIV.
39 Chapter XXVI.

5   THE AUTHOR AND THE BOOK

To the Ill-Disposed Reader:[1]

If any ambitious and ill-disposed arbitrator
Is keen to attack us, as if one might find favour
With a slight slim book, to seek a great or lasting
Name, he is wrong by a long chalk. He's mistaken
And it is shameful. This is not the root of
A tiny man, nor do we now wish to indulge
The learned. That labour was happy and boldly
A greater one will not fear at length to surface.
The primary elements of things are only little.
Furthermore, is it not true that you unfurrow
My brow all the better if I like you
Than if you do your best to make me loathe you?
If these things are not pleasing to your palate
Then perhaps there are other things to please it.
But you do better; don't find fault with my work.

THE AUTHOR

Our author does not give his name. The title page discloses that
the otherwise anonymous book is by 'Le Prieur de S. Pierre' and
that is the only obvious clue in the first edition. But he was not
concerned to disguise his identity. It would be clear to his
readers, one would presume, which Priory of St Pierre was

---

1   Printed at the end of Jean Pierres *Commentaire sur l'Édit des Arbitres* 1564:
   Ad lectorem malignum
     Si quisquam ambitiosus et malignus
     In nos irruere arbiter concupiscat,
     Quasi unus placeat levi libello
     Magnum quaerere vel perenne nomen,
     Longe fallitur, errat atque turpe
     Non hic est hominis scopus pusilli,
     Nec non iam volumus favere doctis,
     Faelix ille labos, opusque maius
     Tandem surgere non timebit audax,
     Ac sunt parva elementa prima rerum.
     Verum quin magis explicas amandus
     Frontem, quam mi odiosus esse pergis?
     Si non haec placeant tuo palato
     At fortasse alii placere possint.
     Sed tu da meliora, non reprende.

referred to and presumably the name of its prior was well known or could be discovered by contemporaries, though it eludes me.[2] Internal evidence strongly suggests that he was of the clergy. More telling, though, is that in the second and later editions the Approbation of the Doctors reveals that their imprimatur is for a book, to be printed for a second time, composed (*composé*) by Sieur Alexandre de la Roche, Prieur de S. Pierre. That is the name, and the only name, under which the book is always catalogued.[3]

But the bibliographers appear to have ignored what immediately follows the academic censors' imprimatur: an extract from the Royal Privilege, granting permission and copyright protection to Sieur de la *Rivière*, who is to be allowed to have the book printed by whatever printer or publisher/bookseller (*libraire*) he likes. It was not unknown for such permission to be granted to someone other than the author. If so, then who was this Sieur de la Rivière?

If there was only one person, there could have been a simple confusion of names. Both are common and perhaps easily confused – 'rock' and 'river'. But other explanations should be eliminated before such an assumption is made. And, despite the consistent attribution of the bibliographers to La Roche, what is there to prefer that name to La Rivière? Who are more likely to have made a mistake, the King's officials or the doctors of the Sorbonne?

There is no help to be found in the French biographical dictionaries.[4] There is nothing under any of the variants of La Roche

2   The scholar-bookseller Jean-Jacques Magis warns me that this assumption may be ill-founded. It was not unusual to choose a false ecclesiastical title as a pen-name, and there could be humour in this one, as suggesting the author was the right-hand man of St Peter, who holds the key to Paradise, which is the avoidance of litigation. But then the doctors would not have granted their approval to 'Sieur Alexandre de la Roche, Prieur de S Pierre'.

3   There is another pseudonymous work attributed to a contemporary La Roche: LA ROCHE Sieur de (pseud) *Lettre au Sieur Morin, visionnaire restaurateur de la science celeste; par le Sieur de la Roche* Libraire de Montpelier Paris 1655 8pp 4o. There is nothing to connect that work to our author. There appears to be one copy only, in the New York Public Library, *National Union Catalogue Pre-1956 Imprints* 1974.

4   None of the standard biographical tools are of any help. There is no Alexandre de la Roche in the enormous compendium of many sources, the *Archives Biographiques Françaises*, edited by Susan Bradley 1993, now in its 2nd edn 1999 in four boxes of microfiche. The new national bibliography, M Prevost, Roman D'Amat, H Tribout de Morembert and J-P Lobies *Dictionnaire de Biographie Française*, had by April 2001 reached fascicle CXII *Langumier – La Rochefoucauld* but there is no entry under La Rivière or La Roche which could possibly be the author, cols979–1017. Nor is there any other entry in other biographical dictionaries for Roche, La Roche or De la Roche (or Rivière) which gives any information.

or La Rivière which would give a clue to our author.[5] But, if the same searches are made under La Rivière, the mystery deepens. First there is a bibliographical entry for a Roch le Baillif, Sieur de la Rivière, who must have been writing 1578–80, nearly a century too early to be our author. Then, in the French equivalent of Burke's *Peerage*,[6] there is an entry for: De la Rivière, branche du Plessis XV, Charles-Yves-Jacques Comte de la Rivière, Marquis de Paulmy, Vicomte *de la Roche* de Gennes, died 1729. What can be deduced from the juncture of the two names? Can it be coincidence?[7] Perhaps the best that can be made of all this is the conjecture that all three appellations may have been correctly applied to the same person in sequence: Alexandre de la Roche, Sieur de la Rivière, Prieur of St Pierre.

Though more may be discovered about the author from church records, the search for a Priory of St Pierre has so far been fruitless.[8] He does not appear to have become a bishop.[9]

5   There is a contemporary legal author and publisher called Simeon de la Roche, whose *Lois, Chartes et Coustumes du Chef-Lieu de la Ville de Mons* was published in Mons by L'Imprimerie de Simeon de la Roche in 1663. There is also a Gilles de la Roche (1621–1668), seigneur de St-André, in Charles Gavard *Versailles: Galeries Historiques* Paris 1838. And a La Roche was *Président de la Cour des Comptes etc* in Montpellier in 1663, see the extraordinary confidential reports on the judiciary, *Notes Sécrètes sur le Personnel de Tous les Parlements et Cours de Compte Envoyés par les Intendants des Provinces à Colbert*, Depping *Correspondance* II 131. Sadly, there is nothing to connect our author with the Jesuit father La Roche of the College of Rheims who, in 1663 or thereabouts, was expelled from the convent of Saint Étienne where he taught, and from the diocese, for preaching the importance of nudity: 'Because Adam felt shame for his nakedness only after he had sinned, the most certain sign of guilt must be any feeling of shame in appearing naked.' Pierre Varin, *Archives Législatives de la Ville de Reims* 1848 Pt2 Statutes vol 2 pp649–50.

6   De la Chenaye-Desbois et Badier *Dictionnaire de la Noblesse* 3rd edn 1872 Vol 17 p143. See also DJ Sturdy *The D'Aligres de la Rivière* 1986 and fn36 below.

7   Another clue may be found in the name of the younger son of the Prince de Conti, François Louis de Bourbon, Prince *de la Roche*-sur-Yon. And Guy de la Roche, Seigneur de la Roche-Guyon, married (before 1408) Perrette de la Rivière, daughter of Baron de la Rivière.

8   My research so far has revealed only that there were a number of Abbeys of St Pierre in France at the time, but no Priory.

9   A search of PPB Gams *Series Episcoporum Ecclesiae Catholicae Quotquot Innotuerunt a Beato Petro Apostilo* 1875 (which is organised only by dioceses within countries, with no index of names), from the middle of the seventeenth century, shows no La Roche (or any variant) and only one De la Rivière, forenamed Michael Poncet, (see below) not to be confused with the judge and member of the law reform commission of that name, mentioned by Chéruel *Journal de D'Ormesson* II p292 for Sunday 4 January 1665. See below

The other source of information is the text itself. The internal evidence shows him to have been an experienced mediator and arbitrator[10] with a substantial practical knowledge of the way the law worked in Paris in his day. He was well aware of what was happening in the world of arbitration in Paris and the rest of France and he even claimed to know something of commercial legal practice in England, as well as Spain, Portugal and Holland.[11] It was not impossible for a prior to have been a professional lawyer in earlier life. His robust criticisms of the way lawyers behave in litigation does not mean that he had no time for them. Indeed, he assumes that the arbitrators he so fervently recommends will always be lawyers if there is any point 'of law or custom. Because, other than that, merchants and other wise and intelligent people, even peasants, can decide any questions relating to their own trade.'[12]

He knows things not likely to be known to a non-lawyer: that it is in the interlocutory stages that the greatest heat tends to be engendered;[13] how the ease with which a matter can be resolved depends on how well the pleadings are drafted;[14] the technical advantages of an agreed settlement over an award[15] and the forms in current use.

His practical experience is not just a matter of implication from his obvious knowledge of legal procedure. He often expressly says that what he is about to describe is something he has experienced himself:[16] 'I have seen a number of lawsuits settled after this fashion' and 'I have seen it often in my own experience' (an inferior calling on a superior to settle); 'I know an *Officier* ... who brought an action'; 'We know from experience ... matters are transferred every day from one *Parlement* to another'; 'I have known

---

also on the change from 'Nosseigneurs' to 'Messeigneurs' as his form of address for bishops. Our author must be distinguished from the Abbé de Saint Pierre of a later generation, also an advocate of arbitration, who was the subject of interest in Voltaire's correspondence with Frederick the Great, at the end of Chapter 3 above.
10 Particularly Chapter XXIII.
11 Chapter XXXIV.
12 Chapter XXIII para 2.
13 Chapter XXI para 5.
14 Chapter XXI para 4.
15 Chapter XXIII para 17, where the detail shows the nature of the author's experience.
16 These examples are taken just from Chapters XXII and XXIII.

mediators ... at this stage propose'; 'I have often seen this succeed' (introducing expert or politically powerful intermediaries); 'I have often seen settlements made which you would expect to be broken'; and he tells the lovely story of the hapless mediator he knew well, who became so friendly with both sides that they resolved their differences despite his ineptitude, just to please him.

Less surprising is the author's personal knowledge of the work of priests and bishops and the manual is full of examples of the success of the good curé, even in simply calling on the congregation in the mass to make up their quarrels before taking communion or, as confessor, going further and refusing absolution. And the author says he has personal experience of the effectiveness of a priest's simple offer, during the sermon, to help anyone with a dispute.[17]

The author must have lived in Paris for a number of years. He knows all about the convention which many highly placed people made to avoid litigation, about the district judge of the *faubourg* who supported arbitration, of the charitable arbitration centre in the parish of St Sulpice, of the activities of the Archbishop and of the *Procureur-Général* on behalf of those in prison there. Most important, he mentions by name some of the leading private arbitrators whom other sources show to have been arbitrating at the time or a few years later. The whole point of such private arbitrations about family property was to avoid the dispute becoming a matter of public knowledge. Only an insider would have known about them.

He cannot have been a young man at the time. He seems to have been in the confidence of the Duc de Sully, who died in 1641 but retired in 1610. From the tone of his writing, quite unlike the subservience of his contemporaries, and from his name, De la Roche Sieur de la Rivière, he is likely to have been from the nobility, as most of those who held high office in the Church were at that time in France. Moreover, he was a close associate of the Prince de Conti, and for a considerable time, because he says in Chapter XV: 'I have often heard him say to those who had the honour of being close to him.' At that time De Conti was governor of Languedoc. He is not afraid to express support for a Huguenot or a Jansenist, or cite as examples those of mixed reputation like the Duchesse de Longueville and the Ducs de

17 Chapter II.

Liancourt and de Luynes. He does not shrink from addressing the King with bold exhortation and only thinly veiled criticism.

There is a curious sentence in Chapter VII: 'We have a good example, a bishop of our France still alive, whose name modesty prevents me from mentioning.'[18] He could mean the Bishop of Luçon. But in the dedication La Roche expressly says that he has overridden that bishop's feelings of modesty. If not the bishop's modesty, could it have been La Roche's? That seems the most likely. But why should La Roche's modesty stop him mentioning anyone by name? Could it be that they were related?

The only possible family connection I have found is to Louis Barbier Rivière, known as the Abbé de la Rivière, who was Bishop of Langres at the right time.[19] He had been regent of the college of Plessis in Paris and then almoner of the Bishop of Cahors, who got him a place with Gaston de France, Duc d'Orléans. He advised Gaston's daughter, Mademoiselle, more favoured with wealth than beauty, in her marriage plans, including setting her sights on England's exiled Charles II.[20]

The entry in the *Bibliographie Universelle*[21] is not fulsome:

> Sharp and clever, but of vile and despicable character; he insinuated himself into the Prince's good books by encouraging his passions and, when he had won his confidence, he abused it by revealing his secrets to Cardinal Mazarin. His intrigues and his weak indulgences, which should have deserved different treatment, won him several rich abbeys and finally the see of Langres, to which a peerage is attached.

He was after a cardinal's hat when he died in 1670. It may therefore have been more than mere modesty which dissuaded our author from mentioning his name. At the time of the book's publication, this Rivière would almost certainly have been Bishop of Langres.

18 The French is ambiguous: 'un Evesque dont la modestie m'empesche de dire le nom' can equally mean: 'a bishop whose modesty prevents me from mentioning his name' or 'a bishop whose name my modesty prevents me from mentioning'. This arises from the French use of a definite article instead of a possessive pronoun.
19 Voltaire thought little of him, Moland *Voltaire* XIV p194. Michael Poncet de la Rivière, Bishop of Angers 1672–1730, is obviously too late. Another Poncet was a member of the Conseil de Justice which drafted the *Ordonnance Civile* 1667, see Chapter 3 above.
20 Sackville-West *Daughter of France* pp81–4.
21 Michaud *Biographie Universelle* new edn Paris Desplaces.

Finally, what is the significance, if any, of the change in the form of address to the Bishops? In the first edition it is 'Nosseigneurs', in the second 'Messeigneurs'. Moreover, the subscription: 'Your very humble, very obedient and very submissive servant' disappears in the second edition. Could this all mean that La Roche had meanwhile been elevated?

Unfortunately there seems no chance of a connection with the later proponent of international arbitration, the more celebrated Abbé de Saint-Pierre, Charles Irénée Castel de Saint-Pierre (1658–1745), whom Voltaire mocked but Frederick the Great admired.[22]

THE BOOK

Bibliography

There appear to have been four editions from 1666 to 1671. The only copy of the first I have been able to find is in the Beinecke Library of Yale University.[23] Its title page reads:

L'Arbitre Charitable, et un moyen facile pour accorder les Procez promptement, sans peine, & sans frais.

L'Eglise demande à Dieu tous les jours:
—— *Extingue flammas litium.*

Seigneur délivrez-nous de procez, et de ces flammes
deuorantes, de haine & d'animosité qui les accompagnent.
Et pour conuier les Charitables à y travailler, le Dieu
de Paix a promis par son Prophete: *Defendez*
l'Oppressé. Secourez la Veuve; Aydez l'Orphelin: Et
quand vos pechez seroient rouges comme écarlatte,
ils deuiendront blancs comme neige, Isaïe Chap. I.

DEDIÉ
A MONSEIGNEUR COLBERT,
Evêque de Luçon.

Par le Prieur DE SAINT PIERRE.

M. DC. LXVI.

22 At the end of Chapter 3 above.
23 It is shown in the *National Union Catalogue Pre-1956 Imprints* 1974; no plates.

No printer's name is stated, nor place of publication. There is first a four-page dedicatory epistle to the Bishop of Luçon (unpaginated, though the first page is marked ãiij), then (separately paginated 1–6) an epistle to 'Nosseigneurs les Archevesques et Evesques de France'. An eight-page unpaginated table of contents comes next, followed by the text, paginated 1–140. Then there is a page which declares:

TABLEAU
DES MISERES
DU PLAIDEUR
Pour persuader le menu Peuple.

La Robe de Cesar percée de coups, fit plus d'impression
sur le Peuple Romain, que l'Eloquence d'Antoine.

Socrate, le plus sage des Payens, crût pour persuader,
que le chemin le plus court, estoit de plaire; Pour cela
Platon dans ses Dialogues le represente debitant ses
Maximes les plus éleuées, en riant & bouffonnant.

C'est pourquoy l'on a aussi, fais mettre icy,
la Figure qui suit.

That may be translated: 'Picture of the misfortunes of the litigant, to persuade the common people. Caesar's robe, pierced with thrusts, made more of an impression on the Roman people than Antony's eloquence. Socrates, the wisest of pagans, believed that to win an argument the shortest way would be most appreciated. Therefore Plato in his Dialogues shows him delivering the loftiest maxims while laughing and playing the fool. That is why the picture which follows has also been put here.'

This clearly calls for a plate, which is missing. It was meant for those who could not read, or at least for those more likely to be swayed by a picture. The second edition has five pictures of arbitrations or mediations, which the author precisely says are for just that purpose.

The bishop to whom the book was dedicated was Nicolas Colbert, brother of Louis XIV's chief Minister, Jean-Baptiste. He was Bishop of Luçon from 1661 to 1671. He is not to be confused with his nephew, Jacques-Nicolas (1654–1707), son of Jean-Baptiste, whose arms as Archbishop of Rouen decorate the binding of this Yale copy. Not even Jean-Baptiste would have appointed his twelve-year-old son a bishop.

Part Three is a facsimile reproduction of the first edition. Part Two is my translation of the second edition 1668,[24] which I have taken as my base. The text of the third and fourth editions does not appear to differ in any material way from the second.[25] Significant differences between the first and second editions, mostly new authorities, are indicated and discussed in the footnotes to Part Two.

The second edition says that many bishops had the first reprinted – though I have been unable to find any evidence –

24 The *Catalogue Générale des Livres Imprimés de la Bibliothèque Nationale: Auteurs* LXXXIX 1926 describes the book thus:

> LA ROCHE Alexandre de *L'arbitre charitable pour éviter les procez et les querelles; ou du moins pour les terminer promptement, sans peine & sans frais.*
> *Cela se fera facilement, si les Evesques & les Curez, les Gouverneurs des Provinces, et les Seigneurs de grand Fiefs, ont la bonté d'estre les Mediateurs, comme ils l'ont esté autrefois, & qu'ils sont obligez de l'estre, suivant l'Evangile, les Peres, les Canons, les Conciles, & les Ordonnances de nos Rois.*
> *Monsieur le Prince de Conty l'a fait dignement, pendant sa vie, dans ses terres & dans ses Gouvernemens.*
> *Et Nostre Monarque, au milieu de tous ses soins, prend bien la peine, de donner des Audiences publiques, jusques aux moindres de ses Sujets, pour terminer promptement leurs Procez & differens.*
> *Aprés un example si illustre, qui refusera de seconder les bonnes intentions de nostre Prince.*
> *Presenté au Roy, l'an 1668.*
> *Par le Prieur de S. Pierre* [Alexandre de la Roche] Paris L Raveneau 1668 In-4, pièces limin., 104 p et pl. 2 ex [F. 12133] et Rés. p. R. 141

Both copies are apparently of this edition. The same entry is in JGT Graesse *Trésor de Livres Rares et Précieux ou Nouveau Dictionnaire Bibliographique* IV 1950. It is on the half-title only that the title L'ARBITRE CHARITABLE appears. The format is small quarto, 23cm x 23cm. The British Library copy is bound in what appears to be a contemporary limp vellum binding. There is a copy of this edition in the New York Public Library and another is mentioned in *Catalogue des Livres Imprimés de la Bibliothèque des Avocats à la Cour d'Appel de Paris* 1880 I p258 no2809: 'L'Arbitre Charitable par Alexandre de la Roche prieur de Saint-Pierre, Paris, Raveneau 1668, in-4.' I know of one copy in private hands and there are probably more.

25 The copy I have used I found in the British Library, to which I am grateful for permission to photocopy it. I have worked from a microfilm transformed into printed hard copy. The entry in the British Library Catalogue Vol 89 [shelf mark 5405 aaa 27] and in VF Goldsmith *A Short Title Catalogue of French Books 1601–1700 in the Library of the British Museum* 1973 is substantially the same as that in the Bibliothèque Nationale's. I am also grateful to the Beinecke and University of Iowa Libraries for providing copies of the first and fourth editions.

and the dedication to the King claims that it had already enjoyed success. The text itself claims that it had also been translated into English, German, Danish and Latin, though not necessarily published in those languages.[26]

The Plates

Bibliophile sources and booksellers' catalogues add little to our knowledge. Brunet[27] says that: 'This book deserves to be preserved because of the felicitous ideas it puts forward.' Indeed! But he continues: 'The plates show the arbitral tribunals which existed then in Paris', when of the five only that showing the King can possibly be there. The others show St Augustine, St Yves, a meeting in Provence, and a provincial governor in his province.

Brunet refers to Techener's catalogue, which adds little to our knowledge of the book or its author.[28] Its confident statements about La Roche seem to be based solely on what can be found from the title page and preliminaries. But it tries to place the plates in their stylistic context: 'They are very interesting from the point of view of manners and costume; drawn and engraved in the fashion of Abraham Bosse, they have not quite the fineness of execution of the master's own work, which they much resemble after his *Works of Mercy*.'

---

26 Chapter I.
27 Jacques-Charles Brunet *Manuel du Libraire et de l'Amateur de Livres* 5th edn 1862 Vol 3 has exactly the same description as the entry in the *Bibliothèque Nationale* catalogue but adds: 'Ce livre mérite d'être conservé à cause des heureuses idées qui y sont émises. Les planches représentent les tribunaux d'arbitrage qui existaient alors à Paris. *Bulletin du Bibliophile* 1857 p213 où le livre est porté à 40 fr.'
28 [Techener] *Bulletin du Bibliophile et Catalogue de Livres Rares et Curieux de Littérature, d'Histoire etc qui se trouvent en vente à la Librairie de J Techener* April 1857, which has only a slightly different description: 'In-4 de 15ff non chiff. et 104p fig d-r, dos de mar. r 40. Rare. Sur le titre même de son ouvrage, l'auteur explique tout au long son système: [it quotes the long title] L'auteur se nommoit Alexandre de la Roche; il était prieur de Saint-Pierre. Il a naturellement dédié son livre au Roi. Les estampes pliées, au nombre de 5, représentent tribunaux d'arbitrages qui existoient alors, ceux du Roi, du prince de Conti et du Curé de Saint-Yves; elles sont très-intéressantes au point de vue de l'histoire des moeurs et des costumes; dessinées et gravés dans le genre d'Abraham Bosse, elles n'ont pourtant pas la finesse d'éxecution des pièces de ce maître, quoiquelles ressemblent beaucoup à la suite des *Oeuvres de Miséricorde*.'

Le *Procureur* from 'L'Oeuvre Gravé d'Abraham Bosse'.
© Ashmoleum Museum, Oxford.

Abraham Bosse was born in Tours in 1602[29] and died in 1676. He produced many books relating to art and architecture, including perspective which he taught at the Royal Academy of Painting from its creation in 1648 until he was expelled for his refusal to join in the adulation of its autocratic director. He set up a competing school which was officially closed down.[30] He carried on his quarrel through invective against the director's toadies and was threatened with imprisonment if he did not stop his criticisms of the Royal Academy. At the time of the publication of *L'Arbitre Charitable* he was living in Paris.[31] To the inexpert eye its plates do not seem close to those of Bosse. They have not his refinement, as perhaps can be seen from the example reproduced here, not of one of his *Works of Mercy*, 'visiting the sick', 'prison visiting' and so on, but of 'L'Avoué' in his office, which is more similar both in subject and execution.[32]

Though the date on the title page of the copy I have worked on is 1668, the Royal Privilege shows that the King's Privy Council granted the privilege of publication on 6 July 1667. This edition received the approbation of the scholarly censors, the doctors of the University of Paris in the Faculty of Theology at the Sorbonne, on 22 October 1667. They say they are giving permission for the book to be printed for a second time. La Roche himself says[33] that the work was first published in 1666 but the

---

29   André Blum *Abraham Bosse et la Société Française au XVIIe Siècle* 1924. The *Biographie Universelle* (1843) V pp124–5 gives the date of birth as 1611.

30   Blum p192 quotes the *arrêt*.

31   'En l'Isle du Palais, sur le quay qui regarde la Mégisserie', Blum p182.

32   Nicole Villa *Le XVIIe Siècle Vu par Abraham Bosse, Graveur du Roi* 1967, plate 96. Researches into Bosse, however, produced another facet of his quarrel with the artistic authorities: arbitration. On 18 July 1660 he wrote: 'To Messieurs the Painters and Sculptors of the Royal Academy at the Louvre Galleries, Paris. I had no idea that the whole Company had intended to show what it has been pleased to grant me of its own accord ... to have chosen arbitrators in a dispute between one of my colleagues and me about a matter which concerns the fundamental practice of our art ... .' Blum pp205–6. He complains about the refusal of due respect to him and the freedom with which those who oppose him grant one another honours. He protests about others plagiarising his work. He says he would be happy to leave the judgment in their hands or even with the director LeBrun, his adversary, provided he puts the award in writing and signs it. This is an example of processes found in many places and times within a guild or professional body, particularly apposite for resolving disputes on technical matters, or, like this one, about aesthetics, passing off of written work, or professional ethics.

33   In the dedication: 'This year, 1666 ...'

first edition was not apparently submitted to the King or the censors and has no epistle to the King.

Though I have found no reference to a third edition, I have used a copy of the fourth, also published by Raveneau Paris 1671, in the University of Iowa Library. It is almost the same as the second edition of 1668, using the same typesetting,[34] and with five of the six same plates. The missing plate is that showing 'The Good *Avocats* and *Procureurs* and Charitable Arbitrators'. Could it be that someone had suggested to the author that he had overstated his authorities there, just a little?

The only changes to the text are the removal of the dedication to Nicolas Colbert, Bishop of Luçon,[35] and some minor alterations to the title page. The second clause is omitted – 'or at least to finish them quickly, without trouble and cost'; and there is the following addition at the bottom:

> With Privilege of the King, Approval of the Doctors, and the Approval of the General Assembly of the Clergy of France, which by its resolution of 17 November 1670 exhorted all the Bishops of the Kingdom to establish in their Dioceses *The Charitable Arbitrator*, and to work by their mediation and that of their Clergy towards settlement of Litigation.
>
> He who received the Privilege consents to this book being printed by anyone who wants to. He has the King's agreement to it being printed in full without the obligation to ask for special permission in different places.

The date, of course, is changed; it is specifically stated to be the fourth edition and to have been presented to the King in 1668. 'He who received the Privilege' was Sieur de la Rivière and not La Roche, if they are two different men.[36]

---

34 For example, at the end of Chapter XVI, the typographical errors *brobité* [for *probité*] and *permier* [for *premier*] remain uncorrected.

35 Though the request to him (at the end of Chapter XXIX) to carry on the good work remains unchanged.

36 The best-known holder of that title in 1670 was Étienne d'Aligres, Sieur de la Rivière, *doyen du conseil du roi*, who succeeded Séguier as *chancelier* in 1674, at the age of 82. His son assisted Louis XIV's law reform commission. The details of their lives show no connexion with arbitration, Sturdy *The D'Aligres de la Rivière* 158–64 and 189–91. They may help to solve the riddle of De la Rivière but not the search for De la Roche.

6   LESSONS FOR TODAY

Apart from the light which the manual shines on attitudes and practices in Louis XIV's France, can it teach any lessons about how mediation and arbitration can be used today to ameliorate the social and economic damage done by litigation and, indeed, by costly formal arbitration?

HOW TO GET THE PARTIES TO SETTLE

It is unlikely that in any community today there will be an institution with the authority that the Church had in France in La Roche's time. It would be unwise to rely on parties in dispute being persuaded by threats of divine intervention in their present lives or sanctions in eternity. Though they may suffer vexations, they are unlikely to understand that they are being punished for their unwillingness to settle disputes. They will not easily be deterred from putting forward the same excuses as they did in La Roche's time: this is not the kind of dispute which lends itself to arbitration; a formal judgment is required; trustees are obliged to litigate, perhaps because there are minors involved; or there are partners or others who must be consulted; or 'other similar pretexts'.[1]

But La Roche has ideas which do not depend on faith. He praises the judges in Brittany and Provence, and in Lyons, Nantes and Clermont, as well as in Paris, who were already offering to refer cases before them to arbitration.[2] He recommends that general legislation be enacted requiring all litigants to deposit a sum of money with the court, both a fine and an amount to cover costs, if they wish to start proceedings without trying first to reach a settlement.[3] Then the one who wanted arbitration

1   Chapter IV.
2   Chapters X and XXIV.
3   Chapter XXV para 10(c). William Sheppard had made a similar recommendation to Cromwell ten years before, NL Matthews *William Sheppard, Cromwell's Law Reformer* 1984 p151.

would insist on this deposit and the one who did not would be deterred by it from litigation.

He provides precedents of a summons to agree to arbitration, with variants for use when the respondent is of higher rank than the claimant, or of lower, or of equal.[4] It would take considerable ingenuity to adapt them for use in most modern jurisdictions, however conservative.

HOW TO CHOOSE MEDIATORS AND ARBITRATORS

Despite his emphasis on charitable *arbitrators*, La Roche insists that the priest or bishop, the provincial governor or great lord, who takes the initiative in procuring a settlement, should not attempt to adjudicate. His responsibility is to mediate, to get the parties together to seek a settlement and eschew litigation. If they have an issue which requires adjudication, then it is the mediator's responsibility to get the parties to sign a compromise, submitting their dispute to others to arbitrate – and it is a good idea to keep a stock of forms handy. The mediator should play no part in the choice of arbitrators, which should be left to the parties entirely, as it would be of a doctor or confessor. But *avocats* from the local Court of Appeal make suitable arbitrators and it is appropriate for the mediator to say so. And, if the parties do not fancy them, then the mediator can recommend a list from another district.[5]

After each side has chosen its arbitrator, they must agree to a third. In default of agreement, the mediator should make two copies of a list of eight or ten persons, well respected in that community, sending one to each party. Then the parties should each signify with a cross which of those names they find unacceptable. If more than one name remains, the mediator can then choose by lot any name which has not been marked with a cross.

Similar methods of selecting an umpire seem to have been widespread. The English courts created much learning on the appointment of the umpire. The arbitrators must make a conscious and unanimous choice, they said, and not throw dice or draw lots or 'play crosses and bones' to decide between their

4   Chapters XXXI, XXXII and XXXIII.
5   Chapter XXI.

candidates. But, by a nice distinction, they held that they could draw one name out of a hat, if the parties had agreed that either of the potential umpires whose names were put in would be fit and acceptable.[6]

WHAT MAKES A GOOD MEDIATOR AND ARBITRATOR?

The qualities are those so amply exhibited by the good curé. Probity first. Ability of course but probity foremost.[7] That must still be so – without that, the greater the mediator or arbitrator's other skills the greater the potential damage. Secondly patience. Often all a party really wants is someone who will listen without interruption or contradiction but with sympathy to a tale of woe. Thirdly Christian charity or love or goodwill; a genuine concern to be of help.

You do not need to be eloquent. You do not need to prepare your arguments too cleverly. In fact, the less you say at first the better. Be prepared to listen to a long complaint. But you must have what La Roche calls the right manner. It is best to be 'ordinary'. You must win confidence. The parties must feel that you would never be satisfied with anything that was not the best for them. That means you must get nothing out of it for yourself. Just think of the doctors! A doctor who is working for charity wants the patient to recover as quickly as possible. Not so if he is working for fees. And mediators and arbitrators are just the same. Of course, there is nothing wrong with honour, or with honours. Moreover, they come cheap. So give long-serving arbitrators some title of prestige. You will always find someone willing to work hard for that.

If you feel that the parties do not respect your authority or position, then recruit helpers who are more powerful to exert their influence on them.[8]

Arbitrators should have all the qualities of a good mediator and then more. The good arbitrator should be knowledgeable

6   Compare my 'Captain Charles Elliot RN, Arbitrator: Dispute Resolution in China Waters 1834–1836' 1998 and *A Miscellany of Disputes* 2000 Chapter 8, citing *Re Cassell* (1829) 9 B & C 624; *European and American SS Co v Crosskey* (1860) 8 CB (NS) 397.
7   Chapters XXII and XXIII.
8   Chapter XXI. Those familiar with contemporary practices in Chinese societies may sense analogues here.

and skilful and have a good reputation for legal knowledge if there is a point of law involved. La Roche is, of course, talking about the arbitrator appointed by that party. If you are appointed, it is your job to make your party see that you have comprehended their case, to go over it with them, exaggerating the arguments in their favour and even suggesting new ones. That will persuade them you are intelligent and well disposed towards them. After that you should tell them the other side's arguments, cursorily and without exaggeration but making sure now that you give them some cause to doubt the strength of their own case.

La Roche points out how important it is, nevertheless, to stamp out the idea that arbitrators represent the parties who appoint them, an erroneous assumption still not completely removed today. Each side's arbitrators should tell those who appoint them that the other side's arbitrators are honourable and trustworthy and listen to their arguments with more attention than they do their own side's.

WHAT ARE THE BEST PROCEDURES?

The rules laid down by the charitable arbitration centre of the parish of St Sulpice in Paris are set out as model rules.[9] But La Roche stresses that local requirements should prevail and practice should be tailored to fit them. The parties should always be asked to sign a written submission to arbitration. He calls that a compromise – the *compromissum* of the civil law – and provides a precedent.[10]

It is a good idea to get the parties to write down in just a few lines exactly what they think they would get if they recovered all they were entitled to, principal, interest and costs. On the other side they should set out what they think the dispute is likely to cost, including the time they are going to spend on it and the profit they would otherwise be making if they were getting on with their business. Then they should hand this memorandum over to someone else to look after. Constant

9   Chapter XXVI.
10   Chapter XXX.

reference to it as costs accumulate during the proceedings will induce an attitude favourable to settlement.[11]

If the paper work is properly done – a *factum* is expertly drafted – there will often be no need for a hearing. A decision can be reached on the papers. If it comes to a hearing the most important first step is to isolate the issues. You may have to wait until the parties have let off steam but the time comes when the arbitrators must take command and insist on relevance. One should never forget that the one who writes the award has a great advantage. One word may be enough to reverse its effect. And make sure that you not only draft the award, or better the settlement, on the spot; you should also get any necessary documents signed there and then, contract and conveyance together. You do not want the parties coming back to you with their squabbles over implementation when they have second thoughts and their goodwill has evaporated.

One recommendation which would be controversial in our contemporary culture of dispute resolution is the one which La Roche recommends as crucial. Never listen to one party's arguments in the presence of the other! Keep them apart at all times, thereby avoiding rancour. You can then work out a solution, with a bit of concealment here and an empty threat there, to which both sides will be glad to agree. Of course this is the common practice in some kinds of mediation. It is hard to imagine a peace agreement for Ireland, or for Israel and Palestine, without it. But to extend it from mediation to formal arbitration hearings would now be considered a breach of natural justice, so close have they come to litigation.

He would also like mediation and arbitration to be compulsory preliminaries to, if not substitutes for, litigation. His proposals for penalties for all those who went straight to litigation may be what failed to find favour with Louis XIV's law reformers. It may have been a matter of policy for them to keep arbitration separate and voluntary.

He assumes throughout that the distinction between mediation and arbitration will be observed. Those whom he enjoins to foster charitable arbitration are instructed to do their best to bring about a settlement but not to go over the line into

11 Chapter XXIII paragraph 11.

adjudication, nor even to suggest specific arbitrators by name. The choice of arbitrators is for the parties: the job of arbitrating is not for the mediator. But La Roche also understands and assumes the natural symbiosis of mediation and arbitration and the need for both processes in the search for the goal – the amicable settlement of disputes.

ENFORCEMENT

At a time when there were complaints that the opportunities for reopening arbitral awards were endless, despite the reforms, La Roche wisely advises the arbitrators to get the parties to incorporate their award in the form of an agreed settlement. An award was subject to appeal but a properly notarised formal agreement was straightforwardly enforceable as such and neither party could object to it on the grounds that were usual in appeals against awards: that the arbitrators were biased, or lacked jurisdiction, or wrongly applied the law, or whatever.

ENVOI

If only by his wit and wisdom, his compound of worldly experience and all-embracing goodwill, La Roche has bequeathed his successors a generous gift. Even if we cannot discover more about his identity, we can still express our affectionate gratitude to the original Charitable Arbitrator by following his precepts and working for a system of amicable settlement of disputes with more success than he seems to have enjoyed.

PART TWO

THE TEXT IN TRANSLATION

The illustration overleaf appears in all editions but the first, though not in the same place. The text reads:

BEHOLD THE GREAT KING LOUIS XIV

He is giving an audience, even to the very poorest of his subjects, to put a prompt end to their suits and differences. Solomon sat on the throne to judge those two poor women who argued about whose child it was. Our Monarch copies him perfectly, and our great Kings and Emperors, Charlemagne among others, and Louis Auguste. Like him they gave public audiences, as they were obliged to do by the express law, and they had it published throughout the realm:

ON THE KING'S AUDIENCE

Our messengers make this known to the counts and the people, that we will sit for one day every week to hear and decide causes; Capitul. add. 1. 4. c. 83.

And the same kings and emperors have prescribed by their laws, which causes should be addressed to the prince:

When one would be oppressed, *they say,* or would be pleading that one had been judged contrary to the Ordinances. For which reason one should go into the presence of the King &c; Capitul. 1. 5. c. 141.

Behold the Great King Louis XIV. © The British Library.

TO THE KING[1]

SIRE,

YOUR MAJESTY *is besought very humbly to grant your support to this manual, which one dares to present to you; because it may augment and preserve Your Majesty's victories, prevent duels, and abolish chicanery, in a way which may stop it reviving. This manual has already had great success and one hopes it will go further, if Your Majesty is willing to lend your authority to giving it effect.*

1. To begin with the Conquests; Your Majesty should be aware that the Flemish and other foreigners, even the peasantry, are persuaded that chicanery is the worst of all France's evils, and if they become Your Majesty's subjects, they will have to eat an ox to save an egg.

2. In the second place, on Duels, who is there who does not know that most of them arise out of passionate and never-ending lawsuits among the nobility. Often the family's blood is drained, tit for tat, and they transform such conflicts into duels.

3. The remedies, which I am trying to provide by this manual for these and similar evils, cannot fail if Your Majesty gives them your support and puts into practice the Laws and Ordinances of the Kings and Emperors who went before you: among them Charlemagne, and Louis le Debonnaire. We can see in their Capitularies that these good Princes, great conquerors and great legislators, applied themselves, like Your Majesty, in particular to bestowing peace on their people, within the Realm, by putting an end to their suits and disputes.

4. To succeed in that, they judged it more useful for the people and easier for the Prince if they forbade suits and disputes, or at least finished them off at birth, rather than requiring the Judges to judge them well and promptly. Those good Princes thought that nearly all of those who had suits or disputes would rather come to an agreement; or at least one of the two would want to; to wit, the weakest or wisest, but he would not dare to show it, for fear of what usually happens, that his opponent or his side would draw back and boast that he was afraid.

5. What would happen, if they had intermediaries or mutual friends, is that the one who wanted peace would first give his word and the

---

1   This epistle to the King does not appear in the first edition, but is in all later ones.

*other would find it hard to refuse to accept, because of the respect and
deference he felt for the Mediators. Just as the wars of Kings, which
are their kind of lawsuit, are ended by the mediation of other Kings,
their neighbours and allies, in the same way the lawsuits of ordinary
people, which are wars for them, could be ended in the same way.*

6. *It was for wise reasons like these that the two great Princes and
Emperors began to give public audiences to their peoples, as Your
Majesty has done, and later instructed the Governors of the Provinces
to do the same. They primarily required the bishops and parish priests
as well to work through their benevolent mediation to bring to a
settlement the suits and disputes of their followers, as they were obliged
to do in obedience to the Gospel, the Fathers, the Canons and the
Councils. And to make their request the easier to obey, these Princes
did them the honour of telling them that they would share with them
the criminal jurisdiction of the Crown:* 'you shall have between you
part of our royal jurisdiction'.[2]

7. *We have in our own time, Sire, seen Monsieur le Prince de Conty do
this properly in his own lands and in his public offices.[3] A great
number of bishops have done it, in every century, and there are those
who have done it in your kingdom. This manual tells of a good curé,
Your Majesty's subject, who, by his benevolent intervention, was able
to bring to a friendly compromise nearly all the disputes and suits in
his parish.*

*What can be done in one parish can be done in all the other parishes
in France, and it would be done if the bishops had the goodwill to
exhort the curés to do it. That is why the author of this manual sent
it to all the prelates in 1666 and dedicated it to the Bishop of Luçon,
because he already practised what this manual preaches. Some other
bishops, as soon as they received it, caused it to be printed and distributed to their curés and since then they have worked on it with great
success.*

8. *But since we found out that Your Majesty yourself, in the middle of
all your cares, had taken the trouble to give public audiences, even to
the lowliest of your subjects, to put a prompt end to their suits and
disputes, your example has fired the zeal of many bishops and*

---

2   *Partem ministerii nostri regalis, per partes habetis.*
3   *Dans ses Gouvernemens.* For De Conti see Chapter 4 above and Chapter XV
     below.

provincial governors. They will very definitely follow Your Majesty's good intentions, if you are prepared to send them a circular letter, like the ones you sent before telling them to undertake the execution of your edicts against duels, of which by far the greater part come, as we have already said, from passionate and never-ending suits. So ask the bishops and governors to intervene to bring about friendly settlements; that is to require them to stop duels. That is why, Sire, I very humbly beg Your Majesty to agree to this circular letter, which should have such good effects.

9. Because you know, Sire, when they see Your Majesty and your governors (above all in the conquered countries) and the bishops and curés, all working in accordance with your instructions on this mission of peace, then the subjects of your recent conquests will no longer be afraid of French chicanery. Foreigners and even enemies of the State will no longer be able to decry the Government for it. They will be persuaded that Your Majesty's design is to abolish chicanery completely and prevent it ever being able to revive. They will see that Your Majesty works in this way by the authority of the Laws and has asked the Church to work by the kindness of the Gospel, which is all the better remedy and will last all the longer because you have the power to support it.

10. Your Majesty's best laws may not be carried out because of the carelessness of the kings that come after you; but, if the governors, the bishops and curés are commanded to do their bit in carrying out these peacemaking Laws, this will last for ever. You will always find among them some benevolent one, whose example will rekindle the others' zeal. The people who are used to the gentleness of this remedy will themselves urge them on, when they start to slack. France will ever bless the name of Your Majesty, from whom it will have received a remedy so gentle and effective in guarding against the greatest of all evils.

11. Henry the Great, Your Majesty's glorious grandfather, entered into the thinking and the plans of those Princes of whom we have just spoken. Like them he worked out that, of the two parties to a suit or dispute, one wants peace but dare not ask for it for the reasons we have given; and that the Kings of France, ever since the Vénalité des Charges, have known that they had no means easier than arbitration to bring lawsuits and differences to a prompt conclusion. For that

*reason they required their people by public Edicts to avail themselves
of that remedy. But their laws have not been carried into effect, because
they fixed no sanctions against those who refused to go to arbitration.*

12. *Therefore that good Prince, according to his great minister and
adviser the Duc de Sully, wished to impose this penalty on anyone who
refused to go to arbitration. There would, for example, be a fine
payable before anyone was allowed to start proceedings. Furthermore,
they would have to deposit an amount for the costs of the suit, or at
least the one who refused arbitration could not expect to receive his
costs. If a penalty such as that were imposed, half the litigants would
ask for it to be imposed and the other half would not dare to refuse
arbitration for fear of the penalty. If the laws are going to be carried
into effect they need to be followed by punishments and rewards. To
get obedience, God promises heaven and threatens hell.*

13. *Your Majesty is begged, if you think it proper, to impose these
penalties of which we speak, at least against those who refuse arbitration when they are asked by gentlemen. By this means, which I
believe to be unique, you will stop their duels, and preserve their
property, which will put them in a position to raise their children and
enrol them in your armies, for the service, honour and glory of Your
Majesty, instead of, as they do now, using up both their wealth and
their time in hanging about the Tribunals and paying court to* avocats
and procureurs.

14. *Your Majesty will again, if it please him, allow me to represent to
you that the poor man complains that he has no hope of justice in
France. He says that an appeal always takes money, even if it is
rendered gratuitously, and the poor man has none. But, Sire, your
kingdom is full of poor men without money, who are oppressed by the
rich and the powerful, and who, as a result, complain that they are
without hope of help or remedy for their evils.*

15. *Henry IV, the Prince ever good, who had a heart full of pity for his
people, considering this misery so worthy of pity, resolved to deliver
the weak from oppression. In 1610 he decreed that in all the courts, in
every jurisdiction of his Kingdom, there should be charitable* avocats
and procureurs, *who would take on poor people's cases for nothing,
following the example which is given by the State in the Republic of
Venice, whose criminal justice system is the wonder of Europe.*

16. *This system has already been established in Provence, by charitable concerns, including the first* Président, *the* Procureur *and the* Avocats-Généraux *of the* Parlement, *and it would have applied throughout France had it not been for the unforeseen death of that good Prince. The widow and orphan, Sire, call on Your Majesty to accomplish this grand design of charity, as you have accomplished your grandfather's other great designs.*

17. *In that case, Sire, the poor will lift up their voice even to the heavens, to extol your praise and one will say of Your Majesty, what the Scripture says of a great Prince:* That the all-powerful right hand of the King has raised a wall of brass for the defence of the weak, which the wickedness of chicanery shall not be able to shake.

18. *In that case, they will say again of Your Majesty, what the same sacred text says of another great Conquering Prince like you, whose encomium was:* That in the midst of his armies, and despite the din and noise of his conquests and his triumphs, he has heard the voice of the weak, who seek his help, and he humbles himself to serve as the eye of the blind and the foot of the lame, *to use the words of the Scripture.*

19. *And in payment, Sire, for all these acts of charity, I wish Your Majesty, what the prelates of this France of ours wished the great emperor Charlemagne. To get him to continue his public audiences, to preserve the good order which he had established to bring to an end the suits and disputes of his people, and to keep the peace for them, the truth is that they told him* (as is recorded in his Capitularies) *that* the prize goes not to those who start but to those who finish. *That the Crown is promised only to him who perseveres.*

20. *This Crown will be given to you, Your Majesty, when you are so firm in your resolve and so prompt in its execution, that all the Princes of Europe will be amazed. They cannot understand how your miraculous conquest of the Franche-Comté was accomplished; how Your Majesty was able to march his armies in the middle of winter, in such weather that other princes had trouble in travelling at all; or how Your Majesty was able in the rigour of the season to attack places, besiege towns, and at last conquer the whole of a great Province in less time than it took to conceive this miracle. For that expedition was accomplished in less than twenty days. This miracle, Sire, can only be*

attributed to the presence of Your Majesty, and to the firmness, vigilance, and vigour that you showed in all your undertakings.

I wish you, Sire, the happy accomplishment of all your other good plans, which you have made for the relief of your peoples, and I am, with the very greatest respect,

SIRE, YOUR MAJESTY'S

most humble, most obedient and most faithful subject and servant,

THE PRIOR OF S. PIERRE

DEDICATED TO MONSEIGNEUR

THE BISHOP OF LUÇON

THE YEAR M. DC. LXVI

MONSEIGNEUR,

Forgive me if I dedicate this essay to you.[4] *I know that to advertise your other virtues offends your modesty, but to whom may I address the means of settling lawsuits and the hatreds and disastrous enmities which follow them except you, Monseigneur, who direct all your attention to settling those in your diocese? You have done me the honour of telling me some of what you have done to this end and that in your zeal you want to be able to ensure that you complete such a holy enterprise. The Apostles' fervent charity suffuses everything you do to bring peace to your flock and to chase off the deadly demon of division and discord who is the unhappy and fruitful source of so many of the*[5] *sins committed in France.*

Here is the good curé, of whom I told you, Monseigneur! I present him to you; stimulated by the same zeal as yours, he has undertaken this great Work of Peace, and succeeded in it, in his parish. There is hardly a single lawsuit there which is not brought to a friendly conclusion by his charitable intervention; hardly any disputes, hatreds, or enmities which he does not settle. His bishop worthily supports him; many neighbouring curés follow his example, and a number of bishops throughout France work towards this Holy Harvest.

This was the practice of the Primitive Church, in France and elsewhere. It still is in the whole of the Eastern Church. Saint Paul, all-divine in his counsel, exhorts the faithful to settle their suits by arbitration. All our kings have asked their subjects to do the same, by public Edicts:[6] *among others Louis XII, called the Father of the People; and that great*

---

4   The first edition of this book names the Bishop of Luçon as 'Monseigneur Colbert' and the only surviving copy I have been able to trace, in the Beinecke Library of Yale University, is 'bound in red morocco with Colbert's episcopal arms' but they are the arms of the later Jacques-Nicolas Colbert, see Chapter 5.

5   Where, as here, the first edition contains additional matter, the footnote will show it thus <thousands of mortal>.

6   <Ordonn. titr. des Arbitr.> Presumably of 1560.

Prince, Henry IV, who had no less goodwill than he, had the same plans, of which a famous author[7] has spoken. Finally, this will support the good intentions of our Incomparable Monarch, who wants to bring peace to his subjects and drive chicanery out of France, and who for so long has applied himself so admirably to this work, this great reform of the legal system, which everyone desires with so much eagerness.

Keep going, Monseigneur; no sooner will your example be known than it will be followed by all the prelates of the kingdom. We are all waiting for you, knowing that your thoughts tend only towards the good of your sheep. For you the Court has no charms; Paris, the capital of the world, beautiful as it is, is like exile to you, because your flock is not there. The embrace of your highly eminent brother, the sweet society of your happy family, the lustre of your glittering fortune, which would dazzle so many other men, have no attraction at all for you.

This year, 1666, you were appointed to the General Assembly of the Clergy. Even though it was not yet over and you were not in the best of health, because the festival of Easter was approaching you covered fifty miles a day on horseback, to get back to your Diocese in time. It is an unsalubrious, marshy place, with not much to recommend it, except that God's will asks it of you, and the dear flock which loving Providence has committed to your guidance. Succeed, Monseigneur, succeed in making it happy! Get for it the greatest of all good things, peace! Settle its suits! Be the Charitable Mediator! Drive out the trouble-making demon, that spirit of tempest and division! You will be working for Heaven, where you seek to build up your treasure. Your reward will be the true crown of honour and glory of which Scripture speaks and which the God of peace keeps for those who work for Him. This I wish you, Monseigneur,

and I remain very sincerely, Monseigneur,
your most humble, most obedient
and greatly obliged servant,

THE PRIOR OF S. PIERRE.

---

7   <M. de Sully.> The Duc de Sully, see Chapter 2.

The illustration overleaf appears in all editions but the first, though not in the same place. The text reads:

THE
GOOD BISHOP
SAINT AUGUSTINE

In his Diocese. He settles suits and disputes. He says that he would give everything else up for this; that it is one of the most important functions of the episcopate.

The Gospel and the Fathers require this of the pastors, Philip 3; John 14; Paul, Romans 12, Corinthians 1; Leo, Epistle 82.

The Eastern Church has retained this holy practice.

The Councils so order all bishops: it must be the concern of bishops to exhort brethren who have differences, whether they be clergy or lay, towards peace rather than to litigation. Carh 4 c26.

Our kings in the past have exhorted the bishops to excommunicate those who refuse to settle their differences following the thundering Councils of Worms[8] *15 c41, Agath c31.* The majority so agreed that whosoever were in hatred, or were in dispute in long drawn out litigation among themselves, and were unable to be brought together in peace, should first be challenged by the priests of their communities to say why, if they were not willing to put an end to their enmities, they should not be excommunicated from the most righteous fellowship of the Church.[9] *C ad 4 c31.*

---

8   'De vorm.', see Chapter VII where it is spelled out.
9   *Placuit ut sicut plerumque fit quicumque odio, aut longinqua inter se lite dissenserint, et in pace revocari, nequiverint a Civitatum primitus Sacerdotibus arguantur; Quid si inimicitias deponere noluerint, de Ecclesiae coetu iustissima ex comunicatione pellantur.*

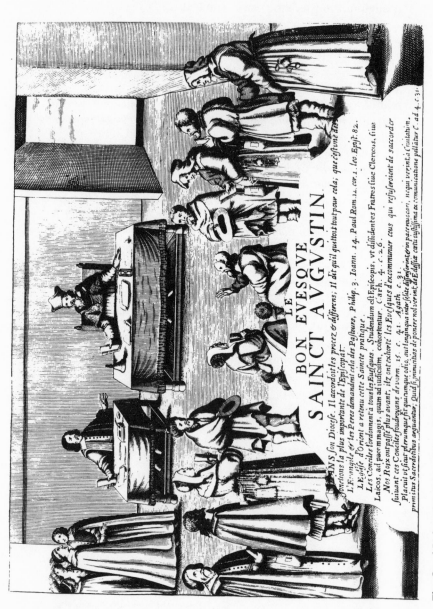

The Good Bishop Saint Augustine. © The British Library.

TO THE
BISHOPS

You are, My Lords, the successors of that divine Shepherd, JESUS CHRIST. He loved his flock so tenderly that, when he had to leave them to return to his Father, he had no more precious present to give them than peace: 'My peace I give unto you',[10] John 14. After his glorious Resurrection, when he was visiting his apostles, and preparing himself for that great entrance into heaven, he nevertheless spoke to them of that peace: 'Peace be unto you',[11] St Luke 24. Moreover, every time he appeared to his beloved disciples, to those princes of the nascent Church, he always wished that same peace: 'Peace be unto you, again Peace be unto you',[12] John 20.

In fact, the repose of the spirit and the tranquillity of the soul are the solid foundations on which the other Christian virtues are built. For how can we listen to the sweet voice of the Lamb amid the din and storms of the passions? How can we hear your pastoral voice, My Lords, amid the thunder and lightning of anger?

Yet today, the condition of most of our poor French people is deplorable. They are eaten up by lawsuits and chicanery. They tear themselves in shreds by their hatreds and irreconcilable enmities, which they couple with wrongs and vengeance and hopelessness, oaths and blasphemies, which they spew up against their opponents, and against Heaven which is innocent of it all.

My Lords, you can stop this stream, this impetuous torrent, of sins and offences, which are the cause of a hundred, no a hundred million, mortal sins committed in France. You can destroy these unhappy thorns, which hinder the fruition of the divine seed, which you are sowing every day in the souls of your sheep, by the holiness of your behaviour, your good advice, your exhortations, the frequent visits which you make in person to your parishes, your holy missions, and a hundred other acts of piety and consummate charity.

---

10 *Pacem meam do vobis.* John 14, 27.
11 *Pax vobis.* Luke 24, 36.
12 *Pax vobis, iterum Pax vobis.* John 20, 21 and 26.

The ground must be prepared if one wants it to bear fruit. You are sowing on the highways *and on the stones*, as the Gospel says, if you cast your seed into a heart set about with lawsuits and moved by anger. And this is all the more deplorable because the poor litigants give up taking the sacraments, and are so weak that they cannot approach them because they cannot forgive, because their souls are full of hatred and vengeance against their adversaries, whom they believe to be the authors of their ruin and their misery. The tribunals of penitence resound with these pleas. Your holy labourers, who work with such zeal in your holy missions, know the punishments which they apply to guide these unhappy souls.

It is easy for you, My Lords, if you undertake the task, to strangle this monster of division and discord. One good curé, of whom I have spoken in this manual, has undertaken this harvest of peace, and God has blessed his plans. In his parish there is neither dispute nor lawsuit which can prevail against him and his charitable enterprise, which means that he is able to bring nearly every one to a friendly settlement. Most of those who have a suit or dispute would like to come to an agreement. In one or two cases only one party wants it, the weaker or the wiser, and does not dare to let the other know for fear of what usually happens, that the other party draws back and boasts that his opponent is afraid. That is when the need arises of a charitable intermediary, who has no interest in the matter and is objective, moved by a spirit of peace, like the good curé and his bishop. That is when the need arises of zealous intermediaries, as all the prelates used to be in the Primitive Church, and as everyone ought to be, following the Gospel, the Fathers, the Canons, the Councils, and the Ordinances of our Kings, which we spoke of before.

The litigant is the man sick of the palsy in the Gospel, by the side of the font, who wants peace. But he has nobody to get it for him. You be the ones, My Lords! Follow the advice of the Gospel! Follow the example of the great number of our bishops, which France has marvelled at! Follow that of St Ambrose and of our charitable St Augustine! He was one of the busiest of prelates; nevertheless he left his studies to work for this harvest, as the most important, he said, of his duties. His successors, and those other bishops of the Church now distressed under the Empire of the Turk, have held on to this holy practice and today it is still one of their more charitable occupations.

In this kingdom, a great number of our bishops are working appropriately on this. Among others there is Monseigneur de Luçon, who leaves behind the apparent delights of the Court and stays banished in a swamp to apply himself to these charitable concerns. He gave public proof in the year 1666.[13] He was appointed to the General Assembly of the Clergy held in Paris and, before it was over, off he set on the long journey home, because the feast of Easter was approaching.

When you start work, My Lords, on this labour of peace, you will be in obedience to the Councils, and will be in support of the intention of our Kings, who, by their Edicts[14] and Ordinances, have required their subjects to put an end to their suits in a friendly way. Above all, you will be supporting the good objectives of our Incomparable Monarch, who has been working for such a long time to reform this unhappy chicanery, with an application worthy of the kings praised in sacred history.[15] In the midst of his concerns, he takes the trouble himself to give public audiences, even to the poorest of his subjects, to put a prompt end to their suits and disputes.

That good Prince has asked you, My Lords, by Letters Circular, to undertake the execution of his Edicts against duels, mostly in the Provinces, arising from suits, passionate and never-ending, among the nobility. In some families there are inheritances which have driven children, fathers, even grandfathers to fight, and the same lawsuits are still going on. Unhappy France, whose chicanery makes you nurture in your bosom such deathless monsters!

The Empire needs a High Priest, if the laws are going to be carried out properly. Princes govern the body but the Church instructs the spirit. That is why the King of Kings, JESUS CHRIST, born on earth, made an alliance with the royal blood, with the High

13 The last sentence of this paragraph reads in the first edition: 'and for the love of his first flock, he has refused the most beautiful, great and rich sees of the kingdom' and a marginal note adds: <l'Archevesché de Rheims.>
14 <Tiltr. ix. des Arbitres.>
15 <Reg. passim>, i.e. in the books of the Bible: Samuel 1 and 2, Kings 1 and 2.

Priest's. You can do it, My Lords! You can boldly undertake to persuade the peoples to obey the Gospel and the Councils, which declare *Anathemas* against those who refuse to settle when they are asked. You can exhort the people to obey our Princes and their Laws, which require them to bring their lawsuits to a friendly conclusion.

Those great Emperors, Charlemagne among others, and Louis le Debonnaire, exhorted the bishops of their time, by their Laws and Ordinances, to work with them for this harvest of peace; and, to make this request all the stronger, they told them that in that way they would be sharing with the Prince the royal functions: 'Part of our royal jurisdiction you shall share.'[16] Capitul 1 2 cap 12.

A sacred resolution has already been made in Paris, by some persons of quality and outstanding virtue, not to take part in lawsuits but to ask the other party in writing to make an amicable settlement and to name arbitrators. In this way a large number of lawsuits are settled every day. If this system is established throughout the kingdom, as you, My Lords, have it in your power to ensure by your holy recommendations, then the lawsuit, that deadly demon of all division, will soon be banished from France.

There are thousands of poor people throughout the kingdom who have lawsuits and are oppressed by the rich or the powerful. They complain with no hope of any help; for justice is not provided without money and the poor have none.

My Lords, you can still cure the ills of this unhappy people. You can request our great Prince to institute throughout France those charitable *avocats* and *procureurs* which have been established in Provence by the Ordinance of Henry IV 1610. They take charge of the litigation of the poor for nothing, and they settle nearly all of it amicably. This is done with complete success in the Republic of Venice. Those who devote themselves to these charitable duties for the length of time required by their laws are rewarded by membership of the Senate, which for them is the supreme honour.

16 *Partem ministerii nostri regalis per partes habetis.* This paragraph is not in the first edition. La Roche seems to have discovered the relevance of this capitulary authority between editions.

By establishing these *avocats* and *procureurs*, My Lords, you will erect *that holy gate of which the prophet speaks*, Jeremiah 1,[17] where the widow and orphan can find safety. For what oppressor, however powerful he may be, will dare to attack the weak? Because they have become more powerful than he is, with the help of the *avocats* and *procureurs*, who will be available in all the tribunals in the kingdom.

All the ill-will of chicanery will not be able to subvert this refuge of the unhappy; it will last forever. Which king would want to do so? And who would dare ask him to? We can see this from our own experience. Since the establishment of *Juges-Consuls*, who are the refuge of merchants, all the Offices of State have become sinecures. Nevertheless, these *Juges-Consuls* have been kept clean of corruption, and stronger than before, because they are *Officiers* who are self-selecting, who ask for nothing but honour by way of reward and who give their time to the public for nothing, with no expectation of any emoluments or fees.

Finally, My Lords, you may bring peace to the whole of France and have it for yourselves, because you have lawsuits like everyone else – you cannot exempt yourselves from them. You have the patrimony of St Peter to look after, and the rights of the Church to defend. If you do this, you will have no lawsuits that you do not want. In the manner which I tell you later, in Chapter XI, you will be able to bring to a settlement those who now are bringing actions, and those who bring them in future. You ought at least to try, for fear of the threats of the fearful Council, which speaks of this matter, and deals with the pastors of those against whom anathema has been pronounced for troubling the peace of the flock by their lawsuits, and which instructs all Christians to seek peace through gentleness, before bringing their brother before the court.

If you follow this path, the great lords will copy you, and settle their suits, and those of their neighbours and their vassals. And generally, everyone will be able to settle their differences according to your example. 'You are the light of the world',[18] as

---

17 This is a misprint for 7 (2 and 6).
18 *Vos estis lux mundi.*

the Holy Text says. As Plato also says: 'the actions of the great are written with rays of sunshine; everybody copies them'.

What happiness it will be for you, My Lords, to be the cause of peace throughout the realm! What joy for you to be relieved of the heavy burden you now carry of the care and conduct of these unhappy matters of chicanery! What satisfaction for those great souls whose spirit is more in Heaven than on earth, who are often torn from the foot of the altar to jump to the demands of some miserable court case! I wish you that peace, My Lords, and I beg you, with the Apostle, to procure it for others.[19]

Approbation of the Doctors

We, the undersigned Doctors in the Faculty of Theology at Paris, certify that we have seen and read a book entitled *The Charitable Arbitrator, and an Easy Means of Settling Suits and Disputes, Without Trouble or Cost*, composed by the Sieur ALEXANDRE DE LA ROCHE PRIEUR DE S. PIERRE, for the said book to be printed for a second time. This book contains nothing contrary to the Catholic, Apostolic and Roman Faith, or against good morals, tending towards the pacifying of dissensions, suits and disputes, which cause great ruin, temporal and spiritual. In this belief we have signed, the 22 October this present year 1667.

L. BAIL   M. GRANDIN

Extract from the Royal Privilege

By the grace and privilege of the King, of the date 29th day of June 1667, signed DENIS, it is permitted to the Sieur de la RIVIÈRE, to have printed by whatever printer and publisher he wishes, a book entitled *The Charitable Arbitrator, and the Means of Ending Suits Promptly, Without Trouble or Cost*, with protection against all other persons, of whatever quality and condition they may be, who pirate or sell pirated copies of the said books, in whole or in part, during the period of seven years, under the penalties contained in the Original.

19 The first edition ends here with a subscription: 'This is, Nosseigneurs, your very humble, very obedient and very dutiful servant, the Prior of S. Pierre.'

Registered in the Book of the Society of Publishers and Printers of Paris, following the Arrest of the Parlement of the 23rd April 1653 and that of the King's Privy Council of the 27th February 1663. The 6th July 1667.

Copies have been provided.

TABLE

Of Contents & of Chapters

CHAPTER ONE

Declaration by the author that he is neither knowledgeable nor eloquent, that his language is rough, that he makes use of boring repetitions, that there is nothing any good in his manual – just the project which is excellent if it is carried out.

That the manual has nevertheless been translated into three languages.
That the Huguenots have had it printed and sent it to their Ministers and the great Lords of their Religion.

CHAPTER TWO

That a good Curé in our France, by his charitable involvement, has managed to settle almost all Suits and Disputes in his Parish amicably.
That the Gospel, the Canons, the Councils and the Ordinances of our Kings, oblige the Pastors to do what the good Curé has done.

CHAPTER THREE

That the greater part of Suits and Disputes will be settled amicably if Bishops and Curés have the charity to be Mediators.
That they are so obliged; that was the practice of the primitive Church which prevailed in France, which it did with plenty of goodwill.
That they can do it without trouble or cost.
That they have only to copy the example of M. le Prince de Conty and do as he did on his estates and in his administrations.
That Litigants, almost all of them, would like a compromise, at least one of them would, to wit the weaker or wiser.
That all that is needed is a Mediator like the good Curé of whom the Manual tells, how he takes the matter in hand and what he says to those who have a Suit or Dispute.

CHAPTER FOUR

What the good Curé does if one of the parties refuses to settle.

CHAPTER FIVE

On the way in which the good Curé resolves Disputes, hatreds and enmities.

How he reconciles families, and neighbours, when there is coldness between them.

CHAPTER SIX

That if they copy the good Curé in all the Parishes of the Kingdom, most Suits and Disputes will be resolved from the start.

That many Bishops have started to establish this practice in their Dioceses, since they found out that the King grants public Audiences on the same matters.

The evils caused by Chicanery.

That it is almost impossible to litigate without giving offence to God, that when they were putting JESUS CHRIST on trial, the wrongs of a maidservant made St Peter deny his good Master, though he was educated in the school of patience itself.

That after such an example the Litigant should stand in dread.

CHAPTER SEVEN

That the Bishops can and should serve as Mediators, to help in the settlement of Suits and differences of those in their Dioceses.

That they are obliged to do so by the Gospel, the Councils and the Ordinances of the Kings.

That a holy Bishop in our France, still alive, in order to resolve a great lawsuit and a passionate dispute between two neighbouring gentlemen, spent part of a night at the door of the one who refused to settle.

That this gentleman gave in to such a great example of charity, and embraced his enemy and settled their dispute; and by his example all those in his canton did the same.

CHAPTER EIGHT

That there are some Bishops who, since they received this Manual, have had it printed and distributed to their Curés.

The order which they have followed in putting it into practice.

That Bishops can have it printed and distributed to their Curés without it costing them anything; the way to find the money.

That many of the Curés of that good Bishop have said that, since the first day they asked in their Sermon that those who had suits or disputes, and wanted them resolved, should come to them and that they would help them, a large number had come the same day and are coming to them as soon as they have a difference.

That if every Curé preached such a Sermon they would see the same result, because virtually everybody wants peace.

CHAPTER NINE

That since they found out that the King gives public Audiences to resolve the differences of his subjects, several Bishops have copied him.

That all can do it without trouble or expense.

That they only have to copy the way in which M le Prince de Conty did it on his estates and in his administrations.

That Bishops, Curés, Governors and great Lords should never themselves be Arbitrators but simple Mediators only, and why.

CHAPTER TEN

Of the difficulties which the Bishops and Curés can find in this work of peace, and the remedies.

That the Judges have begun to authorise these requests for Arbitrations; that the First President of the *Parlement* of Paris, and the ones for Brittany and Provence, send before Arbitrators those who ask for them.

CHAPTER ELEVEN

That the Bishops, too, can bring to an amicable conclusion almost all their lawsuits and that they ought at least to try this method.

That this is what they ought to do except in disciplinary matters, and that they are bound by Councils to do so.

That a Bishop, who had a big lawsuit against his Chapter, summoned it to agree to Arbitrators, and that it was settled immediately.

That another Bishop, who had a big lawsuit against a powerful family, settled it in the same way.

That another Bishop, who was heir and successor to a Bishop who had a large number of lawsuits, advertised that he would like to settle them all, and that is what he did, in a very short time, to the joy of all in his Diocese.

Of the difficulties one can find in nominating Arbitrators, and the remedies.

The distress of a Bishop who had a lawsuit and lost, to him and his flock.

That the Councils treat as anathematised those Pastors who have lawsuits and do not try to settle them amicably.

CHAPTER TWELVE

That Curés and Preachers can and should settle their own disputes amicably.

That the Councils oblige them to, as they do Bishops.

That they are obliged at least to try this way before they start a lawsuit. That it is shameful to see Curés in France that have been away from their Livings for three or four years, on the pretext that they are pursuing some wretched lawsuit.

CHAPTER THIRTEEN

That Monks and Nuns can and should also settle their lawsuits amicably, or at least should try to do so; and that the Councils order them to do so on pain of Anathema.

That they know the complaints that are made about them on this matter, and that the spirit of Chicanery rules in the Cloisters, that it is an excuse to escape from them, and to free themselves from the rule, and that these complaints would cease if they offered to go to Arbitration.

That there are some reformed Religious Communities which have resolved to do this in their Chapters.

CHAPTER FOURTEEN

That Abbés also can and should settle their lawsuits.
That those who have suits against them want that, and why.

CHAPTER FIFTEEN

That Provincial Governors ought to settle their disputes and to offer their mediation in settling lawsuits.
That the Ordinances of the Kings oblige them to do so.
That M le Prince de Conty did so to his credit while he was alive.
That it is still done on his estates by his order.
The way in which he did it, and how he was able to do it without cost, or difficulty, or trouble, or expense.
That good Prince always had a plan to set up a certain Order in his Public Offices, which would have put a stop to all premeditated crime; and a system of criminal justice just as rigorous as that which they have nowadays in Paris, without it costing the king or the people anything.

CHAPTER SIXTEEN

That the Lords of great Fiefs ought to settle the disputes of their vassals and be Mediators to settle their lawsuits, which would be easy for them, and the profit that they will get from this, because their rents will be better paid.
That ordinary gentlemen and the Bourgeois and others can also require their Tenants to settle their lawsuits, and that they will be the better paid for doing so.
That the Lords of Fiefs formerly gave offices to their Judges, that they might render justice to their vassals without charge, and that the written engagement which is still given to the *Chambre des Comptes* in Paris carries such an obligation.
How this practice has changed and how it would be easy for the King to reestablish it.
That the Lords would profit by it, and how there are some who did not want to sell their offices.
That a number of Lords create thousands of *Procureurs*, Notaries and *Sergents* who devour the people and that they would not do

that if the Law were enforced which makes them responsible for their misconduct and that of their Judges.

How it comes about that this Law is not enforced, and the way to put it into practice, and easily.

CHAPTER SEVENTEEN

That the great Lords can settle nearly all lawsuits that they have in their own names, and why.

The miseries of a great Lord who took charge of his lawsuits himself.

The disaster if one does not take charge, and how one is plundered by *Intendants*, Agents or *Solliciteurs*.

That the great Lords are often the cause of the disloyalty of those who serve them because they do not pay them well.

One great Lord's good idea to make them loyal and require them to settle their lawsuits.

CHAPTER EIGHTEEN

That the good Judges can and should settle their lawsuits.

That the *Officiers* know the complaints that are made against them, that they oppress &c, and that their approach is to be feared.

The way to settle their lawsuits and the benefit they will get from that.

CHAPTER NINETEEN

That the lower classes and the weak can and should settle the lawsuits they have with those more powerful than them when they have been assured that they will get more by a lawsuit than by a settlement, and why.

The way in which the inferior ought to persist in such a case.

That the rich and the powerful would not dare to refuse to settle with an inferior if they are requested to do so, and why.

CHAPTER TWENTY

That equals should ask one another to settle, the difficulties they encounter, and the remedies.

When each Curé does no more than bring about the settlement
of fifteen or twenty lawsuits a year, that will settle more than six
hundred thousand a year.

CHAPTER TWENTY-ONE

The manner of choosing Arbitrators, the difficulties one can find,
and the remedies.
That the great Lords, Governors, Bishops and Curés ought never
to be Arbitrators, nor to appoint them, but should leave that to
the free choice of the parties, as they do that of Confessor and
Doctor, and why.

CHAPTER TWENTY-TWO

The qualities of the good Mediator.

CHAPTER TWENTY-THREE

The qualities of the good Arbitrator.
That it is usually the fault of the Arbitrators if the settlement fails,
and why.
That it is much better to get the parties to come to terms than to
make an Award, and why; and the way in which to word the
compromise so that it is hard to disturb.

CHAPTER TWENTY-FOUR

On certain town officials of Lyons, Nantes and Clermont en
Auvergne who, having retired from office, get together on certain
fixed days to settle the lawsuits of the poor and weak.
That people would come from all parts, and the great good that
would do, if only there were in France a number of well-intentioned *Officiers* who could do the same.

CHAPTER TWENTY-FIVE

That in 1610 Henry IV ordained that there should be Charitable
Avocats and *Procureurs* in all the Courts and Jurisdictions of the

Kingdom, who would take charge of the lawsuits of the poor for nothing.

That without that the poor would never get Justice in France, which is not available without money, and the poor have none.

That in Venice there are some charitable *Avocats* and *Procureurs*, and they are greatly honoured.

That such *Avocats* and *Procureurs* have been established first of all in Provence, by the good offices of the First President and the *Avocats* and *Procureurs Généraux*.

That they would have been established throughout France had it not been for the death of that good King, which happened two months after his Ordinance.

That M de Sillery, worthy Chancellor of that great Prince, had that establishment very much in mind.

That, on his instructions, a Counsellor of the *Parlement* of Toulouse wrote on this matter, to show how useful and easy this establishment would be.

The great benefits it would produce.

The Manner in which the charitable *Avocats* and *Procureurs* would be able to settle the lawsuits of the poor, and without trouble.

That M de Harlay, the worthy *Procureur Général* of the *Parlement* of Paris, has established assemblies to have responsibility for Prisons, and to speed up the dispatch of the business of poor prisoners and those who regularly find themselves in those assemblies.

That the poor call on our Monarch to establish those Charitable *Avocats* and *Procureurs* and to carry out the great plan of charity of his Illustrious Grandfather.

CHAPTER TWENTY-SIX

On the assembly of the Parish of St Sulpice in Paris, which settles the lawsuits of the poor.

What has taken place in that assembly.

That in that assembly there are Dukes and Peers and *Cordons Bleus* and Presidents and Counsellors and *Maîtres des Requêtes* &c.

That the Judge of the Parish has assured the assembly that he would contribute to the accomplishment of these good plans.

That the establishment of Charitable *Avocats* and *Procureurs*, established by the King, will produce much more of benefit than these particular assemblies, and why.

CHAPTER TWENTY-SEVEN

The substance of the rules of the said assembly of St Sulpice.

CHAPTER TWENTY-EIGHT

That the settlement of lawsuits will settle a large number of duels. That in the Provinces, most duels arise from the passionate and never-ending lawsuits among the nobility.

That the King by his Letters Circular has required the Bishops to take in hand the execution of his Edicts against duels and that, in the same way that he would require them to intervene to settle the lawsuits of his people, he would require them to stop their duels, because it is the lawsuits that cause them.

CHAPTER TWENTY-NINE

That the Prelates and great Lords who are close to the Prince are begged to ask His Majesty to add his authority to the execution of the above suggestions, if they find anything there of value.

CHAPTER THIRTY

The manner of compromise which the good Curé and M le Prince de Conty make the parties sign.

CHAPTER THIRTY-ONE

The manner of summoning an Arbitration between equals.

CHAPTER THIRTY-TWO

Summons to Arbitration by a great Person to an Inferior.

CHAPTER THIRTY-THREE

Summons to Arbitration by an Inferior to someone more Powerful than him.

CHAPTER THIRTY-FOUR

To create societies and to avoid the lawsuits which in France usually follow.

CHAPTER THIRTY-FIVE

To make commercial contracts and avoid lawsuits.

CHAPTER THIRTY-SIX

Objections to the methods proposed in the two preceding chapters, and responses to them.

The illustration overleaf appears in all editions but the first, though not in the same place. The text reads:

THE GOOD CURÉ S. YVES
BY HIS CHARITABLE INTERVENTION

He managed to bring nearly all suits and disputes
in his Parish to an amicable settlement.
The Councils and the Canons have ordered the Curés and the
Preachers,
as well as the Bishops, to work towards this harvest of Peace.

On Sundays and Feast Days the Priests, before they celebrate the Mass,
should ask if any persons are in dispute,
and if any have between them any litigation which cannot be settled.
And if any such be found, they shall be reconciled at once. Nannet c1.

And our Kings have requested the Curés and Preachers,
by their Laws & Ordinances,
as I have said on the subject of Bishops.

Those who are not turned back to peace
are clearly told by the Priests of the congregation, &c
Capitul. addi. 4 c31

LE BON CVRE' S. YVES,

PAR SON ENTREMISE CHARITABLE,
Il faisoit que dans la Paroisse, les procez & les querelles, s'accordoient
quasi toutes à l'amiable.

Les Conciles, & les Canons, ont ordonné aux Curez, & aux Prestres,
aussi bien qu'aux Evéques, de trauailler à cette moisson de Paix.
Dominicis Festis diebus, Presbyter, ante quam Missas celebrant, interrogent, si aliqui discordantes sint,
qui inter se sedem implacabile habeant. Et, si manifesti fuerint, statim reconcilientur. Nunant. i.
Et nos Roys y ont contede les Curez & les Prestres par leurs Loix & leurs Ordonnances,
comme on l'a dit au suict des Euéques.

De his qui id preestare renuerent, Sacerdotibus subditis, arguantur, &c. Capitul. add. 4. c. 31.

The Good Curé S. Yves. © The British Library.

CHAPTER I

Before getting to the substance, the author reminds you that he is neither learned nor eloquent, that he knows nothing about making books, and that there is nothing good in this one except its intention, which is excellent if carried into effect.

The rest of its contents are ill-ordered, the language is rough, and the author makes use of boring repetitions because he knows no better. Sometimes, though, he uses these repetitions expressly, in the belief that they will better persuade the good curés in the country, to whom it is his principal intention to speak. They have the time, if they have the goodwill, to read this manual, and to put it into practice, to help towards the resolution of the suits and disputes of their parishioners and to bring peace to their flock, like the good curé who is portrayed in this picture.

In the second place, the author intends to speak to those poor litigants who are looking for a way to bring their lawsuits and their woes to a quick end; they will find here the means to help them.

For those intellectuals who think they can get all the arguments out of one word, the author is far too humble to dare to speak to them. He knows that great minds, unless moved by the spirit of goodwill, look for sophistication, the forcefulness of the thoughts, the beauty of the language; that gold for them is badly worked unless it becomes good coin; like a certain grand personage of the past, clever and eloquent, who did not dare to read the Holy Scripture for fear it would spoil his beautiful Latin.

Nevertheless, if those great minds are put in positions of influence, and if they have the goodwill to want to know what this manual contains, to serve their fellows, they should just take the trouble to read the Epistle to the King, and to the Bishops, and the table of contents. That will be enough for them – that contains all the substance of this manual's intention – to spare their time and trouble.

To show how good the project of the manual is, I must tell you that since it was first printed two years ago it has been translated into three or four languages and reprinted in various places.[20]

An English Minister, who was in Paris with his Ambassador, put it into English and sent it to England. A German has also

---

20 For the various editions, see Chapter 5.

translated it and sent it home. The Danish Ambassador has had it translated into Danish, and into Latin, and has sent it to the ministers of his kingdom.

Our Huguenots in France have had it printed, and distributed it in their synods, and sent it to their ministers, and great lords of their religion, with a circular letter asking them to put it into practice. Quite apart from charitable motives, and the glory of God, and the service of our neighbour, they add that they will thereby be doing something very much to the King's liking, because he wants to get rid of chicanery throughout his kingdom. They say that they will be the first to stop it among themselves and that that will contribute to the conquests of our Prince in Flanders, because the peoples of those countries are persuaded that chicanery in France is the worst of all evils, yet one must get involved in it for fear of worse, to divert the hot-headed spirit of the French, who are quite able to engage in civil war. Foreigners will be convinced to the contrary when they see the King, and his subjects, working for the suppression of lawsuits. The Huguenots have done that more easily than the Catholics. They say that their flock is smaller and more united and for that reason they will keep the peace amongst themselves. That will give a good example and will augment or at least maintain their religion. These motives drive them to embrace warmly this work of peace.

This manual has been sent by the author to all the bishops in the kingdom. Some of them have had it reprinted in their dioceses, and have had it read at their ecclesiastical conferences, and all their curés have taken it and put it into practice, with success and blessing.

The Archbishop of Paris, among others, has had it distributed in the conferences which he has set up in his diocese and has given it to the curés in the parishes he has visited. It has been read, in Paris and elsewhere, in various religious communities and they have resolved to put it into practice.

The King himself does today exactly what this manual advises bishops and curés to do. His Majesty grants audiences to all his subjects, even the poorest of them, to put a prompt end to their lawsuits and differences. Following this great example of goodwill, there are bishops and provincial governors and lords of fiefs who have set themselves to imitate him, and with God's help they will imitate him, and keep in mind that that is what is required by the Ordinances of Princes, the Fathers, the Gospel and the Councils.

What a disgrace it would be to the Catholics in France, if one were to see the bishops, curés and great lords condemning the doctrine of the Huguenots, and not working like them for these acts of goodwill, for the settlement of the suits and disputes of their brothers!

CHAPTER II

That a good Curé in our France, by his charitable intervention,
manages to bring nearly all Suits and Disputes
to an amicable settlement

In that, he does nothing, as we have just said in the picture of the good curé, which is not ordained by the Gospel, the Fathers, the Canons, the Councils, and the Ordinances of our Kings.

We have spoken of the Council which provides that on Feast Days and Sundays the curé, before saying the Mass, should enquire who has a lawsuit, and that he should reconcile them before offering the sacrifice.

We have spoken of still other Councils which go further, for they provide that the curés should give them a formal reprimand, and if they refuse to settle, that the bishops should excommunicate them. And what is even stronger, is that two of the greatest of our kings, Charlemagne and Louis Auguste, by their laws have required the bishops and curés to put these Councils into practice.

I am not asking them to do now what they did before; I am only asking them to rouse the people to peace. Hardheartedness is now so great, and the number of litigants so great, that you would need to excommunicate nearly all the kingdom, if you excommunicated all those who have lawsuits.

That is why, with things as bad as they are, I just ask the pastors to call people to peace, and that they should be charitable mediators to settle their differences.

They will be supporting the good intentions of our Monarch, who is the busiest Prince in Europe, and nevertheless gives public audiences, even to the least of his subjects, to bring their suits, disputes and differences to a prompt conclusion.

CHAPTER III

That the greater part of Suits and Disputes will be settled amicably
if our Lord Bishops and Messieurs the Curés
have the Goodwill to be Intermediaries

This general peace could be established throughout the kingdom if our Lord Bishops and Messieurs the Curés had the goodwill to lend a hand. There are those who have already undertaken this with success. It costs no trouble or care or expense, and the reward will be a prize which all the gold on earth could not buy: '*the Treasures of the God of Peace are reserved for them*', as one of the old Fathers says.

1. There is no need to depict the evils of chicanery, as the author can show from the life of Henry IV. The Archbishop of Paris has described them in a couple of words; he said: '*the most stupid people know what they are and have experience of them*'. Indeed, it is today the most lamentable plague on the State, worse than the leprosy which befell the Jews and the locusts of Egypt. It is an evil which ruins both body and soul, and property both temporal and spiritual. It destroys families, which it forces to lead a life languishing at the doors of the law courts and tribunals and which moreover fosters hatred and irreconcilable animosity, blasphemy, despair and deadly vengeance, which are the fruitful and unhappy source of hundreds and hundreds of millions of mortal sins, which Christians today commit in France. You know this, My Lords, at least those of you who make your visitations in person, and who work for the holy missions. The confessors can tell you of the hatred which litigants feel for one another, the desire for vengeance, and the unhappy results which that produces. It goes so far as to separate them from the sacraments and makes them quite unwilling to take them while the lawsuit is on. We will relate to you deplorable examples below.

My Lords, you *and your curés* can cure this evil if you have the goodwill to do the work. You can do it – and the methods I am going to describe to you are easy. We are just waiting for your zeal, principally those of you who, fired with a burning spirit of goodwill, give all your attention to leading your flock and give witness of it by your extraordinary missions, your conferences, your personal visitations throughout your diocese, your assemblies and fraternities of charity for the relief of the poor which have been set up almost everywhere, and finally by a hundred other acts of Christian piety which will make you cherished, loved and honoured by everybody.

What will happen to those who undertake the cure of this unhappy plague, which chicanery inflicts on the body and soul of the Christian, which strips the body of its property and leaves it naked and miserable? The soul is also stripped of that love and friendship which the Christian should feel towards his neighbour, for where is the litigant who loves his opponent? Yet *whosoever hateth his brother is a murderer*, John 3.[21] And most litigants hate him with a deadly hate.

A bishop, a curé, a preacher, the zealous missionaries, would they not be very happy, and would not their harvest be full, if after Advent, or Lent, or an extraordinary mission, they had managed to settle a dozen lawsuits and disputes? If they do what I suggest, they will settle thousands and stop nearly all of them in future and bring peace to their flock. The bishops above all, and curés, will be able to take advantage of it themselves, because they will be able to live without lawsuits and still preserve their own interests, without losing or giving up any of their spiritual or temporal rights.

All this is possible without trouble or cost or doing anything novel of which anyone could complain. One will only be following the practice of the Primitive Church, of our France, and moreover what has been done up to our own times. The Eastern Church still does it. Saint Paul advised it. JESUS CHRIST himself commanded it. Finally, the kings have made it law for their people, by their edicts. And some bishops and curés still practise it in France, with wonderful success.

So that you can see that this has been the practice of our Primitive Church, and can be found in every century, even our own, and of the great prelates which the Church has canonised, who were devoted to these works of charity, it is a good idea to report here the names of some of those charitable bishops, of whom our histories make mention.

21 *Qui odit fratrem suum homicida est.* This is from the first epistle to John, I John 3, 15.

They speak of many, but among them are Saint Marcel and Saint Landry, Bishops of Paris; Saint Martin, Saint Gregory and Saint Gatien, Bishops of Tours; Saint Germain, Bishop of Auxerres; Saint Ouen, Bishop of Rouen; Saint Euverte, Bishop of Orleans.[22]

M de Sale advised it everywhere. Saint Louis, the greatest of our kings, practised it[23] appropriately, divesting himself of his sovereign authority to allow him to play the part of charitable mediator between his subjects. And, as we have said, Charlemagne and Louis Auguste did the same, and instructed their provincial governors, bishops and curés to follow them.

2. Finally, Saint Yves was canonised and all the judges of the kingdom have taken him as their patron saint. He was a curé in France[24] who was full of fire and zeal on behalf of his parishioners and gave all his time to settling their suits and differences. His bishop, who was a holy prelate, fired by the same spirit as he, made him his judge, so that he could make this charity more of a full time profession. As a result, he drove all suits and disputes out of the diocese.

The most glorious act of his life, which earned him altars, is depicted throughout France. He is shown seated in a court of justice, settling a dispute between a poor tramp, dressed in rags, and a rich man. He is not represented holding court and passing judgment, which shows that this is an arbitration and a settlement, which is something better than judgments and sentences. And that is what we ought to believe, since the judges themselves have chosen and brought to light this Throne of Arbitration, as the most glorious action of so holy a life. That is what has earned him the prayers and offerings of poor litigants and of all the people. So there you see sanctified Arbitration, and charitable mediators, and all those who are involved in it. This is a shining example to all the good curés, of our saint who was a curé like them. There is an example to all the great bishops, because his bishop helped him and supported him appropriately. Finally, he ought to be an example to all the good judges, to recommend arbitration, since they have chosen him as their patron.

22 <Surius>.
23 <Mrs. Ste Marthe>.
24 <*de l'Evesché de Treguier en Bretagne*>.

And to show that it is easy to imitate him, and that one can amicably settle nearly all the lawsuits in the kingdom, not only in civil but in criminal matters, so long as they do not entail corporal punishment, this must be presumed to be true and as we have already said.

3. In the first place, in their heart of hearts, nearly all litigants would prefer to come to an agreement, if you except the few who are mad, miserly, or vindictive, or oppress the weak, the widow and the orphan.

At least one of the parties to litigation would prefer peace – the weaker of the two, or the wiser – but does not dare to ask for it for fear that to do so will not prevent it, because in fact, most of the time, the other party then draws back and boasts that his opponent is afraid. He says that he must push on to the end, and does so. The practitioners of chicanery usually advise him to, because that is what suits them.

Of the two parties to the litigation, then, one wants a settlement but has no intermediary. Behold by the font a decent man, who wants peace, but there is nobody who is prepared to get mixed up in it: *he has no man.*[25] If there were somebody, moved by the spirit of God, objective and recognised as such, almost no one would refuse. The good curé practises this at one of the far ends of the kingdom. There is no lawsuit which escapes him and which he does not settle.

His vocation has been extraordinary. He himself had a big controversial case against the preachers of his parish, which caused him a lot of trouble. He was advised to ask them for a settlement and call on them to appoint arbitrators. He did so and they agreed to them with joy, and their lawsuit, which had lasted many years, was brought to a conclusion at once, and to the satisfaction of all parties.

In recognition of such grace, he promised God and the person he had asked to arbitrate that in future he would make every effort to settle other people's lawsuits, particularly those of his parish, and to succeed in that.

5. [26] From the time he had that experience, he would go to the home of his parishioner, and tell him well and simply about the

---

25 *Non habet hominem.*
26 There is no paragraph numbered 4.

substance of it, and that he knew he had a lawsuit on with somebody, and that that did not surprise him because he knew that he had to look after his own. But a Christian might well want to do that if he could, without having to litigate, because you ought to be afraid to give God offence, and that that was nearly impossible when you hated your opponent, when you wished him ill, when you rejoiced if some adversity befell him. You ought to want to keep your own property, without having to get involved in litigation, which produced such unhappiness and was so inimical to the spirit of Christianity,[27] that the Councils had declared an anathema on those who refused to settle. They had declared that it was forbidden to give Communion to those who refused arbitration and that it should be given to those who first asked for peace. These are the words of the Councils: *Therefore, not one of these quarrelling brothers shall dare to approach the altar of the Lord, or partake of the grace of holy communion. But if one shall have agreed to a charitable satisfaction, and the other spurn it, then from that time the former shall be reckoned as a peacemaker within the Church.* Tolet. II c4.[28]

After these words, the most passionate litigant replies that he wants peace and at least on the face of it pretends to. The good curé continues, saying that he has always believed that to be so, but he needs proof, and in this way it will still the voice of those who would be able to say the opposite; and that the shortest, easiest and least contagious way to terminate the lawsuit is accord and arbitration. And he asks him whether he would not very much like to agree to it if the other side consents.

The litigant, who is sensible, replies at once that that is what he would like, and that he consents to it, upon which the good curé makes him sign a compromise, which we will explain later and for which there is a precedent at the end of this book. Next he goes off to the other party's place. If that is within his parish, he tells him the substance of what we have said above, but without telling him straight away that he has already spoken to

27 From here to the end of this paragraph does not appear in the first edition. La Roche appears to have discovered the authorities relating to excommunication of litigants after the first edition.

28 *Horum ergo discordantium fratrum, nullus accedere ad altare Domini audeat, vel gratiam communionis sanctae percipiat, quod si unus alio contemnente ad satisfactionem charitatis cucurrerit, ex eo tempore, ut pacificus intra Ecclesiam reputetur.*

the other side, nor that he has signed the compromise. Otherwise he would take advantage of that, in the belief that the other was afraid, and increase his demand, as one knows from experience. So he must make use of a holy artifice, to make them do good in spite of themselves. If the two parties agree to settle, the good curé makes them sign a compromise, both of them, and puts them in the hands of named arbitrators. I will speak later about how you ought to choose arbitrators, and a third in case they cannot agree, and the difficulties that can arise and their remedies.

If one of the parties is not of the parish, he writes about it to his curé, and by means of his agency does what he would have done himself if that party had been of his own parish.

CHAPTER IV

What the Curé does if one of the Parties refuses to settle

In the first place, whoever it is who refuses a settlement, even if
he is the wickedest and most ill-willed of all chicaners, he never
says to his curé that he has no wish for a settlement, that what
he wants is revenge, or to devour the weak. Nobody wants to give
public proof of his malice or to have his pastor as a witness of
his iniquity.

So he will say that he wants peace. But he will try to find a way
of getting out of it. He will argue: the matter is not at a stage where
it is appropriate to settle it; he has not got the papers; they have
already been produced to the court; he needs to get a formal
judgment; there are minors involved; he has partners and he must
find out what they advise; or put forward other similar pretexts.

If the pretexts are manifestly false, the good curé tells him
nicely and dispassionately, but nonetheless with force and
firmness, that the God of the Just protects the weak and punishes
the wicked; that he makes sport of the plans of the miser, that he
overturns his projects, that he preserved *Naboth's Vineyard*,
despite all the efforts of an unjust power; and finally that the
avenging arm floors the most mighty, that in the olden days he
defeated his enemy with an army of midges.[29] He tells him that
it is not necessary, for a family to be ruined, that it should be
attacked by someone more great and powerful than itself; that it
only needs the loss of property, or the death of a father or
mother, or even of a child, or one of a hundred other misfortunes
which happen every day. In conclusion, it is to blot out the
image of Divine Justice which is written by nature on the heart
of every one: *do not do to another what you would not like to have
done to you.* That is to renounce Christianity and the most
important law which JESUS CHRIST has given us, and shown by
his example: *Love your neighbour as yourself* [30] and *Do good to your
enemies.* And finally that he demands his own damnation every
time he speaks the words of the divine prayer: *Forgive us our
trespasses as we forgive them that trespass against us.*

29 Exodus 8, 21.
30 <S. Math. Cap. 5.>

Not a single litigant has been found, however keen he may be, or so says the good curé, who has dared to tell him that he is not willing to make a settlement. Of course, he will look for all kinds of excuses for getting out of it. But the good curé replies that one can trick men but one cannot trick God. That God plumbs the depths of their hearts – *examining their kidneys and tripes*. If it is true that they want peace, as they bear witness they do, then they must work towards it in a spirit of charity, to remove the obstacles which stand in its way, and to let him know when it is ready and that he will contribute with joy all that he should do as a good pastor and mutual friend.

If the litigant delays, on the other hand, he gives him another little word. And on the great feast days he uses friends as go-betweens. If it is the husband who is behaving badly, he talks to the wife. If it is the wife who is obstinate, he talks to the husband. He waits for the right opportunity. At last, the good curé tells me, there is no lawsuit which can withstand him for more than a year without him settling it. Within that time there is hardly any family which does not suffer some misfortune. Loss of property; a suit or dispute with someone more powerful than they are; death or sickness of a friend or one of the family; neglect or mischief in a matter of business; or the *avocats* and *procureurs*. When you are smitten, then you return to the faith: *vexation will give understanding*, as the Prophet says.[31] You feel the hand of God, which lies heavy on us. You look to Heaven – and to the curé. You tell him your tale of woe. You beg him to resume the conciliation and he does so easily and without trouble.

If there is a suit or dispute between persons so eminent or so obstinate that the voice of the curé is not listened to, the curé writes to his bishop, who intervenes and supports him, with a charity worthy of the zeal of the first pastors of the nascent Church. The good bishop writes to the recalcitrants, sends a messenger to them or speaks to them himself.

---

31 <*L'affliction nous rend sage*, Isaie. c. 28.> The 'holy artifices' are discussed in Chapter I.

CHAPTER V

How the good Curé settles disputes, hatreds and enmities

He settles nearly all disputes quite easily. Once the first heat has gone out of them, nearly everybody would like to be reconciled. It is a lot of trouble to hate, to slander, to seek out opportunities for revenge, and great expense and great cost too, especially if you have to get together a great troop of supporters, and so on.

If disputes are of real importance, he has to do what he does when there is litigation;[32] he has to call friends together. Other disputes, which are not of such great moment, he can manage himself, because they have every confidence in him, since he is devoted to these actions of charity. Moreover, he does not pretend to be anything other than an ordinary man.

The good curé has found a remedy for the animosities and enmities,[33] or rather the estrangements among family members, or neighbours, or others, for which the cause is often trivial but which nevertheless give rise to irreconcilable animosities, and great suits and disputes, which have dangerous consequences. He goes to their homes and tells them that he has found out about their estrangements, and that if they are Christian they must be reconciled. How can they come to the sacraments? They would not want to find themselves at a wedding with clothes with the least dirty mark on them. It is true that, even though there is no hatred left, it is still a bad example. And finally, the God of Peace demands that, when you are at the foot of the altar, you say that you will *give up your offering* and go off and be reconciled with your brother.[34]

And so all these disputes, enmities and estrangements without substance, which are very numerous, evaporate at the first approach of the good curé. Everybody, once they have told their side of the story, declare that they feel no enmity at all, that they are quite ready to meet one another and make it up. The usual

32 <*Pour les querelles de consequence fait nommer Arbitres. Pour les autres, les accommode luy-méme.*>
33 <*Pour les haines et inimitiez, sans fondement luy seul les accommode & comment.*>
34 <Matth. 5.>

place is at the curé's home. His house is *the living altar* of peace and concord.

These reconciled enemies later meet and visit one another's homes, and give one another assistance. And that puts pressure on everybody else to follow their good example.

It is worth noting that the primary quality which you need to settle suits and disputes is to be able to win the confidence of those you speak to.[35] The curé listens to their complaints very patiently, sympathises with their weakness, shares their grief, and in this way gains their confidence and eventually their hearts.

What the good curé can do, so can everybody else. You do not need any special capacity for it, or great eloquence. Just a little bit of patience and a lot of goodwill – God will supply the rest, as we know from experience. It is not the cleverest or most eloquent pastors who always bear most fruit. He often makes use of what appear to be feeble methods: *Out of the mouth of babes*, as the Prophet says,[36] *he takes his honour*. Moses performed prodigies, those miracles worthy of the greatness of the Almighty arm. Yet for all that *his stammering mouth* could not explain them. And so that no one can defy His power, God gives words to those who have good intentions. We shall afterwards tell how curés can find assistance, and of the people who can help them *in this harvest of peace and of concord*.

---

35   <*Pour accorder les Procez et querelles, la patience est nécessaire, & la charité.*>
36   <Psal. 8.>

CHAPTER VI

If one copies the good Curé and his Bishop
in all the Parishes of the Kingdom
there will be scarcely any Suits or Disputes in France

If the order of which we have just spoken were to be established
in all the parishes of the kingdom, following the intention of our
Kings and the Councils, there would be hardly any lawsuits which
did not end amicably. We would dissipate the unhappy enmities
and animosities which accompany them. The greater part of
those who litigate, as we have said, would like to come to an
agreement. All they lack is a charitable mediator. You can see
that from the experience of our good curé. Following his
example, others have done as much, and enjoyed the same
success, inasmuch as they have been motivated by the same
goodwill.

Several bishops have also started to establish the same practice
in their dioceses, following the example of the many holy
prelates in our France, whom we spoke of before. But above all
they have done this since they found out about the audiences
which our King gives for this purpose, even to the poorest of his
subjects.

Our bishops have recognised that the greatest obstacle to their
holy enterprises is division in their flock. Their sheep, moved by
that spirit of chicanery, are not even willing to meet together,
whether it is a question of a work of piety, or hospices, or other
activities to which they are inclined. Even though individually
they are willing to contribute, nevertheless, if they have a
lawsuit, they carry over into it the objectives of whatever it is
they are mixed up in. There are a hundred examples, especially
in small towns.

So we must put a stop to this deadly source of division, hatred
and animosity. Bishops are obliged to do so. They are the Vicars
of JESUS CHRIST on earth. The divine Pastor has recommended
nothing so much as peace: *My peace I give unto you, my peace I
leave with you.*[37] After him, the most beloved of his disciples
preached only of that peace, that union and concord, which

---

37 *Pacem meam do vobis, pacem meam relinquo vobis.* <Joan. 1. 14.>

there should be among Christians: *Love one another.*[38] Finally, the Church, following the wishes of its Husband, has asked its children – and sings every day – *Put out the flames of lawsuits!*[39]

1. Therefore the bishops, who are the vicars of the divine and peacemaking Pastor, cannot copy his example better than by providing peace to their flock. It is rent apart by hatreds and enmities, engendered by lawsuits. Their sheep become wolves[40] which devour one another in chicanery. Nobody is exempt from it. People of good will, who have no intention of attacking anyone, are attacked themselves.[41] I suppose that fear, or the longing to be rid of vexation, makes them agree to the most unjust demands.

2. The preacher, the monk, the curé, even the bishops are dragged from the foot of the altar. Nobody is exempt.[42] They all have to leave, just before the sacrifice, so that they can chase after the demands of some miserable lawsuit.

3. The nobility can no longer serve the King in his armies; the merchant abandons his business; the labourer must give up tilling the field, all so that they can follow some unhappy lawsuit. Even families, brothers and sisters, eat one another up. Children even bring actions against their father and their mother. The courts are full of such actions. And to add to the misfortune, they are long, slow and ruinous. They usually end only when goods or life runs out.

4. What is even more deplorable is the hatred and irreconcilable enmities of the litigants. How can a poor litigant do other than hate the opponent who persecutes him, ruins him, and who every day ascribes to his name a hundred insults in his writs and pleadings and charges him with a hundred false facts? If the fear of God enables us to resist the first attack of these insults, the second shakes us; and it is a miracle if we do not succumb to the third. The insults of *Semei*[43] were the sharp arrows which pierced the heart of poor David.

---

38 *Diligatis alterutrum.* <*Diligamus alter utrum.*> <2 Joan. Cap. 5.>
39 *Extingue flammas litium.*
40 <*Les Brebis par là sont devenus des Loups.*>
41 <*Tout le monde a Procez, qui n'en veut point faise on luy en fait.*>
42 <*Le Procez empesche le Service Divin.*>
43 <Reg. 3.> The story of Shimei cursing David is told in 2 Samuel 16, 5–13; and of his punishment in 1 Kings 2, 8–9 and 36–46.

5. To say that one can litigate without going to these extremities, it is true that God once kept safe three children in the fiery furnace. But these miracles are as rare as they are surprising. And it is trying the mercy of God to expect them. One should stay away from evil and try to destroy its cause.

The Gospel gives us a good example. When they were prosecuting JESUS CHRIST, who was innocence itself, the words of an insolent maidservant ensnared Saint Peter: *he denied his beloved Master thrice, with oaths and blasphemies.*[44] And after the fall of the leader of the apostles, taught in the school of patience itself, will any Christian, weak and lax, claim to be able to stand the false accusations and calumnies of which chicanery is full?

6. We find that even those who bring a suit in good faith, who start off with no hatred or animosity, cannot stop their advocates using certain insulting and offensive terms, and taking advantage of certain tricks, which they say are for the good of the cause. Thereupon they get excited and respond to the insults and in the end they come to those deadly and irreconcilable hatreds and enmities. How can the God of Peace dwell in hearts moved by vengeance? How can your sheep, My Lords, hear your pastoral voice if they are agitated and carried away with anger? How can that divine sowing germinate in their souls, which so many zealous prelates set about spreading every day, by a hundred acts of piety and consummate charity? One must tear out the thistles, therefore, before one can hope for the vine to bear fruit. One must get to the cause of the evil, one must cut down the thorns before one can hope that your divine sowing will produce fruits worthy of your zeal.

---

44 There were apparently two such maids, Matthew 26, 69 and 71; Mark 14, 66–7, 69; Luke 23, 56.

CHAPTER VII

*That the Bishops can and should settle
the Lawsuits and Differences of those in their Dioceses*

The Councils instruct them, as we have said: *the bishops ought to
study how they may bring disputing brethren together in peace,
whether they be cleric or lay*. Carth. 4 c26.[45]

If litigants refuse to do this, the Council of Worms 4 c4
instructs the bishops to excommunicate them, Capitul. L 6 c31.

The Gospel commands just the same: *Make your case! Make a
request! Make a loud complaint! But the servant of God ought not to
litigate*. 2 Tim 2.[46]

And to get the bishops to do this our Kings have said in their
laws that they would share with them the functions of royalty
and help them to do their job well, particularly in bringing peace
to their people. So they ought now to support our Prince who, by
his laws and his audiences, works towards the abolition of
chicanery and the granting of peace to the whole of his kingdom.

Look what the great Emperor Charlemagne said to the bishops
on this subject: *Any one of you shall have a part of our royal jurisdiction, according to your shares etc.*[47] And he asked them to make
it their business, so that the people might live *in equity, peace and
concord, etc*, Capitul. L 2 c12.[48]

And in another place, explaining the functions of royalty, that
great prince said that they principally consisted of listening to
the complaints of the poor and the orphan, *to be father to the
weak, and serve as the eye of the blind and the foot of the lame*.[49]

*To listen to the cries of the poor and of the orphan who has no
helper*, as Job says.[50] In consequence the King, and the bishop

---

45 *Studendum est Episcopis, ut dissidentes fratres, sive Clericos sive Laïcos ad pacem
cohortentur*. The first seven paragraphs are not in the first edition.

46 *Argue, obsecra, increpa. Servum Dei non oportet litigare*. What 2 Timothy 2 says
is (24–5): 'And the servant of the Lord must not strive; but be gentle unto
all men, apt to teach, patient, in meekness instructing those that oppose
themselves ... .'

47 *Unusquisque vestrum, partem Ministerii nostri regalis, per partes habetis &c.*

48 *In aequitate, pace, & concordia &c.*

49 Job 29, 16.

50 Job 29, 12: 'Because I delivered the poor that cried, and the fatherless, and
him that had none to help him.'

who shares his functions, should be, he said, *father of the poor, eye to the blind, foot to the lame.*[51] Capitul. addit. 2 c22.

And so, My Lords, the bishops should support the good intentions of our kings, and principally those of our Prince, who has set them an example. You can do it, My Lords, without trouble or expense. Your flock beg you to, and hold out their arms to you. Not one of them wants anything to do with lawsuits. At least, as we have said, of the two litigants, one would like to come to an agreement, the weaker or wiser. To bring about an agreement, all they lack is a charitable mediator. You be he, My Lords! Do what your curés do! You are already the ones who mediate between God and his people. These unhappy lawsuits are now preventing the French from rendering to his grandeur the adorations which are denied him. Shift these obstacles! It is not too difficult a matter. The good curé has managed it. All the others can do the same. His neighbours have started, and succeeded. In Paris itself there is a curé,[52] famous for his doctrine, piety and zeal, who has tried it and God has clearly blessed his work. Many of our bishops are working on it, and have worked on it through the centuries. The demon of strife does not know how to resist their forces.

We have a good example, a bishop of our France, still alive, whose name modesty prevents me from mentioning,[53] a prelate worthy of the century of Saint Paul. He went looking for a gentleman who had a lawsuit and a fierce dispute with his neighbour. He begged him to settle it and asked for his word. The gentleman refused him, insisting with oaths and blasphemies that he would have his revenge. This good prelate, quite carried away with zeal, declared that he would stay outside his door until God touched his heart. And he did stay there for part of a night, in the torrential rain. The gentleman, once his fury had died down, sent to see whether the prelate was still there and found he was. So this madman, totally won over by such an example of charity, ran to him with tears in his eyes, threw himself down on his knees and begged him for mercy. He said he would go at once and make it up with his opponent and obey all the orders of the holy bishop.

51 Job 29, 16.
52 <M. Poussé.>
53 Could that be because he was a relative? See Chapter 5.

There is no need for such efforts, such heroic actions, My Lords, in settling every lawsuit. Far from it. To settle nearly all lawsuits there is no need of trouble or great pains; just to copy the successes of the good curé and his bishop, and what several prelates have done since they received this manual.

CHAPTER VIII[54]

That there are some Bishops who,
since they received this manual,
have had it printed and distributed to their Curés;
and the order they have followed in putting it into action

1. They had it printed and distributed; they had it read in their seminaries and ecclesiastical conferences; and they have exhorted their curés to put it into practice.

2. They have repeated those exhortations when they have made visitations.

3. Before any of that they had asked them in writing, together with the superiors of convents in their dioceses, to remind their people forcefully, in their sermons and homilies and above all in the confession, of the extent of their obligation to the divine commandment, placed on all Christians, to avoid every subject of hatred and enmity with their neighbour. To remind them also that for that purpose the Councils had instructed them to nominate arbitrators and, if anyone refused, requested that they be excommunicated. And to remind them that our kings had asked the bishops to put these Councils into practice; and had asked all clergy to preach that to their people; because it is said of any litigants who refuse to settle: *They should be clearly told by their parish priests that, if they are not willing to put aside their enmities, they should be driven out of the congregation of the Church.* Agath. c31, Trosl. c12.[55]

4. Above all the good bishops have asked their confessors to inculcate these maxims forcefully in their penitents in the confession. To make sure of that, they should ask them whether they have any lawsuits, or any animosity against their opponents. Hardly anybody will ever confess to that, yet nearly everybody does have some lawsuit and hatred towards his opponent.

5. Not to give them absolution except on the understanding that they bear witness to their opponents that they want a

---

54 The material in this chapter is not in the first edition.
55 *A sacerdotibus civitatum arguantur, quod si inimicitias deponere noluerint, a coetu Ecclesiae pellantur.*

settlement, in obedience to the Councils, the commands of the Church and the instruction of their confessor.

This practice has settled a great many suits and disputes and will always settle them, if the good bishops continue their charitable endeavours.

To prevent the party on the other side taking unfair advantage of these offers of arbitration, it would be a good idea if, at the same time that the written offer is made, the confessor, the curé, or other clergy, sought out the other party to whom the offer of arbitration is made, and told him that it has been made because the confessor ordered it to be made, and that he hopes the other will do likewise.

One of the bishops who has set up this scheme in his diocese has since said that one of the leading magistrates in the kingdom has confessed to him that nothing has ever touched him so much as a good confessor's simple remonstrance on this matter, and on the obligations of his office. It is so true, said the *Officier*, that the tribunal of penitence is something so august and terrible for Christians who approach it in a spirit of humility and submission.

Several curés of this good bishop have said that, since their first sermon on this matter, a large number of litigants have come to tell them that they would like to settle, and have pleaded for them to help them with it. It is enough for the curés, in their sermons, to tell them, sincerely and simply, that whoever would like to settle their differences should go to them, and that they would do all they could to help them. That will produce very good results, from the very first day. We know this by experience.

The illustration overleaf appears in all editions but the first, though not in the same place. The text reads:

THE GOOD PROVINCIAL GOVERNOR
AND THE GOOD SEIGNEUR DE FIEF
M. LE PRINCE DE CONTI

*He settled the suits and disputes within his jurisdiction and his Estates
as our Kings have ordained.
The good Prince, following their example, has also ordained
that this holy practice be continued throughout his Estates.
This Widow shows that he who possessed every virtue
has left it to be done properly.
In his treatise on the duties of the great he has also said
that the great lords are the 'men of their neighbours'
who have no one to protect them or grant them peace. Art 12.*[56]

56 It is not clear what this Art. 12 refers to.

The Good Provincial Governor and the Good Seigneur de Fief M. le Prince de Conti. © The British Library.

CHAPTER IX

That since they found out that the King gave public Audiences
to put a prompt end to his Subjects' Suits and Differences,
some Bishops have followed his example.
That all can do so without trouble.
That the Prince de Conty did so, and gave Audiences for this purpose,
twice a week after dinner.

We have already said that the bishops are obliged to do this and
that the kings have ordained that they should do so, that *they*
should have part of the royal jurisdiction according to their shares, and
that the Gospel, the Fathers and the Councils also ordained it.

If the bishops continue as they have begun, and all the prelates
of the kingdom do the same, there will be scarcely any suit or
dispute which is not settled at birth, and that without trouble.
That is what one of them did in his diocese a long time ago,
copying what the Prince de Conty[57] did in his administrations
and on his estates.

After dinner twice a week he gave an audience of one hour,
which he treated as relaxation. Everyone was admitted, even the
poor, and he settled their disputes himself. If there was litigation,
he made the parties agree on arbitrators in his presence and sign
a compromise, which he sent to the arbitrators with a request to
expedite the matter and come and tell him (*within a fixed period*)
whether they had settled and on what terms.

His secretary kept a register of all these compromises, and the
said parties, especially the poor, had the right to start proceedings
before him, if their adversaries did not carry out in good faith
what they had promised.

This good prince did the same thing among his vassals on his
estates and proceeded similarly in the countryside within his
public offices.

The bishop who copied him did the same thing in his own
place and in the parishes which he visited, so that on the arrival
of this good prelate the weak could threaten the powerful who
were going to bring an action against them. Those who were
suffering waited for these visits with impatience. They left their

57 See Chapter 4; La Roche's spelling is not consistent.

towns and villages and came in droves to meet him and greeted him with shouts of joy, each running up to him, as if he were the Father of all, who brings peace to the whole world. All the bishops could and should do as he does; then they will be cherished and loved and honoured like him.

It should be noted that the bishops, curés, governors and great lords, should never become arbitrators, but only mediators, for the reasons given above and set out in Chapter XV below.

The good bishop has had some of these manuals sent from Paris, for the illustrations, which are persuasive for the common people, and has given them to his curés.

The clergy wanted to pay for this expense and raised the money out of their tithes. One could do that in the same way in all dioceses, so that it would cost neither the bishops nor the curés anything. Or you could simply print them without the illustrations, which would cost less.

CHAPTER X

Of the difficulties that can be encountered on the part
of the Bishops, the Curés or the Parties

If among the bishops there is someone who wants to say that he has not got enough time for this sort of thing, he should remember that Saint Augustine was no less busy than he, and yet he said that he would give up everything else, as it was one of the most important functions of the episcopate. But the Gospel commands it, as we have already said, and the Fathers, the Councils and the kings, and one should obey them. Great revenues are not given by princes to bishops except so that they can discharge their duties properly. And the respect and honour, which everyone gives to them as if they were crowned heads, oblige them to demand of themselves to do all they can to bring peace to their flock.

As for the curés, if you want to say that there are some who have not the goodwill, nor the ability, nor the belief in the principles of their parishioners, then what I say to them is that as far as goodwill goes, everybody ought to feel it. Even the most lukewarm should be inspired by the example of the bishops, the ecclesiastical conferences and the other curés who have applied themselves with zeal and goodwill.

Nobody can make the excuse of lack of capacity. It is only a matter of calling on the parishioners to make peace and offering to be mediator in the settlement of their differences. The curé should never be judge, even if the parties themselves beg him to. He should remain a neutral and simple mediator, so that he does not become suspect to anyone.

He does not need ability nor eloquence, nor the grand manner; all he needs is goodwill. He should not put himself to the trouble of preparing fine harangues to persuade the litigant to make peace. His own miseries are persuasion enough. If they have to speak to eminent persons, who are not afraid of them, God has promised to give words to those who have good intentions. He made use of the apostles to speak before kings. And those apostles were only ordinary folk, poor seamen, called in the Scripture: *the filth and offscouring of the world*. St Paul 1 Corinth.[58]

Moses wanted to refuse the work which God offered him, because he said he did not know how to speak.[59] Aaron was given to him to explain his thoughts. So, if the curé wants to get help, he should take someone from his parish who has a reputation for probity and is prudent. This mediator will be able to settle most of the peasants' differences when they are of little consequence. We know from experience that in the parishes where this is established, the parties will go before him and ask him themselves, to avoid them having to look for arbitrators from a long way off.

In matters in which it is necessary to have recourse to arbitrators, it is a good idea to take them from a jurisdiction other than that where the action began; particularly if you want to appoint judges or *avocats* or *procureurs* as arbitrators.

But if the bishops have set up in their diocese a tribunal of peace, litigants need no longer be afraid of asking for settlement and their adversaries can take no advantage from that. They will be persuaded that that is what they should do according to religious principles, in obedience to the Gospel and their confessor.

And besides, those who ask for peace will have the advantage that no one will be able to accuse them of being chicaners or oppressors, because they have asked for a settlement; and this request should always be made in writing so that evidence is available.

The one who refuses arbitration after having been summoned to it, will be accounted litigious. He will not dare to appear before his bishop or his curé. His family and friends will censure him and he will come to grief. Everybody will be against him and he will be laughed at. Even his wife and children will condemn him, at least in the secrecy of their hearts. So you will find very few people who refuse arbitration, for fear of this happening.

I should not imagine that the good judges will find fault with these requests for arbitration. Would a doctor have the audacity

---

58 *L'ordure et la balieure du monde*: 1 Corinth 4, 13: 'Being defamed, we entreat; we are made as the filth of the world, and are the offscouring of all things unto this day.'
59 *Nescio loqui.*

to give evidence that he was sorry that the plague had ended in his town? Or a surgeon that his neighbour's wound had healed? Moreover they know that agreements to arbitrate are according to the principles of religion, and the Councils, and the exhortations of the bishops and curés. Who would dare to find fault with the Ordinances of our kings, all of which require them to put an end to their differences by means of arbitration? Most of all, now that our Prince works with such application to abolish chicanery in his kingdom, even giving public audiences to the poor, as we have said.

And so that anyone may confidently ask for peace, they have already begun to introduce these maxims in the courts. The first President (of the *Parlement* of Paris, and the ones for Brittany and for Provence) send before arbitrators all those who ask for it, and often even those who do not want it! These great men's only objectives are the Prince's authority and the people's tranquillity. If the Presidents of other *Parlements* copy them, they will soon chop off the head of the deadly monster of chicanery.

CHAPTER XI

That the Bishops can bring their Lawsuits to an amicable
conclusion,
and should do so;
and that they will nevertheless preserve
all their Spiritual and Temporal interests

If they can, they should. We have already said that the Gospel, the Canons and the Councils ordain it for all Christians. But this is how they ordain it especially for bishops: *a bishop should not prosecute in court as a party in his own cause, unless it is to come to the aid of the poor oppressed by force, &c.* Cabilo. sub Carolo c2.[60]

Bishops should never go to court over their own affairs but only in defence of the poor and oppressed.

There is another Council, passed long before that, which forbids them to bring any lawsuit for the protection of their temporal interests, even when they are being attacked: *nor should a bishop be provoked to litigate over transitory matters.* Carth. 4 c19.[61]

The Council well understood that nobody will attack you if you yourself attack nobody and if you show that you are willing to settle your differences amicably. For that reason, another Council forbids them to start an action without first having asked the other side to agree to arbitrators: *If anyone believes that he has business of his own with a bishop, he shall not go before the judges until he has first had recourse to those who are reminded that they ought to heal these things in a family conference. If he does otherwise, he should be deprived of Communion.* Nicaen. c27; Aurelian. 5 c17.[62]

The bishops may rest assured that nobody will fall under this censure, because nobody will start an action against a bishop, without first asking him to agree to arbitrators, if they see that he wants to bring his affairs to a peaceful conclusion. So the bishops have only to give evidence of this to be assured that everyone in their diocese will gladly agree to it.

---

60 *Episcopus ad forum non pergat suae causae suffragaturus, nisi vi pauperibus oppressis succurat.*
61 *Episcopus nec provocatus, pro rebus transitoriis litiget.*
62 *Si quis erga episcopum, se proprium crediderit habere negotium, non prius adeat judices, quam ad eos recurrat, ut familiari colloquio commoniti ea sanare debeant: quod si aliter egerit, communione privetur.*

To make this happen, the following conditions must be met:

1. Christians, by their religious principles, honour, respect and cherish their prelates and want to be on good terms with them;

2. It must also be supposed that the weak usually do not want to have any lawsuits against those who are more powerful, whether in property, in influence, or in friends &c. Now, is it not true that bishops are naturally honoured, and everybody in their diocese considers themselves to be their inferiors? There may be one or two with more property, but the bishops have more influence, because so many people depend on them, spiritually and temporally. Moreover they usually have more support at Court, with the Prince, in the Council. At least that is what everybody thinks. Finally, all Christians have written in their soul: *This is the unction of the Lord: touch it not. Touch not my anointed.*[63] Consequently everybody wants to be well in with them.

I say nothing of those lawsuits which concern discipline and the correction of morals. It is a loving cruelty to chastise the blameworthy. God was as good when he destroyed *Sodom and Gomorrah* as when he fed the Israelites in the desert *with the divine bread, kneaded in Heaven.*[64]

So I speak of the lawsuits which the bishops have either for the rights to feudal honours, against their chapters or others, or for rights profitable and temporal, for the preservation of the patrimony of the Church or of their own. All these lawsuits can be ended amicably if they will only show that they want to do so. Everyone will happily agree to it. And that is just what happened a little while ago.

A bishop who had a big case against his chapter, and gave little consideration to the loathing for chicanery, was complaining one day to one of his friends that he was unhappy and so overwhelmed with business, which he hated, that he would not believe it. His friend advised him to prove it by silencing the voices of his opponents. What he had to do was to offer to his chapter to name arbitrators and to make an offer of settlement of such sum as he liked. He made such an offer through notaries, giving them an authentic deed, which the chapter accepted.

---

63 *C'est l'oing du Seigneur, n'y touchez pas. Noli tangere Christos meos.*
64 *De ce pain Divin, petry dans le Ciel.*

Since then they have had a truce and a suspension of the battle, civilities and compliances have resumed, one to another, and with them the hope of peace and perfect union.

1. If the chapter refused him, then the bishop would be justified before all the world; they would say that he had sought peace and given a good example and the chapter would be blamed for being the cause of the lawsuit and for the disturbance. The summons was drawn up by the notaries. The chapter agreed to the arbitration and at the same time sent a deputation to the bishop for the first time in more than a year. The deputation behaved very properly, with courtesy and cordial affection, and all the canons came round to expressing their joy and satisfaction. The good bishop responded to their courtesies with tears of joy. The reconciliation of hearts and minds was perfectly accomplished. Arbitrators were appointed and the matter ended amicably.

2. Another bishop had a lawsuit for his profitable rights, against a powerful family in his diocese. He had quite a reputation for having a fondness for litigation. He pleaded that this family and their relatives and friends had disparaged him and had secretly stirred up acts of animosity against him. He was advised to use the remedy of which we just spoke, to offer them arbitration. He did so and was accepted. The same day he received courtesies from them and at once they terminated their differences amicably. Since that time the good bishop has not had a single lawsuit where he has not offered straight away to go to arbitration. They always accept. And so, instead of being an object of fear and dread, as he was, and little loved and honoured, he is presently cherished and adored, and rightly so because, as we said, one honours the bishops because of religious principles, but fears them for their wealth and authority. But if war is declared, one leaves behind respect and commits injuries and outrages. Once the sword is drawn, the inferior maltreats the superior if he can.

3. Another bishop did even more. He was the nephew, heir and successor of another good bishop whose enemies said that he counted his lawsuits in hundreds; that he had some in every court and jurisdiction; and that you could see him in the law courts, as the comedian says, more often than in the pulpit. His successor as bishop advertised everywhere that he wanted peace with

everybody. That was his desire and he asked others to have the same sentiments. Arbitrators were named and all was concluded nicely in less than a year. He weeded out the tares that his good uncle had sown, as he said, for twenty years in his vineyard.

In fact, none of the bishops who would prefer to avoid lawsuits need have any, for the reasons we have stated. All the world wants to be on good terms with them; it is up to them to want to be on good terms with all the world. One honours them naturally; one holds them in fear and dread. When an equal or inferior asks for a settlement, one may think that that is from fear. But when a bishop asks for it, one cannot attribute to him anything other than motives of goodwill and paternal charity.

4. On the nomination of arbitrators, there are some who believe that the people on the spot will not be favourable to them, because they think that the Church has enough property, so that they would rather lean to the side of those who have a wife and children. Without stopping to discuss whether such an idea is reasonable, I believe that God has not so totally abandoned the world – and never will – that there cannot always be found everywhere some decent fellow, capable of judging his brother at fault if he has done wrong. Even in *Sodom*, the most abominable city in the world, there was one decent fellow.

Nevertheless, you can choose arbitrators from outside the diocese, *avocats* if you like from the *Parlement* of that jurisdiction. If even they are suspect, because of the differences the bishops sometimes have with that sovereign corps, you can choose *avocats* of another jurisdiction.

Though local customs and usages differ, lawsuits are transferred every day from one *Parlement* to another and still the *avocats* can examine and consult them and are consequently able to judge and decide. This is the old-fashioned way, to have differences judged by unknown persons; and it is still the way in various northern nations.[65]

5. So the bishops can live in peace and without lawsuits, and can bring to a peaceful conclusion those they now have and

65 Here the first edition (p47) continues: 'The judge complete and without stain; the great Melchisedek is depicted in Scripture without father, mother, relations or friends. That is to say, in judging no one had his ear, which applies more to an unknown judge; a stranger from afar, rather than one of that place.'

those they may have in the future. If they can, they should. Apart from the commands of the Gospel and the Councils, should not peace be better than war? What satisfaction is it to a bishop or a great lord to do evil to those with whom he has to live? With a chapter, for example, or a town or community, or different individuals, who would all render to him a hundred courtesies and civilities if it were not for these miserable lawsuits? Instead of the courtesies there are animosities and slanders and calumnies and a hundred bad turns, which are the sad and deadly fruits of these wars of the desk.

6. On top of all that, lawsuits take up all your time, unless you abandon them to the management of agents, *procureurs* or *solliciteurs*, depending on their good faith and often paying very dearly for the faults of their mischief, idleness or ignorance.

If a bishop or other great lord takes charge of the lawsuit himself, he becomes just like any other law court rat, with his hands ever full of waste paper and red tape, and all he can talk about is applications, productions, plaints, replies and exceptions,[66] and other words of that black magic and curse of chicanery.

But the worst is that he must give up all his time to it and thereby lose what is the most pleasant thing in life, and the most precious. The great lords, who have plenty of property in different places, also have plenty of lawsuits in different jurisdictions. And if they want to keep everything in order every day, they become nothing more than postmen and messengers who no sooner arrive than they are gone. They have a hundred letters which they must receive and send every week; memoranda and instructions to prepare; deeds and papers to find with the *procureurs*, notaries and *greffiers*; and all the unhappy weapons to get ready for this miserable war which takes place in the courts and tribunals.

To heap up the misery, this is the wheel of Ixion, turning endlessly, with no hope of an end. Lawsuits are immortal in France, especially before the Council. Against an award there is but one appeal; but against an *Arrest* there are a hundred ways to appeal: *Requeste Civile, Proposition d'Erreur, Contrariété d'Arrests* and a hundred *Incidens en Explication* or *Exécution* – and this is

66 *Salvations*.

how judgments are made in France but not one of them
concluded. The old ones never finish and new ones are begun
every day. So that you are crushed and cannot hope ever to see
the end of it by any ordinary means. This is the lamentable
monster of whom the poet speaks, whose limbs grow again as
soon as they are cut off; you have to fight it all the time but as
soon as one enemy is conquered another one takes its place: *One
overthrown there's no lack of another.*[67]

What a miserable occupation, in which you spend the greatest
of your treasures, time; the most precious thing in the world,
which you can never buy back, and which neither kings nor
princes can grant: *for they have none among their treasures* and in
which they are as poor as their subjects. But above all to a
Christian, and to a bishop, to whom time is given for him to
work for his salvation and that of others, to whom the divine
oracle has said: *While we have time, let us do good.*[68] And which
threatens him, if he does not, that *he will never see His face.*

On top of that, the bishops complain that the judges often
have a grudge against them and that the *Parlements* are not
always on their side. Well, a healthy man needs no doctor. And
a man without lawsuits need have no fear of judges. So it
depends on the bishops, not at all on the judges. But what is
deplorable and deserves to have tears of blood wept over it, is
that when a bishop has a lawsuit it usually means that he has to
abandon his flock and that he sets them a bad example. In order
to carry on the litigation he must give it the better part of his
time. To take care of it he must go to Paris or somewhere. But, My
Lords, who is going to take care of your sheep in your absence?
The Divine Shepherd said a long time ago that the hungry wolf
always bites and wants someone to devour: *he circles round seeking
whom he may devour.*[69] As long as you are in Paris or wherever,
who is going to keep an eye on them? And you know very well,
My Lords, that your flock was given to you and stands to your
account *and you have to give an account, even at the last day!* Will
those of you who have absented yourselves for ages be able to
say to the Eternal Father what the Divine Shepherd, whose

67 *Uno avulso non deficit alter.* <Virgil.>
68 *Dum tempus habemus, operemur bonum.* <Ad Gal. Cap. 6.>
69 *Circuit quaerens quem devoret.* <1 Pet. c. 5.>

disciples you are, said to him: *Here are the sheep which you gave to me and I have lost not one of them.*

Saint Paul, whose thoughts were always divine, and full of fire and love for his brothers, did he not say that it is better to suffer wrong and the loss of property than to bring an action in the courts? *Why would you not rather accept the wrong? Why would you not rather suffer the fraud?*[70] So much is not expected of you today, if you just show that you are only wanting to look after your own interests in a gentle way, without it having to come to the rigours and bitternesses of a lawsuit. The Council thundered their anathema against the pastors who disturbed the peace of their flock by suit or dispute. The bishop can hardly have that kind of thing with those of his diocese. *This is to be spelled out most particularly: that peace and harmony must be preserved at all times between the pastors of the Church and Christ's flock &c. So that if anyone neglects these things, we shall be found to be not pastors then but slaughterers (God forbid!) of Christ's sheep.*[71]

And so, My Lords, when bishops have lawsuits and offer to their opponents to go to arbitration, they do what the seculars have already started to do in Paris and various provinces, what the bishops have done in former times, and what several do today. Offer arbitration and to make a deposit to be forfeit; if your opponents accept, you will preserve your interests in a gentle way, without trouble and without cost, and without shame. You will keep the hearts and affection of all those in your diocese and make it a haven of peace and unity and love.

But if it should happen that some strong-willed enemy of this quietude refuses arbitration, you will have satisfied the requirements of the Apostle's advice and the Council. You will have set a good example. No calumny can accuse you of being motivated by a spirit of anger or avarice. On the contrary, your opponents will be declared enemies of the peace and will bear the anathema of the whole world.

---

70 *Quare non magis injuriam accipitis? Quare non magis fraudem patimini?* <S. Paul. 1 Cor. c. 6.>

71 *Hoc summopere elaborandum est, ut semper inter Pastores Ecclesiarum, & gregem Christi, pax et concordia servetur, &c. ita ut si haec negligantur, non jam Pastores, sed interfectores, (quod absit) Christi ovium inveniamur.*

CHAPTER XII

The Curés and the Preachers also can and should settle their lawsuits amicably

They are Christians, and moreover preachers and pastors, and all the more obliged than others to obey the Gospel, the Canons and the Councils. It is forbidden, as we have said, for bishops to be found in the courts and even bringing actions for their wordly goods, *because they are shepherds*, and the curés are subject to the same prohibition.

And besides, as we have said, the Councils instruct curés and preachers to correct and admonish litigants, and to reconcile them before they say the Mass. How can they do that and have their own lawsuits that they have a duty to settle amicably? How can they admonish and reprimand others for a crime of which they themselves are guilty?

The Council of which we have just spoken in the last chapter, which instructs bishops to live in peace with their flock, applies also to curés. They are shepherds and their lawsuits are usually against their own parishioners over mundane rights.

It is right that they should look after their interests: those who serve the altar should live by the altar. But they must do that in the spirit of Christianity, attempting the way of gentleness before entering into litigation. They must make an offer to go to arbitration; then, if their opponents refuse it, the anathema of the Council of which we spoke will fall upon them.

1. Is it not a shameful thing for Christianity, to have curés who have not been seen in their parishes for three or four years under the pretext that they have been involved in a miserable lawsuit? Yet they nonetheless ask God every day for *their daily bread*, which men cannot do without. They would do better to remember this, that it is said of them *the good shepherd knows his sheep and the sheep know him*. How can the flock know him when he has been away for three years? Soul and conscience change in a moment. When the divine Leader of the Flock of Israel stayed forty days on the mountain, the people worshipped idols in the valley. Nevertheless he prayed for them, and he was busy with God on His affairs. How unhappy it would have made the people

if, like our curés and pastors, he had abandoned them for years at a time to prosecute litigation and chicanery! After only forty days absence, they could scarcely recognise the voice of Moses, they had forgotten his miracles, and found it difficult to obey him. What would they have said to him if he had stayed away for years for leisure and lawsuits?

That is not to say that there are not a number of curés who have litigation forced on them. They have to preserve their property and that of the Church. But they ought to copy the illustrious example of that good curé we spoke of who, moved by the spirit of the Gospel, first asked his adversary for settlement and arbitration – and he got it. Ever since, by a special grace and a holy unction, and by the example of the great Saint Yves, he has undertaken this work of peace and brought to an amicable conclusion all the lawsuits in his parish.

Follow his example, Messieurs, and like him you will be cherished, loved and honoured by all, like him you will be all-powerful in your parishes, in matters spiritual and temporal. Everybody will have complete confidence in you, and honour, profit and property will follow. They are grateful to anyone who cures the sicknesses of the body. Lawsuits *are sicknesses, of the body and the soul*, as a holy Father said, where the ill-will of men and of devils presses on us.

As we have said, when a curé asks for arbitration, and the other side refuses, he will be respected and have the approbation of both the good and the wicked, and his adversary will be condemned by everyone.

CHAPTER XIII

Monks and Nuns also can and should
settle their lawsuits amicably;
and there are some Religious Communities
which have resolved to do so

1. For the same reasons we have stated before, monks and nuns ought to want to terminate their lawsuits amicably and should ask for that to be done. Besides what the Gospels tell all Christians, the Councils speak to them in more specific terms than to others. The one which prohibits pastors from going to law adds: *this is to be observed most strictly by monks.*[72]

Another prohibits them going to law without their bishop's permission. And another absolutely prohibits them litigating for any cause whatever:[73]

Monks are absolutely forbidden to appear in the secular courts without their bishop's consent. Magun. c12

Monks are absolutely forbidden to appear in the secular courts. Remen. c29

Nowadays we do not ask them to do more than to make known their willingness to come to an amicable settlement, and to summon the other side to arbitration, before they start any litigation. They must do this if they want to still the voice of slander. For they know what is said about them, that they give no quarter; that they are so strongly attached to their own interests that they never let go; and that they have it as a maxim that they would rather see a whole family perish than give up a single one of their claims. That maxim is very much against the purity of the Gospel, which instructs us to care for the poor, and even to sell the consecrated vessels we use for the sacrifices, rather than abandon the poor.

To show how far they have distanced themselves from such sentiments, which slander attributes to them, and which says that they will try to find any pretext for leaving the convent and to escape their rule, they must show the contrary by their summons to arbitration. In that case people will be persuaded

---

72 *Hoc de Monachis, maxime observandum est.*
73 *Monachi ad saecularia placita nullatenus veniant, sine consensu Episcopi sui.*
    Monachi, ad placita saecularia nullatenus vadant.

that for them the courts and the world's bustle are a hard ordeal, and that they cherish their retreat and their gentle solitude, where the delights of the soul are to be found, which only breathe from Heaven.

2. There are some religious communities which have formally resolved in their chapters[74] that they will have no more lawsuits, either as plaintiff or defendant, without first taking the written opinion of three advocates and also making a written offer of arbitration. If all other monks and nuns did the same, they would have peace, preserve their property, and still the voice of the complaints which everybody makes about them.

74 *Capitulairement.* This paragraph is not in the first edition.

CHAPTER XIV

That Abbés can easily settle their differences and should do so

1. For the same reasons we have stated in previous chapters, abbés, priors and all other holders of benefices ought to follow the holy maxim and show that they seek peace. Will it not be a great benefit to them to preserve their interests without trouble or cost? To be rid of long and troublesome lawsuits which cost them dear? It is easy for them. Nobody wants to have a difference with them. Everyone knows their power, to say nothing of their rank, their descent and their wealth. Everyone knows they can get support everywhere. Everyone knows that they only have to drop a hint to a judge or a *rapporteur* that they are prepared to resign their benefice in favour of his son or other relative[75] and the mere hope of that makes him listen and treat them with favour. So they can ask for a settlement boldly, with no fear that they will be rejected. When some unfortunate does reject their offer, then they are freed from their duty and will still the voice of those who complain that they oppress everybody with their power, authority and property.

Besides, they are obligated; they are clad in the livery of the Lamb, of the God of Peace, who pays their salary, which is fat enough for several. And so they ought, at least by their example, to work towards extending His Empire, which is entirely one of peace, unity and concord.

75 Scil. the *judge's* son or relative.

CHAPTER XV

That Provincial Governors ought to mediate
to settle the Suits and Disputes of those of their Provinces;
that several have done so and still do

1. Monseigneur the Prince de Conty,[76] that very illustrious Governor, performed worthily in this respect; since he gave himself up totally to God, he gave himself totally to his neighbour.

He took as his motto *that a great man is the man of his neighbour,*[77] that all those who are set up in dignity and authority are not there for themselves but for the public, to whom they owe it to devote their efforts. These are the words of the admirable book which he wrote on *The Duties of the Great.*[78] He says: *A great man ought to consider himself more obliged than other Christians, because by his vocation he is principally the man of his neighbour, being made great only to serve him, to look after his needs, to console him in his afflictions, to correct him in his failings, to do him justice, to rescue him from oppression, and to protect him from violence.*

2. Please God that these sentiments, worthy of eternity, should first be well written on the hearts of all those who are in authority in the kingdom! Please God that all provincial governors should wish to follow the examples and the charity of this great prince! Languedoc and Guienne have seen his house open to all the miserable and unfortunate. He would go to them, when he found out they had a dispute, to make peace between them. When he found out they had a lawsuit, his lively and penetrating mind understood its deadly and unfortunate effects. So, he would request great men to nominate arbitrators and would require the lower classes to do so. He left to them freedom of choice of arbitrators. He himself stuck to the role of mediator. For the choice of arbitrators ought to be as free as the choice of confessor or doctor. One would approach with fear an arbitrator who was a prince, or a Marshal of France, or a provincial governor.

And so he worked on this with so much charity that he brought peace everywhere. He often said, in his bursts of

---

76 See Chapter 4.
77 *Qu'un Grand est l'homme du prochain.*
78 See Chapter 4.

enthusiasm, that if his infirmities and illnesses should prevent him from being able to stay in his provinces to render the services of charity which he owed to his neighbour, with the regularity that they deserved, he would leave his provinces lest he become unfaithful to God, who had given him the grace to understand what his duty was.

We have already said in Chapter IX, on the subject of audiences, that the bishops provide the same arrangements as the good prince did, for the settlement of the suits and disputes of those in their dioceses.

Twice a week after dinner he would grant an audience, as the King does today. Everybody was admitted, with priority to the poor, who are the weakest and have the greatest need of protection. Disputes he would settle himself. As for lawsuits, he would make the parties agree on arbitrators in his presence and sign a compromise. Then his secretary would always have it printed. The good prince would then send this compromise with one of his men to the nominated arbitrators, and ask them to be good enough to hurry up and deal with the parties promptly and find some way of bringing them to a peaceful settlement.

After requiring the arbitrators to behave with kindness and diligence, he would ask them to be good enough to make a report to him within a fixed period.

In this way, governors of provinces, towns and fortresses can settle a great many suits and disputes, without difficulty, without trouble and without cost.

They are obliged to do this in conscience, our laws say. It is certainly true that they ought to make sure that in their provinces all is done for the peace and quiet of their people which would be done by the King if he were there himself in person. If he were there, he would give public audiences; he does so wherever he may be.[79] Provincial governors, therefore, who represent him, ought to do the same. That is why the great King and Emperor Charlemagne said to those with whom he shared the functions of royalty: *They shall have part of our royal authority according to their shares.*[80]

---

79 The remainder of this paragraph is not in the first edition; it represents new authority.

80 *Partem ministerii nostri regalis, per partes habent.*

Now that our prince has given us the lead, who shall refuse to copy and follow his good intentions?[81]

3. The enthusiasm of M de Conty would have gone much further, had not death put a stop to the course of that fine life. I have often heard him say to those who had the honour of being close to him that he had a plan to set up a certain organisation throughout his provinces, by which the least crime would have been found out and punished. By this means, apparently, he would have prevented ninety out of every hundred premeditated crimes, violent deeds and oppressions of the weak. For who would dare to commit such a premeditated crime if he knew that he would be found out and punished? Who would dare to conspire against the King or the State, or to oppress the weak if he thought the prince or the provincial governor was standing next to him?

Yet it would have cost the King or the people nothing to establish this fine organisation, and there would have been no need of new laws. Everything can be done within the Ordinance[82] and following the way in which these things are done in the kingdoms of the East, where law and order are excellent.

4. That prince had yet another fine plan to establish another kind of organisation in all the towns in his provinces, by which the King's commands would be executed promptly and with

---

81 The first edition includes here material not in later editions:

> To defend the people in time of war, and give them justice at any time, the principal obligation of the Prince and the Monarch, pray God for that (that they should judge us and fight for us, *ut nos judicent et pugnent pro nobis*) – an obligation from which Kings cannot dispense themselves, nor the Governors who represent them.
>
> Moreover there are a large number of them who acquit themselves worthily, M the Duc de Vandosme among others in Provence, M the Duc de Longueville during his life in Normandy and the Mareschal de la Meilleraye in Brittany, as long as he lived. The last was lucky enough, during the agitations of the State, to have kept his province in peace and quiet. That general peace was the result of a particular peace which he tried to establish among all the families. When he found out about a dispute or lawsuit, he worked to pacify the disputants with such goodwill and charity that even had he not been the Governor, or Maréchal de France, they would have blindly followed his opinions. His son, M the Duc de Mazarin, follows in the footsteps of his famous father and copies his good examples.

82 It is not at all clear which legislation is referred to. It may be that of Henry IV 1610, or more probably the two edicts of 1560 in the Appendices.

pleasure. The system of justice would be preserved very correctly, particularly in time of plague. Towns would be rebuilt, with public buildings, rivers, roads, ports and harbours. Even more important, manufactures would be established everywhere, bringing succour to the poor and getting rid of beggars. And all without any cost to the King and without requiring any new legislation. Everything could have been done under the Ordinance.

We ought to wait and see how this fine system of criminal justice will be secured under the reign of our incomparable Monarch, who has already begun so well, and who continues his efforts to make his people happy and to get rid of the unfortunate chicanery which disturbs all law and order and our system of criminal justice.

CHAPTER XVI

That the Lords of great Fiefs ought to settle the Disputes of their
Vassals and be Mediators to settle their Lawsuits
That Noblemen and ordinary Bourgeois can require their Tenants
to settle their differences

The great lords ought to do this:

1. For the profit that they will get out of it.
2. For honour and glory and to gain the affection of their vassals.
3. Because it will unburden their consciences.

Monsieur the Prince de Conty did so worthily on all his estates, as I have said, and I have discovered from an *officier* of his house, to whom he recommended it and who is full of enthusiasm for it, that he wished that it should continue to be practised after his death.[83]

Madame the Duchesse de Longueville[84] has established this holy practice on all her estates.

Monsieur the Duc de Liancourt[85] has worked on it with great success; and several other great lords and ordinary noblemen have undertaken it and been successful.

1. It is easy. Nobody dares to refuse the great because of the good or evil they can do. Some respect them, others fear them. Those who are peasants or tenants dare not refuse their masters, gentlemen, bourgeois, or others. Most owe them something and are always in their debt. When they have a lawsuit, they have only to threaten them that, if they refuse to come to an amicable settlement, they will carry out the threat the day after that refusal. That never fails.

I know one nobleman who has an estate on which the peasants were being consumed by litigation and did not pay him. He was advised to take advantage of this remedy. He did so and all the lawsuits were settled in less than three months. Since then they have all lived in peace and the lord has been paid.

---

83 This is confirmed somewhat by De Conty's own manual, see Chapter 4.
84 Chapter 4.
85 Chapter 4.

But if the two peasants who are in dispute are not the vassals, men or tenants of the same master, this is what I have seen another nobleman do. He wrote to the lord or master of whom the other peasant was tenant, pointing out to him that they both shared the same interest in getting an amicable settlement. He tells me that no one has refused him yet. Everybody looks after their own interests. When you have tried it, you find the way is gentle and easy – and costs nothing.

Because litigation is a form of warfare, which is fundamentally about property, but which is accompanied by hatred, animosity and vengeance, and because to revenge yourself you will stop at nothing, the lowly just as much as the great, the peasant, the labourer and the artisan, they all give up everything and devote everything to it.

However, the land is not worked during this war and the artisan does no work. The lord is not paid his rent. So there you have a poor peasant, who has fallen prey to a *solliciteur*, or to the judge and *procureur* of the village. They plunder him and rob him; they subject him to excessive valuations; he must pay high rates of interest to buy time; and in the end they make him pay twice the amount of his rent in costs. In that way, if the lands are not let out, they produce no revenue. If they are let, then the peasants are ruined, the lands lose their value and the rents diminish. So the great lords, out of self-interest, are obliged to prevent lawsuits among their vassals as much as they can.[86]

2. Besides, the great lords are obliged to render these services to their vassals on religious principle and in conscience. They

---

86 The first edition here includes:

> But what is there more glorious and charitable than to end disputes of subjects and neighbours? Moses – great judge as well as great prince – who had learned the lesson from the God of Peace, spent all his days on this holy task. Job, the great patriarch, did just the same. Still today, is not the most honourable activity of kings, and what they do with the most pomp and *éclat*, the offer of their intervention and mediation in ending the wars of neighbouring sovereigns? History is full of Papal legations and embassies of Princes on such matters. So, all the wars of Princes end in a treaty and the litigation of individuals ought to end in an accord.
>
> Can you serve a country better than by bringing peace and abundance to prevail there? The coming of such good Lords is longed for in every land; it is earnestly desired in Heaven. Everybody hopes to find in them the cure for their ills – the widow, the orphan, the weak – all the rich and poor alike – they look on them as that holy asylum of which the Apostle speaks, where everyone finds relief from their unhappiness.

must remember that their estates and their fiefs are only given to them by their sovereigns on condition that they render justice to their subjects, without charge, on the terms of their first grant. Most of them have forgotten that, but it is only fifty years since the King granted all their offices to his *officiers*. And still today, in the *aveus* which they make to the *Chambre des Comptes* of Paris, they are obliged to make mention of that, and that reduces the price of the lease, when the land falls to be redeemed.[87]

Things were different before that unfortunate *Vénalité des Charges* came into effect, introduced by the kings in spite of themselves, and made necessary by the misfortune of wars (*to adopt the language of our Kings and their Ordinances*).[88] That may be excused in our Sovereigns but not in their Lords the *Haut Justiciers*. Before that, all the lords gave to their judges this charge: 'Let the safety of the people be the first law!'[89] That is the first law of princes – to save the people. If they cannot be saved without war, and if the war means that they cannot be saved without getting revenue from the sale of offices, that necessity provides our Kings with an excuse.

But as regards the Lords *Haut Justiciers*, the wars have not altered the nature of their holding of estates, fiefs and jurisdictions. They have a duty to provide justice free, as they did during the term of the first grant to them. They have not lost what they think they have. Suppose that they make ten or twelve thousand *livres* from an office at the time they sell it, the annual income being five or six hundred *livres*. The purchaser does not consider himself obliged in any way to his lord for this sale, or obliged to give his time and trouble for the preservation and increase of his estate. And rightly so. You do not consider yourself obliged to a merchant because you have bought some merchandise from him, which he has sold at as high a price as he could make it fetch.

If the lords granted their offices as they used to, they would be able to pick people of standing, of ability and recognised probity, who could constitute their little domestic senate. Then the

---

87 This sentence does not appear in the first edition, which reads instead: '& les destivoient (*ad Nutum*) c'estoit l'ancien vsage auant cette malheureuse venalité des Charges …' and continues as the later editions do. I guess that 'destivoient' is a mistake for 'destinoient' and that the phrase can be translated 'And so intended them (on the nod)'.

88 <Henry III. Estat de Blois.>

89 *Salus populi prima lex esto.*

responsibilities, the discussions, the advice and the good management of their estate, and the protection of their vassals' interests would be more important to them than the prices for which they could sell their offices. We know that from experience.[90]

There are plenty of lords who have resisted this corruption. The Ducs de Luynes[91] and de Liancourt among others have never been willing to sell them. One of them has gone further. He came into possession of an estate where he found a judge who had bought his office. He paid him back and appointed him with no payment.

3. The lords are responsible before God and before men for the misconduct of their *officiers*. They must give an account, as a great Father of the Church says, 'on the Terrible Day', when the strict Judge shall give favour to no one. In this world they are made strictly liable for the vigorous enforcement of the laws. The Ordinance makes the Lords *Haut Justiciers* responsible for the errors of judgment and misconduct of their *officiers* and ministers, *procureurs*, notaries and *sergents*, and provides that any sentences passed on them shall be executed against the lords of the fiefs, as their joint obligors. This was the practice of all the *Parlements* before the introduction of the *Vénalité des Charges* and before the *officiers* were in possession of great estates, fiefs and jurisdictions. The *Arrest* of the *Parlement* of Paris, among others, is well-known.[92] It was reported by that famous compiler M Loüet,[93] and pronounced *en Robbes rouges* in the form of a *Règlement* of the year 1526.

---

90 This sentence is not in the first edition. Perhaps this experience was recent.

91 Presumably not Charles d'Albert, Duc de Luynes (1578–1621), lover and chief minister of Louis XIII, who had been dead for nearly fifty years, but his successor – De Liancourt's fellow Frondiste. Perhaps La Roche means to include all who hold these two titles. This paragraph does not appear in the first edition.

92 <Ordonnance de Roussillon art. 27.>

93 Georges Louet, from Anjou, was an advocate in Paris in the sixteenth century; counsellor at the *Parlement* of Anjou 1584. He collected and published in 1602 a great number of *arrests*, edited and arranged alphabetically with a commentary, which went through nearly 20 editions, *Biographie Universelle* XXV p147. Author (as Georgius Lovetius) of *Notae ad Commentaria Caroli Molinari in Regulas Cancellariae Apostolicae* Paris Cramoisy 1656 (published posthumously) and part author of *Notae Caroli Molinari, Georgii Louet, Antonii le Vaillant circa Rem Beneficiariam a Celeberrimo Patrono N Sachot Collecta et Ordine Alphabetico Digestae* Paris Guillaume Cavelier 1723.

This *Arrest* merely repeated the Ordinance, which said that all lords of fiefs should remain jointly responsible for the misconduct of their *officiers*.

4. And so, if the King would order, just by an *Arrest du Conseil*, that this *Arrest de Règlement* should be carried out and that in executing it the Lords *Haut Justiciers* should be constrained to make up a roll of the names of their *officiers*, *procureurs*, notaries and *sergents*, in the registry of the *Siège Royal* where they sit, or better where their jurisdiction lies, would not the lords of fief, the very next day, give precise information of the capacity of their judges and other ministers? And above all of their *sergents*, who may be men of property but of whom they say the number is not great? What lord is there who would be willing to be jointly obliged for the sufficiency and probity of all his *procureurs*, notaries and *sergents*? If they undertook that, all the revenues of their fiefs would not be enough to cover it. Now nobody dares to take this on, because most of them are poor, and they have forgotten that their lords are their joint obligors. And those who do remember that, will rightly be afraid that the judges will not find them guilty, because they themselves hold fiefs.

But if the law were renewed and carried out, they would boldly take it in hand. The lord would then have a hundred lawsuits on his hands. To put that right he would reduce the number of all the *procureurs*, notaries and *sergents*, to the smallest number possible and would keep only the most able, the men of most property, and would still take care about those whom they had appointed supervisors and controllers of their actions in their place.

Why is it that the lords of fiefs do not keep down the enormous number of locusts which feed on the people? They make no profit out of them. Most of them are appointed without payment. Would the lord like to remain jointly obliged for the probity of a bailiff whom he would not normally guarantee for five sous? Nevertheless they create thousands of these desk-caterpillars, at the request of the first come. This is the refuge of good-for-nothings and ne'er-do-wells. The mischief has got so bad that there are some who can neither read nor write. They make a mark where their name is written for them. It reminds us that Moses called up the locusts in Egypt just to distress the people, and that those deadly creatures are the results of the anger of God the destroyer.

Finally, if the lords of fiefs were strongly persuaded that they must pay for the misconduct of their *officiers*, they would make sure they committed none. They would carefully enquire about their probity and adequacy, and would assiduously correct them, at least for the future. They would have some regard to their probity and ability and would not sell their offices, as they do now, indiscriminately to the highest bidder, the one who offers most.

But if the King, as he can do, made them render justice free to their vassals, in that case it would mean that they would seek the most respectable men to be judges. In that case it would mean that they would have no difficulty in settling the suits and disputes of their vassals. The judges themselves would work hard for this and, from the first hearing, all their betters would end them if they could. For then they could hope for no *épices*.

The charitable doctor who works for nothing would like to cure his patient on the first visit. The surgeon who has no hope of payment would like to be able to cure the sickness when it first appears.

CHAPTER XVII

*That the Great Lords can settle nearly all their lawsuits
and should do so*

What is more undignified than a great lord with a lawsuit? Who is there so strong above him? As we said of the bishops, if he takes charge himself, there he is like a miserable law clerk, with his hands always full of papers. He receives and writes a hundred chicanery letters. Body and soul he is always in the company of judges, *avocats* and *procureurs*. He suffers a hundred indignities and rebuffs. All this in the hope of winning a miserable little lawsuit, when he would not put up with all that for the chance of getting to Heaven!

For the duration of that disgraceful and punishing war, he must give up all pleasures of body and spirit. He can no longer dream of hunting, of walks, of visits, of the company of friends or books. Days and nights are too short for this unhappy war of the desk.

And so they have much to gain from finishing off most of their lawsuits at birth, and they can do so best at the beginning. They can pursue this course without hatred or animosity, using agents and *solliciteurs* as kings make war through their lieutenants.

So if in the first place you ask for a settlement, your opponent will consent to it because for the most part they are relatives, allies, or friends and continue to see themselves as such despite the lawsuits. But when it comes to the seizure of a country house and the sale of the estates, all intercourse stops. The great hate one another just like the small and they tear one another to pieces. That is why settlement is easier before you get to that stage. So it is best to declare your willingness to settle at the earliest possible moment, even before the action is brought if you can. And if that is not agreed, you should offer to nominate arbitrators and record that fact. After that, if the other side refuses, they cannot blame you whatever happens, loss, ruin, sale of their estate, &c.

If the plaintiff has not offered arbitration, the defendant should do so and the sooner the better, as we have said, but also continuously throughout the proceedings. He can do so. You often see lawsuits settled after the interlocutory proceedings have begun. This request should be made continuously, whenever you can, communicating with your adversary through notaries – more trustworthy than *sergents*. You can use men of honour as intermediaries, people who are friendly and charitable. The man who will only speak to a *procureur*, *solliciteur*, agent or *intendant* may often find himself asking the wolf to save the sheep.

If the great lords do not take charge of their lawsuits themselves, their houses are often ruined. If they abandon their suits to agents, *intendants* or *solliciteurs*, the cost is immense. Besides that, they are exposed to their idleness, ignorance, ill-will, or untrustworthiness. How many houses have been ruined by that sort of thing? There are a hundred examples of it, throughout the kingdom.

You can see the advantage, then, when great lords will have none of such litigation and try to bring it to an amicable end. For them it is easy. Their action is against their inferiors, or their equals, or their superiors. If it is against their inferiors, they have only to ask them to settle and they will agree with pleasure: the weak want peace with the stronger.

If the litigation is with their equals or superiors, it is still easy as we will tell you.

To oblige your *intendants*, agents, or *solliciteurs* to involve themselves completely in your interest, to strive and work to keep them free from litigation, you must copy the great idea discovered by one great lord. He gave his *avocat* and his *procureur* fixed annual appointments, charging them with the duty of keeping him free from the cost of all litigation. And he also gave them certain allowances, calculated according to the number of lawsuits which they managed to settle. In this way they took care not to reject arbitration. They were always the first to ask for it. They worked to get settlements with such keenness that several of those soldiers of chicanery now have to work hard to keep their long drawn out war going.

On top of these ordinary appointments he gave his *intendant* certain other rewards, in proportion to the good services he rendered, and recompensed him handsomely whenever he did something useful and profitable for the house. Unless you are appreciative and pay well, you will never have faithful and well-disposed servants. You will have to pay hand over fist. As the poet said long ago: 'The gods would have no worshippers at all if they did not grant them favours.'[94]

But it often happens that great lords think they are gods, to whom everything is owed but who owe nothing. Flattery has persuaded them that all the world was made for them. What happens to people like that? They get plundered, they get robbed; or at least their affairs are abandoned or neglected. Everything falls into disarray, all is lost. Their houses are seized and sold: 'The best fish are to be found in troubled waters.'[95]

What needs to be done to have faithful and well-intentioned servants? Do what the Oracle said: 'Love if you want to be loved!'[96] To be served well you must pay well. The Holy Father of the family paid the workers in his vineyard, who only arrived to work in the evening, the same as those who came in the morning. The reason was that they worked with more affection and skill; what seemed to be little bore greater profit than the longer labours of the others.

When the great lords follow the example of the wise Father of the family, they will have no lack of faithful and affectionate servants, who will not be looking for ways to raise stumbling-blocks or otherwise impede the friendly settlement of their lawsuits.

If only the great lords would copy the holy resolution taken in Paris by people of high position and eminent quality who have resolved to have no more lawsuits without first offering to the other party a friendly disposition of them, by nominating arbitrators and entrusting them with the matter. Every day a great number are terminated in this way, as we have said and as we know from experience. At least it has this advantage, that you will have tried to find a peaceful solution. If afterwards execution, or imprisonment, or seizure or sale is necessary, neither equals nor inferiors will be able to complain that they have been crushed by connexions or influence.

---

94 *Les Dieux n'auroient point d'adorateurs, s'ils n'etoient reconnoissans.*
95 *La bonne pesche se fait en eau trouble.*
96 *Pour estre aimé il faut aimer.* <Math. c. 20.>

Above all, though, you make this request according to religious principle, because you are a Christian,[97] because those are the orders of the Gospel and the Council which denies the very *Communion* to those who refuse.

---

97 The first edition substitutes for the rest of this sentence:

Because you say every day, or at least you should, 'Our Father, which art in Heaven'; because the Heavenly Father is a God of Peace; because he reigns in Heaven; and because his children ought to seek it on earth. Ask for settlement to this end and you will get it, and riches as well, and abundance. 'But seek ye first the kingdom of God ... and all these things shall be added unto you.' <Math. c. 6> (verse 23).

The first edition then brings in here what in later editions immediately precedes this chapter.

CHAPTER XVIII

That the Officiers, *being respectable people,*
can and should settle their lawsuits

1. You know what everybody says, that the judge's gown is the feather of the eagle, which devours others; that their neighbourliness is that of the wolf, their companionship that of the lion, who wants the lot. No succession is safe because if a judge has any interest in it he wants a share; if he is one of the heirs he wants another, just because he is an *officier*. In the end he wants the lot because he is the stronger.

They know too that there are complaints that in the countryside there is not a meadow or vineyard close to their houses which is safe from them. They grant pardons to the widow and the orphan if they are happy to share with them an inheritance to which they have not the slightest claim. These complaints are often slanders, but the good judges can easily silence the voice of calumny. They have only to offer to the other party to agree on arbitrators and entrust the matter to them. If the other side accepts, the lawsuit is thereupon terminated promptly and without trouble or cost. If the other side refuses, thereupon the judge is protected from the usual criticisms that they are oppressed by his power, his reputation and his connexions.

They may rest assured that nobody will reject arbitration with them, not their equals, nor their inferiors, nor their superiors. Even though they may be superior in birth, in rank, or in property, they all consider themselves inferior to a judge in matters of litigation. That would be to gamble with him *in his own den*, as the popular proverb has it. That would be to have his brothers for judges. They all hold one another's hand, from one end of the kingdom to the other. It is our common cause in which we all have an interest – he is our brother[98] – to strike fear into those of that *métier* and terrify those of that profession.

Inferiors do not have confidence in refusing to settle with a judge. They think of him as a Cyclops, who can eat them up. His proposal of peace will be received as if it had been brought by an angel from Heaven.

98 *Frater noster est.*

As for equals, if they are judges and of the same branch of the profession, they have the same interest in wanting a settlement. They know better than anyone the troubles, the torments of body and soul, of a poor litigant. For them above all, if they have to give up their house and the exercise of their office, then, instead of the profits and honours and prestige that they find there, they must travel far and incur great expense and suffer rebuffs and humiliations just like any other unfortunate litigant.

So, if a judge does not want to, he almost never needs to litigate. As we have said, his inferiors, his equals and his superiors all want to be well in with him. At least nobody seeks to be in his bad books.

CHAPTER XIX

That the Lower Classes and the Weak can usually settle any Lawsuits
they may have with those more powerful than them,
and that they ought to do so

Even when they are assured that they will get more from litigation than from a settlement, they should remember that, if you imprison a great lord, or attach his revenues, or sell up his estates, his family never forgets, as the proverb says, even unto the hundredth generation. They seek revenge against the author of it and on his children and all his family.

When a great lord is stripped of all his property, his birth remains. His family and friends, who have shared in his ruin, will take their revenge sooner or later. They have long arms and a hundred ways of doing harm, like that woman who was annoyed with the poet: 'a thousand arts of injuring'.[99]

If it is the inferior who is defendant, at the suit of a great lord, he is usually pursued by agents, *solliciteurs* or *procureurs d'office*. Gentlemen of honour and respectable people are to be found among them but, for fear of being misunderstood, he should nevertheless address himself directly to the lord in writing. That is what I have often found successful. Whether the lord is at home or away, it is always better to communicate with him in writing *for it is difficult to approach them personally and have a calm hearing*. Explain to him by letter that in his name they have brought such and such an action against you; that you have far too much respect for him to want to have a fight with him; but, because he is just and equitable, and would never wish to crush the weak, that you beg him to name arbitrators; that you are willing to put down a deposit for that purpose; that to bring that about you have informed his *procureur* of this offer; but that just in case he has omitted to advise him of it, you are sending a copy direct to him.

You then put the copy in the envelope with the letter. Make the letter as short as possible and deliver it by hand, for fear that it fall into the hands of those gentlemen who have an interest in

99 *Mille nocendi artes.*

seeing that the litigation is not settled and who might be able to bias the mind of their master.

Now whether the lord is at home or away, if you write to him direct, most people open their letters and packets themselves, if only out of curiosity, and ought to read them themselves and not tell their people what is in them, like most people do. Because that would stop people from daring to write and tell them the truth, and they would become statues, as the Prophet says: *they have ears but will not hear, they have eyes but will not see.*[100] They have eyes and ears but they neither see nor hear and can manage nothing. All is in confusion with them and everybody knows it. There is nobody who is unaware of it.

To conclude, the letter the inferior writes to the lord should be short, as we have said, because we would rather have him read it himself than call his agent or *solliciteur* (who will have dreamed up the affair) to read it. When it calls on his honour and conscience and says that he should not allow the weak who want to settle to be crushed in his name, he will give appropriate orders and his agents will not dare to disobey them.

I have seen a number of lawsuits settled after this fashion and most will be, if the weaker party follows this path.

In fact, how can a great lord, duke, marquis, or other, who is more powerful than his opponent, dare to refuse to come to a settlement with the weaker party who has begged him, who has offered to pay or do whatever the arbitrators award? If the great lord should refuse, he will be taken for the sort of man who lets his men manage his affairs for him, or even for a scoundrel who wants to devour the poor, *and fatten himself,* as the Ancient said, *on the substance of the unfortunate,* which even the wickedest do not want, if you believe what they say.

If a bishop or a curé, for example, were asked by someone to make an amicable settlement, would he dare to refuse? If it were possible that there were some pastors who were such enemies of peace, who loved litigation so much, would they refuse to agree on arbitrators if they were summoned to do so? After that, how could they preach that peace, friendship and unity which there ought to be among Christians? How could they give advice, in

---

100 *Aures habent, & non audient, oculos habent & non videbunt.* <Psalm. 134.> In the King James version Psalm 135, 16–17.

private or in public, in their conferences and on their visits? How could they pronounce the divine words in the most august of our sacraments: *peace be with you?*[101]

How could they want peace for their flock, and yet tear them limb from limb by their bad example, and by the hatreds and dreadful enmities which accompany chicanery? In that case could not one say with the Council that the bishops, curés and pastors should become subject to anathema? *And those who kill Christ's sheep.*[102]

Similarly, if the weak ask a judge for a settlement, or the poor a rich man, how can he refuse? This summons to arbitration will be a pretext to inveigh against them and will give the impression that the litigation is only a pretext for stripping the poor. They will not omit from their invective a denunciation of the life and actions of the *officier* or the rich and powerful man who rejects arbitration. This will be the beginning and the end of the pleas, writs and requests. So there will not be many who refuse. That is why, if the great lord, the bishop, the judge, the rich man does not ask for arbitration first, the weak should not fail to ask for it, and show proof of that, and you will see that that succeeds. I have seen it often in my own experience.

Besides, if the weak or the wise who want a settlement are unlucky enough to be in a parish, bishopric or province, where the curés, bishops or governors do not give any audiences after the example of our Prince, and do not work towards supporting his good intentions, then the one who seeks peace should interpose some friendly persons before these gentlemen, and suggest to them the ways and means. That will oblige them to do it, in spite of themselves. One is happy to be thrown out of the door when it is by an enemy.[103]

---

101 *Pax tecum.*
102 *Et interfectores Christi ovium.* These last two sentences are not in the first edition, more evidence of La Roche's further reading in the authorities.
103 This paragraph is not in the first edition.

CHAPTER XX

That equals also ought to ask one another to settle,
that the wiser will be the first to ask,
that there is no shame at all in that, nor mark of fear,
since in Paris eminent Persons of quality, principle and merit
make a practice of it, following the Gospel and the Councils

Settlement between equals is more difficult than with superiors or inferiors. One is making an overture and who shall take the first step? Although often both parties want it, as we have said, they do not dare to show it for fear the opposing party will take advantage of it and boast that the other is afraid and is begging for mercy. It is true that this is what has often happened up till now. But from this moment on there is nothing to fear by following the example of those illustrious Christians, those gentlemen of Paris, who have taken the holy resolution, following the advice of the Apostle and the Councils, never to take their brother to court without first asking him for peace and an amicable settlement.

When they are persuaded that the request is based on charity and the purity of the Gospel, and is not at all the result of fear or trepidation, nobody is going to take advantage of it. On the contrary, most people will immediately give in to such a great example of humility and Christian charity. You can tell that from experience in Paris and in the provinces where they have begun this holy practice.

1. However, should it happen that people are carried away with anger or vengeance, or are blinded by their own interests, and refuse the offer of settlement out of hand, then the offer is still always advantageous to the one who makes it first.

2. It will have silenced, as we have said, any accusations that the intention was to oppress by power, authority or property. Above all we shall be relieved of the duty which our consciences place on us, which the Apostle advises us of, and which the God of Peace commands us to perform. After that we can leave it to Him to take good care of our interests, our honour and reputation. He may be the God of Peace but he is also the God

of Vengeance. His arm is not foreshortened. He knows how to look after us (*God the Lord of Vengeance*).[104]

Nevertheless, as God often makes use of the ministry of angels and of saints to work his miracles, this is where our bishops and curés ought to work to good effect. They should, by their words and example, root out the false maxim that it is shameful for any Christian to ask for settlement, to want to live happily with his neighbour, to want to live in peace here below, with those we should desire to have as companions in glory in Heaven.

This is how confessors and preachers can work effectively. We have good cause to hope for all this from the zeal and charity of our bishops, who live a completely exemplary life and choose for service worthy curés, and inspire by their example the confessors and preachers and the great number of religious orders, famous for their doctrine and piety. If this holy legion, this abundant army of so many peacemakers, declared war on litigation, its destruction would be assured.

If every man of the Church would only settle one lawsuit a year, how many thousands would be settled? They can do it. Even the least efficient and the least intelligent of preachers, monks and nuns, whom one does not want to discourage, can manage it if you tell them often and carefully enough. You will find the moment when the invalid himself wants to be cured.

One single missionary, inspired by this spirit of peace, settled hundreds of disputes in his missions. Now here is the holy trick which he made use of, when he saw them touched by the sadness of the sinner. If they had lawsuits, he explained to them that this unfortunate and fruitful source had been the dreadful cause of many of the sins they had committed. And it would seem that they were about to commit them again if they did not settle their differences amicably. To this end he made them agree on arbitrators, and sign a compromise, like that you will find at the end of this manual. He always had printed copies of it available. After that, he got them to shake hands and sent the compromise to the arbitrators. Otherwise, once the mission was over, and their fervour had waned, they would return to their litigation and all the confusion which follows, of which there are a hundred examples.

104 *Deus ultionum Dominus*. <Psalm. 93.> (King James 94).

Finally, there is not one single curé who, if he has the charity to apply himself to it, cannot at least contribute by the settlement of fifteen or twenty lawsuits a year. If pastors are men of goodwill they can settle a much greater number. For they are the friends of the penitents, of so many sick and afflicted people, who follow their advice. Nevertheless, as we have said, if each one settled only fifteen or twenty a year, there are more than 30,000 parishes in the kingdom, so that makes more than *six hundred thousand monsters destroyed*, which produce such desolation, as everybody knows, among the flock of the Lord and ruin it.

One can therefore boldly undertake this holy work. We are in the century of peace. Our invincible Monarch[105] has been working for a long time and with so much application on this reform of chicanery. All the people desire it with so much passion. He himself gives public audiences for this purpose; and he strives to get the governors, bishops and curés to support his good intentions.

---

105 Here the first edition inserts: 'has won this for us abroad by his arms and wants to give it to us internally by his laws, for which he ...'. The last sentence is not in the first edition.

CHAPTER XXI

How to choose Arbitrators,
and the difficulties you can find there,
and the remedies

1. Everyone ought to nominate their own arbitrators, as we have already said. If somebody else nominates, you do not have the same confidence as in one you nominate yourself. Besides having to judge, the arbitrator has to persuade and that is the more important. For that you have to have complete confidence in him. That is why mediators, whether great lords or others, should never nominate the arbitrators. This is what the very excellent and very virtuous Prince de Conty did. He drew his maxims from sacred history, which tells us that God commanded the people, through the mouth of Moses, that they had to choose their judges: *judges shalt thou make in all thy gates.*[106]

2. You should choose people of probity and recognised ability, but probity is above all the most necessary because without it there will be few successful settlements. If they have not got this charitable principle, they will not have the patience to listen to the long statements of the parties, which seem to have nothing to do with the substance of the case, yet often prove decisive. In that way the arbitrator works his way into the mind of the party, gains credibility and, as a result, can make a decision and persuade him to accept it.

3. After both sides have nominated an arbitrator, they must agree on a third. If the parties cannot come to an amicable agreement, the mediator will make a list of eight or ten persons of the canton, who are well respected. He will make two copies of this list and send one to each of the parties, who will then mark with a cross in the margin the names he has doubts about and at the bottom he puts the words: *I have doubts about those I have marked with a cross.* Then he gives the list back to the mediator. If you pick eight or ten people with a reputation for probity, it is almost impossible that all of them will be rejected. If only one of them remains who is not rejected, he will serve as the third. If two or three are left, or more, the mediator says so

106   *Iudices constitues in portis tuis;* Deuteronomy 16, 18. <Deut. C. 16.>.

and writes their names on separate slips of paper, which he displays and then puts in a hat in the presence of the parties and then has one drawn by chance.

4. Sometimes you would prefer not to have arbitrators from your own place nor to resort to the *Parlement* where you live. And you may be perfectly justified. I know an officer in a royal regiment who brought an action against someone who had also been an officer and his colleague but no longer was. The latter called on the former, who was the plaintiff, to seek a settlement. The plaintiff agreed on condition that they appointed as arbitrators *avocats* from the jurisdiction of a *Parlement* other than that where they then were. That was because the plaintiff was still an officer and therefore esteemed in all his province but the defendant no longer was. The arbitrators from that place would not have been able to reach a settlement but those of another jurisdiction did.[107]

When some apparent difficulty crops up, this is how you can deal with it. All the *avocats* in France, whatever *Parlement* they belong to, are capable of judging all kinds of questions – of fact, of law and of custom – if the *factum* is well drafted or the pleadings are properly prepared for trial. We know from experience, as we have said before, that matters are transferred every day from one *Parlement* to another where they are prepared for trial and decided.

So the mediator will get the parties to agree, or will draw by chance, the names of the *avocats* and the *Parlement* by which they want to be judged. If the parties do not know anyone, the mediator will get a list of eight or ten of the best known and will draw from it three by chance, or a greater number if the parties so desire.

5. If the proceedings have not yet been prepared for the hearing, that can be done in the place where the parties reside, in the following form. Each party makes an election of domicile before a *procureur* or notary. They then inform one another of

107 At first sight it seems that the author has got into a muddle with the plaintiff and defendant. Surely it would have been the party disadvantaged by retirement who would have sought to arbitrate elsewhere. But I prefer to believe that the author got it right. The one with the unfair advantage took the initiative to transfer the matter to another jurisdiction, where the arbitrators could not be accused of bias and the award had a better chance of acceptance by the parties.

this and produce it and the rest of the interlocutory proceedings follow, except that all should be done with courtesy, which is done with such great bitterness in court. This courtesy is often enough to bring the matter to an end. I have known mediators, and even the parties themselves, at this stage propose ways which allowed them to bring the matter to a successful settlement, there on the field of battle.

6. But, if that does not happen, the proceedings have to move to a hearing, open or private. The mediators will ask the parties to agree on a friend for that.

7. If the case does not require long preparation, and can be judged on the basis of a *factum*, the mediator will prepare one which the parties will agree to and sign.

8. The mediator will require the parties to deposit in his hands the penalty on forfeiture,[108] which will not be reported in the compromise, for fear that what often happens will happen here, that the judges decide to award the sum fixed by this penalty, even though the Ordinance[109] prohibits that.

9. When the proceedings have been properly prepared for trial, or the *factum* is ready, it is sent by the mediator to the agreed *avocats* and their decision is notified to the parties. If there is something particularly difficult for one of the parties to comply with, the mediator will try to ameliorate it by whatever means goodwill may suggest.

At last, after providing all the good offices of a true friend, in the sight of Heaven and not of Earth, he pronounces the award. If anyone refuses to acquiesce in it, he sends to the one who does acquiesce the sum which has been deposited as a forfeit.

---

108 See 'What are the Best Procedures' in Chapter 6.
109 This appears to be a reference to the last paragraph of the 1560 Edict of François II on the execution of arbitral awards, set out and discussed in Chapter 2.

CHAPTER XXII

The duty of a good Mediator

We have just told one party what to do when the parties are in agreement to settle amicably. But it is more difficult when it is necessary to drag such consent out of the parties.

1. You have to persuade them and that is the big problem. However, it is easy to achieve your purpose if you have the good intentions of the good curé we told you about, the zeal of his bishop[110] and of that good prince the provincial governor.

2. All sorts and conditions of persons are able to be mediators: a neighbour, a friend, even a person a long way beneath those whose dispute you want to settle. Even if the mediator cannot manage it himself, he may be able to get someone else who can. However great a lord he may be, a sick man knows very well that the lowliest person wishes him health and will do what he can to get it for him.

3. But to be a good mediator you need more than anything patience, common sense, an appropriate manner, and goodwill. You must make yourself liked by both parties and gain credibility in their minds. To do that, begin by explaining that you are unhappy about the bother, the trouble and the expense that their litigation is causing them. After that, listen patiently to all their complaints. They will not be short, particularly the first time round.

4. You must have the wisdom and discretion not to say anything to upset the one you first talk to, however poor his case seems. Just tell him that all this is having a bad effect on his reputation, that his enemies, or those who are ill-informed, are telling stories about the matter to his discredit and that is giving a very bad impression. Tell him that, if he settles, these rumours will stop and he will be able to make people see he is quite a different person from what his enemies put about.

5. What if there is someone whose cause is so good that you can have no doubt that he has been oppressed, persecuted, stripped of his property by the proud or insolent? The offence strikes to the quick if the mediator does not show that he is

---

110 For the rest of the sentence the first edition substitutes: 'who supports him so worthily'. There is no mention of the provincial governor.

concerned for his interests, and has compassion for him. He will tell him privately, face to face if he can, that everyone knows the wrong and the injustice he has been done, and that everyone is complaining about it and wants peace for him.

If the party asks the mediator to speak in these terms to his adversary, the mediator replies that he would willingly do so if that would serve his cause; but that it would only irritate his opponent and hinder a settlement because it would make the mediator himself suspect. So he says that he will speak to him and get friends to intervene and say all that is necessary. The mediator says, however, that he hopes that the party will not disclose anything he has said about his opponent, otherwise the mediator will be obliged not to stand by it, because that would aggravate the affair rather than ameliorate it. The mediator would thenceforth be seen to be like a party. That would ruin everything. So in the end the confessor and the consultant are bound by the same confidentiality – but it is a confidentiality that they can take advantage of.

6. A great deal of skill is needed to find ways of dealing with the difficulties presented by the nomination of arbitrators, the conditions on which the proceedings may be suspended, and a hundred other problems which can be encountered. If the intermediary does not have all the insights necessary for the job, or lacks the necessary authority, he should take advice from sensible persons, or interpose powerful persons who command the respect and fear of the parties and to whom they would not dare to break their word.

I have often seen this succeed. Just one instance out of many was between persons of high estate and in a matter of great consequence. The mediator was not of their weight, so he interposed powerful persons and the matter was settled even though the parties had been very passionate about it.

7. Finally, the mediator ought to have an inexhaustible supply of goodwill. That is to say that all his actions, words and thoughts ought to be inspired by that divine love that the Christian ought to feel for his neighbour and that nature itself inspires in us: *Do unto others what you would have them do unto you.*

8. Those who act on these principles bear with patience the complaints, the disgruntlement, the grievances, even the ingratitude of those to whom they have rendered services. On the other hand, sometimes everything seems fine with a mediator, when

in fact there are faults. I know of another important matter, between eminent persons, where the mediator, who was not of their station in life, negotiated between them for a long time but made some big mistakes. They told him so, at least they complained to him often. Nevertheless they forgave him everything. He was always welcome, eating and drinking with all the parties. At last he was the cause of their settlement, really because he always acted on the lofty principles of goodwill and love for one's neighbour.

This fire divine inspires us, makes us active, patient, eloquent and ingenious. This is the *divine gold* of the Apostle, which the smoke of calumny knows not how to blacken. This is the *living spring* of which the Prophet speaks, which refreshes and delights those who work in the light of the great God of Peace.

9. And so, if all those who have power and authority, and all those who have access and credibility, intervene to settle suits and disputes, we shall soon destroy the monsters of division. We have shown you how they can do all this, our Lord Bishops,[111] curés, the zealous missionaries, the preachers (those faithful interpreters of the purity of the Gospel), the confessors (charitable doctors of the most secret ulcers of the soul) who take the trouble to enquire of their penitents whether they have any lawsuits and whether they hate their adversaries, because most people never confess that.

Finally we ask them in their sermons, homilies and confessions to follow the system which the good bishop introduced into his diocese, of which we spoke in Chapter VIII, and they will soon see peace established everywhere.[112]

111 'Nosseigneurs' here in all editions.
112 Instead of this last paragraph, the first edition has:

> any more than the soldier would confess to having sworn an oath [*d'avoir iuré*], the *officier* of having been corrupt [*preuariué* – which I take to be a mistake for *prévariqué*], the merchant of having been guilty of usury, hardly anybody owns up to the sins of their trade. The litigant more than anyone always thinks he is right, that even his hatred is just and legitimate. So when his confessor takes the trouble to ask him questions, he finds the soul of this poor litigant all gangrened [*cangrenée*] with hate, enmity and violent lust for vengeance, so that, with these ulcers, he often does not let him approach the sacraments, to multiply his diseases at the place of their cure. So governors of provinces would do well to settle litigation. The great lords and *Haut Justiciers* should do it for their vassals. Ordinary gentlefolk, bourgeois, and the least person who has a tenant or a peasant below him, can require him to settle his differences amicably, as we have said in previous chapters.

CHAPTER XXIII

Of the qualities of the good Arbitrator

1. He should be patient like the good mediator and prudent like him, and above all charitable like him. That is where he ought to start, to continue and to finish. If he has other thoughts or interests it will be a miracle if he succeeds. Sooner or later someone will complain about him and about his judgment. We see this happen every day.

On the other hand, to the one who works according to the principles of divine love, the small are worthy of the same consideration as the great; strangers and unknowns are as dear as family and friends.[113] So arbitrators should remember what is commonly said about them, that in ninety-nine out of every hundred matters which fail to settle it is the fault of the arbitrator. That is to say it is their lack of goodwill for the parties.

2. The good arbitrator ought as well to be knowledgeable and skilful, and should be held in esteem for that, that is to say if there is any point of law or custom. Because, other than that, merchants and other wise and intelligent people, even peasants, can decide any questions relating to their own trade.

3. He ought to give the parties free access. The judges of whom sacred history speaks, elected by the people, by the commandment of Moses, were seated *at the gate of the camp*.[114] Job settled differences *at the door of the Temple*, that is to say in a place to which access was free and convenient for everybody.

4. You are master of the place once you have won over the governor. You are master of the will of the poor litigant once you have gained his affection. For that it is necessary to show him goodwill and friendship and a great desire to help him. You should begin by listening quietly, as we have said, and though he says a lot of things which are irrelevant to the matter, you must listen with patience, at least the first time round, to win credi-

---

113 Cf *Hesiod, Homeric Hymns, Epic Cycle, Homerica* with an English translation by HG Evelyn-White 1936 'Works and Days' 213: 'Those who give straight judgments to outsiders and their own people alike and do not stray from the straight and just, their city prospers and the people in it flourish.'
114 <Deut. Cap. 16.>

bility in his mind. Afterwards you can act differently. Once the poor invalid has been persuaded that you feel goodwill towards him, he will accept whatever you may say.

5. To make him see that the arbitrator has comprehended his case, go over it with him, exaggerate the arguments in his favour, even suggest some new ones. That will persuade him that you are intelligent and well-disposed towards him. After that you can tell him the arguments which the other side pleads to the contrary, though cursorily and without exaggeration but nevertheless in a way, if they are good, that gives him cause for doubt. Finally, tell him – and persuade him – that you will do whatever you can to support his interests and procure peace for him.

6. In the provinces, in many districts, they have a bad habit of treating a party's arbitrator as if he were the party himself, and often with dislike, hatred and abuse. This bad habit must be rooted out. It is easy. The arbitrators need only tell those who have nominated them that they have to go and visit the arbitrators nominated by the other side to seek their cooperation. They should say that they are honourable men in whom they may have confidence. They should point out that the arbitrators from the other side must listen to them with more patience than they do their own side, giving more weight to their arguments and showing them goodwill and friendship and a great desire to contribute to their settlement.

This favourable reception will totally win them over, so much more than in the courts where you usually have to put up with the rebuffs of the judges and their staff – you cannot talk to them, they will not listen.

7. In the provinces, arbitrations are usually held in taverns, after the German fashion. But, as one of their historians says, 'drinking produces good settlements but it also produces good disputes'. Now arbitration is a holy and sacred thing, and something more venerable than mere judgment. Because, as well as judging, you are trying to reconcile their hearts. That is why it is better to choose a place which is worthy of the sanctity of the enterprise. So you should assemble at the home of one of the arbitrators, or the curé of the parish, or in some convent. The consecrated ministers who live in these holy places are angels of peace who will support the arbitrators.

8. Once the arbitrators are assembled, it is best to start by deciding what is the fundamental point at issue, with the same rigour with which that would be decided in the courts. That is not always done in the provinces. On the contrary, they often begin by proposing expedients. They keep changing the subject. Intelligent and clever arbitrators, when they are ill-willed, take advantage of that.

9. If the point in issue is decided upon with rigour, and you then find that the parties do not want to stick to it, you have to look for compromises and expedients, whatever they might be – a thousand écus, for example, may have to change hands to make them happy, in return for some advantage, perhaps because they have business with a man who is powerful, or full of chicanery, or rapacious. In order to defend himself, he may have to spend a great deal of money, to give up his business, commerce, or the management of his estates, thereby losing all the profit that he would have made if he had not been involved in litigation.

10. Similarly it is worth a thousand écus to such a person to be rid of one opponent so that he can take on another, because he has another matter on with powerful people, with whom he is finding it hard to come to an agreement, so that he must go to great expense. Even if he wins after such expense, he will never get back a third of what he has paid out, to say nothing of the waste of time, the stress, the household left to its own devices, and all the profit he would have been able to make had it not been for this unfortunate matter.

11. I have often seen settlements made which you would expect to be broken, but an arbitrator with wonderful expedients and goodwill has discovered a holy trick to persuade the most opinionated. He has them write a memorandum in four lines, stating what they would recover, principal, interest and costs, if they were to win exactly the judgments and *arrests* they want.

12. On the other side he gets them to set out the expenses it must cost them, the time they must devote, the profits which they will lose during the period of litigation &c. Then he hands this memorandum over to them, or to their wife or one of their friends and asks them to look after it until the litigation is concluded, to see whether it was accurate. The most opinionated yield eventually, either in the arena or some time later. The most

hot-headed are capable of thinking these things through. But these compromises have to be made voluntarily by the parties, not just by the arbitrators. They ought not to be depriving one party of an advantage so that they can give it to the other. They ought to judge as they would be judged. But after imposing this discipline on them they can tell the parties to relax.

13. There is one very important thing which the arbitrators should watch out for. That is they should almost never allow the parties to plead their cause in one another's presence, even if it is not necessary to take evidence on certain matters in secret, because very often the eyes, or the expression, are dumb witnesses, and unexpected questions and answers reveal the truth.

But apart from that, one should never allow it. The reason is that even the best proceedings are still accompanied by a little bit of acrimony – *everyone looks after his own interests on that subject*. When the parties come to speak in the presence of the other side, they interrupt one another, they get one another excited, they irritate one another, and straight away it comes to insults, abuse and reproaches, bile erupts and the arbitrator is no longer master of the situation. Anger, vanity and vengeance are passions stronger even than the avarice and selfishness which are the usual causes of these proceedings.

So the arbitrators should not allow the parties to talk together in front of them. It is even a good thing to keep them in separate rooms, from which you can call them as the need arises. When they speak to their own arbitrator, they speak gently as they would to their friend or to a judge. And they gently receive the compromises the arbitrator proposes. If they find there something they feel they must reject, they disclose the inconveniences without getting excited. They would not be able to do that if the other party were present, for fear he might take advantage of them. We see this happening every day, and many an arbitration has failed because the parties have got angry and have swapped insults in the presence of their arbitrators.

14. You must also watch out for another thing which is of great importance. The arbitrator who holds the pen must be competent and above all a decent man, because it is a maxim among the clever ones in this business, that he who is master of

the pen is as good as master of everything. He only needs to change one word to reverse the meaning of the award.

15. If possible, the arbitrators should themselves take the trouble to prepare the award or the compromise which is mediated. At least they should make the necessary notes, and should note down what has been decided in articles. Some notaries, however clever they may be, find it hard to understand the substance of a matter the first time they hear it told them.

16. As far as you can, you should not leave anything to the last minute in these arbitral awards or compromises. You should do on the spot all you can to complete them. For example, if a debtor promises to pay in instalments, or a lump sum out of an inheritance, you should make the contract and conveyance by the same deed. If a son makes a promise of dowry to his mother, or brothers make a partition, the *designation* should also be made on the spot and the conveyance at the same time by the arbitral award. Otherwise there may be a real risk that further proceedings will be necessary, or further recourse to the same arbitrators, doubling the trouble for them and for the parties.

17. Because it should be the arbitrators' intention to bring peace and as far as possible prevent any occasion for a lawsuit, it is better to get the parties to make a compromise rather than making an arbitral award. It is more difficult to appeal against a compromise than against an award, even one you have acquiesced in. Corruption is so widespread that on an award you can obtain an order for relief,[115] and then you can plead *for ever and a day*. You see thousands of lawsuits of that kind.

18. It is true that you can also get an order for relief against a compromise but, quite apart from the fact that that is difficult and given more grudgingly, the point is that, once the matter has been disposed of, you are afraid to make a compromise in general terms without setting out your reasons in detail, on the off chance you will not know how to recover, because you will not be able to reveal what the question was between the parties, if it should happen that one party claims to have been wronged. For example, if it is a question of the execution of an *arrest*, and whether it is valid, you may have mentioned a particular sum which the compromise requires in general terms: *by means of the*

115 *Lettres pour estre relevé.*

payments heretofore made and of sums received, which the parties did
not wish to be set out in detail, and for other cause, Titius[116] *declares*
Maevius quit of the execution of his arrest, in principal, interest and
costs.

19. If it is a question of accounts, which are a matter only for
the parties to the compromise, then you should declare that the
parties are between themselves quit of all matters up to this day,
and likewise of anything else that the matter has disposed of.

In addition to the fact that it is difficult to get relief against
compromises made in this way, which the arbitrators do not
have to sign, it has another advantage for the arbitrators. Often,
to further the appeal, the appellants make a song and dance
about the wrongs done to them, alleging that the *avocats* and
arbitrators dealt with them with ignorance or ill-will. But if their
names do not appear, and instead of an arbitral award there is
only a compromise, which none of the arbitrators has signed,
they cannot say anything about it.

Finally, the arbitrators, judges of gentleness and peace, ought
to have the same goodwill and charity for others which they
would like to receive were they in similar circumstances. They
should remember that there is nothing more worthy of honour
among men than to have a reputation for such great ability and
probity that people are prepared to submit themselves voluntarily to them. That was the most noble ambition of the great
senators of Rome, and princes of the land, at the end of their
days, to see their fellow citizens come to them and accept them
as the judges of their differences. They preferred that private
esteem to their trophies and triumphs. They had defeated their
enemies by force but had won the hearts of their people by
gentleness.

Sacred history depicts for us the great patriarch Job, the
almighty sovereign, settling the disputes of his people at the door
of the temples, and commends him more for those actions than
for all the rest of his outstanding qualities.

Solomon, the wisest of kings and of men, was esteemed more
for his qualities as a judge, gentle and peacemaking, than for all
his other virtues. That was what drew to him the crowned heads,

---

116 Titius and Maevius are two of the stock characters of the Roman law
teacher, equivalent to the modern X and Y.

and the Queen of Sheba, to pay homage to him at the foot of his throne. It was his award and the arbitrator's stratagem which appeased the two mothers in the sharing of the child, which have caused him to be worthy of the praises of all the centuries, both past and still to come. That single act has received more eulogies than all the victories and triumphs of the conquerors. Charlemagne is praised more in history for the audiences he gave to his people than for his victories, and rightly so, because those audiences were concerned only for the good of the people, who took more of a part in them than they did in the victories of the prince. Similarly the audiences which our King gives bring him more praise than all his conquests.

20. Therefore, no one should think that the position of arbitrator is beneath him. Saint Louis[117] also, one of the greatest of our kings, made this his particular profession. History tells of him taking singular pleasure in rendering justice to his peoples and in finding ways of settling their differences. He would doff the rank of sovereign to assume that of arbitrator.

Finally, all the great saints and all the great prelates of which our history speaks gave up everything else to concentrate on the work of this holy undertaking.

21. On that basis, everybody ought to hold in honour this role of charitable arbitrator and mediator. There are, thank God, throughout the kingdom, persons of eminence and position and virtue who have devoted themselves to it. In Paris we have among others three famous people who have held the highest offices of the State, Messieurs de Morangi, de Boucherat and le Nain.[118] Their houses are open to all. Their virtue has set up in their homes tribunals of peace. Their ability, their goodwill and their patience soothe the most excited of minds and find ways of resolving the most difficult of differences. If their example is followed throughout the kingdom, and everybody in his place imitates those great men, the monster of chicanery will soon be smothered.

---

117 Louis IX.
118 Chapter 4.

CHAPTER XXIV[119]

That in various Provinces at various times
persons of quality have assembled
to serve as Arbitrators for the poor

In the town of Lyons, in Nantes in Brittany and in Clermont in the Auvergne, certain honorary *officiers* used in the past to devote themselves to this holy practice. And there were *avocats, procureurs* and notaries who joined them and served as their *greffiers*.

This is what brought such people of high reputation in the countryside to devote themselves to this charitable work. Rich people were always asking them to be their arbitrators and that took up all their time. But they resolved to be better employed; they thought better of themselves by working for Heaven and looking after the poor, bringing their suits and differences to an amicable conclusion. They would get together for this purpose twice a week at the house of the senior, and make that known at once throughout the district. Everybody hurried there, rich and poor alike, and anybody who refused to go when called before them was considered a wicked man. It was a common proverb among the people: 'will you trust the good arbitrators?' Their doors were open to all the wretched. Their houses, as Aristotle (*that living altar*) says, were where the weak rushed in crowds.

In one morning they would decide more suits than the *Siège du Lieu* would dispose of in a month, just like the *Juges-Consuls* do now. At this early stage of the proceedings there was often only one document to look at. But by the time they are well prepared, 'according to all the court forms' as they say, there are mountains of waste paper, and it takes a long time to find out the truth which they take such trouble to conceal.

However none of these meetings of charitable and voluntary arbitrators have continued up to our times. They ended with the death of those zealous workers who composed them, in default of a spiritual generation which would have cooperated with their curés and bishops and had the support of the authority of their Prince.

---

119 This matter is in Chapter IV of the first edition.

Now we are going to speak of other charitable consultants and arbitrators, which Henry IV established in Provence and wanted to set up throughout the kingdom.

The illustration overleaf is found in the second edition but not in the first or fourth. I have not seen a third edition. Its omission from later editions may indicate La Roche's recognition that it overstates his case, and that the charitable arbitrators, *avocats* and *procureurs* were never established in Provence. The problem is discussed in Chapter 2 above. The text reads:

THE GOOD *AVOCATS* AND *PROCUREURS* AND CHARITABLE ARBITRATORS

There were some established in Provence who took care of the suits of the poor for nothing, and brought almost all of them to an amicable conclusion, following the intention of the Ordinance of Henry IV of 6 March 1610. *The first President at that time, and the King's men in this* Parlement *of Provence, put this Ordinance promptly into Practice. That good Prince had resolved to bring it into operation throughout France* after the example of Venice, *but death prevented that. The poor and the weak ask our Monarch to complete this great plan of charity, as he has completed the other great plans of his Grandfather, in both peace and war. Unless he does so, whatever reforms he makes, the poor cannot hope for justice in France, to say nothing of getting it free. So, you need to have money and the poor have none. But our Monarch with one word, by one Ordinance, by means of these charitable Arbitrators and* Procureurs, *can build for the poor that invincible fortress of which Scripture speaks, where the weak, the widow and the orphan can find safety. Jeremiah c15.*

LES BONS ADVOCATS ET PROCVREVRS, ET ARBITRES CHARITABLES.

IL y en a d'établis en Prouence, & permettroit soin des procés des pauures gratuitement, & les accordantqui tous à l'amiable, suiuant l'intention & l'ordonnance d'Henry IV. du 6 Mars 1610. Le premier President, lors, & le gens du Roy dudit Parlement de Prouence, firent promptement executer cette Ordonnance.

Ce bon Prince a nostre resolu de la faire executer par toute la France à l'exemple de Prouence, la mort l'en empécha.

Les pauures, & les foibles, conurent nostre Monarque, à achauer ce grand dessein de Charité, comme il achoue ces aubres grands desseins, de son Auril, & en paix, & en guerre.

Sans cela, qu'elque reforme qu'on faße, le pauure ne pais & pourra de pairse la rendre egualitement. Donc il faudra de l'agent, & le pauure n'en a pas.

Mais n'importe Monarque, peut à imo parole, & d'une seule Ordonnance (par ces Advocats & Procureurs charitables) bastir au pauure (cette forteresse invincible) dont parle JE² remur, ou le foible, la veuue, & l'Orphelin seront en seurté Ierem. C. 15.

CHAPTER XXV

That in the year 1610 Henry IV ordered that there should be estab-
lished an Assembly of Charitable Consultants and Arbitrators, of
Avocats *and* Procureurs,
in all the Courts and Jurisdictions of the Realm,
which would take care of the affairs of the poor for nothing
That M the Chancellor de Sillery[120] *had his heart in this*
establishment
That he asked M De Laujorrois,[121] *Counsellor at the* Parlement *of*
Toulouse, to write something on this matter, which he did,
and published it
What has stopped such establishments being set up throughout France
What was done in Provence, where the first President at that time,
and the King's Men in the Parlement *of that Province, set up that*
establishment, which is easy to do in the rest of the Kingdom,
without it costing the King or the People anything
The great benefits that would produce

That great Prince Henry IV had a heart full of sympathy for his
subjects, especially the poor, who are exposed to the wrongs of
the great, and of whom it is said that the kings are their principal
saviours and defenders, from whom God will demand an exact
reckoning, *on the terrible Day of Judgment,* to use the words of the
Apostle. That good Prince's plan, as his great confidant and
minister[122] told us, was to publish, on his return from the wars

---

120 Nicolas de Broulart Marquis de Sillery (1544–1624) negotiated the treaty
      which ended the war with Spain in 1598, then the divorce of Henry IV
      from Marguerite de Valois and his marriage to Marie de Medicis. He was
      appointed Garde des Sceaux in 1604 and Chancelier de France in 1607.
      Colleague and rival of the Duc de Sully. He was manoeuvred out of
      power by Maréchal d'Ancre in 1612, recovered his position of influence
      under the Duc de Luynes but worked unsuccessfully against the rise of
      Richelieu and fell from power just before he died. It was said that he
      knew no Latin. Henry IV quipped that, being advised by such a
      Chancellor and a Constable (De Montmorency) who could not read or
      write, he could get quickly to the bottom of the most difficult business.
      Dictionnaire des Personnages Historiques Français; Michaud *Biographie*
      Universelle Vol 39.
121 Chapter 2.
122 The Duc de Sully, see Chapter 2. <M. de Sully dans ses memoires> but I
      cannot find there any reference to such a plan.

in Germany, the reform of the legal system, that he already had everything drafted, and that the King himself had corrected it and added a recommendatory postscript in his own hand.

1. But, seeing that the weakness of the poor could not wait so long for a remedy, before he left for that war, on 6 March 1610 he ordered that there should be established, in all the courts and jurisdictions of the kingdom, a council of charitable *avocats* and *procureurs*, who would take care of the suits of the poor for nothing, and who would make it their business without getting anything for it. But out of fatherly goodwill that great Prince promised to give offices and privileges to those charitable ministers to recompense them for their trouble.

2. M de Sillery, worthy Chancellor of such a Prince, also had his heart in this establishment, so much that, in order to advance its implementation, he asked M De Laujorrois, Counsellor at the Parlement of Toulouse, who was fired by the same zeal as he was, if he would be willing to write something on this subject, to show how useful it would be and how easy to put into practice, which he did in that same year of 1610 and had it published.[123]

3. The demon which is the enemy of peace and quiet in France took from us that incomparable Monarch two months later, by a sad and untimely death which prevented the continuation of the implementation of that charitable plan. Wars, within and without the kingdom, which have afflicted France ever since, have prevented it till now.

4. But now we are in the age of miracles. Our invincible Monarch, for whom Heaven has reserved the execution of the great plans of his grandfather, labours for this reform of the great chicanery which all the people desire so much. The poor and the weak should have the hope that he will keep them specially in his dreams. If not even this assembly of charitable *avocats* and *procureurs*, consultants and arbitrators is set up, then I am afraid the poor will never taste any of the sweet fruits of this reform. They are stripped of all their property, denuded of all relief. Their condition is so desperate that it is no good for them to be beside the font if our Prince, the charitable physician of all ills, does not provide the men to immerse them therein.

123 See Chapter 2.

There is a fine example of this plan being put into action in the Parish of Saint Sulpice[124] in Paris, which for the first time in the year 1666 set up an assembly to provide relief for the poor. It only lasted one year but helped two to three thousand poor people, of whom many had fallen into extreme poverty as a result of litigation. Among them was a father, unfortunate and unhappy, who had been stripped of all he had, in favour of his only son, who left him to die of starvation, and perish in misery, on a handful of straw, at the age of eighty five.

The father had been a merchant in Paris and, to get a better marriage for his son, he had given him all his property which amounted to more than eighteen thousand livres. He kept only the furniture for one room and a subsistence amount, and left the son with an obligation to pay off six or seven hundred livres' worth of debts which his firm had incurred.

The ungrateful and unnatural son had his father imprisoned in the name of a moneylender, took away all his furniture on the pretext of looking after it, and refused to pay him the agreed amount of the pension. For four years he failed to pay.

The poor father, now thus naked and abandoned, asked the legal system for relief. He obtained three judgments at the *Chastelet*, but the wretch of a son appealed them. He was non-suited by two contradictory *arrests* but resisted execution. The father obtained ten others but the son did not waste a moment in making all these *arrests* illusory. As all the property was movable, and all he feared was corporal constraint, he absconded to a distant province and put his acquisitions in the name of his children, who were still in the cradle. His poor father of eighty five was left naked and dying for four years on a handful of straw. Of all his property, all that was left was a bag full of papers – twelve *arrests* in one hand but no bread in the other.

What a travesty of justice! What shame on the chicanery of our France, crammed full of judges but this unhappy and unfortunate father can find no relief against the ingrate son. If Henry IV's plan had been put into practice, if there had been in every

---

124 Instead of the rest of this sentence and the next, the first edition has: 'of which we spoke before'. The first edition, dated 1666, already refers to the Assembly of Saint Sulpice, which the second says met for the first time in that year. The first says it met in 1665, and increases even these unlikely numbers, see below Chapter XXVI paragraph 1.

town an assembly of charitable *avocats* and *procureurs*, this father would soon have been relieved, and a hundred thousand other unfortunates like him who groan throughout France.

6. For example, the charitable council of Paris would write to that of the town where the wretched son had gone to hide. They would take him prisoner and he would pay up. Better still, of a hundred lawsuits of this kind, or other similar vexations inflicted on the weak, just the fear of this assembly would prevent ninety of them. The attacker, the one who hopes to get some advantage from his opponent's poverty, seeing these assemblies established, would not dare to do it. He would know that he was fighting not against the feeble arm of the poor man but against the almighty hand of the Prince which supports him, which is like struggling against the strength of the angel.

There is nothing easier than to set up charitable *avocats* and *procureurs* in all the courts and jurisdictions of the kingdom. That can be done without cost either to the King or to the people and without depriving the poor of the benefit of Henry IV's plan, which is so liberal and charitable, which would have granted offices to the charitable arbitrators. That would be better but the enterprise would work without it.

The number of matters would not be so great as might at first appear. As we have said, all the rich who now attack the poor in the hope of taking advantage of their poverty would not then do so.

7. A great number of the lawsuits of the poor, more than a third or a half – one might as well say nearly all – would be amicably settled at the outset, if they did what we said earlier. A Christian, and above all a poor man, ought to try to preserve his interests without getting into the acrimony of litigation. Just as a person entering a hospice must first make confession before he can receive the other benefits, it would be a good thing if the charitable council began with a summons to arbitration. That would stop the rich from complaining that they were being harassed and overwhelmed by the power of the council. Otherwise there would be few rich people who would be willing to settle. The poor man, with the support of the council, would be stronger than them and than even the greatest of the powerful.

In all the towns, in all the tribunals of the kingdom, there would be charitable protectors who would work for nothing and devote themselves to this work with more zeal and diligence than they give to their own affairs. What they did for nothing and on charitable principles they would do as well as they could.

However influential they may be, the rich do not have so much of an advantage outside their own areas. They even find it hard to understand what is going on and to know how to behave; and hard to find people who are loyal and well-disposed towards them. If they have to travel afar, they cannot avoid the trouble and expense of leaving their house, where there is always something useful to be done. So there will be hardly any rich man who, seeing the poor man supported, will not consent to a settlement with good will.

8. If there are two poor people who have an action against one another, they will have it settled for them whether they like it or not.

9. Besides that, the poor have a lot of litigation which is ill-founded. People without property get attached to hopes which they are unwilling to give up, tormenting the rich and wasting time which they ought to be using to earn their living. This assembly of charitable consultants will provide a cure for this disorder. If the poor refuse to have their lawsuits settled, they will have to give them up; and if they consent, the rich will have peace and the poor the time to earn their living.

10. So you can see that it will be better if fewer lawsuits are pursued. Almost all the business of this charitable assembly will be consultations and arbitrations. However, on the litigation which cannot be avoided, it will not be necessary to spend any money, yet profit will flow to the worthy *avocats* and *procureurs*, as I will show you later.

(a) Nobody will start any litigation unless they have been well advised and have found that advice acceptable. If the action appears to be well-founded and well-prepared, nobody will lose too much. Consequently, the poor man's opponent will be condemned in costs and so he will be able to reimburse himself for any advance he may have made.

(b) Here is a way to avoid paying anything in advance. You do not usually have to pay any money except to *huissiers*, *greffiers*, or receivers of *épices*, and they can give credit until after the judgment in the matter. They know they can make no profit out of the litigation of the poor, if it is not pursued, which it will not be, and if it is not maintained by someone, which it cannot be, unless they themselves contribute by providing this facility by granting credit for a period. That being so, there is no need to spend any money.

(c) What would be even better would be if you could work it so that all these proceedings were done for nothing, as is done for the hospices. Nevertheless, everybody has to make a living even though it makes everything venal. So it will be enough if they provide credit terms and wait for their money until after judgment has been given.

But the most certain way would be for them to ask the King to ordain that anyone who refuses to settle after being summoned to nominate and agree on arbitrators, and who prefers war to peace, shall be bound to deposit, without any hope of recovery or applying for it back, a considerable sum to be used to pay the costs of the litigation, and to a fine for the benefit of the hospice. In default of making this deposit within three days, if an application is made, the sum applied for shall be forfeit, and the defaulter shall be found liable in costs on a simple request. Moreover, if it is the defendant to whom the application is granted against his opponent, prohibitions are available against the judges, making them subject to the penalty of a civil action and of responsibility for all costs, damages and interest for contravening this Ordinance, which is something they do every day with regard to the penalty bonds carried by a *compromissum*, from which they discharge those who appeal against arbitral awards.[125]

The Ordinance must impose the same penalty against the *avocats* and *procureurs* who employ prejudicial defences, and must allow the parties to assign the matter to the council, by virtue of the declaration, without other *pareatis*.

11. How are the charitable *avocats* and *procureurs* to be recompensed? You do not pursue an action if you have not considered the matter carefully and decided that you have a good chance of winning, and that you will be recompensed for your trouble and preparation of documents by the losing party. That is fair. Each should live by his labour. On top of that, to reward them for the

---

125 This paragraph and the next are not in the first edition.

time they devote to consultations and arbitrations, the King can grant them privileges and offices, as he has to some directors of hospices, such as exemption from the duties of guardianship and trusteeship, billeting of soldiers, watch and ward, military service, and anything else which the Prince considers more appropriate. These charitable workers cannot be rewarded enough.

12. The Republic of Venice is so well organised that it is the miracle of law and order in Europe. There they have gone much further. Besides charitable *avocats* and *procureurs* they appoint famous magistrates to be the guardians and trustees of the poor. This work is so honourable among them that the sovereign authority rewards it by membership of the Senate.

So, if the King believes it to be appropriate, *avocats* who have given twenty years of this charitable service could be admitted to membership of the *Parlements* with the rank of honorary Counsellors. That is the recommendation of M De Laujorrois, Counsellor of Toulouse, who has written about the fundamentals of this matter. *Procureurs* who have rendered similar services could be rewarded by membership of the *Maisons de Ville*, with the rank of Counsellors, or Past Mayors or Aldermen.

On top of that, this work will make them plenty of friends, who will do good turns for them and their families, and their reputation and esteem will be known by all. This will mean that the rich will give them their business, from which they will profit.

But above all they will have the real reward that you get from doing good deeds, that joy which is felt by charitable souls and unknown to souls which are hard and ungrateful. They know they are working for Heaven, for the liberal God, whose promises are not false, who for the least action done for him or for the poor, *whom he calls his members*, promises riches which will never be exhausted.

So it remains only for our King to set up these assemblies of charitable *avocats* and *procureurs*. He will find workers everywhere, who will happily offer themselves.[126] For this he only needs to renew the Ordinance of Henry IV and in particular

---

126 The rest of this and the next paragraph is replaced in the first edition by:
    'It only remains for those glorious ministers, who so worthily help him to govern the State, to put this holy idea into his mind; it only remains for M the Chancellor to lend a hand to add to his glory for ever.'

to ask the *Premiers Présidents* and the King's men in the *Parlements* to set up such establishments in their jurisdiction, as has been done in Provence, and report their prompt action to his Majesty within six months, and each will undertake this with enthusiasm.

The *Procureur-Général*[127] of the *Parlement* of Paris (*worthy of the ancient senate of Rome when it exercises its authority on the King's behalf*), without having been asked, has already set up assemblies where he appears regularly, to take special care of the prisons, and to deal expeditiously with the affairs of the prisoners.

So that France keeps in mind the obligations it owes to our incomparable Monarch, it is a good idea to draft regulations for the conduct of these assemblies, to be read every six months. These regulations should have at the top the Ordinance and the illustrious name of our great Prince Louis XIV.

And so, France will always remember his fatherly charity, for ever his name will be blessed and venerated by all, the weak, the downtrodden, the widows, the orphans, and all the poor people who are oppressed, whether by the might of a governor or a great lord or a man of the robe, or a petty tyrant of a gentleman. Eventually, all the desolate and abandoned souls, of which France is full, will have recourse to these assemblies, as to secure refuges, which the charitable hand of our Prince has prepared for them. This will be the holy anchor, which will save them from shipwreck. As the payment for such a heroic action he will have the reward promised by the Apostle, *the sum of all the joys*, which shall last for ever and ever.

---

127 M Harlay; but there is some evidence of his coolness towards such assemblies outside his control, see Chapter 4 above.

CHAPTER XXVI

Rules of the Assembly of the Parish of St Sulpice in Paris, which takes care of the deserving poor;[128] *and which has been the first also to take care of their lawsuits and try to settle them amicably*
The Cause & the End of this Assembly

We have already spoken of this assembly in the preceding chapters. It is only the shadow, the appearance, an imperfect sketch of those assemblies of charitable *avocats* and *procureurs* which Henry IV had planned to set up. For those would have had the authority of the Prince and would have been armed to say with a forerunner – 'carving out laws with the sword' – which the powerful would not be able, and would not dare, to resist. But the charitable workers of the special assemblies of this parish can only work with apprehension because they are open to censure, to mockery, to slander and calumnies from everybody. They are like the poor disciples, well intentioned but timid, who went about stealthily, *secretly for fear of the Jews*.[129] However these assemblies are capable of doing a great deal of good, while we wait for our Prince to establish those of his grandfather, whose foundations cannot be shaken.

1. This is what has taken place in the parish of St Sulpice. The assembly of the deserving poor survived, as we said, for only one year.[130] It helped three or four thousand of them, most of whom had fallen into extreme poverty through the misfortune of litigation and chicanery. What is even more regrettable is that very many of them had given up the observation of the sacraments and were unwilling to draw near, confessing that their souls were so full of rancour, hatred and animosity against their opponents that they felt unable to forgive them. They considered them to be the authors of their ruin and the disastrous cause of their poverty, their shame and their suffering, and of all the miseries which come with the ruin of a family.

---

128 *Des pauvres honteux* – the poor too ashamed to beg.
129 *Clam propter metum Judaeorum*. The second corrects the first edition's error '*mecum*' to '*metum*'.
130 The first edition has: 'which lasted only last year, 1665; it helped four or five thousand, of whom ...'.

2. The curé,[131] who loved so tenderly even the least of his parishioners, like the most devoted father loves his only son, begged and pleaded with the assembly of the worthy poor to look for a remedy for such great evils. At first, the size of the enterprise amazed everybody. There is hardly anyone in France with property who does not also have some litigation. They want nothing to do with it, but they are forced to. The smallest lawsuit is long, slow, contagious and distressing. So everyone assessed the difficulty of the enterprise from his own experience and considered it impossible. At first nobody was willing to embark on it.

But in the end goodwill swept their reservations away. The poor father we discussed earlier asked for relief against his ingrate son, who had stripped him of all his property and left him to die of hunger, cold and misery, on a handful of straw, at death's door, eighty-five years of age. This matter moved even the least tender hearts. The curé took advantage of his opportunity and, with a zeal as great as that of the pastors of the early Church, as great as that of our good curé St Yves, put fire into the most lukewarm.[132]

3. In the end the assembly for the deserving poor resolved to take care of their lawsuits and above all to seek ways to settle them amicably. From the time this resolution was taken, and it became known how nature makes great efforts to remedy great evils, it hastened to labour on this holy work. A host of famous people became arbitrators there, eminent in rank and every kind of virtue: dukes and peers, *cordons bleus*, the King's lieutenants in the provinces, the premier *officiers* of the royal household, marquises, presidents then in office, counsellors, even *avocats* and *procureurs*, counsellors of state and *maîtres des requêtes*, and finally eminent people who had been ambassadors and a great number of other persons of goodwill whose names are all reported in the assembly's register.

4. Monsieur le Bailly de St Germain, who is the sole judge of that *faubourg*, as great as any of the greatest towns of the kingdom, showed his pleasure and offered his services. He

---

131 The first edition, not here but at p38, names him as M Poussé.
132 Here the first edition adds: 'he had two famous right hand men, MM De Couder and D'Acol, who relieved our Curé of some of his laborious but charitable duties'.

approved and supported this sensible initiative every time he was asked. This good judge, enlightened and fired by goodwill, knows that you lose nothing by helping the weak; that magistrates get no great profit from poor people's litigation; that no one can bring an action without money; that you can relieve yourself of their importunings if you settle them amicably. And even if there may be some loss involved, that the God of Charity will ensure their reward. He stripped Saul for his avarice and heaped Solomon with good things for his liberality and the magnificence of the Temple he built so proud. With even greater justification will he reward those who protect the poor, who are his very limbs and his living temples.

5. If in all the towns of the kingdom there were charitable assemblies, until such time as the King established those of his grandfather by his authority, there would be a safe harbour for the weak, the wretched and the oppressed. They are easy to set up if My Lords the bishops have the goodwill to involve themselves. Almost everywhere their charity has set up parish assemblies which take care of the sick and the deserving poor. They only have to be asked to follow the example of the parish of St Sulpice and a number of intelligent persons will join them. They only have to ask the other curés to follow in the track of that famous curé of Paris. Even if in their town there is no assembly for the deserving poor, they can still set up an assembly of charitable counsel.

Everywhere there is somebody who is well intentioned and quite ready to be an ambassador for peace when he is asked and given support. You do not need any great ability for this work, as we have said. All you need is a little bit of goodwill. Goodwill is simple but its arguments are strong and persuasive. Even if you do not have the ability to decide difficult questions you can still be a mediator and get agreement on arbitrators. So you will find peace workers everywhere who will worthily support the good intentions of the bishops and the curés until such time as it pleases our great Prince to establish the assemblies of charitable *avocats* and *procureurs* of his illustrious grandfather Henry.

Then we shall be able to say of our invincible Monarch that his goodwill has built *that fortress in the house of Israel* for the protection of the weak which all the malice of men shall not be able to throw down.

CHAPTER XXVII

The Substance of the Regulations of the said Assembly

I will not set out here what would be useful for the provinces, to avoid too great length, and because what is good for Paris may not be suitable elsewhere. Everybody should make regulations according to the environment and the needs of the place where they reside. I shall be content to show the essence of those of Paris.

1. The purpose is, as far as possible, to prevent the poor from wasting their time in litigation, so that they can use it to earn their living.

2. To bring that about, before giving them any assistance, they are asked if they are willing to come to an amicable settlement if their opponent will. If they refuse, you give up on them.

3. If proceedings have not yet commenced, then before they are started you ask the other side whether they are willing to have a settlement and, if they consent, you nominate arbitrators.

4. If the arbitrators picked by the assembly of the poor are unacceptable to the rich party, the poor party nominates others.

5. The poor man is required to be bound by the arbitral award and will never be helped to bring an appeal, even if the cause of complaint is clear as daylight.

6. If the poor man's rich opponent refuses to settle, then he is deprived of every pretext for complaint that he is being harassed or tormented by the poor man giving him notice, by a declaration before notaries, asking him to have compassion on his weakness, setting out that he has already asked him to settle amicably and is now asking him again, and declaring that if he brings an action against him he remains ready at every stage of the proceedings to come to a settlement.

7. If the poor man's case is found to be bad when it has been sent to arbitration, the arbitrators will condemn him without pity. God ordains: *you shall have no pity for the poor in your judging.*[133] Their cases are often ill-founded. People without anything latch on to hopes which they find hard to let go.

---

133 *Pauperis non misereberis in judicio.* <Exod. C. 13.>

8. But if on the contrary it is found that their case is a good one[134] but that it cannot be settled without giving in a bit, you can arrange that. For example, a hundred écus in ready money are of more value than a hundred and twenty after a long wait.

9. If you have not been able to settle a matter before it goes to litigation, three *avocats* should be consulted, the best known in that place. If you think they are good, ask the opinion of the *avocats* and *procureurs* of the assembly and also ask them what it would cost, but so that the said assembly does not have to make any advances.

10. You appoint one *procureur* and one *avocat* at the bar of that place and at the *Parlement* of appeal, and you pay them for their attendance from beginning to end. If they are not willing to make any voluntary allowance, the saving of one party's costs is not an excessive price to pay for prompt expedition, and the payment contributes to that.

11. If the poor party has a good case and it is well conducted, then clearly he will lose very little from it, because if he wins the *procureur* will be paid from the advances of the poor person's opponent, who has lost.

12. But as even the best cases sometimes fail, the costs can be taken from those who have won. The best thing is for the assembly to pay the costs but in the Provinces there are a number of well intentioned persons, who are not rich, who may be keen to form such holy assemblies but are put off by fear of the cost.

13. In the big towns, it would be good to have a *solliciteur* as security and to pay him generously. His support and attention will help to bring matters to a prompt conclusion, above all those which can be settled amicably, of which there will be a large number. The poor man who is starving to death, or the weak who is suffering oppression, now would they not like to have a

---

134 Instead of the rest of this paragraph, the first edition has:

> it is a good idea to be flexible and arrange for some allowance from one party, who wants the lot but often has nothing. Then the poor litigant is quite content to get the better part of his debt and for you to obtain for him some peace, and time to get on with his work and earn a living. If he had not been rescued he would usually have not got any of it.
>
> Besides, if you want to get all you are strictly entitled to, you will not make many settlements. By being a bit flexible you will make a hundred times as many.

well disposed *solliciteur* to whom they would make only a small payment after they won their case?

14. These assemblies would have a secretary, who would keep a register of their deliberations. The *placets* which the poor would present would be distributed and their affairs would be examined before they spoke to the assembly.

15. They would assemble every fortnight in the house of the local curé, or at least in his presence or that of some other ecclesiastic, a clerk who would preside on his behalf and hear the arguments in turn without distinction of rank. Goodwill makes everybody equal and the great elevate themselves by abasing themselves.Those famous persons in Paris, who are the first people in the State, do this with dignity in these assemblies.[135]

16. The bishops will be requested also to be kind enough to visit these assemblies when they are making their visitations, to kindle and inspire their zeal.

17. Finally, those gentlemen who would like to help the poor should remember above all that they are working for God the peacemaker, who is also the God *kind and humble*, and that the good servant copies the master, and so should take good care to ensure that they say and do nothing which might offend the parties or the judges.[136]

18. To conclude, the charitable workers ought to prepare themselves patiently to suffer the insults, the reproaches, and the ingratitude of rich and poor. A long time ago the Apostle told us that God promises only persecution here below to those who follow the purity of the Gospel 'they shall suffer persecution'[137] but in return the same Apostle promises that reward in Heaven which shall last for ever and ever: your reward is plenteous in the heavens.[138]

---

135 The first edition has 'Assemblées de Charité'.
136 The first edition has 'Juges des pauvres'.
137 *Persecutionem patientur.* <Math. cap. 5> (10–12).
138 *Merces vestra copiosa est in coelis.*

CHAPTER XXVIII

That the settlement of Lawsuits will prevent a large number of Duels

In the provinces nearly all duels arise from the quarrels and hatreds and animosities which are caused by litigation worked up by the nobility about the honorific rights of fiefs, jurisdictions, pre-eminences, hunting rights, &c between neighbours. When you are involved in litigation you are always at war, with the enemies at the gates. Even if the masters are wise, their men are not. There is always some quarrel between them. They meet one another all the time on the road or in the village, and then they fight. If you hide, you fear you will attract harassment. And so, in spite of yourself, you are forced to come to blows. Friends take sides and one quarrel starts a hundred and the wounds bleed for a long time.

There are a hundred dreadful examples of this throughout the kingdom. To add to the misfortune, because litigation lasts for ever in France, the hatreds and the quarrels also become immortal. There are families where the grandfathers, fathers and grandchildren have been killed in duels arising out of the same litigation, which has still not yet finished.

So if you could bring this litigation to an amicable settlement, you would stop these quarrels and the unfortunate duels which follow. If our curés and bishops, our governors and great lords had the goodwill to be intermediaries, they would smother these monsters at birth. All the nobility want this. The most restive would like it. They would ask their enemies for it if they dared and if they could avoid losing face.

It is for our great King to complete his miracle, one of the greatest of his reign, that is to have stopped the course and the fury of these single combats, a madness as old as the nation. They sucked it in with their mother's milk. They saw it confirmed by the examples of the most valiant of men. They boast that they are descended from the ancient Gauls who crossed the Alps and who went to dare the Romans, going into their camp to challenge them to single combat.[139]

---

139 <Florus>. L. Annaeus Julius Florus (116AD) wrote annals praising the deeds of famous Romans.

In fact, if you do no more than follow your natural impulses, this is the most noble of combats and the most worthy of glory. That is why the Church and the authority of the Prince ought to work all the harder to remove all its causes.

Up till now no one has found a better remedy than to make the nobility sign the King's declaration against single combat. Similarly, if you make them sign a declaration that in the future they will have no litigation at all without the plaintiff first offering arbitration before starting an action. If there were a fine against anyone refusing to do so, payable in a lump sum, they would all happily sign that declaration, because they are all afraid of litigation and are worried by it, and so you could put a stop to it and the hatreds and quarrels which give birth to duels.

This way seems still gentler and easier to carry out and ought to last a longer time. For many have only signed the King's declaration against duels with reluctance and have trouble in carrying it out. If wars and disturbances break out, and we have a Prince less firm than ours is now, I am afraid we shall fall back into our old error, and duels would once again just count as bravery.

But the declaration against litigation only seeks to ensure that it is brought to an amicable conclusion. Everybody will happily sign it and put it into effect. Once we get accustomed to the gentleness of this remedy, it will last for ever. This consensus and this good example will help to stop other duels and quarrels which arise from other causes. This is why those who have the honour to be close to the Sovereign are begged to inspire these feelings in him. The Marquis de la Motte-Fenelon[140] above all ought to help in this. He is the one who has worked so worthily and so long and with such happy success, in that he has persuaded a large number of the most gallant men at Court and has got them to sign a condemnation of these combats, even before the Prince had condemned them.

---

140 This cannot be François de Salignac de la Mothe Fénélon, the author, archbishop, royal tutor and proponent of quietism, who was born in 1651. It is presumably his father. The marginal heading in the first edition reads: 'Le Marquis de la Motte Fenelon, a aresté le cours des Duels, par les bons Conseils qu'il a donné au Roy.'

CHAPTER XXIX

That the Prelates and Great Lords who have access to the King are asked to request him to help to put into effect the advice below, if he finds any good in it

Those who have the honour of having access to kings and to the *Throne of Power* of which Scripture tells, have the peoples' destinies for good or evil in their hands and should give the princes good advice. We have revealed the deplorable state of France, ravaged by chicanery, by long drawn out litigation which ruins families and the unfortunate hatreds and enmities which consume Christians. We have revealed how everybody yearns for the destruction of this monster of division and discord and cries to Heaven and to the King for it; that everybody wants to have their litigation settled amicably; at least they want it two to one – the weakest and the wisest. We have revealed that the Gospel, the Fathers, the Canons, the Councils and the Ordinances of the Kings and Emperors ordain it.

We have again revealed that, since the *Vénalité des Charges*, all the kings have made edicts abolishing chicanery and simplifying litigation, but that they have not been carried out at all by the judges, who have an interest in contravening them, because that is how they get their profit. I am afraid that they will continue to contravene them in the future, because of the difficulty of punishing those guilty of such contravention and of setting the reforms on a solid enough foundation so that they cannot be shaken by neglect or avarice, or by the needs of the kings who succeed our incomparable Monarch.

Therefore we have revealed that nothing at all has been put into practice of all the great reforms of chicanery made by the Estates General of Orleans and of Blois and the Assemblies of Moulins, and since then by Louis XIII of happy memory. Chicanery has come down to our time in all its purity. *Juges-Consuls* – commercial arbitrators – have been established. They are elected judges, who judge without *épices*, on the spot, and without *avocats* or *procureurs*, like the greater part of all nations do. Now, whenever somebody tries to oppose or suppress the *Consuls*, the merchants, the towns, the corporations, and the provinces where there are Estates make submissions to the kings, who grant them because they have an interest in doing so.

At the same time it would appear, and some people believe, that if the King ordered the edicts of the kings who preceded him concerning arbitrations to be put into effect and imposed penalties on those who refused, nearly all litigation would end in amicable settlement, in as much as half the litigants would like a settlement, as we have said, and would boldly ask for one, and the other half would not dare refuse it because of the fine they would have to pay in cash.

In this way, all those who are now involved in litigation would ask one another for settlement, as the merchants have asked to be referred to the *Consuls*, ever since the Edict[141] was published. Thus, in a trice you would see throughout the kingdom a general suspension of warfare between all the litigants. The *Palais* and the *Tribunaux* would become deserted. You would find there a deep silence, a pleasant solitude. And so the ill-will of the centuries to come would be able to do nothing against this remedy. Because people accustomed to the gentleness of arbitration, if anyone tried to suppress it, would make their submissions to the kings, asking them to maintain it, as the merchants have done for the maintenance of their *Consuls*. But it is not for me to go so far ahead. It is for the King and the gentlemen who work with him in that glorious reform of the State. It is to them that Heaven has handed out the flaming torches which are kept for those, as Scripture says, who are called within the sanctuary.

Nevertheless, since one must bear with the expressed wishes and recommendations of those who have good intentions, it would appear that arbitration would end most litigation. Nature suggests it, and the law of nations, and the practice of all those who want to escape from the *Palais* and the *Tribunaux*. Great or small, learned or illiterate, they say if they have a dispute: find a friend to settle it!

Kings and princes make agreements with other sovereigns to end their wars, which are the litigation of crowned heads. So our laws and customs counsel and ordain arbitration. Associations of merchants throughout the world make it their first principle that if they have a difference they submit it to arbitrators.

141 <Édits des Consuls>. The consular jurisdiction in Paris was established by
       an Edict of 1563.

We know this also from experience, in the person of the good curé who has discovered the secret of settling his parishioners' lawsuits; and of the good bishops who settle their own and those in their diocese; and of the great lords, who also settle their own and those of their neighbours and vassals; and finally of those gentlemen who in the same way settle those of the poor.

And so if the Prince ordains that the edicts on arbitration made by the kings who preceded him be carried out, with a penalty on those who refuse, everyone will hasten to take this cure because, as we have said, half the litigants would like to settle and the other half would not dare to refuse for fear of the penalty. Soon you would see everybody at peace, the Church, the nobility, the merchant, the peasant and the labourer. That will be the day when France can say, as Rome once said of Augustus in the raptures of regard they had for that prince: 'It is a god who has made life easy for us', Virgil.[142] He has given us a profound peace. He has shut down the temple of war, division and discord. That was the acme of happiness for the Romans.[143]

So then one would say of our King what the Scripture said of a great prince: 'He made peace over the earth and Israel rejoiced with a great joy. And all the old people sat in the streets and talked of the good things of the earth; and the young people clothed themselves in glory and the robes of war and each one sat under his own fig tree and there was none who could make them afraid.'[144] Macab c14. He made peace on the earth, at which Israel greatly rejoiced, the old men talked of husbandry and commerce and the young prepared for war. And each could sit in peace in the shade of his fig tree. And there was no one who troubled their repose, that is to say that among them they had no litigation, no *huissier* and no *sergent* who could strike fear into them.

All that remains is to ask our Prince to be willing to complete his miracle and to contribute to this by renewing the edicts on arbitration, with a penalty on those who refuse to be summoned to it; and to provide for the poor by consenting to the setting up

142 *Deus nobis haec otia fecit*. Virgil *Eclogues* 1, 6. <Virgil>.
143 <Tacite>.
144 *Fecit pacem super terram, & laetatus est Israel laetitia magna, & Seniores in plateis sedebant omnes & loquebantur de bonis terrae, & Iuvenes induebant se gloriam & stolas belli, & sederit unusquisque sub siculnea sua & non erat qui terreret eos*. <Macab. C. 14>.

of the charitable assemblies of his grandfather to settle their lawsuits.

I beg My Lords the Prelates, who have the honour of being close to His Majesty, to inspire in him these sentiments. I plead with the Archbishop of Paris, who, during the fine life of Henry IV was one of the first to depict the misfortunes of chicanery and to raise hopes of a cure. He knows that in that republic of earlier times,[145] so well ruled and ordered, it was forbidden to expose the evils of the state without at the same time proposing a remedy and undertaking a cure.

I also beg the Bishop of Luçon[146] to contribute to such a holy undertaking, for which he has worked with such zeal and goodwill, to pacify the lawsuits and differences of all those in his diocese.

Finally I make my plea to all the wise and virtuous prelates who are close to the Prince and ought to work to make the unhappy victims sacrifice at the foot of the altar their duels, hatreds and animosities, which are so worthy of being sacrificed by the hands of those who every day offer to God the sacrifices of peace.[147]

---

145 Athens.
146 Nicolas Colbert to whom the first edition was dedicated, see Chapters 4 and 5.
147 The first edition has here 'Fin'. The forms which follow are for some reason separately paginated, the text ending at p144 and the forms starting 'Façon du Compromis' at p137.

CHAPTER XXX

The Making of the Compromise

This is what the good curé of whom we have spoken gets those of his parish who consent to an amicable settlement to sign. He always tries to impress on anyone who signs on the spot, after a gentle remonstrance, that he should only sign it if he has thought about it for a long time.

You can add to or subtract from the compromise which follows, or the summons to arbitration which comes after it, whatever you consider appropriate according to the usage and the style of that part of the country where the parties are.

Furthermore, the shorter and simpler the compromise the better. It will often be more trouble to draft a compromise to suit the objections of the parties, who so easily get excited, than to judge the substance of the matter.

COMPROMISE

The undersigned have come to an agreement as follows to terminate amicably the proceedings commenced or to be commenced between them concerning the execution of & *for that purpose M* *of* *has named as arbitrator Mr* *of* *; and Mr* *of has named as arbitrator Mr* *of* *and for third arbitrator they have agreed on Mr* *of* *.*

[But if they have not agreed on the third arbitrator when they sign the compromise, you can say: *and on a third arbitrator to be hereafter agreed by the parties*. They will then have the trouble of agreeing on one agreeable to both parties, or else the curé, the mediator or the arbitrators will require them to choose one, as is said in Chapter XXI on the choice of arbitrators.]

And the said parties will take instructions from their arbitrators to produce to them within *each and every of their documents and will deposit for this purpose the sum of* *to be forfeited in case of appeal to the one who acquiesces in the award; with every power that they give to the aforesaid arbitrators to judge and award; desiring that their award should be executed according to the provisions of the Ordinance*[148] (if one really has a mind to reach a settlement, one

148 Presumably the Edict of 1560 on the execution of awards, see Chapter 2.

can add) *and also the aforesaid parties, in the event of an appeal, desiring that the appellant should not be able to get or claim any costs and that he will deposit the sum of*   *to vacate the appeal &c. Make a duplicate &c.*

If you like, you can then deliver the compromise to a notary to be put in proper form.

CHAPTER XXXI

Summons to Arbitration between Equals

It is better to have this done by notaries whenever possible, rather than by *sergents*, for the reasons aforesaid.

Before us, notaries &c.

Duly appeared and submitted before us Mr   *of*   *who has declared to us that proceedings would be commenced between him and Mr*   *of*   *for the following reasons:*

to terminate these proceedings promptly, easily, without trouble and without cost, and to promote peace, unity and friendship between the parties, as there should be between Christians, the aforesaid deponent makes an offer to the aforesaid Mr   *of*   *to agree to arbitrators and to deposit for that purpose the sum of*   *, summoning the said Mr*   *to declare whether he is agreeable to nominate on his part and to so declare by deed before notaries within*   *days electing to this end his domicile to be at*   *and affirming that in case the said Mr*   *refuses settlement, that he will be the cause of all the evils which result from the litigation, and affirming also that that will make him liable for all the damages, interest, and expenses.*

In respect of which the said deponent has requested us to prepare this Deed and to deliver it to the said Mr   *[or to Mr*   *his Procureur in this Cause] to notify him and to deliver to him copies of the present declarations, offer and affirmations and has signed before us, the said notaries, &c.*

Accordingly we, the said notaries, certify that we have served this on the said Mr   *at*   *o'clock on this day, there being there*   *, and speaking to*   *we have notified and delivered a copy of the above and the summons to reply &c.*

CHAPTER XXXII

Summons to Arbitration from a Superior to an Inferior

This needs to be added to the one between equals:

And in so far as the said Mr   of   may be able to plead that he has an action against one who is more powerful than he is, in property, credit or connexions, to show that the said deponent does not intend to take advantage of his birth, property, credit or connexions, and that his only desire is to preserve what is his, the said deponent makes an offer to agree to arbitrators &c.

If it is a bishop or curé or other person of the Church who makes the summons, it is as well to add here that one makes it in the sight of Heaven, &c. and I have seen some so expressed.

CHAPTER XXXIII

Summons of an Inferior to one more Powerful than him

This should be added to the summons between equals:

And in so far as the pursuit of the said action will cause the ruin of the said   and of his poor family, who have not the property, nor credit, nor connexions of the said   , the said proponent begs and entreats him to terminate the said action promptly, without trouble and without cost, and to have the charity to nominate arbitrators, &c.

I have often seen this sort of summons succeed but, as I have said, it is necessary after creating this document to serve it on the *procureur* of the powerful party, to oblige him to see that it reaches that great lord's own hand.[149]

---

149 This is where the first edition ends, except for an unpaginated page which reads:

PICTURE OF THE MISFORTUNES OF THE LITIGANT
To persuade the common people

Caesar's robe, pierced through with thrusts, made more of an impression on the people of Rome than Anthony's eloquence. Socrates, wisest of the pagans, believed that, if you wanted to persuade, your argument should take the shortest route, which is why Plato in his Dialogues describes him reeling off his loftiest maxims while laughing and playing the fool.
That is why I have put here the following picture.

But no plate exists in the only copy I have found, see 'The Book' above, Chapter 5.

CHAPTER XXXIV

To create Partnerships but avoid the Litigation which usually follows in France

This is what they do in Spain, Portugal, England and Holland:

1. If the partnership is for more than one year, you provide that if one of the partners happens to die before the end of the first year, his heir will take no share either in the profit or the loss; but that he will be reimbursed by the other partners, principal and interest, by reason of the aforesaid provision, reckoning from the time of payment in.

2. You also provide that they account from year to year, so that if things go wrong and if one of the partners then happens to die, his heir equally will have no share in either profit or loss but will only be reimbursed, principal and interest, since the last reckoning, and if there has been none, since the day of payment in.

3. And in case the heir shall come into possession of some partnership property, and litigation or dispute arises about its return, then you provide as I am going to tell you in the next chapter.

CHAPTER XXXV

How to make commercial contracts and avoid Litigation

1. All commercial contracts are either for less than five hundred livres or for more. If they are for less, you can provide that, in the event of litigation or difference, each party shall nominate a friend and those two will make a report to the *Juges-Consuls* nearest to the residence of the parties; and they will make a final decision, as a judgment of last resort, in accordance with the Edict which created the said *Consuls*.[150]

2. If the commercial contracts are for more than five hundred livres, you can equally provide that each shall nominate his friend, but in the role of arbitrator, to be judged by them, jointly with the nearest *Juges-Consuls*, with a promise to deposit a sum to be forfeit, and that should there be an appeal, the appellant shall not be able to be allowed to plead:

(a) unless he has paid the forfeit;
(b) unless he has executed the arbitral award – principal, interest and costs – in the terms of the Ordinance;[151]
(c) the appellant is obliged to deposit an amount for the judgment of the appeal;
(d) the appellant cannot hope to get his costs.

With those conditions you get few appeals.

---

150 Of 1563 for Paris.
151 Presumably the Edict of 1560 on the Execution of Arbitral Awards, see Chapter 2.

CHAPTER XXXVI

Objections against the two preceding Chapters and the replies

The first objection might be that the arbitrators may make a mistake and to prevent an appeal would do wrong to the one who suffers loss thereby.

The second might be that, in the case of large partnerships, there would be great inconvenience if they had a large loss one year and a large profit the next, and that it would not be fair to the heirs or to the partners.

The answer is that it is true that it might produce inconvenience and loss for somebody. But it avoids litigation, which is the worst of all evils. To put out a fire you pull down part of the house. To escape the storm you throw a part of the cargo into the sea.

Another answer might be that it is also true that inconvenience may arise from preventing appeals from arbitral awards; but is not their time what merchants value most, and to have a mind free to concentrate on their business? Litigation lasts for ever in France. It robs you of all your time and brings with it vexation and upset. It empties the pocket and brings the merchant into disrepute.

Where is the trader, however little his stock, and his hope of profit, who would be willing to leave France, and leave behind his house, his wife, his children and his business, to go off to the Indies to seek a thousand *écus* to turn into two, with all the uncertainty of finding them there? Nevertheless he would make the voyage to the Indies two or three times rather than not see the end of some miserable litigation in France, especially if he is at the *Conseil*.

The maxims of the great traders of neighbouring kingdoms are to avoid lawsuits and disputes. This is a good example. A Dutchman living in one of our towns gave his only daughter (who was very rich) in marriage to a French merchant who had expectations of a hundred thousand on succeeding his father. Nevertheless, before the marriage, the Dutch merchant obliged his future son-in-law to renounce his right to succeed to his father's estate, because it was involved in litigation. He would rather make a hundred thousand livres by his business than get ten thousand francs out of an inheritance subject to litigation.

The proverb of the Turks in the matter of litigation is very true. They say that it is better to lose early than to win late. In fact, after ten years of litigation, even if you win, will you get the tenth part of what you have had to spend and what you have lost by being forced to neglect your house and your business?

And so, we must learn from others' experience. Neighbouring peoples, who shun litigation and who follow the maxims of which we have spoken in their commercial contracts and partnerships, live in peace and quiet, doing good business everywhere in the world and getting immense wealth.

PART THREE

THE TEXT IN FACSIMILE

L'ARBITRE
CHARITABLE,

Et vn moyen facile pour accorder les Procez
promptement, sans peine, & sans frais.

L'Eglise demande à Dieu tous les jours :

—— Extingue flammas litium.

Seigneur délivrez-nous de procez, & de ces flammes
deuorantes, de haine & d'animosité qui les accompagnent.

Et pour conuier les Charitables à y travailler, le Dieu
de Paix a promis par son Prophete : *Defendez l'Op-*
pressé, Secourez la Veuve ; Aydez l'Orphelin : Et
quand vos pechez seroient rouges comme écarlatte,
ils deuiendront blancs comme neige, Isaïe Chap. 1.

DEDIÉ
A MONSEIGNEVR COLBERT,
Evêque de Luçon.

Par le Prieur DE SAINT PIERRE.

M. DC. LXVI.

A MONSEIGNEVR

COLBERT

EVESQVE DE LVÇON.

ONSEIGNEVR;

Pardon ſi ie vous dédie ce diſcours ; ie ſçau qu'on offenſe voſtre Modeſtie, quand on publie vos autres vertus; mais à qui pouuoir mieux addreſſer le moyen d'accorder les

EPISTRE.

Procez, & ces haines & inimitiez funestes qui les suiuent,
qu'à vous, MONSEIGNEVR, qui donnez tous
vos soins pour accommoder ceux de vostre Diocese ; vous
m'auez fait l'honneur de me dire vne partie de ce que vous
faites pour cela, & ce que vostre zele souhaiteroit pouuoir
faire pour acheuer vne si saincte entreprise ; vous faites
tous vos efforts enflamé de cette ardente charité des Apo-
stres, pour procurer la Paix à vostre troupeau, & en chas-
ser ce demon fatal de diuision & de discorde, qui est la
source malheureuse, & feconde de mille & mille pechez
mortels qui se commettent dans la France.

Voicy ce bon Curé, dont ie vous ay parlé que ie vous pre-
sente, qui animé du mesme zele que le vostre, a entrepris
ce grand Ouvrage de Paix, & y a reüssi ; dans sa Par-
roisse, il n'y a quasi point de procez, qui ne se termine à
l'amiable par sa charitable entremise, point de querelles
de haines & inimitiez qu'il n'accommode ; son Euesque le
seconde dignement, plusieurs Curez voisins imitent son
Exemple, & nombre d'Euesques dans la France trauail-
lent à cette saincte Moisson.

C'estoit la pratique de la Primitiue Eglise, dans
la France & ailleurs, ce l'est encores de toute l'Eglise d'O-
rient ; Sainct Paul tout diuin dans ses conseils, exhorte les
fideles à terminer leur Procez à dire d'Arbitres ; tous n

Ordonn. titr.
des Arbitr.

Roys y ont conuié leurs Sujets, par des Edicts publics
Louys XII. entr'autres surnommé le Pere du peupl
Henry IV. ce grand Prince, qui n'auoit pas moins
bonté que luy, auoit les mesmes desseins, à ce que dit

Mr de Sully.

autheur Illustre, & enfin ce sera seconder les bonnes inte
tions de nostre Incomparable Monarque, qui veut den

EPISTRE.

la Paix à ſes Suiets, & chaſſer la chicane de France, qui pour cela trauaille il y a ſi long-temps ; & auec vne application admirable, à cette grande reformation de la Iuſtice, que tout le monde ſouhaite auec tant de paſſion.

Continuez donc, MONSEIGNEVR, voſtre exemple ne ſera pas ſi-toſt ſçeu qu'il ne ſera ſuiuy de tous les Prelats du Royaume; on attend tout de vous ; dont toutes les penſées ne tendent qu'au bien de vos Brebis ; la Cour pour vous n'a point de charmes, Paris la Capitale du monde, toute belle qu'elle eſt, vous paroiſt vn exil, par ce que voſtre troupeau n'y eſt pas ; les careſſes d'vn frere ſi éleué & ſi éminent, la douce ſocieté d'vne famille ſi vnie, les brillans d'vne fortune ſi éclatante, qui pourroit ébloüir tant d'autres, n'a point d'attraits pour vous.

Cette année vous eſtiez deputé à l'Aſſemblée generale du Clergé, elle n'eſtoit pas finie, & neantmoins par ce que la feſte de Paſques approchoit, auec vne ſanté mal aſſeurée, vous fiſtes des trente licuës par iour, & à cheual, pour vous rendre dans voſtre Diocese ; C'eſt vn lieu mal ſain, vn païs de marais, qui ne peut auoir rien d'agreable, que la ſeule penſée que Dieu vous y demande, que le cher troupeau y eſt, que ſa prouidence amoureuſe a commis à voſtre conduite ; acheuez, MONSEIGNEVR, acheuez de le rendre heureux, procurez luy le plus grand de tous les biens, qui eſt la Paix, accordez ſes Procez, ſoyez ſa Mediateur Charitable, chaſſez ce demon perturbateur, l'eſprit de tempeſte & de diuiſion, vous trauaillerez pour Ciel, ou vous cherchez à faire vos Threſors, & pour recompenſe vous aurez cette Couronne d'honneur & de gloire

EPISTRE.

*solide dont parle l'Escriture, que le Dieu de paix reserue à
ceux qui trauaillent pour luy, ie vous la souhaite,*
MONSEIGNEVR, & *suis tres-parfaite-
ment,*

MONSEIGNEVR,

Vostre tres-humble, tres-obeïssant,
& tres obligé seruiteur,
LA PRIEVR DE S. PIERRE.

A NOSSEIGNEVRS

LES ARCHEVESQVES ET EVESQVES
de France.

NOSSEIGNEVRS;

Vous estes les Successeurs de ce Diuin Pasteur, Iesus-Christ sur terre, a aimé son troupeau tendrement, & quand il la fallu quitter, il n'a point eu de present plus precieux à luy faire que la Paix, *Pacem meam do vobis* : visitant ses Apostres au milieu des ioyes, & ne pensant plus qu'à cette entrée triomphante dans les Cieux, il ne leurs a parlé que de cette Paix, *Pax vobis*; & enfin toutes les fois quasi qu'il s'est apparu à ces chers Disciples, à ces Princes de l'Eglise Naissante, il ne leurs a souhaité que cette mesme Paix, comme le Comble de tous les biens, *Pax vobis, iterum pax vobis*; & en effet le repos d'esprit, & la tranquillité de l'ame, c'est le fondement solide, sur lequel s'esleuent les autres vertus Chrestiennes, car comment pouuoir entendre la douce voix de l'Agneau parmy le bruit & les tempestes des passions? Comment pouuoir ouïr vostre voix Pastorale, NOSSEIGNEVRS, parmy les foudres & les tonnerres de la colere?

Et neantmoins, c'est auiourd'huy l'estat déplorable

E

Ioan. cap. 14.

S. Luc. cap. 24.

Ioan. c. 20.

de la plus part de nos pauures François, ils se déuo-
rent en procez & en chicane, ils se déchirent par ces
haines & inimitiez irreconciliables qui les accompagnent, par ces iniures, ces vengeances, ces desespoirs,
ces sermens & blasphemes qu'ils vomissent contre leurs
Parties, & contre le Ciel qui en est innocent. Vous
pouuez, NOSSEIGNEVRS, arrester le cours de
ces torrens impetùeux de pechez & d'offences, qui
sont cause de cent & cent millions de pechez mortels
que l'on commet en France, vous pouuez, NOSSEI-
GNEVRS, destruire ces espines malheureuses, qui
empeschent cette diuine semence de produire, que
vous allez répandant tous les iours dans les ames de
vos Brebis, par la saincteté de vos mœurs, par vos
bons conseils, vos Exhortations, vos visites frequen-
tes que vous faites en personne dans vos Parroisses,
par vos sainctes Missions, par vos Conferences, & par
cent autres actions de pieté & charité consommée.

Il faut preparer la terre si on veut qu'elle produise,
c'est semer dans les grands chemins, *& sur les pierres*,
comme dit l'Euangile, que de parler des affaires du
Ciel à vn cœur assiegé de procez & animé de colere;
ce qui est de plus déplorable, nombre de ces pauures
plaideurs quittent l'vsage des Sacremens, & aduoüent
leur foiblesse, qu'ils n'en peuuent approcher, qu'ils ne
peuuent pardonner, qu'ils ont l'ame pleine de haine &
de vengeance contre leurs Parties qu'ils croyent les
autheurs de leur ruine & de leurs miseres ; les tribunaux de penitence retentissent de ces plaintes, vos
Ouuriers sacrez qui trauaillent auec tant de zele dans
vos sainctes Missions, sçauent la peine qu'ils ont à
conduire ces ames desolées.

Il est facile, NOSSEIGNEVRS, si vous l'en-

treprenez, d'étouffer ce monstre de diuision & de dif-
corde; ce bon Curé dont ie vais parler, a entrepris
cette moisson de Paix, & Dieu a beny ses desseins; il
n'y a point de Procez dans sa Parroisse qui luy resiste,
par son entremise, quasi tous s'accordent à l'amiable,
la pluspart de tous ceux qui ont procez dans le cœur
voudroient estre d'accord, du moins de deux Parties
qui se plaident, l'vne le desire, la Partie la plus foible, ou la plus sage, mais on n'ose le témoigner, de
crainte comme il arriue d'ordinaire, que Partie aduerse
ne recule, & ne se vante qu'on a peur; il ne faudroit
donc qu'vn Entremetteur charitable, sans interest, sans
passion, animé de l'esprit de Paix comme ce bon Curé,
& son Euesque qui le seconde dignement; il ne faudroit que des Entremetteurs zelez, comme l'ont esté
tous ces Prelats de la Primitiue Eglise, & ce grand
nombre que nostre France a admirez, dont parle nos
Histoires.

Le Plaideur est le Paralitique de l'Euangile, au bord
de la Piscine, qui desire la Paix, mais il n'a point
d'homme qui la luy procure, soyez-le, NOSSEI-
GNEVRS, suiuez le Conseil de l'Apostre, suiuez
l'exemple de ces grands Euesques de ce Royaume,
suiuez ceux de Sainct Ambroise entr'autres & Sainct
Augustin, le plus occupé de tous les Prelats, qui
quittoit ses estudes pour trauailler à cette Moisson,
comme la plus importante, ce dit-il de toutes ses fonctions; ses Successeurs & ces autres Euesques de l'E-
glise maintenant desolée sous l'Empire du Turc, ont
retenu cette sainte pratique, & c'est encore auiour-
d'huy vne de leurs plus charitable occupation.

En France nombre de nos Euesques y trauaillent
aussi dignement, MONSEIGNEVR de Luçon entr'autres

4

qui fe tient relegué dans vn Marais pour cela, & qui par l'amour qu'il a pour fon premier Troupeau, a re-fufé les Euefchez du Royaume, les plus beaux, les plus grands, & les plus riches.

Quand vous trauaillerez, NOSSEIGNEVRS, à ce faint Ouurage, vous feconderez l'intention de nos Roys, qui par leurs Edits & leurs Ordon-nances, ont conuié leurs Suiets à terminer leurs Pro-cez à l'amiable; fur tout vous feconderez les bons deffeins de noftre Incomparable Monarque, qui a des entrailles de mifericorde pour fes Sujets, qui tra-uaille il y a fi long-temps à la reformation de cette malheureufe chicane, & auec vne application digne des Roys, dont l'Hiftoire facrée fait les éloges.

L'Empire a befoin du Sacerdoce, pour que les loix foient bien executées, les Princes commandent au corps, mais l'Eglife perfuade les efprits, c'eft pour-quoy le Roy des Roys, Iefus-Chrift Naiffant fur ter-re, a fait alliance du fang Royal auec le Sacerdotal. Vous pouuez donc, NOSSEIGNEVRS, entre-prendre hardiment de perfuader les Peuples, d'obeïr à nos Princes, d'executer leurs Ordonnances, de ter-miner leurs Procez à l'amiable.

A Paris il s'y eft defia fait vne faincte refolution parmy nombre de perfonnes de qualité & de vertu éminente, de n'auoir plus de Procez que l'on ne con-uie fa Partie par efcrit à s'accommoder à l'amiable, & à dire d'Arbitres; par cette voye, grand nombre de Procez s'accordent tous les iours, fi cela s'eftablit par tout le Royaume, & vous le pouuez, NOSSEI-GNEVRS, par vos fainctes infpirations, le Procez, ce demon fatal de toute diuifion, fera bien-toft banny de la France.   Vous

Vous pouuez , NOSSEIGNEVRS, conuier noftre Grand Prince à executer les bonnes intentions, & les Ordonnances de fon Ayeul Henry IV. ce Prince d'eternelle memoire; il ordonna le 6. Mars l'an 1610. que dans toutes les Villes , Cours & Iurifdictions du Royaume, il y auroit des Confultans & Arbitres charitables, qui prendroient foin des Procez des Pauures gratuitement.

Cela eft eftably dans la Prouence, & ne la pû eftre par tout le refte de la France , par cette mort funefte & precipitée, qui arrefta le cours des glorieux deffeins de ce Monarque ; l'honneur & la gloire de l'execution en eft referuée à noftre Grand Roy.

Ce fera lors, que l'on dira de luy, qu'il a bafty *ce port facré*, dont parle le Prophete, ou le foible, la veufue, & l'orphelin feront en feureté ; Ce fera lors, que ces ames defolées, opprimées, & abandonnées de tout le monde, qui gemiffent à milliers par toute la France, coureront en foule à ce faint azyle: Ce fera lors que le pauure éleuera fa voix iufques au Ciel, & fera retentir les Eloges de noftre Prince, qu'on dira de luy, ce que dit l'Efcriture d'vn grand Roy, que fa *droite toute puiffante a éleué vn mur d'airain, pour la deffenfe du foible*, que la malice de la chicane, & toute la corruption des fiecles prefens & auenir ne fçauroit efbranler ; Car en effet qui fera le Roy qui l'ofera renuerfer ? ny qui font ceux qui l'oferoient demander? Nous le voyons par experience, les Iuges Confuls, azyle des Marchands, ils ont fubfifté au plus fort de la corruption.

Enfin, NOSSEIGNEVRS, vous pouuez procurer la Paix à toute la France, & la procurer à vousmefme, vous auez des Procez comme les autres, vous

Ier. c. 1.
& 15.

ne pouuez vous en exempter, vous auez le Patrimoine de Sainct Pierre à conferuer, & les droits de l'Eglife à deffendre, vous le ferez & n'aurez point de Procez fi vous voulez, par le moyen que ie diray cy-apres; vous pourrez accorder ceux qui font intentez, & ceux qui s'intenteront à l'aduenir, & neantmoins conferuer vos interefts, & au Temporel & au Spirituel : à voftre exemple les Grands Seigneurs pourront accorder les leurs, & ceux de leurs Voifins, & leurs Vaffaux; les Petits & les Egaux & generalement tout le monde pourront accorder leurs differents, *Vos eftis lux mundi*, comme dit le texte facré, & les actions des grands, comme dit auffi Platon, font efcrites *auec les rayons du soleil*, & tout le monde les imite.

Quel bon-heur pour vous, NOSSEIGNEVRS, d'eftre la caufe de la Paix generale du Royaume ? Quelle ioye pour vous d'eftre déchargez de ce pefant fardeau, du foin & de la conduite de ces malheureufes affaires de chicane ? Quelle fatisfaction pour ces grandes ames, dont l'efprit eft plus dans le Ciel que dans la terre, qui fouuent font arrachez du pied des Autels, pour courir à la follicitation d'vn miferable Procez ? ie vous fouhaite cette Paix, NOSSEIGNEVRS, & vous coniure *auec l'Apoftre* de la procurer aux autres, c'eft

NOSSEIGNEVRS,

Voftre tres humble, tres-obeïffant
& tres foûmis feruiteur,
LE PRIEVR DE S. PIERRE.

TABLE.

CHAPITRE I.

QVe tous les Procez quafi du Royaume fe peuuent terminer à l'amiable, fi NOSSEIGNEVRS les Euefques
& Mrs les Curez ont la charité d'eftre les Entremetteurs. fol. 1

TABLE

TABLE
CHAP. V.

CHAP. VI.

CHAP. VII.

CHAP. VIII.

TABLE

TABLE

CHAP. XVIII.

CHAP. XVI.

TABLE

Façon du Compromis.

FIN.

QVE TOVS LES PROCEZ
se peuuent accommoder à l'amiable, si NOSSEIGNEVRS les Euesques & Messieurs les Curez ont la Charité d'estre les Entremetteurs.

CHAPITRE PREMIER.

Qu'vn bon Curé dans nostre France le fait, & accorde ceux de sa Paroisse, & que son Euesque le seconde dignement.

ETTE Paix generale se peut establir par tout le Royaume, si NOSSEIGNEVRS les Euesques, & Messieurs leurs Curez ont la charité d'y contribuer : Il y en a qui l'ont déja entrepris auec vn succez admirable ; il n'en coustera ny peine, ny soin, ny dépense ; & la recompense sera d'vn prix, que tout l'or de la terre ne sçauroit payer, *les Thresors du Dieu de la Paix*

A

(ce dit vn ancien Pere) font referuez pour eux.

Il n'eft pas befoin de dépeindre les malheurs de
la chicane, l'Autheur illuftre de la vie de Henry
IV. M. l'Archeuefque de Paris, les a repre-
fentez en deux mots, il dit (*que les plus ftupides,
les connoiffent & les reffentent*) & en effet c'eft auiourd'huy la playe la plus déplorable de l'Eftat,
pire que la lepre des Iuifs, & les fauterelles d'E-
gypte, c'eft vn mal qui ruine le corps & l'ame, les
biens temporels & fpirituels, qui détruit les familles, qui fait mener vne vie languiffante aux por-
tes des Palais & Tribunaux, & enfin qui produit
ces haines & animofités irreconciliables, ces blaf-
phemes, defefpoirs, & ces vengeances funeftes;
qui font la fource feconde & mal-heureufe, de
cent & cent millions de pechez mortels, que les
Chreftiens auiourdhuy commettent en France,
Vous le fçauez, NOSSEIGNEVRS, du
moins ceux qui font leurs vifites en perfonne, &
qui trauaillent à ces Miffions faintes : Les Confeffeurs vous peuuent dire, la haïne des Plaideurs
les vns contre les autres, leurs defirs de vengeance?
& les fruits malheureux que cela produit, iufques à s'éloigner des Sacremens, & n'en vouloir
point approcher pendant le procez, dont nous rap-
porterons cy apres des exemples déplorables.

Vous pouuez, NOSSEIGNEVRS, &
Meſſieurs vos Curez, remedier au mal, ſi vous auez
la charité d'y trauailler, chacun endroit ſoy : Vous
le pouuez, les moyens ſont faciles que ie vais
déduire, on attend cela de voſtre zele, principalement de ceux, qui animez de ce feu ardent de
charité, donnent tous leurs ſoins à la conduite
de leur Troupeau, qui le témoignent par ces Miſ-
ſions extraordinaires, ces Conferences, ces Viſites en perſonne par tout leur Dioceſe, ces Aſſemblées & Confrairies de charité pour le ſoulagement
des pauures qu'on a eſtabli quaſi par tout, & enfin
par cent autres actions de pieté Chreſtienne, qui
les fait cherir, aimer & honorer de tout le monde.

Que ſera-ce s'ils entreprennent la gueriſon de
cette playe mal-heureuſe, que la chicane fait
dans le corps & l'ame du Chreſtien, elle dépoüille
le corps de ſes biens, le rend nud & miſerable, l'a-
me eſt dépoüillée de ſes vertus, de cét amour &
amitié qu'vn Chreſtien doit auoir pour ſon prochain, qui eſt le Plaideur qui aime ſa partie ?

Vn Eueſque, & vn Curé, vn Predicateur, ces
Miſſionnaires zelez, apres vn Aduent, ou vn Ca-
reſme, ou vne Miſſion extraordinaire, ne ſe trou-
ueroient-ils pas bien heureux, & leur moiſſon
bien ample, s'ils auoient accordé vne douzaine de

Procez, & de querelles, & par le moyen que ie
propoferay, ils en accorderont des milliers, & à
l'aduenir les empêcheront quafi tous ; donneront
la Paix à leur Troupeau, & les Euefques fur tout
& les Curez en ioüiront eux-mefmes, pourront
viure fans Procez, & neantmoins conferuer leurs
interefts, fans rien perdre ny relafcher de leurs
droits fpirituels, & temporels.

.Tout cela fe peut fans peine, & fans frais, &
fans rien faire de nouueau, dont perfonne fe puiffe plaindre ; on ne fera que fuiure la pratique de la
primitiue Eglife, de noftre France, & d'ailleurs qui
eft venuë iufques à nous. Celle que l'Eglife d'Oriët
pratique encore aujourd'huy, celle que Saint Paul
a confeillée, & que Iefus-Chrift mefme a commandé, enfin ce que les Roys ont ordonné à leurs
peuples, par leurs Edits, & ce que des Euefques
& des Curez pratiquent encore dans la France,
auec vn fuccez merueilleux.

Et pour faire voir que ç'a efté la pratique de la
primitiue Eglife parmi nous, & qu'il s'eft trouué
dans tous les fiecles, mefme dedans le noftre, de
grands Prelats que l'Eglife a canonizé, qui fe
font addonnés à ces Oeuures de Charité, à accorder les Procez & differends de leur Troupeau, il
eft bon de rapporter icy le nom de quelques-vns
de

de ces dignes Euesques, dont nos histoires font mention.

Ils nous parlent de plusieurs, mais entr'autres, de Saint Marcel, & Saint Landry, Euesques de Paris.

De Saint Martin & S. Gatien Euesques de Tours, *Surius.*

S. Germain Euesque d'Auxere.

S. Oüen Euesque de Roüen. *S. Greg. de Tours.*

S. Euuerte Euesque d'Orleans.

Monsieur de Sale le conseille partout, S. Louis *Mrs Ste Marthe.* le plus grand de nos Roys l'a dignement pratiqué, il se dépoüilloit de l'authorité Souueraine, pour prendre la qualité de mediateur charitable parmi ses suiets.

Enfin Saint Yues a esté Canonizé, & tous les Iuges de ce Royaume, l'ont pris pour leur Patron ; c'estoit vn Curé de nostre France, de l'Euesché de Treguier en Bretagne, il estoit tout de feu & de zele pour ses Parroissiens, il donnoit tout son temps, pour accorder leurs Procez, & differends ; Son Euesque qui estoit vn Saint Prelat, animé du mesme esprit que luy, pour donner vne carriere plus ample à sa charité, il le fit son Iuge, ce fut lors qu'il chassa du Diocese tous les Procez & toutes les querelles.

B

L'action la plus éclatante de sa vie, & qui a
merité des Autels, elle est dépeinte par toute la
France ; on le represente assis dans vn Tribunal
de Paix, qui accorde vn pauure gueux, couuert
de haillons, auec vn homme riche ; on ne le represente pas, tenant ses Audiances, n'y donnant
des Iugemens, c'est à dire que l'Arbitrage & l'accord, est quelque chose de plus excellent, que
les Arrests & les Sentences ; Et en effet nous le
deuons croire, puisque les Iuges mesme ont choisi & fait dépeindre ce Throsne d'Arbitrage, comme l'action la plus glorieuse d'vne vie si sainte,
c'est ce qui luy a fait meriter les vœux & les prie-
res des pauures Plaideurs, & de tous les peuples;
Voila donc l'Arbitrage sanctifié, les Mediateurs
charitables, & tous ceux qui s'en meslent, voila vn exemple illustre à tous les bons Curés, nostre saint a esté Curé comme eux, Voila vn
exemple à tous les grands Euesques, le sien la
aydé, & la dignement secondé ; & enfin ce doit
estre l'exemple & le Patron de tous les bons Iuges, puis qu'ils l'ont choisi pour cela.

Et pour faire voir qu'il est facile de l'imiter,
& qu'on peut accorder à l'amiable tous les Procez quasi du Royaume en matiere Ciuile & en
matiere Criminelle, ou n'escheoit punition cor-
porelle, il faut supposer comme il est vray.

Premierement, que tous les Plaideurs quaſi, dedans le cœur, voudroient eſtre d'accord, ſi vous exceptez quelque furieux, auare ou vindicatif, qui oppriment le foible, la veufue, & l'orphelin.

Tous les Plaideurs quaſi vou-droiẗ eſtre d'accord.

Du moins de deux parties qui ſe plaident, vne voudroit accord, la plus foible, ou la plus ſage, mais on n'oſe le demander, de crainte que cela ne l'empeſche, car en effet, la pluſpart du temps, partie aduerſe recule, ſe vante qu'on a peur, dit qu'il faut pouſſer à bout, & le fait, les Miniſtres de chicane ſont d'ordinaire de cét aduis, & les y conuient.

De deux qui plaident vn du moins veut accord, le plus foible, ou le plus ſage.

De deux parties donc qui ſe plaident, vne ſouhaite l'accord, mais elle n'a point d'Entremetteur, voila l'homme de bien au bord de la Piſcine, qui ſouhaite la Paix, qui ſouhaite l'accord, mais il n'a point d'homme qui s'en meſle (*non habet hominem*) qui l'aide, qui l'aſſiſte, qui ſerue d'Entremetteur; s'il y en auoit vn, pouſſé de l'eſprit de Dieu, ſans intereſt & reconnu pour tel, perſonne quaſi ne le refuſeroit; vn bon Curé le pratique dans vn des bouts du Royaume, il n'y a point de Procez, qui luy échappe, & qu'il n'accorde, ſa vocation a eſté extraordinaire, il auoit vn Procez grand & animé, contre les Preſtres de ſa Parroiſſe, qui luy donnoit bien de la peine, il fut conſeillé de leur demander accord, & les

fommer de conuenir d'Arbitres ; il le fit & ils y
confentirent auec ioye , & leur Procez qui euſt
duré longues années , fut terminé ſur le champ,
& auec ſatisfaction de toutes les Parties.

En reconnoiſſance d'vne telle grace, il promit
à Dieu , & à celuy qui l'auoit conſeillé , de faire
à l'aduenir tous ſes efforts, pour accorder les Procez des autres, principalement ceux de ſa Parroiſſe
& pour y paruenir.

Q'il y a
vn Curé
qui ac-
corde tous
les Procez
de ſa Par-
roiſſe, & ſa
façon.Dés qu'il en ſçait vn , du moins à l'approche
des grandes Feſtes, il s'en va chez ſon Paroiſſien,
luy dit en ſubſtance bonnement & ſimplement,
qu'il a ſçeu qu'il a Procez auec vn tel, qu'il ne
s'eſtonne pas de voir des Procez, qu'il faut conſeruer le ſien, mais qu'vn Chreſtien, doit ſouhaiter de le pouuoir faire s'il pouuoit, ſans eſtre obligé de plaider, parce qu'il eſt bien à craindre que
Dieu n'y ſoit offenſé , qu'il eſt quaſi impoſſible,
qu'on ne haïſſe ſa partie, qu'on ne luy ſouhaite du
mal, qu'on ne ſe ré;oüiſſe s'il luy arriue quelque
aduerſité, & partant qu'on doit deſirer de pouuoir conſeruer ſon bien, ſans eſtre obligé d'auoir
Procez, dont les ſuites ſont ſi malheureuſes & ſi
ennemies de l'Eſprit du Chriſtianiſme : le Plaideur
le plus outré, répond qu'il le ſouhaite , il en fait
ſemblant, du moins en apparence.

Le

Le bòn Curé continuë, dit qu'il l'a toûjours creu, mais qu'il faut en donner des marques, que par ce moyen il fermera la bouche à ceux qui pourroient dire le contraire, que la voye la plus courte la plus aisée, & la moins courageuse pour terminer les Procez, est l'accord & l'Arbitrage, & luy demande s'il ne veut pas bien y consentir, si sa partie y consent?

Le plaideur qui est sage, répond d'abord qu'il le souhaite, & qu'il y consent, là dessus ce bon Curé luy fait signer vn compromis, dont sera parlé cy aprés, & qui est raporté à la fin de ce liure: il s'en va ensuitte chez l'autre partie; si elle est de sa Paroisse, luy represente en substance ce qui est dit cy-dessus, sans neantmoins luy dire d'abord auoir parlé à sa partie, ny qu'elle ait signé le compromis, il pourroit en tirer auantage, croire qu'on le craint, & faire le renchery, on le voit par experience, il faut vser d'vn saint artifice, pour leur faire du bien malgré eux; si les deux parties consentent de s'accommoder, le bon Curé leur fait signer le compromis, & le met entre les mains des Arbitres nommez. Ie diray cy apres comme on doit choisir les Arbitres, & le tiers, si on n'en conuient à l'amiable, les difficultez qui peuuent naistre, & les remedes.

C

Si l'vne des parties n'eft pas de fa paroiffe, il en écrit à fon Curé, & fait par fon Miniftere ce qu'il feroit luy mefme, fi elle en eftoit.

Mais fi l'vne des parties confent de s'accommoder, & que l'autre le refufe, voicy ce qu'il fait; premierement celuy qui refufe, fut-il le plus méchant & le plus malin de tous les Chicaneurs, il ne dira iamais à fon Curé qu'il ne veut point d'accord, qu'il veut fe vanger, ou deuorer le foible, perfonne ne veut auoir vn témoin public de fa malice, ny fon pafteur pour témoin de fon iniquité.

Il dira donc qu'il fouhaite la paix, mais il cherchera des efloignemens, que l'affaire n'eft pas en eftat de pouuoir eftre accommodée, qu'il n'a pas fes papiers, qu'ils font produits, qu'il faut auoir vn Iugement par les formes, qu'il y a des Mineurs, ou bien, qu'il a des Conforts, qu'il fçaura leurs aduis, ou autres pretextes femblables.

Ce que dit le Curé à ceux qui ne veulent pas s'accommoder. Si les pretextes font vifiblement faux, le bon Curé leur dit bonnement, & fans emportement, mais neantmoins auec force & vigueur, que le Dieu des Iuftes, protege les foibles, & punit le méchant, qu'il fe rit du deffein de l'auare, qu'il renuerfe fes projets, qu'il a conferué *la vigne de Nabot*, malgré tous les efforts d'vne puiffance iniuſte, & enfin que ce bras vangeur terraſſe les plus forts, qu'il a défait autrefois ſes ennemis auec vne armée de moucherons, qu'il ne faut pour renuerſer vne famille, qu'eſtre attaqué par vn plus grand, qu'il ne faut qu'vne perte de biens, la mort d'vn pere ou d'vne mere, ou celle d'vn enfant, & cent autres malheurs qui arriuent tous les iours ; & pour concluſion que c'eſt effacer l'image viuante de la Iuſtice Diuine, que la nature a graué dans le cœur de tous les hommes ; (*ne fais à autruy ce que tu voudrois ne t'eſtre pas fait :*) que c'eſt renoncer au Chriſtianiſme, & à la loy la plus importante que I. C. nous aye donnée, & monſtrée par ſon Exemple (*aymés voſtre prochain comme vous meſme*) *& faites du bien à vos ennemis :* Et enfin que c'eſt demander ſa condemnation toutes les fois que l'on prononce les paroles de cette Oraiſon Diuine (*pardonnez nous nos offences, comme nous pardonnons à ceux qui nous ont offenſé.*

s. Math. cap. 5.

Il ne s'eſt point trouué de Plaideur, quelque animé qu'il fut (comme nous auons dit) qui aye oſé dire à ce bon Curé, qu'il ne vouloit point d'accord, mais il cherche diuers pretextes pour éloigner : à cela le bon Curé répond encore, qu'on peut tromper les hommes, mais qu'on ne peut pas tromper Dieu, qu'il ſonde le fonds des cœurs (*ſcrutans renes & corda*) que s'il eſt vray que l'on

Il n'y a point de Plaideur qui oſe dire à ſon Paſteur ne vouloir point d'accord.

souhaite la Paix, comme on le témoigne; qu'on aye à y trauailler en esprit de Charité, pour oster les obstacles qui l'empeschent, & l'auertir quand il en sera temps, & qu'il y contribuëra auec ioye comme bon Pasteur, & amy commun.

Si cela tarde aux rencontres, il dit encore quelque petit mot ; & aux grandes Festes interpose leurs amis : si le mary fait le mauuais, on s'adresse à la femme, si la femme est animée, on s'adresse au mary, il prend son tour ; enfin ce bon Curé m'a dit, qu'il n'y a quasi point de Procez qui luy resiste vn an, & qu'il n'accorde : Sous ce temps là il n'y a guiere de famille où il n'arriue quelque affliction ; perte de biens, Procez, ou querelle auec plus puissant que soy, mort ou maladie d'vn amy, ou de quelqu'vn de la famille, negligence ou malice des gens d'affaires, Aduocats ou Procureurs; on est touché, on r'entre en soy, *Vexatio dabit intellectum*, comme dit le Prophete, on sent la main de Dieu qui s'appesantit sur nous, on a recours au Ciel, & à son Curé, on luy compte sa douleur, on le prie de renoüer l'accommodement, il le fait lors facilement & sans peine.

L'affliction nous rend sage.
Isaie c. 28.

S'il y a Procez ou querelle entre personnes si éminentes ou si animées, que la voix du Curé
n'y

n'y ſoit pas écoutée , il écrit à ſon Eueſque , qui
s'entremet & le ſeconde, auec vne charité digne
du zele de ces premiers Paſteurs de l'Egliſe naiſ-
ſante , ce bon Eueſque leur écrit , leur enuoye,
ou leur parle.

Si le Curé n'eſt pas écouté, l'E-ueſque le ſeconde.

CHAPITRE II.

*De la maniere que ce bon Curé accorde les querelles,
les haïnes , & inimitiez.*

POVR les querelles, il les accorde quaſi toutes , & facilement, paſſé la premiere chaleur,
quaſi tous voudroient eſtre d'accord ; il y a de la
peine à haïr , à médire , à chercher les occaſions
de ſe venger, & ſoûuent grande dépenſe & grands
frais , principalement quand il faut faire amas
d'amis , s'attrouper , &c.

Si les querelles donc ſont de conſequence , il
s'y prend comme il fait aux Procez , il leur fait
conuenir d'amis. Mais pour les autres qui n'ont
pas grand fondement , il les accommode luy-
meſme , on a toute creance en luy, depuis qu'il
s'eſt adonné à ces actions de charité ; auparauant
il ne paſſoit que pour vn homme du commun.

Pour les querelles de conſe-quence fais nommer Arbitres.

Pour les autres, les accommo-de luy-mé-me.

Pour les haïnes & inimitiez , ou plûtoft les froideurs entre parens , voifins , & autres , dont la caufe eft fouuent legere , & neantmoins qui font les commencemens de ces haïnes irreconciliables , de ces grands Procez & querelles , dont les fuittes font dangereufes ; ce bon Curé y a trouué remede , il va chez eux , dit qu'il a fceu leurs froideurs , qu'il faut fe reconcilier , qu'on eft Chreftien; comment approcher des Sacremens? qu'on ne voudroit pas fe trouuer à la Nopce auec vn habit où il y auroit la moindre tache; quand il feroit vray qu'il n'y auroit point de haïne, qu'il y a toufiours mauuais exemple ; & qu'enfin le Dieu de PAIX commande , quand on feroit aux pieds des Autels , qu'on ait *à quitter fon Offran-de* , & s'aller reconcilier auec fon frere.

Toutes ces querelles donc les inimitiés & froideurs fans fondement , dont le nombre eft grand , fe diffipent à la premiere approche de ce bon Curé , tous répondent apres auoir vn peu plaidé leur Caufe , qu'ils n'ont aucune haïne, qu'ils font tous prefts de fe voir & embraffer. Le lieu ordinaire eft chez luy , fa maifon eft , *l'Au-tel viuant* , de paix & de concorde.

Ces ennemis reconciliez fe voyent enfuite, fe

vifitent & fe rendent feruice ; eela conuie tous les autres à fuiure ce bon exemple.

Il eft à remarquer que la premiere qualité ne-ceffaire pour accorder les Procez & querelles, c'eft de gagner creance fur l'efprit de ceux à qui on parle ; ce que ce bon Curé fait dignement , il écoute leurs plaintes auec beaucoup de patience, compatit à leur foibleffe , prend part à leur dou-leur , & par ce moyen gagne l'efprit, & en fui-te difpofe du cœur.

Pour ac-corder les Procez & querelles, la patience eft necef-faire, & la charité.

Ce que fait ce bon Curé, tous les autres le peuuent faire, il ne faut pas grande capacité pour cela , ny grande éloquence ; vn peu de patience, & beaucoup de charité , Dieu fuppléra au refte; on·le voit par experience , ce ne font pas les Pa-fteurs les plus habiles & les plus éloquens , qui font toufiours le plus de fruit ; il fe fert fouuent de moyens qui paroiffent foibles (*de la bouche des enfans* , ce dit le Prophete, *il tire fes loüänges*) Moyfe faifoit des prodiges, ces miracles dignes de la grandeur du bras du Tout-puiffant, & neantmoins *fa bouche begayante* ne.les pouuoit ex-pliquer , & ainfi que perfonne ne fe défie de fes forces , Dieu donne des paroles à qui a de bon-nes intentions , & puis nous dirons cy-apres, comme les Curez pourront trouuer de l'ayde, &

Ce que fait vn bon Curé, tous les autres le peuuent faire.

Pfal. 8.

des gens qui les foulageront *dans cette moiſſon de paix & de concorde.*

CHAPITRE III.

Si dans toutes les Parroiſſes du Royaume on imite ce bon Curé & ſon Eueſque , quaſi plus de Procez ny de querelles en France.

SI l'ordre dont nous venons de parler eſtoit eſtably dans toutes les Parroiſſes du Royaume , quaſi point de Procez qui ne ſe terminaſt à l'amiable , & ces haïnes & animoſitez mal-heureuſes qui les accompagnent ; la pluſpart de tous ceux qui ſe plaident , comme nous auons dit, voudroient eſtre d'accord ; il ne manque qu'vn mediateur Charitable , on le voit par l'experience de ce bon Curé ; d'autres à ſon exemple ont commencé à en faire autant , & reüſſiſſent auec ſuccés plus ou moins , à proportion de la Charité qui les anime.

Pluſieurs Eueſques ont auſſi commencé à eſtablir la meſme pratique dans leurs Dioceſes , à l'exemple de ce grand nombre de ſaints Prelats de noſtre France, dont nous auons parlé cy-deuant, ils ont bien veu que le plus grand obſtacle à leurs

ſaintes

faintes entreprifes, eftoit la diuifion de leur Troupeau, leurs Brebis animées par cét efprit de chicane, ne veulent pas feulement fe rencontrer en-
femble, quoy qu'il foit queftion d'œuure de pieté, d'Hofpitaux ou autres entreprifes, à quoy ils
ont inclination ; & quoy que chacun en particulier voudroit y contribuer, neantmoins s'il y
a Procez, on trauerfera les deffeins de celuy qui
s'en mefle. Cent exemples de cela, fur tout dans
les petites Villes.

Il faut donc faire tarir cette fource funefte de
diuifion, de haïne & d'animofité ; les Euefques
y font obligez, ils font les Succeffeurs de Iefus-
Chrift fur terre ; ce diuin Pafteur n'a rien tant recommandé que la paix (*pacem meam do vobis, pa-*   Ioan.1.14.
cem meam relinquo vobis) & apres luy le plus ancien de fes Difciples n'a prefché que cette paix,
cette vnion & concorde, qui doit eftre entre les
Chreftiens (*Diligamus alter vtrum* ;) & enfin l'E-   2. Ioan.
glife, fuiuant les fentimens de fon Efpoux, y   cap.5.
conuie fes Enfans, & chante tous les iours comme nous auons dit, *Extingue flammas litium.*

Et ainfi les Euefques qui font les Succeffeurs   *Les Brebis*
de ce Pafteur diuin & pacifique, ne peuuent   *par là font*
  denenus
mieux imiter fon exemple, qu'en procurant la   *des Loups.*
paix à leur Troupeau ; il eft déchiré par les haï-

Tout le monde a Procez, qui n'en veut point faire on luy en fait.

nes & inimitiez, que les Procez y engendre, leurs Brebis font deuenuës des Loups qui fe deuorent en chicane, perfonne ne peut plus s'en exempter, les gens de bien qui ne veulent attaquer perfonne, font attaquez ; on efpere que la crainte, ou l'enuie de fe redimer de vexation, leur fera confentir les demandes les plus iniuftes.

Le Procez empefche le feruice Diuin.

Le Preftre, le Religieux, le Curé, les Euefques mefmes font tirés du pied des Autels ; perfonne n'eft exempt, il faut tout quitter, iufques aux Sacrifices, pour courir à la follicitation d'vn miferable Procez.

Empefche la Noblef-fe d'aller aux Armées. Empefche & diuertit le Marchand, & le Laboureur.

La Nobleffe ne peut plus feruir le Roy dans les Armées, le Marchand vacquera fon Commerce ; il faut que le Laboureur quitte la culture de la terre, pour la fuite d'vn mal-heureux Procez ; enfin les parens, les voifins, les freres & les fœurs s'entre-deuorent ; les enfans mefme plaident pere & mere, les Tribunaux font pleins de tels Procez ; & pour comble de mal-heur, ils font longs, lents, & ruineux, & d'ordinaire ne finiffent qu'auec le bien ou la vie.

Le plus dé-plorable, font les haines & vengean-ces.

Ce qui eft de plus déplorable, c'eft la haïne & les inimitiez irreconciliables de ceux qui fe plaident ; & en effet, comment eft-ce qu'vn

pauure Plaideur pourra ne haïr par sa Partie qui
le persecute, qui le ruïne, & sous le nom de qui
on luy chante tous les iours cent iniures, dans
les écrits & Plaidoyers ? & à qui on suppose
cent faux faits ? si la crainte de Dieu nous fait
resister à la premiere attaque de ces iniures, on
est ébranlé à la seconde, & c'est vn miracle si on
ne succombe pas à la troisiéme ; les iniures de
(*Semei*) furent des fléches acerées qui percerent Reg. 5.
le cœur du pauure Dauid.

De dire que l'on peut plaider sans en venir à *Qu'à moins*
ces extremités, il est vray que Dieu a vne fois *d'vn mi-*
conserué trois Enfans dans vne fournaise arden- *racle, on*
ne peut
te ; mais ces miracles sont aussi rares que surpre- *qu'on ne*
nans, & c'est tenter la misericorde de Dieu que *baisse sa*
de s'y attendre ; il faut s'éloigner du mal, & tas- *Partie.*
cher d'en détruire la cause.

On voit que ceux qui plaident de meilleur foy, *Les Aduo-*
qui au commencement ne sont portés d'aucune *cats &*
Procureurs,
haïne, ny animosité ; il n'est pas en leur pou- *malgré les*
uoir d'empescher leurs Aduocats & Procureurs *Parties, di-*
d'vser de certains termes iniurieux & offençans, *sent des*
iniures.
& se seruir de certaines ruses, qu'ils disent estre
pour le bien de la Cause ; là dessus on s'anime,
on répond aux iniures ; & enfin on vient à ces
haïnes & inimitiez funestes & irreconciliables.

Comment eft-ce que le Dieu de Paix pourra
habiter dans ces cœurs animez de vengeance?
Comment eft-ce que vos Brebis (NOSSEI-
GNEVRS) pourront oüir voftre voix Pafto-
rale, & eftre troublés & tranfportés de colere ? Comment eft-ce que cette diuine femence
pourra germer dans les ames; que tant de Prelats
zelés (vont répandans tous les iours) par cent
actions de pieté & charité confommée. Il faut
donc arracher les Chardons, auant que de pouuoir efperer que la vigne fructifie, il faut aller à
la caufe du mal, il faut couper ces épines auant
de pouuoir efperer que voftre diuine femence pro-
duife des fruits digne de voftre zele.

Vous le pouuez, NOSSSEIGNEVRS,
fans peine & fans frais, vos Brebis vous en prient,
& vous tendent les bras ; ils fouhaitent tous de
n'auoir point de Procez, du moins, comme nous
auons dit, de deux qui fe plaident, vn voudroit
eftre d'accord, le plus foible ou le plus fage ; pour
les accorder, il ne leur faut donc qu'vn Mediateur Charitable ; foyez-le (NOSSEIGNEVRS)
faites que Mrs vos Curez le foient auffi, vous l'e-
ftes dé-ja entre Dieu & fon Peuple ; ces malheureux Procez empefchent maintenant les François de rendre à fa Grandeur les adorations qui
luy font deus : oftez ces obftacles, la chofe n'eft
plus

plus difficile , ce bon Curé a reüſſi , tous les autres en peuuent faire autant, ſes voiſins ont commencé , & reüſſiſſent. Dans Paris meſme il y a M. Pouſſé.
vn Curé illuſtre par ſa doctrine , ſa pieté & ſon zele qui l'a entrepris, & Dieu benit viſiblement ſon
ouurage ; nombre de nos Eueſques y trauaillent,
& nombre y ont trauaillé dans tous les ſiecles.
Le Demon perturbateur ne ſçauroit reſiſter à
leurs armes ; nous en auons vn bel exemple,
d'vn Eueſque de noſtre France , qui eſt encore
viuant , dont la modeſtie m'empeſche de dire le
nom. Prelat digne du ſiecle de ſaint Paul ; il al- *Exemple*
la trouuer vn Gentil-homme qui auoit vn Pro- *heroique de*
cez & vne querelle animée contre ſon voiſin , il *la patience*
le prie de s'accommoder , & demande ſa parole; *& humili-*
ce Gentil-homme la luy refuſe , auec ſermens & *ſé a'vn*
blaſphêmes qu'il s'en vangeroit ; ce bon Prelat *Eueſque,*
tout tranſporté de zele , luy proteſta qu'il de- *pour accor-*
meureroit à ſa porte , iuſques à ce que Dieu euſt *der vn Pro-*
touché ſon cœur ; & en effet, il y paſſa vne par- *cez, &*
tie de la nuit , qu'il pleuuoit à torrens ; ce Gen- *querelles*
til-homme reuenu de ſa fureur , enuoye à la por- *animée.*
te , voir ſi ce Prelat y auoit reſté , on l'y trouua;
alors ce furieux entierement gagné par vn tel
exemple de charité , court à luy les larmes aux
yeux , ſe iette à ſes genoux , luy crie mercy , dit
qu'il eſt tout preſt d'embraſſer ſon ennemy , &
d'obeïr à tous les commandemens du ſaint Eueſque. **F**

Il ne faudra pas , NOSSEIGNEVRS,
de ces efforts , ny de ces actions heroïques pour
accorder chaque Procez ; bien loin de cela , pour
les terminer quafi tous, il ne faudra ny peine, ny
grand foin, imiter feulement ce bon Curé & fon
Euefque qui reüffiffent ; pour cela , fi vous le iugez à propos, affemblez M^{rs} vos Curez en forme
de Synode ; remonftrez leur combien cette moiffon de Paix eft grande & glorieufe , combien on
contribuëra au feruicę de Dieu , au falut du prochain , & au fien particulier ; que ce fera fecon-
der les bonnes intentions de noftre Prince , qui
fouhaitte d'abolir la chicane , & qui trauaille à
cette reformation il y a fi long-temps ; qu'outre

Biens &
honneurs
aux Curez
qui accor-
deront les
Procez.

cela, honneur, gloire & biens temporels en viendront aux Curez , on fçait gré , & on a recon-
noiffance pour fon bien faicteur : les Arbitres &
Mediateurs font refpectés , feruis & honorés , &
pour mieux leur faire conceuoir l'ordre qu'ils auront à tenir , leur donner vn autant de ce liuret,
ou en faire vn meilleur (il ne fera pas difficile)
cela leur apprendra , & leur infpirera vne fainte
methode pour faire ces actions de Charité; qu'on
le faffe en efprit de foûmiffion & détachement,
& Dieu benira l'ouurage ; ie parle dans cét efprit , ie fçay que mes lumieres font foibles, mais
la connoiffance & l'experience malheureufe que
i'ay des miferes de ceux qui plaident , m'ont ou-
uert la bouche.

Outre cela, vous pouuez, NOSSEIGNEVRS, perfuader fortement par les Confeffeurs & Predicateurs, qu'vn Chreftien eft obligé de fouhaiter & trauailler pour accorder ces Procez à l'amiable, puis qu'il luy eft commandé d'aimer fon prochain, à peine de damnation eternelle ; & qu'il eft comme impoffible de fe pouuoir defendre de haïr ceux auec qui on a Procez, que l'on croit nous perfecuter & ruiner ; car de dire que l'on plaidera fans haïr fa Partie, ny fans rien dire qui bleffe la Charité, c'eft vouloir faire croi-re qu'au milieu des flammes on pourra fe garentir de la chaleur du feu ; qu'on pourra fouffrir les iniures & la ruine de fes biens, fans en auoir de la douleur & du reffentiment, contre ceux que l'on croira en eftre les autheurs, en voicy vn bel exemple. *Qu'on ne peut refifter aux iniures dont la chicane eft pleine.*

Pendant qu'on faifoit le Procez à Iefus-Chrift, l'innocence mefme, les iniures d'vne fimple Seruante firent trébucher faint Pierre, il renia fon cher Maiftre, *Il iura & blafphema* ; & apres vn tel exemple, apres la cheute du premier des Apoftres, inftruit dans l'Efcole de la patience mefme, vn Chreftien foible & tiede, dira qu'il pourra fouffrir fans s'émouuoir, les iniures & les reproches fauffes & calomnieufes, dont la chicane eft pleine ? C'eft tenter Dieu, que de s'expofer à vn tel peril ; s'il faut vn miracle de fa Toute- *Que faint Pierre y a fuccombé.*

puiffance pour nous en garentir, c'eft vouloir marcher fur les eaux, parce que l'Apoftre bien aimé y a marché vne fois : la Sageffe Diuine nous a dit (aydez vous, & ie vous aideray) efloignés vous du mal, & ie vous garentiray, & au contraire elle vous menace que qui s'expofera au peril y perira, & ainfi c'eft offencer Dieu mortellement, que de s'expofer à vn danger euident de l'offencer, *qui amat periculum in illo peribit.*

Eccl. cap.3.

Mais quand on feroit affeuré de fes forces, n'eftce pas commettre le peché que d'eftre la caufe que d'autres le commettent, fi vous pouuez fouffrir la perte de vos biens, & les iniures, fans vous émouuoir, & fans murmurer, eftes vous affeuré que voftre partie le pourra faire ; & fi elle ne le fait pas, n'eftes-vous pas la caufe de fon peché & de fon crime ; (*ab alienis parce feruo tuo*) n'eft-ce pas des crimes des autres, & de ceux dont il eft la caufe, dont ce Grand Roy aduoüe eftre coupable, & dont il demande pardon.

Pfal. 18.

Si ces veritéz eftoient fortement imprimées dans le cœur de nos pauures François, on n'auroit pas de peine à leur perfuader, qu'vn Chreftien doit chercher tous les moyens pour terminer à l'amiable fes Procez & differens ; mais fur tout quand il en eft requis, que fa partie le demande,

il

il ne peut le refufer, fans offence.

C'eſt ce qui a fait que depuis peu dans Paris des perſonnes de toutes qualités, des ames hautes & eſleuées, ont introduit cette ſainte pratique, dont nous auons parlé, de n'auoir plus de Procez qu'ils ne faſſent offre à leur partie, & par écrit, de les terminer à l'amiable & à dire d'Arbitres. Nous dirons à la fin de ce liuret, en quels termes ces offres doiuent eſtre conceües, & quelle formalité il faut obſeruer pour cela; ſuffit de dire maintenant que cette pratique chreſtienne accorde vn grand nombre de Procez, & que ſi elle eſt ſuiuie par tous les gens de bien du Royaume, ce ſera l'eſtoille qui deuance le Soleil, & le Precurſeur des doux fruiĉts de la reformation de noſtre Prince, qui nous promet la deſtruĉtion de ce demon fatal de Chicane.

Apres que, NOSSEIGNEVRS, les Eueſques auront perſuadé les peuples, qu'ils doiuent ſouhaiter & trauailler à accorder leurs differens, ils doiuent encore perſuader leurs Curés, & ſe perſuader eux-meſmes, qu'ils ſont obligés en conſcience à trauailler auſſi à ce bon ouurage; qu'ils doiuent défricher la vigne, & arracher les épines qui la ſuffoquent, que le Diuin Paſteur leur a dit (*Paſce oues meas*) paiſſez mon troupeau;

que ce n'eſt pas le paiſtre, que de laiſſer le loup au milieu des brebis, de les abandonner à ce de-mon furieux & rugiſſant, à cét éſprit de tempeſte & de Chicane, qui ruine le corps, l'eſprit & l'a-me de ce troupeau que Dieu a commis à voſtre conduite.

Et vous, NOSSEIGNEVRS, & M. vos Curés, vous receuez par aduance, pour recom-penſe de ces ſoins, les richeſſes, les honneurs, les reſpeᶜts, que tous les peuples vous rendent, meſ-me les teſtes Couronnées, & c'eſt pour vous que le Ciel reſerue encore ces recompenſes eternelles, que Dieu promet par ſon Prophete à ceux qui ſecourent l'oppreſſé, la veufue & l'orphelin.

C'eſt vn re-
ché ce dit
S.Paul a'a-
uoir Procez
ſeulement.

Saint Paul tout Diuin dans ſes penſées, tout de feu & de zele pour le prochain, nous enſeigne en cette matiere, ce que nous deuons faire, n'eſt-il pas honteux (ce dit il) de voir des Chreſtiens,

S Paul.
2.c. cap. 6.

auoir des Procez enſemble (*iam quidem omnino delictum eſt in vobis, quod iudicia habetis inter vos*): Donc ſi on ne peut s'empêcher d'en auoir, il faut du moins les accorder promptement, & les ter-miner à l'amiable.

Apprenez leur ce langage, NOSSEIGNEVRS, inſpirés leur ces ſentimens, apres cela ils con-uiendront facilement d'Arbitres, ſi vous auez

la bonté & M^{rs}. vos Curés d'eſtre les Mediateurs;
on en a ainſi vſé dans toute la primitiue Egliſe;
Vous le ſçauez, NOSSEIGNEVRS , & comme
ces grands Docteurs & ces grands Eueſques, &
de noſtre France, & d'ailleurs, ont tout quitté pour
cela.

Qu'on ne craigne pas qu'on y trouue à redire,
les Roys, comme nous auons dit, ont conuié tous
leurs ſujets à terminer leur Procez à l'amiable, &
à dire d'Arbitres, recours à l'Ordonnance, & c'eſ-
ſtoit l'vn des deſſeins de Henry IV. à ce que dit
M. de Sully , d'abolir la Chicane par cette meſme
voye.

Toutes les coûtumes quaſi de nos prouinces
y conuient auſſi les peuples, ſur tout les parens,
parce que diſent nos Loix, qu'ils ſont de meſme
ſang ; les Chreſtiens ne ſont-ils pas tous de meſme ſang ? ne ſont ils pas tous racheptez du ſang
l'Agneau immolé pour eux ? tous les François ne
ſont ils pas de meſme famille ? tous enfans du
meſme Roy & du meſme Prince, qui doiuent
tous trauailler également dans leur condition,
pour le bien de l'Eſtat, & le repos des Peuples.

Les Eſtats Generaux d'Orleans ayans ces meſmes penſées, demanderent au Roy Charles IX.
pour empêcher la ruine du Commerce dans la
France, qu'il luy plût de donner des Arbitres aux

Marchands, qui font leurs Iuges Confuls; La conferuation des autres ordres du Royaume , n'eft-
elle pas d'auffi grande confequence à l'Eftat , &
au Prince , que celle des Marchands? l'Eglife, la
Nobleffe , & fur tout les payfans & laboureurs
de terre fource de toutes les richeffes? ne doiuent
ils pas eftre conferuez, enfin l'an 1560. à la Re-
quefte defdits Eftats Generaux, Charles IX. donna des Arbitres forcés aux Marchands, qui font
leurs Iuges Confuls, & cela les a conferué autant
qu'ils l'ont pût eftre pendant la corruption, tous
les Royaumes voifins fe feruent de ce remede,
toutes les focietez en France mefme , ont pour
fondement en cas de different, que l'on conuiendra d'Arbitres, témoin celle que l'on vient de faire pour le grand Commerce des Indes.

Parmy les Grecs & les Romains, pendant la fplen-
deur de ces Republiques, il falloit conuenir d'Arbitres, comme dit Plutarque, dans la décadence de ces
Empires, la Chicane s'y fourra auec tous les autres
vices; enfin nos Roys encore aujourd'huy ne terminent leurs differens que par la voye d'Arbitrages, apres leurs combats fanglans, & leurs guerres funeftes, les fouuerains amis communs s'entremettent, & les accordent à l'amiable; la nature cette premiere Iuftice plus puiffante que les
Loix, grauée pas les mains de Dieu dans le cœur
des hommes , leur dit à tous , & leur fait fouhaiter,

Arbitres donnés aux Marchãds, les Iuges Confuls. l. 1560.

Societé des Indes vent que l'on conuienne d'Arbitres

Les Roys terminent leurs guerres par Arbitrage.

haiter, de terminer leurs differens par la voye de douceur, témoin que le langage des grands, des fçauans, des petits & des fimples, s'accordent tous en ce point là, accordez vous, pres vn amy qui vous accommode.

Et ainfi que nos Prelats ne croyent rien faire qui ne foit agreable au Roy, que l'Eglife ne commande, & que leur deuoir & la Charité ne defire d'eux.

Pour y paruenir donc apres y auoir exhorté vos Curés & les auoir perfuadés, il ne vous reftera, NOSSEIGNEVRS, dans vos vifites, qu'à y exhorter le peuple en public & en particulier, & s'il y a quelque affaire fi animée, ou perfonnes fi puiffantes, que la voye du Curé n'aye pû toucher, vous aurez la bonté de vous entremettre, leur parler, leurs écrire, ou interpofer perfonnes agreables, fages & intelligentes comme font déja plufieurs dans leurs Diocefes.

De plus pour aduencer ce diuin ouurage, il fera bon dans les Euefchez, ou il y à des Conferences reglées tous les mois, parmy les Ecclefiaftiques, que les Curés propofent les difficultés qu'ils auront trouuées dans cette entreprife, & qu'on y cherche les remedes.

H

Les Euesques dans leurs visites prendront a ussi la
peine s'ils leurs plaist de s'enquerir du progez qu'y
auront fait les Curés , leurs donneront les aduis necessaires, & réchaufferont leur zele; s'il s'en trouue
quelques vns peu capables de cét employ, qu'ils ne
perdent pas courage, on peut leur donner de l'aide,
il ne faut qu'vn peu de bonne volonté; l'Histoire
Sacrée nous apprend, que Moyse voulut refuser
la conduite du peuple, parce qu'il auoit de la peine à parler ;(*nescio loqui*) Aron luy fut donné pour
expliquer ses pensées.

Si dans la Parroisse il n'y a point de Prestre qui
aye les talens pour cela , prier quelque Gentil-
homme, ou autre quel qu'il soit, il suffit d'estre
bien intentionné, Dieu s'est seruy pour parler deuant les Roys de pauures mariniers, pauures pe-
cheurs, pauures Apostres, appellés dans l'Escriture, (*l'ordure & la balieure du monde*) le Prophete
n'vsa point d'Eloquence à Dauid ; pour persuader vn Roy & luy faire voir l'enormité de son
crime , il ne se seruit que d'vne comparaison commune, d'vn méchant homme, riche & opulent;
qui auoit nombre de brebis , & neantmoins qui
auoit dérobé celle d'vn pauure homme, qui n'en
auoit qu'vne ; cette seule parole fit voir à ce Prince la grandeur de son offense, excita sa douleur,
& luy fit faire vne penitence exemplaire.

S. Paul.
I. Cor.
cap. 4.

Reg.

Et ainſi que les Curés ne craignent pas de mettre la main à l'œuure, il ne faut qu'vn peu de
bonne volonté, Dieu fera le reſte, il donnera des
paroles à qui n'en a point, il ſecondera les bonnes
intentions, il touchera les cœurs les plus inſenſibles,
qui eſt l'ouurage de ſa grace : ces bons Curés vont
eſtre bien ſecondez, il s'eſt pris à Paris vne ſainte
reſolution (comme nous auons dit) parmy grand
nombre de perſonnes de qualité, & eminentes en
vertu, & en pieté, qui d'abord qu'ils ont Procez,
ſomment leurs parties de nommer Arbitres, &
offrent de conſigner pour le dedit, cela a accordé
vn grand nombre de Procez, & en accorde tous
les iours, & en accordera vne infinité, ſi cét exemple eſt ſuiuy dans les Prouinces ; il ſe fera ſi,
NOSSEIGNEVRS les Eueſques, & Mr. les
Curés y trauaillent, & le perſuadent, & la raiſon nous l'auons déja dite de deux parties qui ſe
plaident, vne du moins voudroit accord, la plus
foible, ou la plus ſage, mais on n'oſe, comme
nous auons dit le demander à cauſe que la partie
aduerſe recule, ſe vante qu'on a peur, & que l'on
croit ſa cauſe mauuaiſe.

Mais quand on ſera perſuadé qu'on demande
cét accord par principe de religion, à cauſe qu'on
eſt Chreſtien, enfans du Dieu de Paix, qu'on y
eſt conuié par les Eueſques, Curés, & Paſteurs,

qui oſera le refuſer ? qui voudra auoir ces perſonnes Publiques & Illuſtres pour témoins de ſes
haïnes, animoſitez & iniuſtices?

Ceſar dans ſes Commentaires.

C'eſt vne erreur, ce que l'on dit communement,
que le François ayme le Procez par temperament,
qu'vn ancien l'a dit il y a long temps dans
ſon Hiſtoire (*Galli cauſi dici*) Comme ſi le Soleil en France nous ſeroit funeſte, qu'il produiroit
le Procez, comme ſa chaleur produit les metaux
dans la terre, comme ſi l'air en France ſeroit rem-

Qu'il n'eſt pas vray que les François, ayment le Procez par temperament.

ply d'atomes de Chicane; que les François malheureux reſpireroient des leur naiſſance ? cette
opinion eſt bonne pour ceux de la Secte de ces
Philoſophes, qui manient l'écritoire, qui viuent
des playes, & des vlceres du peuple; mais quand
tout cela ſeroit vray, que depuis Ceſar, depuis
15. & 16. cent ans, la Chicane ſeroit en vogue
en France, ce pauure Royaume a eſté bien plus
de temps dans l'aueuglement, dans l'erreur du
paganiſme, des 4. & 5. mille ans; & neantmoins
apres tant de ſiecles le Pere des Lumieres l'a éclairé du flambeau de la Foy, & ſes enfans la portent auiourd'huy à toutes les nations de la terre.

De meſme ſi on a creu iuſques à preſent, que
demander accord à ſa partie, eſtoit vne marque
de crainte, & de laſcheté, que c'eſtoit crier mer-

ſy,

cÿ, il eft temps de changer de maxime, nous fommes au fiecle des grands exemples ; quand vous feriez affeuré que cette demande d'accord ne feroit pas fuiuie de la paix, vous ne deuez pas laiffer de la demander ; il vous en arriuera trois grands biens ; Le premier, vous eftes Chreftien, & obligé d'aymer voftre prochain comme vous mefme, à peine de damnation ; vous aurez recherché la paix, vous vous ferez acquitté de voftre deuoir enuers ce Dieu clair-voyant que l'on ne trompe pas, & vous ioüirez de cette paix & repos d'efprit interieur, que les méchans ne gouftent point, & qui eft referuée aux enfans du Ciel.

Demander accord, produit trois grands biens.

2. Outre cela, comme c'eft l'ordinaire des Chicaneurs, pour exciter la haïne des Iuges contre leurs Parties, de dire qu'on les accable par la puiffance, les biens, ou l'efprit ; calomnies qui fouuent font de fortes impreffions, cette demande d'abord fermera la bouche à toutes ces iniures.

3. Celuy mefme qui aura refufé de terminer à l'amiable, aura eftime pour fa Partie, & ne fera pas long-temps fans en auoir douleur, & rechercher la paix. Le Procez eft vne guerre.longue, lente, penible & ruineufe, quand elle feroit fuiuie de la victoire ; auant d'y paruenir il y a de mauuais pas à franchir, & cependant vous

I

n'oſeriez vous plaindre , ſi vous auez refuſé l'accord ; amis , parens , femme & enfans , vous re-
prochent que vous eſtes la cauſe de vos maux,
que vous auez refuſé la paix , & enfin on la demande.

Et pour concluſion , qu'on ne craigne pas que
les bons Iuges trouuent mauuais cette demande
d'accord. Vn Medecin oſeroit-il témoigner auoir
regret de ce que la peſte ceſſe dans ſa Ville ? Vn
Chirurgien , de ce que la playe de ſon voiſin
n'eſt pas cangrenée ? le Iuge ſe ſert de ce remede
dans ſes propres affaires ; il le conſeille à ſes parens & à ſes amis ; il ſert d'inſtrument tous les
iours pour terminer leurs affaires à l'amiable ; il
ne faut pas croire que la maſſe du ſang du corps
des Officiers de France ſoit ſi fort corrompuë;
qu'il ne reſte plus aucune partie qui ſoit ſaine.
Il y a tant de gens d'honneur , & de gens de bien
parmy eux ; il eſt vray que depuis que le malheur de nos Guerres a introduit & toleré cette
funeſte venalité des Charges , pour ſe ſeruir des
termes de nos Roys , & de leurs Ordonnances.
Les Offices ſe ſont multipliés à l'infiny , tout le
monde en a voulu auoir , parce que , honneur,
gloire , & richeſſes s'y rencontrent , & parmy ce
grand nombre il s'y trouue des méchans , qui ſouhaitent la durée & multiplicité des Procez , parce que profit leur en vient : neantmoins il y eñ

Henry III.
Eſtats de
Blois.

à pluſieurs , & en grand nombre , Magiſtrats Que les Iu-tres meſme auront eſtimé pour celuy qui aura deman-dé accord. tres dignes & tres iuſtes , qui ſont éloignés de ces ſentimens , les méchans meſme dans le cœur ne ſçauroient vouloir du mal à vn homme qui aura demandé accord , qui aura voulu ſe ſauuer du naufrage. La Iuſtice n'eſt-elle pas la fille du Ciel ? Le doigt du Tout-puiſſant l'a grauée dans l'ame de tous les hommes ; l'image de l'iniquité ne la peut effacer ; & apres tout cela , quand quelques-vns y trouueroient à redire , le bras du Seigneur eſt-il racourcy ? N'eſt-ce pas luy qui ti-re noſtre ſalut de noſtre perte ? N'eſt-ce pas luy qui a defendu Dauid dans la Cauerne , auec vne 1. Reg. 10. 24. foible toile d'araignée , contre la colere d'vn grand Roy armé , puiſſant & animé ?

Et ainſi qu'on demande la Paix hardiment, ſans craindre de paſſer pour des lâches , ny ſans craindre d'offenſer les Iuges ; il y en a meſme qui ont commencé à introduire cette ſainte maxime dans les Compagnies Souueraines , ils renuoyent deuant amis, les Parens , les Conſorts , & ceux qui le demandent ; le premier Preſident, entr'au- Premier Preſident de Breta-gne . & de Prouence, ordonnent ſouuent l'Arbitra-ge. tres du Parlement de Bretagne, & celuy de Pro-uence ; ces deux hommes illuſtres, ces deux gran-des Ames n'ont pour but que l'authorité du Prin-ce , & le repos des Peuples ; ſi les autres Preſi-dens ſuiuent leur exemple ; ſi les autres Parle-

mens les imitent, on aura bien-tost écrasé la tê-
ste du Serpent.

CHAPITRE IV.

Des Consultans & Arbitres Charitables, qu'à Pa-
ris & dans les Prouinces, il y en a eu en diuers
lieux, & qu'il y en a encore qui defendent le
Pauure gratuitement, & taschent d'accorder leurs
Procez à l'amiable, suiuant l'intention & l'Or-
donnance de Henry IV. du 6. Mars 1610.

En Prouen-
ce, Arbi-
tres, &
Consultans
Charita-
bles.

NOvs auons dé-ja dit, que dans la Prouence, il y a par tout de ces Consultans & Arbitres Charitables, & qu'il y en auroit par toute la France, sans cette mort déplorable de ce
grand Prince, Henry quatriéme, qui arriua deux
mois apres cette Ordonnance toute diuine.

En Breta-
gne & à
Lyon, au-
trefois des
Consultans
Charita-
tables.

Dans la ville de Nantes en Bretagne, & à
Lyon sur le Rhosne, des Officiers honoraires
d'eux-mesme s'adonnerent autrefois à ce saint
exercice; ils virent que les riches les prioient tous
les iours d'estre leurs Arbitres, & qu'ils y em-
ployoient tout leur temps ; ils songerent à faire
mieux, à trauailler pour le Ciel, à secourir le
Pauure,

Pauure, à terminer leur Procez à l'amiable ; ils s'affembloient pour cela deux fois la Sepmaine chez leur Ancien, leur porte eftoit ouuerte à tous les miferables ; leur maifon eftoit comme dit A-riftote, c'eft Autel viuant, ou les foibles cou-roient en foule.

En vn matin ils iugeoient plus de Procez, que le Siege du lieu n'en faifoit en vn mois, les Pro-cez naiffans, il n'y a fouuent qu'vn Acte à voir, ou deux, mais quand ils font bien inftruits comme l'on dit, par toutes les formes du Palais, ce font des montagnes de Paperaffe, il faut bien du temps pour chercher la verité, qu'on a pris tant de peine à déguifer.

Cependant ces deux faintes Affemblées, & de Lyon, & de Nantes ne font point venuës iuf-ques à nous, elles finirent par la mort de ces ou-uriers Charitables qui les compofoient ; faute de cette generation fpirituelle, pour n'auoir pas eu de liaifon auec les Curés & les Euefques.

Dans Paris, cette année 1666. on a auffi refo-lu d'affifter le Pauure, fuiuant l'intention & l'Or-donnance de Henry quatriéme. L'Affemblée en-tr'autres de Parroiffe de faint Sulpice, qui prend foin des pauures honteux, a formé le deffein de prendre auffi le foin de leurs Procez, & tafcher

K

de les accorder à l'amiable : ce qui les a conuié,
c'eſt qu'ils ont veu, que l'Année derniere ils
auoient aſſiſté trois à quatre mille Pauures, qui
la pluſpart eſtoient tombez dans l'extréme pauureté, par le malheur du Procez & de la Chicane, & ce qui eſtoit de plus déplorable, nombre
d'eux s'eſtoient éloignés des Sacremens, & n'en
vouloient plus approcher, auoüans auoir le cœur
plein de haïne & d'animoſité contre leur Parties
qu'ils croyoient les autheurs de leur ruine & de
M. Pouſſé. leurs miſeres. Le ſaint Paſteur de ces ames deſolées, ſongea à remedier au mal par ſa cauſe, &
conuia l'Aſſemblée de Parroiſſe, qui prenoit déja le ſoin de ſoulager leur pauureté, de prendre
auſſi celuy d'accorder leur Procez.

La difficulté de l'entrepriſe faiſoit peur à tout
le monde, mais vn pauure pere vint à la trauer-
ſe, qui demanda ſecours contre vn fils ingrat,
à qui il auoit donné tous ſes biens pour le mieux
marier, & qui ne luy auoit payé il y auoit quatre ans la penſion qu'il s'eſtoit reſeruée ; qui le
laiſſoit nud & moribond ſur vne poignée de paille, âgé de 85 ans. Ce fut alors que l'Aſſemblée
par vn tranſport de zele, proteſta qu'elle feroit
tous ſes efforts pour aſſiſter ces miſerables, & cela a ſi bien reüſſi, que ce fils meſme, ingrat &
dénaturé, qui n'auoit pas eu de honte de plaider

son pere , & l'abandonner vn si long temps, s'est rendu à vne simple parole de son Curé , plus puissante que douze Arrests qu'auoit son pere contre luy , parce que la parole de ce bon Pasteur estoit animée de Charité.

Ie mettray à la fin de ce Liure les Reglemens de cette Assemblée , & le nombre illustre des personnes qui l'a composent, dont il y en a qui sont des premiers de l'Estat.

Si dans toutes les Villes du Royaume il y auoit de pareilles Assemblées , quel bon-heur & qu'elle assistance pour les Pauures ? Vous le pouuez , NOSSEIGNEVRS , & M^{rs} vos Curez, vostre Charité a quasi par tout establi des Assemblées qui prennent soin des pauures honteux , & des malades ; Conuiés ces mesmes Assemblées, de vouloir aussi prendre le soin d'accorder leurs Procez , & les terminer à l'amiable ; nombre de Personnes intelligentes se ioindront à eux , comme ils ont fait à Paris, ainsi que nous dirons cy-apres.

Quelle plus grande Charité , quelle action plus approchante de la Diuine , que d'assister des miserables , dont on ne peut esperer aucune récompense ? Combien dans le Royaume y a-il de personnes intelligentes & capables;

Combien de Iuges & d'Aduocats bien intention-
tionnez , Qui fongent à la retraite dés que Dieu
les touche ? mais tandis que Moyfe prioit fur la

Exodi.

Montagne , Iofué combattoit dans la plaine ; il
mettoit la main au glaiue , & deffendoit le Peuple , il en faut pour la vie actiue auffi bien que
pour la complatiue , à moins d'vne vocation extraordinaire ; il femble que Dieu demande de
nous que chacun fe fauue dans fa condition , que
chacun fanctifie fa profeffion , & c'eft reffembler

Matth.
cap. 5.

à ce feruiteur ingrat de l'Efcriture , *d'enfoüir le*
talent fous la terre , & cacher la lumiere fous le boi-
ceau , Le Pilote doit - il abandonner le Vaiffeau
pendant la tempefte , & pour fe fauuer feul ; expofer les autres ? C'eft décrier la profeffion des
Officiers que de l'abandonner , dés que Dieu
nous donne quelques bons mouuemens ; c'eft
faire croire qu'on ne peut y faire fon falut , que
le meftier eft plus dangereux pour la confcience,
que celuy de la guerre auec tous les defordres qui
la fuiuent ; & neantmoins nous voyons que l'vn
des plus celebres Conciles de noftre France a de-

De his qui
arma pro-
ijciunt in
pace (Ec-
clefia) pla-
cuit abfti-
nere eos à
communio-
ne.
Can. 3.
Arelat. 1.

claré *Anathemes,* ceux qui fous pretexte de pieté,
quittoient la profeffion des Armes , & abadon-
noient l'exercice de leurs Charges , & la deffen-
ce des Peuples ; à plus forte raifon la profeffion
de la Iuftice ne doit pas eftre abandonnée fous
pretexte de pieté , pouuant dans cét employ rendre

dre de si grands seruices au prochain , & aux
miserables.

Qu'on l'entreprenne donc hardiment, que ces
Arbitres charitables ne craignent pas que les Iuges s'en offensent, parce que leurs profits pourroient diminuer , les Procez des pauures ne se
poursuiuent point faute d'argent , & partant
quand on les accordera , les Iuges n'y perdront
rien : mais quand ils y perdroient, ils doiuent se
souuenir que le Dieu de Paix, est celuy des
richesses, que le Dieu de Iacob, est celuy de l'a-
bondance, qu'il comblera la famille du bon Iuge,
d'honneurs & de richesses (*Gloria & diuitiæ in* *Le Iuge*
domo eius); & enfin ils ne doiuent point craindre *iuste aura*
la disette, ils ont pour caution le plus grand des *des richesses.*
Roys, & des Prophetes, que le iuste ne sera ia- *Psal. 13.*
mais abandonné , & que ses enfans ne seront ia-
mais dans la disette, (*non vidi iustum derelictum* *Psal 36.*
nec semen eius quærens panem.)

Et neantmoins s'il arriuoit que l'on voulût
mal à ces charitables Pacificateurs, que quelqu'vn d'eux fut persecuté, qu'il attende l'assistance du Ciel pour qui il trauaille ; le secours ne
manquera pas, la parole du Dieu vangeur y est
engagée (*Qui trauaille pour moy ie le protegeray*) *Le Dieu*
il fera des miracles plutost que d'y manquer, les *vangeur.*

L

ours defcendront plutoft de la montagne, que le
prophete foit abandonné, mais auffi que ces
ouuriers de Paix, Protecteur des pauures, & de
l'orphelin, le faffent auèc efprit de douceur & de
fimplicité, auec efprit de prudence & de fageffe,

fans choquer ny les Iuges, ny les parties aduerfes;
(*difcite à me quia mitis fum & humilis corde*) qui
trauaille pour le Dieu de Paix & de Charité, il
doit imiter fa patience & fon humilité.

CHAPITRE V.

Que les Euefques peuuent terminer leur Procez à
l'amiable, viure en Paix, & neantmoins con-
feruer leurs interefts, & au fpirituel &
au temporel.

ILs le peuuent & le doiuent ; pour faire voir
qu'ils le peuuent, il faut fuppofer comme il eft
vray, 1. que les Chreftiens par principe de Religion, honorent, refpectent, & cheriffent leurs
Prelats, & fouhaitent d'eftre bien auec eux.

2. Il faut fuppofer encore que le foible pour
l'ordinaire voudroit bien n'auoir point de procez
auec le plus fort, en biens, en credit, en amis, &c.
Or eft il que les Euefques font naturellement ho-

norés, refpectés & cheris à caufe de leur Caracte-
re, & dans leurs Diocefes tous fe croyent leurs inferieurs; fi vn ou deux fe trouue auoir plus de
bien qu'eux , les Euefques ont plus de credit , à
caufe de tant de monde qui dependent d'eux , &
au fpirituel & au temporel , & d'ailleurs ils ont
fupport en Cour , aupres du Prince, au Confeil;
& ailleurs , enfin tous les Chreftiens ont graué
dans l'ame (*c'eft l'oing du Seigneur, n'y touchés pas*)
Noli tangere Chriftos meos , & partant tous fouhaitent d'eftre bien auec eux , & n'auoir point de
Procez ny differens. Ie ne parle point des Procez
pour la difcipline & correction des mœurs, ceux
là font neceffaires , & c'eft vne cruauté charitable
de chaftier les coupables, Dieu eft auffi bon quand
il foudroye , *Sodome & Gomore* , comme· quand
il nourrit les Ifraëlites dans le defert , *de ce pain*
Diuin , qui fut petry dans le Ciel.

Ie parle donc des Procez qu'ont les Euefques,
ou pour des droits honorifiques contre leurr Chapitres, ou autres, ou pour des droits vtiles & temporels , pour la conferuation du patrimoine de
l'Eglife, ou pour le leur propre : Tous ces Procez
fe peuuent terminer à l'amiable, qu'ils témoignent
feulement, qu'ils le fouhaitent tous y confentiront
auec ioye ; & voicy ce qui eft arriué depuis peu,
vn Euefque qui auoit vn grand Procez, & animé

contre fon Chapitre , & vn peu en eſtime de ne
haïr pas la chicane, ſe plaignant vn iour à vn de
ſes amis, qu'il eſtoit malheureux, accablé d'affaires, qu'il les haïſſoit, qu'on ne le croyoit pas, cét
amy le conſeilla d'en donner des preuues , & fermer la bouche à ſes ennemis, que pour cela il euſt
à faire offre à ſon Chapitre de nommer des Arbitres , & conſigner pour le dedit telle ſomme qu'il
voudroit, & que cét offre ſe fit par des Notaires,
pour qu'il en reſtât vn acte authentique, que ſi le
Chapitre l'acceptoit, dés ce moment , il y auoit
tréue & ſuſpenſion d'armes, ciuilités & complai-
ſances de part & d'autre , & eſperance de Paix,
& vnion parfaite.

Que ſi le Chapitre le refuſoit , l'Eueſque eſtoit
iuſtifié vers tout le monde, que l'on diroit qu'il
auroit cherché la Paix , & donné bon exemple,
& le Chapitre blaſmé d'eſtre la cauſe du Proçez
Vn Eueſque & du deſordre. La ſommation ſe fit par des No-
ſomme ſon
Chapitre taires, le Chapitre accepta l'Arbitrage & auec ioye,
de conuenir
d'Arbitres, deputa en meſme temps vers l'Eueſque , qu'on
& on s'ac-
commode à n'auoit veu il y auoit plus d'vn an, la deputation
l'amiable,
auec la ioye fut ſolemnelle pleine de ciuilité & d'affection cor-
de tout le
monde. diale, tous les Chanoines en particulier le vindrent
auſſi trouuer, témoignerent leur ioye & leur ſatisfaction, ce bon Eueſque répondit à leurs ciuilités, auec des larmes de ioye; la reconciliation ſe fit
par

parfaite des cœurs & des esprits, les Arbitres se
nommerent, & l'affaire se termina à l'amiable, ce
remede n'est pas difficile, l'épreuue n'en coustera
rien.

Vn autre Euesque auoit vn Procez, pour des
droits vtiles, contre vne famille puissante de son
Diocese, il estoit aussi en estime de ne haïr pas le
Procez, il se plaignoit que cette famille, leurs parens & amis, le décryoient, & soubs main luy
suscitoient cent mauuaises affaires; il fut conseil-
lé d'vser du remede, dont nous venons de parler,
de leurs offrir Arbitrage, il le fit, il fut accepté,
le mesme iour il receut cent ciuilités d'eux, &
ensuitte terminerent leurs differens à l'amiable, &
du depuis ce bon Euesque n'a point de Procez,
qu'il n'offre d'abord l'Arbitrage, qu'on accepte
toûjours, & ainsi de craint & redouté qu'il estoit,
& peu aimé & honoré, il est presentement chery
& adoré, & la raison, parce que, comme nous
auons dit, on honore les Euesques par principe
de Religion, & qu'on les craint à cause de leurs
richesses & authorité, mais quand la guerre est
declarée on sort du respect, & on se porte aux
iniures & aux outrages: l'épée tirée, l'inferieur s'il
peut mal traitte le superieur.

Vn autre Euesque fit bien plus, il estoit néueu,
heritier, & successeur d'vn autre bon Euesque,

M

(marginal note:) Vn Euesque qui
auoit pro-
cez contre
personnes
puissantes,
offrit l'Ar-
bitrage, on
l'accepta,
& on s'ac-
corda auec
grades ci-
uilités qu'õ
rendit à
l'Euesque.

dont les ennemis difoient, qu'il comptoit fes Proccez par centaines, qu'il en auoit en toutes Cours & Iurifdictions, qu'on le voyoit au Palais, *comme dit le Comique*; plus fouuent que le Preteur; l'Euefque fucceffeur fit publier par tout, qu'il fouhaïtoit la Paix auec tout le monde, qu'il l'a defiroit, & conuioit les autres d'auoir les mefmes fentimens; Arbitres furent nommez, & tout fut terminé par la douceur, à moins d'vn an; il arracha

Vn Euefque heritier & fucceffeurd'vn autre Euefque qui a uoit nôbre de procez, offre arbitrage à tous, & accorde auec tous.

la zizanie que fon bon oncle, ce dit-on, auoit femé pendant vingt ans, dedans fa vigne; & en effet tous les Euefques qui voudront n'auoir point de procez, n'en auront pas, tout le monde fouhaïte d'eftre bien auec eux, il ne refte qu'à eux de vouloir eftre bien auec tout le monde; on les honore naturellement, on les craint, & on les redoute; quand vn égal ou vn inferieur demande accord, on peut croire que c'eft par crainte, mais quand vn Euefque le demande, on ne peut l'attribuer, qu'à des mouuemens de bonté & de charité paternelle, tous le reconnoiffent pour fuperieur au fpirituel & au temporel, & tous fouhaïtent la Paix auec luy.

Pour la nomination des Arbitres; quelques-

Les Euefques peuuent auoir pour fufpects les

vns croyent que ceux des lieux ne leur font pas fauorables, qu'ils penfent que l'Eglife a du bien affés, qu'il faut plutoft pancher du cofté de ceux

qui ont femme & enfans, fans m'arrefter à dif-
cuter, fi cette penfée eft raifonnable, ie croy que
Dieu n'a pas fi fort abandonné le monde, & iamais ne l'abandonnera, qu'il ne fe trouue tous-
jours quelque homme de bien par tout, capable
de condamner fon frere, s'il eft coupable : dans
Sodome la ville du monde la plus abominable, il
s'y trouua vn homme de bien.

Neantmoins on peut choifir des Arbitres hors
du Diocefe, des Aduocats fi on veut du Parlement du reffort, & fi encore ils font fufpects, à
caufe des differens, que les Euefques ont quelquefois auec ces corps Souuerains, on peut choifir
des Aduocats d'vn autre reffort ; quoy que les coûtumes & vfances locales foient differentes, neantmoins on euoque tous les iours des Procez d'vn
Parlement, qu'on renuoye dans vn autre, & les
Aduocats les inftruifent & les confultent, & partant capables de les iuger & decider ; c'eftoit l'ancienne façon, de faire iuger les differens par gens
inconnus, c'eft encore la façon de diuerfes nations
du Septentrion, ce Iuge entier & fans tache, ce
grand *Melchifedec* eft depeint dans l'Efcriture
fans pere, fans frere, fans parens & fans amis;
c'eft à dire qu'en iugeant il n'auoit acceptation de
perfonne, ce qui conuient encore mieux à vn Iuge
inconnu, eftranger & efloigné, qu'à celuy qui
eft du pays.

Les Euesques donc peuuent viure en Paix & sans Procez, terminer à l'amiable ceux qu'ils ont à present, & ceux qu'ils pourront auoir cy-apres, s'ils le peuuent, ils le doiuent, & pour l'amour d'eux, & pour l'amour du prochain, & pour l'amour de ce grand Dieu de Paix & de charité qui les y conuie; la Paix ne vaut elle pas mieux, que la guerre? quelle satisfaction a vn Euesque, & a vn grand Seigneur, d'estre mal auec ceux auec qui il y a à viure? auec vn Chapitre; par exemple, ou vne Ville, vne Communauté, & diuers particuliers? qui tous luy rendroient cent ciuilités & complaisances sans ce malheureux Procez, & au lieu de ciuilités, ce ne sont que haïnes, médisances, calomnies, & cent mauuais offices, qui sont les fruits malheureux & funestes de ces guerres d'écritoire.

Les miseres des Euesques & grands Seigneurs qui ont Procez.

Outre cela il y faut donner tout son temps, ou les abandonner à la conduite d'Agens, Procureurs, ou Solliciteurs; dépendre de leur bonne foy, & payer souuent bien cherement les fautes de leur malice, paresse, ou ignorance; que si vn Euesque, ou autre grand Seigneur, prend soin luy mesme de ses Procez, il deuient comme vn rat de Palais, les mains tousiours pleines de paperasses, il ne parle plus que de Requestes, productions, griefs, contredits, saluations, & autres mots de cette magie noire & maligne de chicane.

Mais

Mais le pis, c'eſt qu'il y faut donner tout ſon temps, & y perdre ce qu'il y a dans la vie de plus agreable, & de plus pretieux; les grands Seigneurs, qui ont beaucoup de biens, & en diuers lieux, ont beaucoup de Procez, & en diuers endroits, s'ils veulent eux meſme y donner l'ordre, tous les iours, ce ne ſont que poſtes & meſſagers, qui partent, ou qui arriuent, cent lettres qu'il faut écrire & receuoir toutes les ſémaines, dreſſer memoires & inſtructions, chercher actes & papiers chez Procureurs, Notaires, & Greffiers, & preparer tous ces outils malheureux de cette miſerable guerre, qui ſe fait dans les Palais & Tribunaux.

Pour comble de miſere c'eſt icy la roüe d'Ixion, tourment ſans fin, & ſans eſperance qu'il finiſſe, les procez ſont immortels en France, contre vne Sentence il n'y a qu'vn appel, mais contre vn Arreſt, cent moyens de ſe pouruoir, Requeſte Ciuile, propoſition d'erreur, contrarieté d'Arreſts, & cent incidens en explication ou execution; & ainſi les procez ſe iugent en France, mais ils ne ſe terminent point; les vieux ne finiſſent pas, & il s'en fait tous les iours de nouueaux, de ſorte qu'il ne faut eſperer d'en voir iamais la fin par les voyes ordinaires. C'eſt ce monſtre déplorable dont parle le Poëte, dont les membres coupez renaiſſent en meſme temps, il

N

faut toufiours combattre, vn ennemy vaincu, vn
autre prend fa place.

————— *Vno avulfo non deficit alter.*

Miferable occupation ; où l'on employe le plus
grand de tous les biens, qui eft le temps; la chofe du monde la plus precieufe, que l'on ne peut
acheter, que les Roys ny les Princes ne peuuent
donner, qu'ils n'ont point dans leurs threfors,
comme dit le Sage, & dont ils font pauures auffi
bien que leurs Sujets; mais fur tout à vn Chreftien & à vn Euefque à qui le temps eft donné,
pour operer fon falut & celuy des autres, à qui
l'Oracle Diuin a dit (*Dum tempus habemus, opere-*
mur bonum) & qu'il menace s'il ne la pas fait,
que iamais *il ne verra fa face,* qu'à iamais cette
lumiere diuine fera éclipfée pour luy.

Perte du
temps que
lesRoisne
peuuent
reparer.

Ad Gal.
cap. 6.

Outre cela les Euefques fe plaignent que les
Iuges leurs en veulent, que les Parlemens ne font
pas toufiours pour eux, vn homme fain n'a pas
befoin de Medecin, vn homme fans procez ne
craint point les Iuges, il dépend donc des Euefques de ne dépendre point des Iuges; mais ce qui
eft déplorable, & qui merite d'eftre pleuré auec
des larmes de fang, c'eft quand vn Euefque a des
Procez, il faut d'ordinaire qu'il abandonne le

Troupeau, & qu'il luy donne mauuais exemple,
il faut pour leur conduite, qu'il y donne la meilleure partie de son temps pour les solliciter, qu'il
aille à Paris ou ailleurs; Cependant, NOSSEI-
GNEVRS, qui aura soin de vos Brebis en vostre absence? Le Diuin Pasteur a dit il y a long-
temps, que le loup affamé raude tousiours, & veut
en deuorer quelqu'vne (*circuit quærens quem deuo-* 1. *Pet. c. 5.*
ret) tandis qu'on est à Paris ou ailleurs, com-
ment y auoir l'œil? & neantmoins le Troupeau
vous a esté donné par compte, vous le sçauez,
NOSSEIGNEVRS, & vous le rendrez par
compte iusques à la derniere. Ceux qui font ces
longues absences pourront-ils dire au Pere Eternel
ce que luy a dit ce Diuin Pasteur, dont vous estes
les Successeurs? Voicy les Brebis que vous m'a-
uez données, & ie n'en ay perdu aucune.

Saint Paul tousiours diuin dans ses pensées, &
tout de feu & de charité pour ses freres, n'a-t-il pas
dit qu'il vaudroit mieux souffrir l'iniure & la perte
des biens, que de s'en plaindre en Iustice? (*quare* S. *Paul.* 1.
non magis iniuriam accipitis? quare non magis fraudem Cor. *c.* 6.
patimini?) on n'en demande pas tant auiourd'huy,
qu'on témoigne seulement qu'on voudroit bien
conseruer ses interests par la voye de douceur,
sans estre obligé d'en venir aux rigueurs & aux
aigreurs du procez, faites donc, NOSSEI-

GNEVRS, ce que des *Seculiers* ont defia commencé à faire dans Paris, & en diuerfes Prouinces, faites ce que des Euefques ont fait autrefois , & ce que plufieurs font encore auiourd'huy, offre Arbitrage à tous ceux auec qui vous auez procez , & offre de configner pour le dédit; fi vos parties l'acceptent , vous conferuerez vos interefts doucement fans peine & fans frais, & fans fcandale ; vous conferuerez le cœur & l'affection de tous ceux de voftre Diocefe , vous en ferez vn séjour de PAIX *d'vnion & de charité.*

Mais quand il arriueroit que quelque opiniaftre ennemy de fon repos refuferoit l'Arbitrage, vous aurez fatisfait au confeil de l'Apoftre, vous aurez donné bon exemple , la médifance ne pourra plus vous accufer d'eftre animez de l'efprit de colere ou d'auarice ; au contraire, vos parties feront declarées ennemies de la PAIX, ils feront *des anathemes* à tout le monde.

CHAP. VI.

CHAPITRE VI.

Les Curez & les Preſtres peuuent auſsi accorder à l'amiable la pluſpart de leurs Procez.

PRemierement ils ſont Chreſtiens, & Dieu a parlé à eux, & l'Eſcriture comme au reſte des Chreſtiens, mais outre cela, les Curés ſur tout, y ſont obligez, ils ſont Paſteurs & les ſeconds des Eueſques, ils doiuent procurer la Paix du troupeau (*Opere & ſermone*) par les actions & les paroles ; mais les actions, c'eſt vn langage muet, & efficace, comme dit vn ancien plus fort que le diamant, qui imprime des caracteres dans le cœur qui ne s'effacent iamais ; cependant il s'en trouue qui ſont abſens des années entieres, il y en a qui n'ont eſté dans leurs Paroiſſes il y a des 3. & 4. années ſous pretexte de la ſuite d'vn miſerable Procez, & neantmoins ils demandent à Dieu tous les iours *ce pain quotidien,* dont les hommes ne ſe peuuent paſſer, ils doiuent donc diſtribuer ce meſme pain, & tous les jours à leur troupeau & à leur brebis, ils doiuent encore ſe ſouuenir, qu'il eſt dit d'eux, (*Que le bon Paſteur con-*

Des Curez abſens des leurs Paroiſſes des trois années, pour la ſuite d'ũ Procez.

O

noit fes brebis, & que fes brebis le connoiffent) comment le connoiftre apres 3. années d'abfence, l'ame
& la confcience changent dans vn moment; ce
diuin conducteur du troupeau d'Ifraël pour s'eftre
arrefté quarante iours fur la montagne, le peuple

Moyfe a-
pres qua-
rante iours
n'eft plus
connu, &
les Pa-
fteurs, cô-
ment le fe-
ront ils a-
pres de lô-
gues ab-
fences ?

idolatre dans la vallée, & neantmoins il prioit pour
luy, & traitoit auec Dieu de fes affaires; qu'auroit fait ce peuple mal-heureux, fi comme nos
Curés & nos Pafteurs on l'auoit abandonné des
années entieres pour fuiure des Procez, & de la
chicane ? apres 40. iours d'abfence feulement on
a peine à connoiftre la voix de Moyfe, on a ou-
blié fes miracles, & on a de la peine à luy obeïr,
que luy auroit on dit s'il auoit efté abfent longues
années, pour fes plaifirs, ou fes Procez ?

Ce n'eft pas qu'il n'y aye nombre de Curés qui
ont des Procez forcés, il faut conferuer leur bien
& celuy de l'Eglife, mais ils doiuent imiter cét
exemple illuftre de ce bon Curé, dont nous auons
parlé, qui le premier pouffé par l'efprit de l'Euangile a demandé accord & Arbitrage à fa partie, & l'a obtenu, & du depuis par vne grace fpe-
ciale, & vne fainte onction à l'exemple du grand
S. Yues, a entrepris cét ouurage de Paix, & termine à l'amiable tous les Proces de fa Paroiffe;
imités fon exemple M^{rs}, vous ferez comme luy
cheris, aimés, & honorés de tout le monde, vous

ferez comme luy tous puiſſans dans vos paroiſſes, au ſpirituel & au temporel, tout le monde
aura confiance entiere en vous : honneur, profit,
& biens en viendront, on ſçait gré à qui guerit
les playes du corps, les procez *ſont des playes, &*
du corps & de l'ame, comme dit vn ſaint pere,
que la malice des hommes & des demons, nous
imprime ; & enfin comme nous auons dit,
quand vn Curé aura demandé Arbitrage, & qu'on
l'aura refuſé, il ſera eſtimé, & aura l'approbation
des bons & des méchans, & ſa partie ſera con-
dannée de tout le monde.

CHAPITRE VII.

On trouuera à la fin de ce liure la forme de ces de-
mandes d'Arbitrages ; & la forme du compromü.
Les Religieux & Religieuſes peuuent auſſi
accorder leurs Procez.

L ES Religieux & Religieuſes doiuent pour   Religieux
les meſmes raiſons qu'on a dit cy-deuant,   & Religieuſes
demander & ſouhaiter de terminer leurs Procez   doiuent
à l'amiable, quand il n'y auroit que pour fermer   taſcher
d'accom-
la bouche à la médiſance car; ils doiuent ſçauoir   moder
que l'on a dit d'eux, qu'il n'y a point de quar-   leurs Procez à l'a-
tier, auec eux qu'ils ſont ſi fort attachés à leurs   miable.

intereſts, que iamais ils ne demordent, qu'ils tiennent pour maxime , qu'il vaut mieux que toute
vne famille periſſe que de ſe relacher d'vn ſol de
leurs pretentions ; maxime qui ſeroit bien contraire à la pureté de l'Euangile , qui ordonne pour

Que leurs ennemis diſent d'eux, qu'ils ai-mét mieux qu'vne fa-mille pe-riſſe, que relaſcher vn ſol de leurs in-tereſts. ſoulager le pauure, de vendre iuſqu'aux vaſes ſa-
crés, qui ſeruent aux Sacrifices , plutoſt que de
l'abandonner ; pour faire voir qu'ils ſont bien
eſloignés de ces ſentimens, que la calomnie leur
attribuë, qui dit auſſi qu'ils ne cherchent qu'vn
pretexte de Procez pour ſortir du Conuent, & ſe
diſpenſer de la Regle, qu'ils faſſent voir le contraire ; comme il y a des procez forcés auant de plaider ſoit en demandant ou deffendant, qu'ils faſſent offre de les terminer à l'amiable , & à dire

Les Reli-gieux de-mandans Arbitrage ferót voir qu'ils ai-ment la Paix. d'Arbitres, ils fermeront la bouche aux méchans,
& les feront faire ; ils feront voir qu'ils n'ont
point de procez que malgré eux, & quand ils en
ont qu'ils ſouhaitent de les terminer promptement , que les palais pour eux , & le tracas du
monde , eſt vne rude épreuue, qu'ils cheriſſent
leur retraite, & leur douce ſolitude , où ſe trouuent les delices de ces ames, qui ne reſpirent que
le Ciel , & à qui la terre eſt vn exil bien penible.

CHAP. VIII.

CHAPITRE VIII.

Que les Abbez peuuent facilement accommoder
leurs differents.

POur les mefmes raifons que nous auons dites aux Chapitres precedens, les Abbés, Prieurs, & tous autres beneficiers doiuent fuiure cette fainte maxime, & témoigner qu'ils veulent la paix, ne fera-ce pas vn grand bien pour eux, de conferuer leurs interêts, fans peine & fans frais ? eftre déchargés de ces longs & penibles Proces, qui leur coutent fi cher, cela leur eft facile, perfonne ne veut auoir different auec eux, on connoît leur pouuoir & leur puiffance, outre leur qualité, leur naiffance & leurs biens; on fçait qu'ils trouuent fupport par tout ; ils n'ont qu'à infinuer à vn Iuge, ou à vn Rapporteur, qu'ils refigneront au fils, ou au parent, la feule efperance les fait écouter & traiter fauorablement : & ainfi qu'ils demandent accord hardiment fans crainte d'eftre refufés; & quand quelque malheureux le refuferoit, ils fe feront acquitez de leur deuoir, & fermeront la bouche à ceux qui fe plaignent qu'ils

Que les Abbés Prieurs & autres Ecclefiaftiques peuuent accorder leurs Procez, & neantmoins conferuer leurs interefts.

P

vexent tout le monde par leur pouuoir, leur puiffance, & leurs biens ; outre cela ils y font obligés, ils font parés de la liurée de l'Agneau, de ce
Dieu de Paix, ils font à la folde, & qui eft bien
graffe pour plufieurs, ils doiuent donc du moins
par leur exemple trauailler à eftendre fon Empire, qui eft tout de Paix, d'vnion, & de concorde.

CHAPITRE IX.

Que les Gouuerneurs des Prouinces font obligez d'ac-
corder les Procez & les querelles de ceux de
leurs Gouuerneurs, que plufieurs l'ont fait,
& le font encore.

M. le Prin-
ce de Cô-
ty accor-
doit les
Procez &
querelles
de ceux de
fon Gou-
uernement

MOnfeigneur le Prince de Conty, ce tres
illuftre Gouuerneur, s'en eft acquitté dignement dix ans auant mourir ; depuis s'eftre
donné tout à Dieu, il fe donna tout au prochain.

Il tenoit pour maxime (qu'vn grand eft
l'homme du prochain) que tous ceux qui font
conftituez en dignité & authorité ne font pas à
eux, qu'ils font au public, & qu'ils luy doiuent
tous leurs foins, voicy les termes de cét admirable Liure qu'il a compofé du Deuoir des Grands,

Vn Grand (ce dit-il) doit s'y croire plus obligé qu'vn autre Chreſtien , puiſque par ſa vocation il eſt principalement l'homme du prochain, n'eſtant fait que pour luy ; pour le ſoulager en ſes beſoins, le conſoler dans ſes afflictions, le corriger dans ſes manquemens, luy rendre iuſtice, le tirer de l'oppreßion, le garentir de la violence.

Pleût à Dieu que ces ſentimens dignes de l'Eternité fuſſent graués bien auant dans le cœur de tous ceux qui ont authorité dans le Royaume? pleût à Dieu que tous les Gouuerneurs des Prouinces vouluſſent imiter les exemples de la charité de ce grand Prince ? Le Languedoc & la Guyenne ont veu ſa maiſon ouuerte à tous les miſerables & malheureux, il alloit au deuant dés qu'il ſçauoit vne querelle, il l'appaiſoit : dés qu'il ſçauoit vn Procez, comme ſon eſprit vif & penetrant en connoiſſoit les effets funeſtes & malheureux, il prioit les grands de nommer des Arbitres, & obligeoit les petits d'en conuenir , il en laiſſoit la liberté du choix , & ne ſe reſeruoit que la qualité de mediateur ; car le choix des Arbitres doit eſtre libre , comme celuy du Conſeſſeur, & Medecin, on approcheroit auec crainte d'vn Arbitre qui ſeroit Prince, Mareſchal de France, ou Gouuerneur de Prouince; enfin il y trauailloit auec tant de Charité , qu'il mettoit la Paix

Deſſein de M. le Prince de Conty de quitter ſes Gouuernemeus, &

par tout, & il a dit fouuent dans les tranfports de fon zele, que fi fes infirmités & maladies l'empefchoient de pouuoir demeurer dans fes Gouuernements, & rendre les feruices de Chaarité qu'il deuoit au prochain, auec l'affiduité qu'il defiroit, qu'il quitteroit fes Gouuernemens pour n'eftre pas infidele à Dieu, qui luy auoit fait la grace de connoiftre quel eftoit fon deuoir.

Et en effet les Gouuerneurs font les images des Roys dans les Prouinces, & obligez d'y faire ce que les Souuerains y feroient s'ils y eftoient en perfonne, deffendre les peuples en temps de

guerre, & leur rendre iuftice en tout temps, obligation principale du Prince & du Monarque, demande à Dieu pour cela (*Vt nos Iudicent & pugnent pro nobis*) obligation dont les Roys ne peuuent fe difpenfer, ny les Gouuerneurs, qui les reprefentent; auffi il y en a grand nombre qui s'en acquitent dignement, M. le Duc de Vandofme, entr'autres dans la Prouence,

M. le Duc de Longueuille pendant fa vie dans la Normandie, & le Maréchal de la Meilleraye en Bretagne pendant qu'il a vécu; ce dernier fut affés heureux pendant les agitations de l'Eftat, pour auoir maintenu fa Prouince dans la Paix & le calme, cette paix generale fut vn effet de la paix particuliere qu'il tafchoit d'eftablir

dans

dans toutes les familles, dés qu'il fçauoit vne querelle, ou vn procez, il trauailloit pour pacifier ces differens auec tant de bonté & de Charité, que quand il n'auroit esté, ny Gouuer-uerneur, ny Marefchal de France, on auroit fuiuy aueuglement fes fentimens; fon fils M. le Duc Mazarin fuit les traces de ce pere illuftre, & imite fes beaux exemples.

Plufieurs autres Gouuerneurs, & grands Seigneurs dans la France, trauaillent à cette riche moiffon, dont les fruits fe gouftent dés la terre, par les acclamations des Peuples; & que l'on fauourera dans le Ciel pendant tout le cours d'vne Eternité: quel feruice plus grand peut-on rendre au Prince, que de maintenir fes Peuples dans la Paix, fource de tous biens? (*Salus populi prima lex efto*) Quel feruice plus grand peut-on rendre aux Peuples, que d'accorder leurs Procez & differens, leurs querelles, leurs haïnes & animofitez, leur procuier cette paix domeftique qui conferue leurs biens, & le repos du corps & de l'efprit? Ces obligations font des chaînes qui attachent les cœurs fans fe pouuoir délier, & font forgeées *de ce métail diuin*, dont parle *Platon*, qui ne fe trouue pas dans la terre, mais qui vient du Ciel.

Obligations font des chaînes forgées d'vn métail diuin.

Q

Le zele de ce grand Prince , M. de Conty
alloit bien plus loin , fi la mort n'euſt arreſté
le cours de cette belle vie , ie l'ay oüi dire à
ceux qui auoient l'honneur de l'approcher ſouuent ; il auoit deſſein d'eſtablir vn certain ordre dans l'eſtenduë de ſes Gouuernemens , par
lequel le moindre crime euſt eſté ſçeu & puny , & par ce moyen apparemment de cent crimes premedités , violences & oppreſſions qui
ſe font ſur le foible , il en euſt empeſché qua-
tre-vingt dix ; car qui oſeroit commettre vn
crime premedité , s'il eſtoit aſſuré qu'il fut ſçeu
& puny ? Qui oſeroit auoir conſpiré contre le
Roy ny l'Eſtat , ny opprimer le foible , s'il
croyoit auoir le Prince preſent deuant luy , ou
le Gouuerneur de Prouince ? Et neantmoins
pour eſtablir ce bel ordre , il n'en couſteroit rien
au Roy ny au Peuple , & n'y auroit rien de
nouueau à ordonner, le tout ſe peut tirer de l'Ordonnance , & la façon de l'execution de ces
Royaumes d'Orient , ou la police eſt merueil-
leuſe.

Ce Prince auoit encore vn autre beau deſſein , d'eſtablir auſſi vn certain ordre par toutes les villes de ſes Gouuernemens , par lequel

les commandemens du Roy auroient efté executés promptement , & auec affeƈtion ; la police par tout tres exaƈte , principalement en
temps de pefte ; les Villes reparées , les édifices
publics , Riuieres , Chemins , Ports & Haures;
mais fur tout , on auroit eftably des Manufa-
ƈtures par tout , fecouru le pauure & banny la
mendicité , fans qu'il en euft rien coufté au
Roy , & fans rien ordonner de nouueau , le
tout de mefme euft efté tiré de l'Ordonnance.
Nous deuons attendre de voir cette belle police fous le Regne de noftre incomparable Monarque , qui a defia fi bien commencé , & qui
continuë fes foins pour rendre fes Peuples heureux , & bannir cette malheureufe chicane qui
renuerfe tout ordre & toute police.

pour vne police exaƈte, & n'euft rien coufté au Roy.

CHAPITRE X.

Que les grands Seigneurs peuuent accorder la pluſpart
de leurs Procez, & qu'ils le doiuent ; que pluſieurs
le font ; qu'ils peuuent auſſi accorder la pluſpart
des Procez de leurs vaſſeaux , & qu'ils le doi-
uent ; que M. le Prince de Conty le faiſoit dans
ſes Terres ; que Madame la Ducheſſe de
Longueuille le fait , M. le Duc de Liancourt , &
pluſieurs autres ; que de ſimples Gentils-hommes
le font auſſi , auec ſuccés.

QV y a-il de plus indigne d'vn grand Seigneur, que d'auoir des Procez ? Qu'y a-
t-il qui ſoit ſi fort au deſſous de luy ? S'il en
prend ſoin luy-meſme (nous l'auons dit au ſuiet
des Eueſques) le voila deuenu vn miſerable
Clerc de Palais , les mains touſiours pleines de
papiers , qui reçoit & qui écrit cent lettres de
chicane , dont l'eſprit ou le corps eſt touſiours
chez les Iuges, Aduocats ou Procureurs ; qui
ſouffre cent indignitez & rebutades ; qui ſouffre
cent outrages & humiliations , dans l'eſperance
de gagner vn miſerable Procez , qu'ils n'auroient
garde

garde de souffrir pour gagner le Ciel.

Pendant cette guerre honteuse & penible, il
faut renoncer aux plaisirs du corps & de l'esprit,
il ne faut plus songer à la chasse, aux prome-
nades, aux visites, à l'entretien des amis ny des
Liures, les iours & les nuits sont trop courtes
pour cette malheureuse guerre d'escritoire : Ils
ont donc grand interest de la terminer, ils le
peuuent, sur tout dans le commencement, la
pluspart de leurs Procez dans leur naissance, se
poursuiuent sans haïne ny animosité, par des
Agens & Solliciteurs, comme les Roys font la
guerre par leurs Lieutenans ; si d'abord donc on
demande accord, partie aduerse y consentira,
la pluspart sont parens, alliez, ou amis, &
continuent à se voir nonobstant leurs Procez;
mais quand on vient à la mine, à faire sauter
le Chasteau, qu'on vient à la saisie, & à la vente
des terres, tout Commerce cesse, on se haït
comme les petits, on se déchire à belles dents;
C'est pourquoy l'accord est plus facile auant
qu'on en soit-là, & ainsi tout le plutost qu'on
pourra, mesme auant le procez intenté, si on
peut, qu'on declare ses pretentions, & en cas
de contestation, qu'on offre de nommer Arbitres, & consigner pour le dedit : le refusant

R

apres cela , quoy qu'il luy arriue, perte, ruine, vente de terre, &c. ne peut plus ſe plaindre de ſa partie.

Si le demandeur n'a pas offert Arbitrage, que le deffendeur le faſſe, le plutoſt c'eſt auſſi le mieux, comme nous auons dit, & neantmoins dans toute la ſuitte du Procez, on le peut faire, on a veu ſouuent des Procez accordés, qu'on auoit commencé a rapporter; que cette demande ſe faſſe touſiours, quand on pourra parlant à la Partie par des Notaires plus croyables que des Sergens, qu'on entremette en outre gens d'honneur, perſonnes amies & Charitables; qui ne parle qu'à vn Procureur, Solliciteur, Agent ou Intendant, parle ſouuent au loup, de conſeruer la brebis; ſi les grands Seigneurs ne prennent ſoin eux meſme de leur Procès, leur maiſon ſouuent ſont ruynées; ſi on les abandonne à des agens, intendants ou ſolliciteurs, la dépence eſt immenſe; outre cela on eſt expoſé à leur pareſſe, ignorance, malice ou infidelité, combien par la de maiſons ruinées, cent exemples déplorable de cela, par tout le Royaume.

On voit donc l'intereſt qu'ont les grands Sei-

gneurs de n'auoir point de Procez, & taſcher de
les terminer à l'amiable ; cela leur eſt facile;
ils plaident contre leurs inferieurs, égaux, ou
ſuperieurs, ſi contre leurs inferieurs, ils n'ont
qu'à demander accord, on y conſentira auec
ioye, le foible ſouhaite la Paix auec le plus
fort.

S'ils ont Procez auec leurs égaux, ou ſuperieurs, cela leur eſt encore auſſi facile, nous
venons de le dire.

Mais pour obliger leurs intendans, agens
ou ſolliciteurs, d'entrer entierement dans leurs
interêts, ſouhaiter & trauailler pour les exempter de Procez, il faut imiter vne belle inuen-
tion trouuée par vn grand Seigneur : à ſon
Aduocat & Procureur il bailloit certains gages reglés par an, à la charge de le tenir quitte de tous frais de procedure, & leur bailloit
en outre vn certain preſent reglé à vne ſomme, pour chaque procez, qu'ils luy accordoient, par ce moien ils n'auoient garde de
refuſer l'Arbitrage, ils eſtoient les premiers à
le demander, & trauailloient à la paix auec autant d'ardeur, que pluſieurs de ces ſoldats de
chicane trauaillent maintenant à tirer la guerre
en longueur.

Pour ob-
liger les
intendans,
agens, &
ſollici-
teurs, à
eſtre fide-
les.

A fon intendant outre fes gages ordinaires,
il donnoit encore certains prefens à proportion
des autres bons feruices qu'il luy rendoit , &
le récompenfoit largement , s'il faifoit quelque
chofe d'vtile & de profitable pour la maifon;
à moins d'eftre reconnoiffant & payer liberale-
ment , on n'aura iamais de feruiteurs fideles &
affectionnés, on fe payera par fes mains, le Poëte l'a dit il y a long temps (*Les Dieux n'auroient*
point d'adorateurs, s'ils n'eftoient reconnoiffans)

Mais il arriue fouuent que les grands feigneurs
croyent eftre des diuinités , à qui tout eft deu
fans rien deuoir , la flaterie leur a perfuadé que
tout le monde eftoit fait pour eux , & qu'arri-
ue-t'il à ces gens la ? on les pille , on les volle,
ou du moins on abandonne, & on neglige leurs
affaires ; tout va en defordre , & tout perit, les
maifons fons faifies , & venduës , *la bonne pefche*
fe fait en eau trouble : que faut-il donc faire pour
les auoir fidelles & affectionnés ? faire ce qu'a
dit l'Oracle (*pour eftre aimé il faut aimer*) pour
eftre bien feruy , il faut bien païer. Ce Diuin
Pere de famille recompenfa les ouuriers de la
vigne qui n'eftoient allés que du foir , comme
ceux qui y eftoient allés du matin, & la raifon
parce qu'ils auoient trauaillé auec plus d'affection & d'adreffe , & que ce peu en apparence
profitoit plus , que le long trauail des autres.

Math.c.20.

Quand

Quand les grands Seigneurs imiteront ce sage Pere de famille, ils ne manqueront point de Seruiteurs fidels & affectionnez, on ne cherchera point à leur susciter des embarras, ny empécher que leurs procez s'accordent à l'amiable. Enfin que les grands Seigneurs imitent cette sainte Resolution qui s'est prise à Paris, par des Personnes de condition, & d'eminente vertu, qui ont resolu de n'auoir plus de procez, qu'ils n'offrent à leur Partie de les terminer à l'amiable, de nommer des Arbitres, & consigner pour le dedit. Il s'en termine tous les iours vn grand nombre par cette voye, comme nous auons dit, qu'on en fasse aussi l'experience, on en tirera du moins cét auantage, qu'on aura cherché la paix; & si apres cela il faut faire executer, emprisonner, saisir ou vendre; ny les égaux ny les inferieurs, ne se pourront plaindre, qu'on est accablé par les amis ou par la puissance.

Mais sur tout, qu'on fasse cette demande d'accord par principe de Religion, parce qu'on est Chrestien, parce que l'on dit tous les iours, ou du moins qu'on le doit dire (*Nostre Pere qui est aux Cieux*;) que ce Pere Celeste est le Dieu de paix, qu'elle regne dans le Ciel, & que ses Enfans la doiuent chercher sur terre; deman-

S

dez accord en cette veuë, & vous l'obtiendrez, & les richeſſes de plus & l'abondance : (*Primum quærite Regnum Dei, & omnia adjicientur vobis.*)

Matth.c.6.

Que les grands Seigneurs peuuent & doiuent accorder les procés de leurs Vaſſaux.

Ce n'eſt pas aſſez que les Grands Seigneurs puiſſent accorder leurs procez, ils peuuent encore accorder la pluſpart de ceux de leurs Vaſſaux, & le doiuent faire. 1. Pour le profit qui leur en viendra. 2. Pour l'honneur & la gloire, & pour gagner l'affection de leurs Vaſſaux. 3. Pour la décharge de leur conſcience, Monſeigneur le Prince de Conty le faiſoit dignement dans ſes terres, & a voulu que cela ſe pratiquaſt apres ſa mort, ie l'ay ſceu d'vn Officier de ſa maiſon, à qui il l'a recommandé, & qui eſt tout de zele pour cela. Madame la

Noms de pluſieurs qui le font.

Ducheſſe de Longueville a eſtably cette ſainte Pratique dans toutes ſes terres ; Monſieur le Duc de Liancour y trauaille auec benediction, & pluſieurs autres grands Seigneurs & ſimples Gentil-hommes l'ont entrepris, & reüſſiſſent.

Le moyen d'obliger les Payſans & les Fermiers d'accorder leurs procez.

Cela eſt facile, perſonne n'oſe refuſer les Grands, à cauſe du bien & du mal qu'ils peuuent faire ; les vns les honorent, les autres les craignent : Pour ce qui eſt des Payſans & des Fermiers ils n'oſeroient refuſer leurs Maiſtres, Gentilshommes, Bourgeois, ou autres ; la pluſpart leurs doiuent, & font toûjours en leur reſte, il n'y a qu'à les menacer, quand ils auront procez, s'ils refuſent de les accommoder à l'amiable, qu'on les fera executer le lendemain de leur refus, & n'y manquer pas. Ie connois vn Gentilhomme qui a vne terre, dont les Payſans ſe mangeoient en procez, & ne le payoient pas, il fut conſeillé de ſe ſeruir de ce remede, il le fit, tous procez furent accordez en moins de trois mois, & du depuis eſt fort bien payé.

Mais ſi les deux Payſans qui ſe plaident ne ſont pas Vaſſaux, Hommes, ou Fermiers du meſme Maiſtre, voicy encore ce que i'ay veu pratiquer à vn excellent Gentilhomme, il écriuoit au Seigneur ou au Maiſtre de qui l'autre Payſan eſtoit Fermier, luy remontroit qu'il auoit pareil intereſt que luy, qu'il s'accommodaſt à l'amiable, il m'a dit qu'aucun ne l'auoit iamais refuſé, chacun ſe rend à ſon intereſt, qu'on en faſſe l'experience, la voye eſt douce & facile, & n'en couſtera rien.

Comme le procez eſt vne eſpece de guerre, qui a pour fondement le bien, mais qui eſt accompagnée de haine, d'animoſité & de vangeance ; & que pour ſe vanger on n'épargne

rien, le Petit comme le Grand, le Payſan, le
Laboureur, l'Ouurier quitte tout, & donne
tout pour cela : Cependant la terre n'eſt pas
labourée, pendant cette guerre l'Ouurier ne
trauaille pas, & le Seigneur n'eſt pas payé de
ſa ferme, & ainſi voila vn pauure Payſan en
proye au Solliciteur, au Iuge, & Procureur de
Village, on le pille, on le volle, on luy fait
des apprecis exceſſifs, on vſuraſſe pour luy donner terme, enfin on luy fait payer en frais le
double de ſa ferme, & de là, ſi les terres ſont
en recepte, voila des non-valeurs, ſi les terres
ſont affermées, voila des Payſans ruinez, les
terres ſe décrient, & les Fermes diminuënt. Les
grands Seigneurs donc par leur propre intereſt
ſont obligez d'empécher les procez tant qu'ils
pourront parmy leurs Vaſſaux.

Mais qui a-t'il de plus glorieux & de plus
charitable, que de terminer les differens de ſes
Sujets & de ſes Voiſins. Moyſe ce grand Prince, auſſi-bien que grand Iuge, qui auoit apris
ſa leçon du Dieu de la Paix, paſſoit toutes les
journées à ce ſaint Exercice. Iob ce grand Pa-
triarche en faiſoit autant, & encore aujour-
d'huy l'employ le plus honorable des Roys, &
qu'ils font auec plus d'éclat & de pompe, n'eſt-
ce pas d'offrir leur mediation, & entremiſe,
                                              pour.

pour accorder les Guerres des Rois leurs voisins, qui sont les procez des Souuerains. L'Histoire est pleine des Legations des Papes, &
des Ambassades des Princes pour tels sujets, &
enfin toutes les guerres des Princes se terminent par vn traité, & les procez des particuliers
se deuroient terminer par vn accord.

Peut-on plus obliger tout vn Pays que d'y
faire regner la Paix & l'Abondance ? L'arri-
uée de ces bons Seigneurs est souhaitée dans
leurs Terres, elle est demandée au Ciel auec
instance, chacun espere y trouuer le remede à
ses maux, la Veuve, l'Orphelin, & le Foible,
generalement les Petits & les grands, les re-
gardent comme cét azile Sacré dont parle l'A-
pôtre, où chacun trouue le soulagement de
ses miseres.

Outre cela les grands Seigneurs sont obligez de rendre ces seruices à leurs Vassaux, par
principe de Religion, & de conscience; ils doiuent se souuenir que leurs Terres & leurs Fiefs
ne leur ont esté données par les Souuerains,
qu'à la charge de rendre justice à leurs Sujets,
& gratuitement, aux termes de la premiere
Concession ; la pluspart s'en sont oubliez,
neantmoins il n'y a que cinquante ans qu'ils

Les Sei-
gneurs
hauts Justi-
ciers obli-
gez de ren-
dre justice
à leurs Vas-
saux gra-
tuitement.

T

donnoient tous des gages à leurs Officiers, &
les destituoient (*ad Nutum*) c'estoit l'ancien vsage auant cette malheureuse venalité des Charges, introduite par les Rois malgré eux, &
soufferte par le malheur des guerres (pour vser

des termes de nos Rois & de leurs Ordonnances) ce qui peut estre excusable dans nos Souuerains, ne l'est pas dans les Seigneurs hauts
Iusticiers, (*Salus populi prima lex esto*) c'est la premiere Loy des Princes de sauuer le peuple ; si on
ne pû le sauuer sans la guerre, & cette guerre si
on ne la pû faire sans tirer argent de la venalité
des Charges, la necessité sert d'excuse, à nos
Rois.

Mais à l'égard des Seigneurs hauts Iusticiers, les guerres n'ont pas changé la nature
de la donation de leur Terres, Fiefs, & Iurisdictions ; ils doiuent la justice gratuitement,
comme ils faisoient au terme de la premiere
Concession, ils n'y perdroient pas ce qu'ils
croient ; Supposé qu'ils tirent d'vn Office par
exemple dix ou douze mille liures quand ils les
vendent, sont cinq ou six cens liures de rente ;
l'acheteur ne se croit point obligé à son Seigneur pour cette vente, ny obligé de donner
son temps, & sa peine pour la conseruation &
augmentation de sa Terre, & auec raison, on
ne se tient pas obligé à vn Marchand pour

auoit acheté de luy vne marchandise, qu'il a venduë tout le plus cher qu'il a pû ; Mais si les Seigneurs donnoient leurs Charges, ils seroient choix de Personne de condition, de capacité & probité reconnuë, qui seroient leur petit Senat domestique, dont les soins, les conseils, les avis, & la bonne conduite de leur Terre & conseruation de leurs Vassaux, vaudroient bien plus que l'interest des sommes qu'ils vendent leurs Offices.

De plus les Seigneurs sont responsables deuant Dieu & deuant les hommes, des maluersations de leurs Officiers ; ils en rendront compte, comme dit vn grand Pere de l'Eglise, *au Iour Terrible*, que ce Iuge rigoureux ne fera grace à personne : dés ce monde ils y seroient estroitement obligez, si les Loix estoient dans leur force & vigueur. L'Ordonnance rend les Seigneurs hauts Iusticiers, responsables du mal jugé, & des maluersations de leurs Officiers & Ministres, Procureurs, Notaires, & Sergens, & veut que les condamnations, qui interuiendront contre eux, soient executez contre les Seigneurs des Fiefs, comme leurs Cautions solidaires ; ç'a esté la pratique de tous les Parlemens auant la venalité des Charges, auant que les Officiers possedassent les grandes

Les Seigneurs hauts Iusticiers sont responsables & cautions solidaires des maluersations de leurs Officiers.

Terres , Fiefs & Iurifdictions. L'Arreſt entr'autres du Parlement de Paris eſt celebre, rap-

Mr Loüet. porté par ce Compilateur illuſtre , prononcé
en Robbes rouges en terme de Reglement, il
eſt de l'an 1526.

Ordonnã-
ce de Rouſ-
ſillon art. Par cét Arreſt on n'a fait que repeter l'Or-
27. donnance, que tous les Seigneurs de Fiefs , de-
meureront reſponſables ſolidairement des maluerſations de leurs Officiers.

Si le Roy dont par vn Arreſt du Conſeil
ſeulement , ordonnoit que cét Arreſt de Reglement fuſt executé , & qu'en execution , les
Seigneurs hauts Iuſticiers fuſſent condamnez
de mettre vn Rolle du nom de leurs Officiers,
Procureurs , Notaires , & Sergens , au Greffe
du Siege Royal d'où ils releuent , où ſont en-
clauez , les Seigneurs de Fief dés le lendemain ,
Si on con- ne feroient-ils pas vne information exacte de
damnoit les
Seigneurs la capacité de leurs Iuges & autres Miniſtres?
pour les ſur tout de leurs Sergents, qui peuuent eſtre
maluerſa-
tions de gens de bien , mais dont on dit que le nombre
leurs Offi- n'eſt pas grand ; Qui eſt le Seigneur qui vou-
ciers, ils les
reduiroiét droit eſtre Caution ſolidaire de la ſuffiſance &
à vn petit probité de tous ces Procureurs, Notaires , &
nombre. Sergents ? s'ils eſtoient entrepris, tout le reuenu du Fief , ne ſuffiroit pas pour payer pour
eux,

maintenant on ne les entreprend pas , parce
que la pluſpart ſont pauures , & qu'on a ou-
blié que leurs Seigneurs ſont leurs Cautions
ſolidaires ; & quand on s'en ſouuiendroit, on
craint auec raiſon , que les Iuges ne les con-
damneroient pas , parce qu'eux-meſmes ont des
Fiefs.

Mais ſi la Loy eſtoit renouuellée & executée, on les entreprendroit hardiment , le Seigneur auroit cent procez ſur les bras : pour y
remedier, il reduiroit tous ces Procureurs, Notaires , & Sergens au plus petit nombre qu'il
pourroit , ne laiſſeroit que les plus capables, &
les plus gens de bien, & encore prendroit caution d'eux , qui ſeroient autant de ſurueillans,
& controlleurs de leurs actions ſur les lieux.

Pourquoy eſt-ce que les Seigneurs de Fiefs ne
ſuprimeroient pas tout ce nombre monſtrueux
de Procureurs, Notaires, & Sergens , Sauterelles qui deuorent le peuple, dont ils ne tirent
aucun profit, la pluſpart ſont pourueus gratuitement? le Seigneur voudroit-il demeurer Caution ſolidaire de la probité d'vn Sergent, qu'il
ne voudroit pas d'ordinaire cautionner de cinq
ſols ? neantmoins on crée des milliers de ces
Chenilles d'écritoire, à la priere du premier venu ; c'eſt l'azile aujourd'huy des Féneans &
Vauriens, le deſordre eſt allé ſi auant qu'il y

V

en a qui ne ſçauent ny lire ny écrire, ils ont vne marque ou leur nom eſt graué. Qu'on ſe ſouuienne que Moyſe ne fit naiſtre ces Sauterelles en Egypte, que pour la deſolation du peuple, & que ces productions funeſtes, ſont des effets de la colere du Dieu deſtructeur.

Enfin ſi les Seigneurs des Fiefs eſtoient fortement perſuadez, qu'il faudra payer pour les maluerſations de leurs Officiers, il feroient ce qu'ils ne font pas; ils s'informeroient exactement de leur probité & ſuffiſance, & y remedieroient ſoigneuſement; du moins à l'auenir, ils auroient quelque égard à la probité & capacité, & ne vendroient pas indifferemment comme ils font leurs Charges au plus offrant & dernier encheriſſant.

Mais ſi le Roy les obligeoit, comme il le peut, à faire rendre juſtice à leurs Vaſſaux gratuitement. Ce ſeroit pour lors, qu'ils chercheroient pour Iuges tous les plus gens de bien; ce ſeroit pour lors, qu'ils n'auroient pas de peine, à accorder les procez & querelles de leurs Vaſſaux; les Iuges y traualleroient euxmeſme, & tout de leurs mieux, dés la premiere audiance, s'ils le pouuoient, ils les termineroient : car il n'y auroit point d'eſpices à esperer. Le Medecin charitable & gratuit, voudroit pouuoir guerir le malade, dés la premiere visite ; le Chirurgien, qui n'espere point de payement voudroit pouuoir guerir la playe, dés le premier appareil.

CHAPITRE XI.

Que les Officiers , gens de bien , peuuent & doiuent accorder leurs procez à l'amiable.

ILs sçauent tous ce qu'on dit d'eux , que la Soutanne est la plume de l'Aigle qui deuore les autres ; que leur voisiné est celuy du Loup , leur societé celle du Lyon , qui veut tout auoir ; qu'il n'y a point de succession en seureté ou vn Iuge a interest , qu'il veut auoir vne portion parce qu'il est heritier , qu'il veut en auoir vne autre , parce qu'il est Officier , & enfin qu'il veut tout auoir , parce qu'il est le plus fort ; ils sçauent encore que l'on se plaint, qu'à la Campagne , il n'y a ny Pré ny Vigne auprés de leurs maisons , qui soit en seureté , qu'ils font grace à la veufue & à l'orphelin quand ils se contentent de partager auec eux la succession où ils n'ont aucun interest ; ces plaintes souuent sont des calomnies, mais

Plaintes que l'on fait des Iuges , & de leur voisiné.

les bons Iuges. peuuent facilement fermer la
bouche à la médifance ; il n'y a qu'à faire offre à fa partie de conuenir d'Arbitres, & configner pour le dedit ; fi la partie l'accepte, voila vn procez promptement terminé fans peine,
& fans frais ; fi la partie refufe, voila le Iuge
à couuert de ces declamations ordinaires, qu'on
eft opprimé par fa puiffance, par fon credit,
& fes amis.

Ils font affeurez, que perfonne ne refufera
l'arbitrage auec eux, ny leurs égaux, ny leurs
inferieurs, ny leurs fuperieurs ; quoy que fuperieurs en naiffance, en qualité, ou en biens ;
tous fe tiennent inferieurs à vn Iuge en matie-
de procez, c'eft ioüer auec luy, comme dit le
Prouerbe, dans fon Tripot ; c'eft auoir pour
Iuges fes Confreres, tous fe tiennent par la
main, d'vn bout du Royaume à l'autre; c'eft
la caufe commune (*Frater nofter eft*) tous y ont
intereft, de faire craindre ceux du meftier, de
faire redouter ceux de la profeffion.

Les inferieurs donc n'ont garde de refufer
de s'accommoder auec vn Iuge, ils le confi-
derent comme le Cyclope qui le peut deuorer,
leur propofition de paix, fera receuë, comme
fi vn Ange l'apportoit du Ciel.

Pour

Pour les égaux, s'ils sont Iuges, & de mesme mestier, ils ont mesme interest de souhaiter l'accord, ils sçauent mieux que personne les peines, les tourmens de corps & d'esprit d'vn pauure plaideur ; pour eux sur tout, quand il faut quitter la maison & l'exercice de la charge, qu'au lieu de ces profits, ces honneurs, & ces respects, qu'ils trouuent chez eux, il faut aller au loin faire dépense, & souffrir rebufades, & humiliations comme les autres miserables plaideurs.

Et ainsi si vn Iuge veut, il n'aura iamais de procez ses inferieurs, comme nous auons dit, ses égaux, & superieurs, souhaitent tous d'estre bien auec luy, du moins personne ne cherche à y estre mal.

CHAPITRE XII.

Que les Inferieurs & les Foibles, peuuent d'ordinaire accorder les procez qu'ils ont auec plus puissant qu'eux, & qu'ils le doiuent.

ILs le doiuent, quand bien ils seroient asseurez d'obtenir par procez plus que par accord, vn grand Seigneur qu'on emprisonne, ses reuenus qu'on arreste, ou ses terres que l'on vend, il ne s'en oublie iamais, on s'en souuient, comme

X

dit le Prouerbe, iufques à la centiéme generation, & on cherche à s'en vangerfur l'Autheur, fur les Enfans ou les Parens.

Quand vn grand Seigneur feroit dépoüillé de tous fes biens, la naiffance luy refte, & fes Parens & fes amis, qui prennent part en fa ruine, & s'en vangent toft ou tard, ils ont les bras longs, & cent moyens pour faire mal, comme cette femme irritée du Poëte, (*Mille nocendi artes.*)

Si l'Inferieur eft deffendeur, & attaqué par vn grand Seigneur, d'ordinaire il eft pourfuiuy par vn Agent, Soliciteur, ou Procureur d'Office, il s'en trouue nombre de ces Mrs qui font gens d'honneur & gens de bien; mais neantmoins de crainte de fe méprendre, qu'on s'adreffe directement au Seigneur, qu'on luy écriue, voicy ce que i'ay veu fouuent reüffir; que le Seigneur foit dans le pays ou abfent, luy écrire: (car on a peine à les approcher, & auoir audience paifible) qu'en fon nom on luy a fait vn tel procez, qu'on l'honore trop pour vouloir auoir conteftation auec luy, mais comme il eft iufte & equitable, & qu'il ne voudroit pas accabler le foible, le prier de nommer des Arbitres, que l'on fait offre de configner pour le dedit, que pour y paruenir, on a fait fignifier ces offres à fon Procureur.

mais de crainte qu'on ne luy en donne pas l'auis, qu'on luy en enuoye vne copie.

Qu'on mette cette copie dans le pacquet auec la lettre, la plus courte qu'on pourra, qu'on la fasse tenir en main, de crainte qu'elle ne tombe entre les mains de ceux qui ont interest, que les procez ne s'accordent pas, ils pourroient preuenir l'esprit du Maistre. Que le Seigneur donc soit sur les lieux ou absent, qu'on luy écriue directement, la pluspart quand ce ne seroit que par curiosité ils ouurent leurs lettres & pacquets; & deuroient les lire, & non pas s'en rapporter à leurs gens, si leur fidelité n'est à l'épreuve : car cela empéche qu'on n'ose leur dire ny écrire la verité, & deuiennent les statuës, dont parle le Prophete (*aures habent, & non audient, oculos* ^Psal. 134. *habent & non videbunt*) ils ont des yeux, & des oreilles, & ils ne voyent ny n'entendent ; & ne donnent ordre à rien.

Pour acheuer que la lettre que l'inferieur écrira au grand Seigneur soit courte, comme nous auons dit, car il l'aura plûtost leuë qu'il n'aura appellé son Agent ou Solliciteur, quand il aura conçeu l'affaire, & qu'il y va de son honneur & de sa conscience, de ne souffrir pas qu'en son nom, on accable le foible qui demande accord,

il donnera ſes ordres, & ſes Agens n'oſeronty
contreuenir. I'ay veu nombre de procez termi-
nés de la ſorte, & la pluſpart ſe termineront, ſi
le foible prend cette voye.

Et en effet, comment eſt-ce qu'vn grand Seigneur, Duc, Marquis, & autre, qui eſt plus puiſſant que ſa partie, oſeroit auoir refuſé d'accorder
auec le foible, qui l'en prie, qui offre de payer
ou faire tout ce que les Arbitres ordonneront?
ſi le grand Seigneur refuſe, il paſſe pour vn homme qui ſe laiſſe gouuerner à ſes gens d'affaires,
ou bien paſſe pour vn méchant homme, qui veut
deuorer le pauure, & s'engraiſſer, comme dit vn
Ancien, de la ſubſtance du malheureux, ce que
les plus méchans ne veulent pas que l'on croye
d'eux.

Si vn Eueſque par exemple eſtoit prié par
quelqu'vn de ſon Dioceſe d'accorder à l'amiable, oſeroit-il le refuſer? S'il eſtoit poſſible qu'il
y euſt des Eueſques ennemis de la paix, qui ai-
maſſent les procez, oſeroient-ils refuſer de conuenir d'Arbitres s'ils en eſtoient ſommez? Apres
cela comment pouuoir prêcher cette paix, cette
vnion & amitié, qui doit eſtre entre les Chreſtiens? Comment la pouuoir conſeiller en particulier ny en public, dans les Conferences ny
dans les viſites? Comment pouuoir prononcer
ces

ces paroles Diuines dans le plus Augufte de nos
Sacremens (*Pax tecum;*) Comment fouhaiter la
paix au Troupeau , & le déchirer par le mauuais
exemple, & par ces haines & inimitiez funeftes
qui accompagnent les procez ?

De mefme fi le foible demande accord à vn
Iuge, le pauure à vn homme riche, comment
pourra-t'on le refufer ? cette fommation d'Arbitrage fera vn pretexte de declamer contre
eux, & fera impreffion; que le procez n'eft qu'vn
pretexte pour dépoüiller le pauure, on n'oublie-
ra pas dans cette declamation de décrire la vie
& les actions de l'Officier, ou de l'homme riche
refufant arbitrage, ce fera le commencement
& la fin des plaidoyers, des écrits, & follicita-
tions, & ainfi peu le refuferont; C'eft pourquoy fi le grand Seigneur, fi l'Euefque, fi le
Iuge, fi l'Homme riche ne demande le premier
l'Arbitrage, que le foible ne manque pas de le
demander, qu'on en faffe l'épreuue, & on verra
que cela reüffira, i'en ay veu fouuent l'experience.

Y

CHAPITRE XIII.

Que les égaux aussi doiuent s'entre-demander accord, que le plus sage le demandera le premier, qu'il n'y a plus de honte à cela, ny marque de crainte, depuis qu'à Paris des Personnes eminentes en qualité, en vertu, & en merite, le pratiquent.

L'Accord entre les égaux est plus difficile, on est sur la demarche à qui fera le premier pas, quoy que souuent les deux parties le souhaitent, comme nous auons dit, on n'ose le témoigner, de crainte que partie aduerse n'en tire auantage, ne se vante qu'on a peur, que l'on crie mercy, & il est vray que jusques à present, cela est arriué souuent ; mais d'oresnauant cela n'est pas à craindre, apres l'exemple de ces Illustres Chrestiens, de ces Messieurs de Paris, qui ont formé cette sainte Resolution suiuant le conseil de l'Apostre, de ne point traduire son frere au Tribunal, qu'auparauant il ne luy aye demandé la paix, & l'accord à l'amiable.

Quand on sera persuadé que cette demande a pour fondement la charité, & la pureté de l'Euangile, que ce n'est point vn effet de la peur ny de la crainte, personne n'en tirera auantage, au contraire, la plufpart d'abord fe rendront à vn fi grand exemple d'humilité & charité Chreftienne : on en voit l'experience dans Paris, & dans les Prouinces où l'on a commencé cette fainte Pratique.

Cependant quand il arriueroit que des gens transportez de colere ou de vengeance, ou aueuglez par leurs interefts, refuferoient d'abord l'accommodement, la demande en fera toûjours auantageufe à celuy qui le premier l'aura faite. 1. Il aura fermé la bouche, comme nous auons dit, à toutes ces declamations, que le deffein eft d'opprimer par la puiffance, l'authorité, ou les biens; mais fur tout, nous nous ferons acquitez de ce que noftre confcience demande de nous, de ce que l'Apoftre nous confeille, de ce que le Dieu de la Paix nous commande; apres cela, laiffons luy hardiment les foins de nos interefts, de noftre honneur, & reputation; s'il eft Dieu de Paix, il eft Dieu de Vengeance, fon bras n'eft pas racourcy, il fçaura nous deffendre (*Deus vltionum Dominus.*)

Les égaux doiuent s'entredemander accord, le bien qui leur en arriuera.

Pfal. 93.

Neantmoins comme Dieu foûuent fe fert du Miniftere des Anges & des Saints pour ope-

Que les E-
uesques &
Curez doi-
uét icy tra-
uailler for-
tement.

rer ses merueilles. C'est icy où Nosseigneurs les
Euesques, & Messieurs les Curez doiuent trauailler dauantage à déraciner cette fausse maxime, qu'il est honteux à vn Chrestien de demander accord, de vouloir bien viure auec son
Prochain, de vouloir viure en paix icy bas auec
celuy que nous deuons souhaiter d'auoir dans
le Ciel pour compagnon de la gloire. C'est à
quoy les Confesseurs & Predicateurs doiuent
trauailler dauantage ; nous auons sujet de tout
esperer, du zele & de la charité de nos Euesques, dont la vie est toute exemplaire, qui
nous choisissent de dignes Curez, qui animent
par leur exemple les Confesseurs & Predicateurs ; & ce grand nombre d'Ordre de Religieux, illustres en doctrine & en pieté : Si cette
sainte Milice, si cette Armée nombreuse de tant
de gens pacifiques, declarent la guerre aux procez, la destruction en est asseurée.

Si chaque Homme d'Eglise n'accordoit
qu'vn procez par an, combien de milliers est-
ce qu'on en accorderoit ? ils le peuuent, les
moins capables & les moins intelligens, Prestres, Religieux, & Religieuses ; qu'on ne se
rebute pas, qu'on en parle souuent & prudem-
ment, on trouuera le moment que le malade
mesme souhaitera la guerison.

Vn.

Vn feul Miffionnaire , animé de cét efprit
de Paix , dans fes Miffions , les accorde à
centaines ; mais voicy la fainte Rufe , dont il
fe fert quand il les voit touchez de la douleur du peché ; s'ils ont des procez, il leur re-
prefente que cette fource malheureufe & feconde , a efté la caufe funefte d'vn grand
nombre qu'ils ont commis , & qu'apparemment ils commettront encore , fi le different
ne s'accommode à l'amiable , pour cela il
leur fait conuenir d'Abitres, & figner vn compromis, pareil à celuy qui eft à la fin de ce
Liure , dont il a toûjours des Copies imprimées , & aprés cela , il les fait embraffer : car
autrement la Miffion finie , la ferueur paffée,
on retourne au procez , & à tous les defordres qui les fuiuent , cent exemples de cela.

Enfin il n'y a point de Curé, s'il a la
Charité de s'y appliquer, qui ne puiffe du
moins contribuër à accorder fix ou fept procez par an. Si les Pafteurs font gens de bien,
ils ont des Amis, des Penitens, tant de perfonnes malades, & dans l'affliction, qui fuiuent leurs confeils, & neantmoins quand
chacun n'en termineroit, comme nous auons
dit, que fix ou fept par an. Il y a trente-

Z

mille Paroiſſes dans le Royaume , ce ſeroient plus de deux cens mille Monſtres d'é-
touffez, qui produiſent ces deſolations , que
tout le monde connoiſt parmy le troupeau du
Seigneur, & qui le défigurent.

On peut donc hardiment entreprendre ce
ſaint Ouurage , nous ſommes au ſiecle de la
Paix , noſtre Inuincible Monarque nous l'a
procurée au dehors par ſes Armes , & veut
nous la donner au dedans par ſes Loix, pour
cela il trauaille, il y a ſi long-temps , & auec
tant d'application à cette reformation de la
Chicane , que tous ſes peuples ſouhaitent
auec tant de paſſion.

CHAPITRE XIV.

*La façon de choiſir les Arbitres , des diffi-
cultez qui peuuent s'y trouuer,
& des remedes.*

1. CHacun doit choiſir ſon Arbitre, nous l'a-
uons dit ailleurs; quand vn autre les nô-
me, on n'a pas en eux la côfiance qu'on a en ceux
qu'on a choiſis. L'arbitre, outre qu'il doit juger,
il doit perſuader qu'il eſt le principal , & pour

cela il faut qu'on aye toute creance en luy;
C'est pourquoy les Mediateurs, grands Seigneurs ou autres, ne doiuent iamais nommer les Arbitres; c'est ce que faisoit tres-
excellement ce tres-vertueux Prince Monsieur de Conty, il auoit puisé ces maximes
dans l'Histoire Sacrée; elle nous dit que Dieu
commanda au peuple, par la bouche de Moyse, qu'il eust a choisir ses Iuges. *Iudices constitues in portis tuis.*

Deut. c. 16.

2. On doit choisir des gens de probité &
capacité reconnuë, mais la probité sur tout
est la plus necessaire, sans cela peu d'accom-
modemens reüssissent, sans ce principe de
Charité, on n'a pas la patience d'écouter les
longues plaintes des Parties, qui en apparence ne sont rien au fond de l'affaire, & neantmoins qui souuent le décident: car par ce
moyen l'Arbitre s'insinuë dans l'esprit du plaideur, gagne creance, & ensuite en dispose.

On doit choisir gês de probité sur tout.

3. Il faut conuenir d'vn tiers, apres auoir
nommé chacun son Arbitre: si les parties n'en
peuuent tomber d'accord à l'amiable, le Mediateur fera vne liste de huit ou dix personnes
du canton le plus en estime, fera deux copies
de cette liste, en baillera vne à chacune des

Comment choisir le tiers quand il s'y trou-ue difficul-té.

parties, qui marqueront d'vne Croix à la marge, ceux qui leur feront fufpects, & au bas mettront ces mots, *l'ay pour fufpects ceux que i'ay croifez*, puis rendront la lifte au Mediateur; il eft quafi impoffible de huit ou dix perfonnes en eftime de probité, que tous foient recufez, quand il n'en refteroit qu'vn qui ne le feroit pas, il feruira de tiers, s'il en refte deux ou trois, ou plus grand nombre, le Mediateur le dira, & écrira leurs noms en des billets feparez qu'il mettra dans vn chapeau, & les fera tirer au fort par les parties.

Que l'on ne veut pas quelquefois conuenir d'arbitres fur les lieux, ny du Reffort de fon Parlement, & auec raifon.

4. Quelquefois on ne veut pas conuenir d'Arbitres fur les lieux, ny du reffort du Parlement où l'on demeure, & peut y auoir raifon pour cela ; i'ay veu vn Officier de Compagnie Souueraine qui fit procez à vn autre qui auoit efté Officier, & fon Confrere, mais ne l'eftoit plus, ce dernier euocqua, le premier qui eftoit le demandeur, rechercha accommodement, l'autre y confentit, mais qu'on euft à prendre des Aduocats pour Arbitres du Reffort d'vn autre Parlement que celuy où ils eftoient, parce que le demandeur eftoit Officier, & que le défendeur ne l'eftoit plus, les Arbitres des lieux n'auoient pû les accorder, ceux d'vn autre Reffort le firent.

Quand

Quand il arriuera donc quelque difficulté
semblable, voicy comme l'on pourra faire, tous
les Aduocats en France, de quelque Parlement
que ce soit, sont capables de iuger toutes sortes
de questions, de fait & de droit, de Coustume
ou d'Vsance localle, quand le Factum est bien
dressé, ou le Procez bien instruit; on le voit par
experience, comme nous auons dit ailleurs, on
éuoque tous les iours des Procez d'vn Parlement
qu'on renuoye dans vn autre, ils y sont instruits
& iugez.

Le Mediateur donc fera conuenir aux Parties, ou tirer au sort par quels Aduocats, & de
quel Parlement ils veulent estre iugez; si les Parties n'en connoissent aucun, le Mediateur y é-
crira pour auoir vne liste de 8. ou 10. des plus
fameux, & en fera tirer 3. au sort, ou plus grand
nombre, si les Parties le desirent.

Comme l'on pourra conuenir d'Aduocats d'vn autre Ressort.

5. Si le Procez n'est pas instruit, on le pourra
instruire sur les lieux en la forme qui suit; on
fera élection de domicile chacun chez vn Procureur ou Notaire, là on se communiquera,
on produira, & on y fera le reste de l'instruction
ordinaire, à la reserue qu'il faudra faire auec douceur, ce qu'on fait au Palais auec beaucoup d'ai-

On pourra instruire le Procez sur les lieux, & l'enuoyer iuger ailleurs.

A a

greur; cette douceur sert souuent à terminer l'affaire, ie l'ay veu, les mediateurs, les amis communs, les parties mesmes pendant ce temps-là, proposent quelquefois des expediens qui peuuent les accorder sur le champ.

6. Cependant si cela n'arriue pas, & qu'il faille pour l'instruction faire Procez verbaux, monstrées ou veus ; les Mediateurs feront aux parties conuenir d'vn amy pour cela.

7. Si le Procez ne demande pas longue instruction, & qu'il se puisse iuger sur vn Factum; le Mediateur en fera dresser vn, dont les deux parties conuiendront, & qu'ils signeront.

Consigner le dedit sans en parler dans le compromis, & pourquoy. 8. Le Mediateur fera aux parties consigner entre ses mains, la peine du dedit, qui ne sera rapportée dans le compromis, de crainte qu'il n'arriue, ce qui est souuent arriué que les Iuges condamnent de rapporter la somme touchée pour cette peine, quoy que l'Ordonnance le deffende.

9. Le Procez mieux instruit, ou le Factum sera enuoyé par le Mediateur aux Aduocats conuenus, & leur iugement notifié aux parties, & s'il y a quelque chose de rude ou de difficile pour l'vne des parties, le Mediateur tasche-

ra de l'adoucir par les expediens, que sa Charité luy suggerera.

Enfin apres auoir fait tous bons offices de veritable amy en veu du Ciel, & non de la Terre, il prononcera le iugement, & s'il y en a vn qui refuse d'acquiescer, il baillera à l'acquiesçant la somme consigné pour le dedit.

CHAPITRE XIV.

Du deuoir du bon Mediateur.

NOvs venons de les dire, parce que les parties ont consenty de s'accorder à l'amiable, mais le plus difficile, c'est ce qu'il faut faire auparauant pour cela, il faut les persuader, & c'est la grande peine ; cependant il est facile d'en venir à bout, si on a les bonnes intentions de ce bon Curé dont nous auons parlé, & le zele de son Euesque qui l'assiste si dignement.

Outre cela, toutes sortes de personnes & de toute sorte de condition sont capables de cette mediation, vn voisin, vn amy, vne personne même beaucoup au dessous de ceux qu'on voudroit d'accord, s'il ne le peut par luy-mesme, il peut

Toute sorte de personnes capables d'estre Mediateurs, par soy ou par autruy,

exciter des personnes qui en seront capables, vn malade trouue bon, quelque grand Seigneur qu'il puisse estre, que le moindre luy souhaite la santé, & tasche de la luy procurer.

1. Mais pour estre vn bon Mediateur, il faut sur tout, patience, prudence, adresse & charité ; il faut se rendre agreable aux parties, gagner creance sur leur esprit, pour cela commencer par les plaindre, qu'on a douleur du mal, de la peine, de la dépense que leur cause leur Procez, apres cela écouter patiemment toutes leurs plaintes qui ne seront pas courtes.

Grande patience necessaire au Mediateur.

2. Il faut auoir la prudence & la discretion de ne rien dire qui choque d'abord celuy à qui on parle, quelque mauuaise que sa cause paroisse; mais seulement on luy peut dire que cela fait grand tort à sa reputation, que ses ennemis, ou les mal informés, racontent la chose autrement, que cela donne de mauuaises impressions ; & qu'enfin s'il s'accommode, que ces bruits cesseront, & qu'il fera voir qu'il est tout autre que ses ennemis ne publient.

Grande prudence, ne rien dire qui choque.

3 S'il y a quelqu'vn, dont la cause soit si bonne qu'on n'en puisse douter, opprimé, persecuté, dépoüillé de son bien, par le puissant ou l'insolent;

Témoigner à l'oppressé qu'on a douleur

l'infolent ; c'eft l'offencer au vif, fi le Mediateur ne témoigne entrer dans fes interefts ; il luy dira donc en particulier , & feul à feul, s'il fe peut, que tout le monde fçait l'iniure & l'iniuftice qu'on luy fait , que tout le monde le plaint , & luy fouhaite la paix , &c.

S'il prie le Mediateur d'en parler en ces ter-mes à fa partie, il luy répondra qu'il le feroit vo-lontiers, fi cela feruoit au bien de la caufe, mais que cela ne feruiroit qu'à l'irriter & empefcher l'accommodement, qu'il luy dira & fera dire par amis interpofez tout ce qui fera neceffaire pour cela. Cependant qu'il le prie qu'il n'aye point à redire ce qu'il luy a dit de fa partie , autrement qu'il feroit obligé de n'en demeurer pas à vn, car cela aigriroit l'affaire au lieu de l'adoucir , que de Mediateur on le regarderoit dores-en-auant comme la partie, que cela romproit tout accord, & qu'enfin le Confeffeur & le Confultant doi-uent le fecret , mais auffi que le mefme fecret leur eft dû.

Il faut encore beaucoup d'adreffe pour trou- uer des expediens aux difficultez qui fe prefen- tent, foit pour la nomination des Arbitres, l'affignation du lieu de l'Arbitrage , les con- ditions de la furceance des procedures , & cent autres difficultez qui peuuent se rencontrer , si l'entremeteur n'a pas toutes les lumieres necessaires pour cela , ou qu'il n'aye pas toute l'autorité qu'il faudroit ; il prendra conseil de personnes sages , ou interposera personnes puissantes pour qui les Parties auront respect & crainte , & à qui elles n'oseroient manquer de parole ; i'ay veu cela reüssir souuent , vne fois entr'autres , entre personnes de grande qualité , & pour vne affaire de grande consequence ; le Mediateur n'estoit pas de leur poids , il interposa personnes puissantes , & l'affaire s'accommoda , quoy que les Parties fussent bien animées.

Grande Charité necessaire, & c'est le principal. Enfin , le bon Mediateur doit auoir vn fonds inépuisable de Charité , ce doit estre le fondement de l'édifice , le corps du Palais , & le dome ; c'est à dire que toutes ses actions , ses paroles & ses pensées doiuent estre animées de ce diuin amour , que le Chrestien doit auoir pour son prochain , & que la nature mesme nous inspire , *Rendez à autruy les seruices, que vous voudriez vous estre rendus.*

On trouue tout bon d'vn Mediateur charitable, iusques à ses fautes. Ceux qui agissent par ces principes , souffrent auec patience , les plaintes , les murmures , les doleances , les ingratitudes mesme de ceux à qui ils rendent seruice , & en reuanche on trouue tout bon de ces Mediateurs , quand bien ils fe-

roient des fautes ; ie l'ay veu en vne affaire d'importance , & entre perſonnes éminentes , le Mediateur n'eſtoit pas de leur qualité , il negotia la
paix entre-eux vn long-temps, il faiſoit de grandes fautes à ce que l'on diſoit, du moins on s'en
plaignoit ſouuent , neantmoins on luy pardon-
noit tout , il eſtoit touſiours le bien venu , beu‧
uoit & mangeoit auec toutes les parties ; & enfin fut la cauſe de leur accommodement, & cela , parce qu'il agiſſoit par ces principes releués de
Charité & d'amour pour le prochain : ce feu di‧
uin nous anime , nous rend actifs , patiens , éloquens & ingenieux ; c'eſt là cét *Or diuin*, de l'A‧
poſtre , que la fumée de la médiſance ne ſçauroit noircir ; c'eſt là cette *eau viue* , dont parle
le Prophete , qui rafraiſchit & delaſſe ceux qui
trauaillent dans la veuë de ce grand Dieu de la
Paix.

Et ainſi que tous ceux qui ont pouuoir & authorité , & tous ceux qui ont accés ou creance
s'entremettent d'accorder les Procez & les querelles , on aura bien-toſt eſtouffé ces monſtres de
diuiſion : nous auons fait voir comme NOSSEI-
GNEVRS les Eueſques y peuuent tout , Mrs les
Curés , ces Miſſionnaires zelez , ces Predicateurs , ces fidels Interpretes de la pureté de l'E‧
uangile , ces Confeſſeurs medecins Charitables
des vlceres les plus ſecretes de l'ame , qu'ils pren-

nent la peine d'interroger leurs Penitens s'ils ont
Procez, s'ils haïſſent leurs parties, car la pluspart ne s'en confeſſent iamais, non plus que le
Soldat d'auoir iuré, l'Officier d'auoir preuariué,
le Marchand d'auoir vſuraſſé, perſonne quaſi ne
ne ſe confeſſe des pechez de ſa profeſſion; le Plaideur ſur tout croit touſiours auoir raiſon, que ſa
haïne meſme eſt iuſte & legitime; que le Con-
feſſeur donc prenne la peine de l'interroger, &
il trouuera l'ame de ce pauure Plaideur toute cangrenée de haïne, d'inimitié, & de deſirs violens
de vengeance, & neantmoins auec ces vlceres,
il ne laiſſe pas d'approcher ſouuent des Sacremens, & augmente ſes playes au lieu de les
guerir : enfin les Gouuerneurs de Prouince peuuent beaucoup pour l'accommodement des Procez, les grands Seigneurs, les hauts Iuſticiers
vers leurs vaſſaux, les ſimples Gentils-hom-
hommes, les Bourgeois, & le moindre qui a vn
Fermier, ou vn Payſan ſous luy, peut l'obliger d'accorder ſes differens à l'amiable, ainſi
que nous auons dit aux Chapitres precedents.

*Le Plai-
deur ne
ſe confeſſe
quaſi ia-
mais de
haïr ſa
partie, que
les Con-
feſſeurs
doiuent
les inter-
roger là
deſſus.*

CHAP.

CHAPITRE XV.

Des qualitez du bon Arbitre.

1. IL doit estre patient comme le Mediateur, prudent comme luy, & sur tout Charita- ble comme luy; c'est par là qu'il doit commen- cer, qu'il doit continuer & qu'il doit finir; s'il a d'autres pensées ou d'autres interests, c'est vn miracle s'il reüssit, & tost ou tard on se plain- dra de luy & de son iugement; on voit cela ar- riuer tous les iours, au contraire, qui agit par ces principes du diuin amour, les petits luy sont aussi considerables que les grands, les estrangers & inconnus aussi chers que les parens & les a- mis; enfin que les Arbitres se souuiennent, ce que l'on dit d'ordinaire, & qui est vray, que de cent accords qui manquent, il y en a quatre- vingt dix, qui manquent par la faute des Arbi- tres; c'est à dire faute de bonté & de Charité pour les parties.

(marginnote) Arbitre doit estre patient, charita- ble & pru- dent.

2. Le bon Arbitre en outre doit estre sçauant & habile, & en estime de cela; c'est à dire s'il est question d'vn point de Droit ou de Coustume, car hors de cela les Marchands, & autres gens sages

(marginote) Sçauant en sa profes- sion.

C c

& intelligens peuuent decider les questions de
leur profession.

Accès libre.
Dent.
cap. 16. 3. Il doit donner vn accez libre aux parties,
les iuges dont parle l'Histoire Sacrée, éleus par
le peuple, par le commandement de Moyse, estoient
assis *à la porte du Camp* ; Iob accommodoit les
differens *à la porte du Temple*, c'est à dire dans vn
lieu, dont l'accez estoit libre & commode à tout
le monde.

Témoi-
gner ami-
tié & écou-
ter pa-
tiemment. 4. On est maistre de la place, quand on a gai-
gné le Gouuerneur, on est maistre de la volonté
du pauure plaideur quand on a gagné son affection; pour cela, il faut luy témoigner bonté &
amitié, & vn grand desir de l'aider, il faut com-
mencer par l'écouter paisiblement comme nous
auons dit, & quoy qu'il dise beaucoup de choses,
qui ne font pas à la cause, il faut l'écouter auec
patience la premiere fois, pour gagner creance
sur son esprit, apres cela on pourra en vser àutre-
ment, passé que ce pauure malade sera persuadé
qu'on a bonté pour luy, il trouuera bon tout
ce qu'on luy dira.

Témoi-
gner qu'ō
a consceu
l'affaire. 5. Pour faire voir que l'Arbitre a conceu son
affaire la luy repeter, exagerer les raisons, qui
font pour luy, & mesme luy en dire de nouuel-

les, cela le perfuadera fortement, qu'on eft intelligent & affectionné; apres cela on pourra luy
dire les raifons, que fa partie allegue au contraire, mais comme en paffant & fans exageration,
d'vne façon neantmoins fi elles font bonnes, que
cela luy donne fujet de douter, & enfin luy dire,
qu'on fera fon poffible, pour foûtenir fes interefts, & luy procurer la Paix.

6. Dans les prouinces en beaucoup d'endroits,
on a cette mauuaife coutume, qu'on regarde l'Arbitre de fa partie, comme fa partie mefme, & fouuent auec auerfion, haïne & injures; il faut déraciner cette mauuaife habitude, il eft facile, les
Arbitres n'ont qu'à dire à ceux qui les ont nommés, qu'ils ayent à aller voir & folliciter les Arbitres nommés par leurs parties, & ceux-cy il faudra les écouter auec plus de patience, que les autres, exagerer leurs raifons, & leur témoigner
bonté & amitié, & grand defir de contribuer à
leur accommodement.

Dans les Prouinces on regarde fouuent l'Arbitre de partie aduerfe comme fô ennemy. Le remede a ce mal.

Cét accueil fauorable gaigne entierement les
cœurs, d'autant plus que dans les Palais, on n'a
d'ordinaire que des rebufades des Iuges, & de
leurs miniftres.

7. Le lieu de l'Arbitrage d'ordinaire dans les

Prouinces s'assigne dans les cabarets, à la mode d'Allemagne; mais comme dit vn de leurs histo-riens en beuuant, il s'y fait bien des accords, mais aussi il s'y fait bien des querelles; & puis l'Arbitrage est vne chose sainte & sacrée, & quel-que chose de plus auguste que de iuger simple-ment, car outre que l'on iuge, on tasche de re-concilier les cœurs, c'est pourquoy il est bon de choisir vn lieu digne de la sainteté de l'œuure, on s'assemblera donc chez l'vn des Arbitres, ou chez le Curé de la paroisse, ou dans quelque Conuent, & puis ces ministres sacrés, qui sont des Anges de paix seconderont les Arbitres.

Ou as-signer le lieu de l'Arbi-trage.

On doit comencer par iuger la questiõ.

8. Les Arbitres assemblés, il est bon de com-mencer par iuger la question au fonds, & à la rigueur, comme on feroit au palais, ce qu'on ne fait pas tousiours dans les Prouinces, on com-mence souuent par proposer des expediens, on trauaille à batons rompus, & les Arbitres intel-ligens, & spirituels, quand ils sont malins en tirent auantage.

Apres on peut pro-poser des expediéts.

9. La question iugée à la rigueur, si l'on voit que les parties ne s'y voudroient pas tenir, on cherche lors des temperamens & des expediens, tel ne doit, que mille écus par exemple, qui se-roit heureux, de donner quelque chose d'auantage,

par-

parce qu'il a affaire à homme puiſſant, chica-
neur ou deuorant, qu'il faudra pour ſe deffendre faire grande dépenſe, & quitter ſon trafic,
ſon commerce ou ſes menages, & manquer à
gagner, ce que l'on gagneroit ſi on n'auoit pas
des Procez.

De meſme il eſt dû mille écus à telle perſon- *Qu'il eſt quelquefois auantageux de perdre.*
ne, qui ſeroit heureux d'en quitter vne partie
pour auoir l'autre, parce qu'elle a affaire auſſi à
perſonnes puiſſantes de difficile conuention, qu'il
faudra faire grande dépenſe, & quand on ob-
tiendroit auec dépens, on ne retirera pas le tiers
de ce qu'on y aura mis, ſans parler de la perte du
temps, de la geſne d'eſprit, de la maiſon abandonnée, & de tous les profits qu'on auroit pû
faire ſans cette malheureuſe affaire.

I'ay veu ſouuent des accords ſe faire que l'on *Artifice d'vn Arbitre Charitable pour perſuader l'accord.*
croyoit rompus, vn Arbitre merueilleux en ex-
pediens & en charité, auoit trouué vn ſaint artifice, pour perſuader les plus opiniaſtres, il
leur faiſoit vn memoire de leurs pretenſions en
quatre lignes, du principal des intereſts & dépens, ſuppoſant qu'ils obtiendroient Sentences
& Arreſts tout comme ils voudroient.

De l'autre coſté il leur mettoit la dépenſe qu'il
Dd

leur faudroit faire , le temps qu'il y faudroit
employer , les profits qu'on manqueroit à faire
pendant ce Procez &c. La gesne d'esprit , l'a-
bandon de la maison &c. Et enfin leurs bailloit ce memoire , ou à la femme , ou à vn de
leurs amis , & les prioit de le garder iusques a-
pres le Procez finy , pour voir s'il auroit dit
vray , les plus opiniastres se rendoient , ou sur le
champ , ou quelque temps apres , les plus em-
portez sont capables de ces meditations.

Que les
Arbitres
ne doiuent
quasi ia-
mais souf-
frir les
parties
plaider
l'vne de-
uant l'au-
tre, &
pourquoy.
   9. Il y a vne chose de tres-grande consequence à
quoy les Arbitres doiuent bien prendre garde,
qui est de ne souffrir quasi iamais que les parties
plaident leur cause en presence l'vne de l'autre ,
si ce n'est qu'il faille les interroger sur certains
points en secret , dont les yeux souuent ou le
visage sont des preuues muettes , & dont les demandes ou les réponses non preueuës font voir la
verité.

   Mais hors de cela , iamais on ne le doit souffrir , & la raison , parce que le meilleur Procez
est tousiours accompagné d'vn peu d'aigreur (que
chacun se consulte là dessus) & quand les parties viennent à parler en presence l'vne de l'autre , on s'interrompt , on s'échauffe , on s'aigrit,
& incontinent on vient aux iniures , aux outrages & aux reproches , la bile émeuë , on n'est

plus maiſtre , la colere , la vanité & la vengeance ſont des paſſions plus fortes que l'auarice &
l'intereſt , qui ſont d'ordinaire la cauſe des Procez.

Et ainſi que les Arbitres ne ſouffrent pas les
parties parler enſemble deuant eux , il eſt bon
meſme qu'ils ſoient en chambres ſeparées , d'où
on les appellera ſi on en a beſoin ; quand on parle à ſon Arbitre, on parle auec douceur , comme
à ſon amy & à ſon Iuge , les expediens qu'il
propoſe on les reçoit auſſi doucement , & ſi on
y trouue à redire , on fait voir les inconueniens
ſans ſe mouuoir ; ce qu'on ne feroit pas ſi la partie eſtoit preſente , de crainte qu'elle n'en tiraſt
auantage , on voit cela arriuer tous les iours , &
beaucoup d'arbitrages auoir manqué pour les
parties s'eſtre miſes en colere , & s'eſtre dites des
iniures en preſence de leurs Arbitres.

10. Il faut encore prendre garde à vne choſe Que l'Ar-
qui eſt de tres-grande conſequence , que celuy bitre qui
des Arbitres qui tiendra la plume ſoit habile , & tout, ſoit
ſur tout qu'il ſoit homme de bien , car c'eſt vne homme de
maxime parmy les intelligens dans ce meſtier, pourquoy.
que qui eſt maiſtre de la plume , eſt quaſi maiſtre de tout , il ne faut qu'vn mot de changé
pour renuerſer tout le ſens d'vn iugement.

Que les
Arbitres
doiuent
eux-mef-
mes d ef-
fer leurs
iugemens.

11. S'il eft poffible que les Arbitres prennent la peine eux-mefme de dreffer le iugement
ou la tranfaction qui interuiendra , du moins
qu'ils faffent tous les *Nota* , & ce qui aura efté
decidé par articles ; les Notaires quelques habiles qu'ils foient , ont peine à conceuoir vne affaire à fond dés la premiere fois qu'ils en entendent parler.

Qu'on ne
laiffe
point de
queuë aux
Sentences
arbitrales.

12. Tant que l'on pourra qu'on ne laiffe point de
queuë à ces Sentences arbitrales ou tranfactions,
qu'on execute fur le champ tout ce qui fe pourra executer ; comme par exemple fi vn debiteur
promet payer en rente ou en fond d'heritage,
qu'on faffe la defignation & le tranfport par le
mefme acte ; fi vn fils promet tant à fa mere
pour douaire, ou à fes freres pour partage, que
la defignation fe faffe auffi fur le champ, & le
tranfport par la Sentence arbitrale , autrement il
y aura bien à craindre qu'il ne faudra vn fe-
cond Procez pour l'executer, ou qu'il ne faille
recourir aux mefmes Arbitres, qui feroit double
peine pour eux & pour les parties.

Au lieu de
Sentence
arbitrale,
faire tran-
figer les
parties.

13. Comme le deffein des Arbitres doit eftre
de donner la paix , & d'empefcher autant qu'il
leur eft poffible , tout pretexte de Procez , au
lieu de donner des Sentences arbitrales, le mieux
eft

est de faire transiger les parties, il est plus difficile de se pouruoir contre vne transaction, que contre vne sentence, quoy qu'on aye acquiescé, la corruption est si grande, qu'on obtient lettres pour estre releué, & ensuitte on peut plaider cent & vn an, on voit des Procès à milliers de cette nature.

Il est vray qu'on peut aussi prendre lettres pour estre releué, contre vne transaction, mais outre que cela est plus difficile, & de plus mauuaise grace, c'est que l'on peut, si la matiere y est disposée, faire la transaction en termes generaux, sans rien expliquer par le détail, en sorte qu'on ne sçauroit se releuer, on ne peut faire voir dequoy il estoit question entre parties, & en quoy on pretend auoir esté laisé; comme par exemple s'il est question de l'execution d'vn Arrest, & qu'à y valloir, on a touché quelque somme, la transaction peut porter en termes generaux, (*au moyen des payemens cy-deuant faits, & des sommes receües, que les parties n'ont pas voulu estre articulées par le détail, & pour cause ; Titius declare quitter Mæuius de l'execution de son Arrest, en principal, interests & dépens.*

S'il est question de compte, qui ne regarde que ceux qui transigent, declarer que les parties s'entre-quittent de toutes affaires iusques à ce iour,

Façon de transactiõ difficile a casser.

& ainfi du refte, fi l'affaire y eft difposée.

Outre qu'il eft difficile de fe releuer contre des
tranfactions, faites de la forte, ou les Arbitres ne
doiuent pas figner, il en vient vn autre bien aux
Arbitres, fouuent fous la caufe d'appel on leur
chante des iniures, les Aduocats & les Iuges les
traitent d'ignorans, ou de méchans ; quand leurs
noms ne paroiftront point, qu'au lieu d'vne Sentence Arbitrale, il n'y aura qu'vne tranfaction,
qui ne fera point fignée d'eux, on ne pourra que
leur dire.

Enfin, ces Arbitres, ces Iuges de douceur, ces
Anges de Paix, doiuent auoir la mefme bonté,
& la mefme charité pour les autres, qu'ils voudroient, qu'on eut pour eux en pareille rencon-
tre ; ils doiuent fe fouuenir, qu'il ny a rien de
plus honorable parmy les hommes, que d'eftre en
eftime de capacité & de probité fi grande, que
les peuples s'y foûmettent volontairement, c'eftoit la plus noble ambition de ces grands Se-
Les arbi- nateurs de Rome, & Princes de la terre,
tres, fort fur la fin de leurs iours, de voir leurs Ci-
honorez
chez les toyens venir à eux, & les prendre pour Iuges de
Romains. leurs differens, ils preferoient cette eftime fecrete
à leurs trophées, & leurs triomphes ; ils auoient
vaincus leurs ennemis par la force, mais ils auoient

gagné les cœurs de leurs peuples par la douceur.

L'Histoire sacrée nous dépeint ce grand Patriar- Iob fort loüé dans l'Escriture pour cela.
che Iob & souuerain tout ensemble, accordant
les Procez de ses suiets à la porte des Temples, &
luy donne plus de loüanges pour ces actions,
que pour le reste de ses qualités eminentes.

Salomon le plus sage des Roys & des hom- Salomon estimé pour cela.
mes, fut plus estimé pour cette qualité de Iuge
doux & pacifique, que pour toutes ses autres vertus; c'est ce qui attira les testes Couronnées, la
Reyne de Saba, à luy venir faire hommage au
pied de son Trosne; c'est ce Iugement & cét expedient d'Arbitre, qui appaisa les deux meres sur
le partage de l'enfant, qui luy a fait meriter les
loüanges de tous les siecles, qui ont passé, & de
tous ceux qui les suiuront, cette seule action a
plus receu d'eloges, que toutes les victoires, &
les triomphes des Conquerans.

Et ainsi que personne ne croye, que la quali- S. Louys accordoit les procez.
té d'Arbitre, soit au dessous de luy : S. Louis l'vn
des plus grands de nos Roys, en faisoit profession
particuliere, l'histoire le dépeint prenant vn plai-
sir singulier à rendre Iustice à ses peuples, & a
trouuer des expediens pour accommoder leurs
differens, il se dépoüilloit de la qualité de Souue-

rain, pour prendre celle d'Arbitre.

Enfin tous ces grands saints & ces grands Prelats, dont parle nostre Histoire, ont tout quitté, pour trauailler à ce saint exercice.

Apres cela tout le monde doit tenir à honneur cette qualité d'Arbitre, & de mediateur Charitable, graces à Dieu il y en a, par tout le Royaume, d'eminens en dignité & en vertu qui s'y addonnent ; à Paris entr'autres, nous en auons trois celebres, qui ont passé par les premieres charges de l'Estat, Messieurs *de Morangi*, *de Boucherat*, *& le Nain* ; leur maison est ouuerte à tout le monde, leur vertu a esleué chez eux le tribunal de la Paix, leur capacité, leur bonté, & leur patience, adoucit les cœurs les plus animés, & trouue des expediens pour terminer les differens les plus difficiles, si leur exemple est suiuy par tout le Royaume, & que chacun dans sa condition imite ces grands hommes, ce monstre de Chicane sera bientost estouffé, pour iamais ne renaistre.

CHAP.

CHAPITRE XVIII.

Que l'an 1610.

Henry IV. ordonna qu'il seroit estably vne Assemblée de Consultans & Arbitres Charitables, d'Aduocats & Procureurs, dans toutes les Cours & Iurisdictions du Royaume, qui prendroient soin des affaires des pauures gratuitement.

Que M. le Chancelier de Sillery, auoit cét establissement fort à cœur.

Qu'il conuia M. Lauiorrois Conseiller au Parlement de Thoulouze, d'écrire sur cette matiere, qu'il le fit, & l'Imprima,

La cause qui a empesché cét establissement par toute la France.

Qu'on l'a fait en Prouence, qu'il est facile de le faire dans le reste du Royaume, sans qu'il en couste rien au Roy, ny au peuple.

Les grands biens que cela produira.

CE Grand Prince Henry IV. auoit des entrailles de commiseration pour tous ses Suiets, principalement pour les pauures qui sont exposés aux iniures des grands, dont il disoit que les Roys sont principalement les Tuteurs & Deffenseurs, & dont Dieu leurs demandera vn compte

Ff

plus exacte, *au iour terrible de ses Iugements,* pour se seruir des termes de l'Apostre : le dessein de ce bon Prince à ce que nous dit son grand Confi-dent & Ministre, estoit à son retour des guerres d'Allemagne, de publier la reformation de la iu-stice, qui estoit toute dressée pour cela, & que ce grand Roy auoit luy mesme corrigée & apostillée de sa main.

M. de Sul-ly dans ses memoires

Mais voyant que la foiblesse des pauures ne pouuoit pas attendre vn remede si long, auant de partir pour cette guerre, le 6. Mars 1610. il ordonna qu'on establiroit dans toutes les Cours & Iurisdictions du Royaume, vn Conseil d'Ad-uocats & Procureurs charitables qui prendroient soin des Procez des pauures gratuitement, & les poursuiuroient sans en rien prendre, & la bonté paternelle de ce grand Prince, promit de don-ner des gages & des priuileges à ces Ministres cha-ritables pour recompense de leurs peines.

Henry IV a ordonné vn conseil d'Auocats & Procu-reurs Cha-ritable en chaque Iurisdictiõ pour def-fendre les pauures gratuite-ment.

M. de Sillery digne Chancellier d'vn tel Prin-ce, auoit cét establissement si fort à cœur, que pour en aduancer l'execution, il pria M. l'Au-jorrois Conseiller au Parlement de Thoulouze, qui estoit animé du mesme zele que luy, de vou-loir traiter cette matiere, ce qu'il fit, en ladite an-née 1610. & la fit imprimer.

M. le Châ-celier de Sillery le souhaitoit passionne-ment, & pria M. Lauiorrois Conseiller d'en faire vn traité.

Le demon ennemy du repos de la France nous enleua cét Incomparable Monarque deux mois apres, par vne mort funeste & precipitée, qui arresta le cours de l'execution de ce dessein charitable; & les guerres du dedans & du dehors du Royaume, qui ont affligé la France du depuis, l'ont empesché iusques à present.

Mort de Henry IV. empescha l'executió

Mais nous voicy au siecle des miracles, nostre Inuincible Monarque à qui le Ciel a reserué l'execution des grands desseins de son Ayeul, a donné la paix au dedans du Royaume, & fait trembler ses ennemis au dehors, & en mesme temps il trauaille à cette reformation de la chicane tant desirée de tous les peuples ; les pauures doiuent esperer & les foibles, qu'il songera aussi particulierement à eux, & en effet, à moins qu'on n'establisse cette Assemblée d'Aduocats & Procureurs, Consultans & Arbitres charitables, il y a à craindre que les pauures ne gousteront point les doux fruits de cette reformation, ils sont dépoüillez de tous biens, dénuez de tout secours, leur foiblesse est si grande qu'ils ne leur sert de rien d'estre au bord de la Piscine, si nostre Prince medecin charitable de tous nos maux, ne leurs donne vn homme qui les iette dedans.

Cela est reserué à nostre Roy

La reformation de la iustice inutile aux pauures, si le Roy n'establit ce Conseil Charitable & pourquoy

En voicy vn bel exemple qui a donné lieu à ce deſſein de l'Aſſemblée du conſeil charitable de la Parroiſſe de S. Sulpice dont nous auons parlé cy-deuant, c'eſt vn pere malheureux & infortuné, qui s'eſt dépoüillé de tous ſes biens en faueur d'vn fils vnique, qui le laiſſe mourir de faim, & perir de miſeres, ſur vne poignée de paille, agé de quatre vingt cinq ans.

Vn pere malheu-reux, abā donné par ſon fils, apres luy auoir don-né tous ſes biens. Ce Pere eſtoit marchand à Paris, pour mieux marier ce fils, il luy donna tous ſes biens, qui ſe montoient à plus de dix huit mille liures, il retint ſeulement les meubles d'vne chambre, vne ſom-me pour viure, & l'obligea de payer 6. ou 7. cents liures de debtes ſeulement qu'il y auoit dans la maiſon.

Ce fils ingrat & denaturé fit empriſonner ſon pere ſous le nom d'vn creancier, enleua tous ſes meubles, ſous pretexte de les conſeruer, & a refuſé de luy payer la ſomme ſtipulée pour ſa penſion; il y a 4. ans qu'il ne la payée.

Ce pauure pere ainſi nud & abandonné, de-manda ſecours à la Iuſtice, il obtint 3. Senten-ces au Chaſtelet; ce fils malheureux ſe porta ap-pellant, il eſt débouté par 2. Arreſts contradi-ctoires, il s'oppoſe à l'execution, le pere en a ob-tenu dix autres, mais ce fils indigne de voir le

iour,

iour, pour rendre tous ces Arrests illufoires, comme tous fes biens font en meubles, & qu'il ne craint, que la contrainte par corps, il s'en eft allé dans vne Prouince efloignée, & y a fait des acquets fous le nom de fes enfans, qui font encore au berceau, & ce pauure pere âgé de 85. ans, eft refté nud & moribond, il y a 4. ans fur vne poignée de paille: pour tous biens, on ne luy voit qu'vn fac plain de papiers, & douze arrefts dans vne main, mais dans l'autre il n'a pas de pain.

Le pere obtient 12. Arrefts, que le fils rend illufoire.

Qu'elle illufion à la Iuftice ? quelle honte à la Chicane de noftre France ? tout eft plein de Iuges, & ce pauure pere malheureux & infortuné, ne trouue point de fecours contre ce fils ingrat; fi le deffein de Henry IV. eftoit executé, s'il y auoit en chaque ville vne affemblée de ces Aduocats & Procureurs Charitables, ce pere feroit fecouru, & cent mille autres miferables comme luy, qui gemiffent par toute la France.

L'affemblée par exemple du Confeil Charitable de Paris, écriroit à celuy de la ville, ou ce fils malheureux, qui fuit fon pere & le iour s'eft allé cacher, on l'arrefteroit prifonnier, & il payeroit; bien plus de cent Procez de cette nature, ou autres vexations pareilles, que l'on fait aux foibles, la feule crainte de cette affemblée en empefche-

Si l'ordonnance de Henry IV. eftoit executée par tout, le riche n'oferoit vexer le pauure.

Gg

roit, quatre vingt dix; celuy qui attaque, qui
efpere tirer auantage, de la pauureté de fon ennemy, ne l'oferoit faire voyant ces affemblées efta-
blies, il fçauroit, qu'il n'a plus à combatre le
bras foible du pauure, qu'il eft fouftenu de la
main toute Puiffante du Prince, que c'eft lutter
contre la force de l'Ange.

Il n'eft rien plus facile, que d'eftablir ces Aduocats & Procureurs Charitables dans toutes les
Cours & Iurifdictions du Royaume, cela fe peut
fans qu'il en coufte rien au Roy ny au peuple,
& fans rien prendre du pauure, le deffein de Henry IV. auffi liberal, que Charitable, eftoit de
leur donner des gages, & ce feroit le mieux,
mais l'eftabliffement fe peut fort bien faire fans
cela.

1. Le nombre des affaires ne fera pas fi grand
comme il paroift d'abord, tous les riches comme
nous auons dit, qui attaquent dans l'efperance
de tirer aduantage de la foibleffe du pauure, ne
le feront pas.

2. Grand nombre de leurs procez, plus d'vn
tiers ou vne moitié, on peut dire quafi tous, s'ac-
commoderont à l'amiable dés leur naiffance, faifant ce que nous auons dit cy-deuant; vn Chreftien & fur tout le pauure doit tafcher de confer-

Tous les
procez
quafi des
pauures
s'accorde-
ront; le

uer ſes intereſts , ſans venir aux aigreurs du procez , pour cela comme en entrant dans les Hoſpitaux , la Confeſſion precede les autres aſſiſtances
qu'on y reçoit, il ſera bon que le conſeil charitable commence par vne ſommation d'Arbitrage,
& pour empeſcher auſſi que le riche ne ſe plaigne
qu'il eſt vexé , & accablé par la puiſſance de ce
conſeil, & ainſi il y aura bien peu de gens riches
qui ne conſentent auec ioye à l'accommodement,
le pauure ſouſtenu de ce Conſeil ſera plus fort
que luy & que les plus grandes puiſſances ; dans
toutes les Villes , dans tous les Tribunaux du
Royaume, ils auront des Protecteurs, des Aduocats & Procureurs charitables & gratuitement, &
qui s'y employeront auec plus de zele & de diligence qu'ils ne feroient pour leurs propres affaires, ce que l'on fait volontairement & par principe de charité on le fait tout le mieux que l'on
peut.

 Les Riches quelques puiſſans qu'ils puiſſent
eſtre n'ont pas cét aduantage hors de leurs pays,
ils ont peine à auoir habitude & connoiſſance, &
ſur tout gens fidels & affectionnez, s'il faut aller
au loin, ils ne le peuuent qu'auec peine & dépenſe, & abandonnans la maiſon ou il y a touſiours quelque choſe d'vtile à faire pour eux, &
ainſi il n'y aura quaſi point de Riche, qui voyant
le pauure ſouſtenu , ne conſente de bon cœur

Marginal note: riche n'o-
ſeroit re-
fuſer ces
Aſſem-
blées.

à l'accommodement.

3. Si ce font deux pauures qui fe plaident,
on les accommodera quand ils ne le voudroient
pas.

4. Outre cela les pauures ont nombre de
procez qui ne font pas bons, les gens fans biens
fouuent s'attachent à des efperances, dont ils ne
veulent pas démordre, tourmentent les riches, &
perdent le temps qu'ils deuroient employer à gaigner leur vie ; l'Affemblée de ces Confultans charitables remediera à ce defordre, s'ils refufent de
s'accommoder, on les abandonnera, s'ils y con-
fentent le riche aura la paix, & le pauure le
temps de gaigner fa vie.

5. Et ainfi l'on void qu'il reftera bien peu de
procez à pourfuiure, toute la peine quafi de cette
Affemblée charitable fera pour des Confultations
& des Arbitrages ; Cependant pour les procez
qu'il faudra pourfuiure, cela fe pourra fans rien
débourcer, & mefme profit en viendra à ces dignes Aduocats & Procureurs, comme ie diray
cy-apres. 1. on ne pourfuiura point de procez
qu'on n'aye bien confulté, & qu'on n'aye trou-
uez bons, apparemment les procez eftans bons &
bien inftruits, on n'en perdra guere, & partant
la Partie du pauure fera condamnée aux dépens,

&

& ainſi on ſe remboursera des aduances qu'on aura faites , 2. Voicy vn moyen pour ne rien auancer , il n'y a d'ordinaire argent à débourſer qu'aux Huiſſiers , aux Greffiers ou Receueurs des Épices , ils peuuent faire credit que le Procez ne ſoit iugé , ils ſçauent qu'ils ne tireroient aucun profit du Procez du pauure, s'il n'eſtoit pourſuiuy, qu'il ne le ſera pas, s'il n'eſt aſſiſté de quelqu'vn, qu'il ne le peut eſtre, s'ils n'y contribüent par leur facilité, en donnans terme & credit; cela eſtant , il n'y a rien à débourcer. 3. On pourroit faire quelque choſe de mieux, que toutes ces expeditions ſe donnaſſent gratis, comme on fait pour les Hoſpitaux , neantmoins il faut que tout le monde viue, puis que tout a eſté rendu venal ; & ainſi cela peut ſuffire de donner terme & credit, attendant que le Procez ſoit iugé.

Rien à débourſer aux Aduocats, & Procureurs charitables, & comment.

6. Pour recompenſe à ces Aduocats & Procureurs charitables , 1. Comme on ne pourſuiura point de Procez qu'on n'aye conſulté, & trouué bon , & qu'apparemment on gagnera , on ſera rembourſé de ſes peines & écritures, par la partie qui aura perdu ; cela eſt iuſte, chacun doit viure de ſon trauail ; outre cela , pour le temps que l'on donnera aux Conſultations & Arbitrages : le Roy peut donner des priuileges & des graces comme il a fait

Priuileges deſdits Aduocats, & Procureurs charitables.

H h

à des Directeurs d'Hospitaux, exemption de Tutelle & Curatelle, logement de Gens de Guerre;
exemption du Guet & de Garde, d'arriere-Ban,
ou tels autres que le Prince iugera plus à propos,
enfin on ne peut trop recompenfer ces ouuriers
charitables.

Priuileges
de ceux de
Venife. A Venife, cette Republique fi bien ordon-
née, le miracle de la police de l'Europe, on eft
allé bien plus loin, car outre ces Aduocats &
Procureurs charitables, on commet d'illuftres
Magiftrats, qui font les Tuteurs & Curateurs
des pauures, & cét employ eft fi honorable parmy eux, qu'il eft recompenfé de l'authorité Souueraine, de l'entrée de leur Senat ; & ainfi fi le
Roy le iuge à propos, les Aduocats qui auroient
vingt années de ce feruice charitable, pourroient
auoir entrée dans les Parlemens, en qualité de
Confeillers honoraires ; c'eftoit l'auis de M. Lauiorrois Confeiller de Thouloufe, qui a traitté
cette matiere à fonds ; & les Procureurs qui auroient rendus de pareils feruices pourroient eftre
honorés de l'entrée dans les maifons de Villes,
en qualité d'Echeuins ; outre cela cét employ
leur fera nombre d'amis qui leur rendront de
bons offices à eux & à leur famille, leur reputation & leur eftime fera connuë de tout le monde, cela fera que les riches leurs adrefferont leurs

affaires ; dont gr|and profit leurs viendra.

Mais fur tout ils auront cette recompenfe fo-
lide, dont on eft payé content faifant les bonnes
actions, cette ioye que reffentent les ames Charitables, & qui eft inconneuë aux ames dures &
ingrates, enfin on trauaillera pour le Ciel, pour
ce Dieu liberal dont les promeffes ne font point
trompeufes, qui pour la moindre action, qu'on
aura faite pour luy & pour les pauures, *qu'il ap-*
pelle fes membres, promet des richeffes qui ne ta-
riront jamais,

Et ainfi il ne refte qu'à noftre bon Roy d'eftablir ces Affemblées d'Aduocats & Procureurs
Charitables, il trouuera des Ouuriers par tout,
qui s'y offriront auec ioye, Il ne refte qu'à ces glorieux Miniftres, qui l'aident fi dignement à gouuerner l'Eftat, à luy infpirer cette fainte penfée, il ne refte qu'à M. le Chancellier à y contribuer pour immortalifer fa gloire à iamais ; & afin
auffi que la France à iamais fe fouuienne des obligations qu'elle aura à noftre Incomparable Monarque, il fera bon de dreffer des reglemens pour
la conduite de ces Affemblées, qui fe lieront de
6. mois en 6. mois, & que ces Reglemens portent
à la tefte, l'Ordonnance & le nom Illuftre de noftre grand Prince Louys X I V.

Et ainſi à iamais la France ſe ſouuiendra de ſa
Charité paternelle, à iamais ſon nom ſera beny
& ſera en veneration à tous les peuples ; les foibles, les oppreſſez, les veufues, les orphelins, ces
pauures gens opprimées, ou par la puiſſance,
d'vn Gouuerneur, ou d'vn grand Seigneur, ou
d'vn homme de robbe, ou d'vn petit tyran de
gentilhomme : enfin toutes ces ames deſolées &
abandonnées, dont la France eſt pleine, auront
recours à ces Aſſemblées, à ces aziles aſſeurés,
que la main Charitable de noſtre Prince leurs aura
dreſſées, ce ſera l'ancre ſacrée, qui les ſauuera
du naufrage : & pour le payement d'vn
action ſi heroïque, il aura la recompenſe, que
promet l'Apoſtre, *le comble de toutes les ioyes*, dont
la durée n'aura point de fin.

CHAP.

CHAPITRE XVI.

Reglemens de l'Affemblée de Parroiffe de S. Sulpice à Paris, qui prend foin des pauures honteux; & qui a formé le deffein, de prendre auffi le foin de leurs Procez, pour tâcher à les accorder à l'amiable.

La caufe & la fin de çette Affemblée.

NOus auons déja parlé de cette Affemblée dans les Chapitres precedens, ce n'eft que l'ombre, la figure, & vn crayon imparfait de ces Affemblées d'Aduocats & procureurs Charitables que Henry IV. auoit deffein d'eftablir, car ceux cy auroient l'authorité du prince, & feroient armées pour parler auec vn ancien, *du glaiue tranchant des loix*, à qui les puiffances ne peuuent & n'ofent refifter; mais les Affemblées particulieres de paroiffe, de quelques ouuriers Charitables ne trauaillent qu'auec crainte, ils font expofés à la cenfure, aux railleries, à la médifance & aux calomnies de tout le monde, ils reffemblent à ces pauures Difciples bien intentionnez, mais timides, qui ne marchoient qu'en cachette, (*Clam propter mecum Iudæorum*) cependant ces

Ii

Assemblées sont capables de faire vn grand bien attendant qu'il plaise au bras tout puissant de nostre Prince, d'establir celles de son ayeul, dont les fondements ne pourront estre ébranlés.

La cause del'Assemblée qui prend soin des procez des pauures, & qui les accommode à l'amiable.

Voicy donc ce qui a donné lieu à celle de la Parroisse de S. Sulpice, l'Assemblée des pauures honteux vit que l'année derniere 1665. elle en auoit assisté 4. à 5. mille, dont la pluspart estoient tombez dans l'extreme pauureté, par le malheur du Procez & de la chicane, & ce qui estoit de plus déplorable, grand nombre d'eux, auoient quitté l'vsage des Sacremens, & n'en vouloient plus approcher, auoüans qu'ils auoient l'ame pleine de fiel, de hayne, & d'animosité mortelle contre leur parties, & ne pouuoient leur pardonner, qu'ils les regardoient comme les autheurs de leur ruine, & la cause funeste de leur pauureté, de leur honte, de leur souffrance, & de toutes les miseres, qui accompagnent vne famille ruinée.

Personne au comencemét, n'en vouloit estre.

Monsieur le Curé qui aime aussi tendrement le moindre de ses Parroissiens, comme le pere le plus passionné aimeroit son fils vnique, il conuia & coniura l'Assemblée des pauures honteux de chercher remede à de si grands maux; la grandeur de l'entreprise estonna d'abord tout le monde, il n'y a quasi personne en France, qui aye du bien, qui n'aye Procez ; qui n'en veut point faire, on luy en fait, le moindre est long, lent, couageux, & penible, chacun donc iugeant de la difficulté de l'entreprise par sa propre experience, la croyoit impossible, & d'abord personne ne s'y vouloit embarquer.

Mais enfin la Charité l'emporta, ce pauure pere vint en auant dont nous auons parlé, qui demanda du secours contre ce fils ingrat, qui la dépoüillé de tous ses biens, & qui le laisse perir de faim, de froid & de miseres, sur vne poignée de paille, moribond, âgé de quatre vingt cinq ans ; cet objet émeut les cœurs les moins tendres, M. le Curé se seruit de l'occasion, son zele aussi grand que celuy des Pasteurs de l'Eglise naissante, aussi grand que celuy de nostre bon Curé S. Yues, échauffa les plus tiedes, il eut deux illustres seconds, M. de Couder & D'acol, qui le soulagent d'vne partie des fonctions penibles & Charitables de sa Cure.

Enfin l'Assemblée de ces pauures honteux, resolut de prendre soin de leurs Procez, & sur tout de chercher les moyens de les accorder à l'amiable ; dés que cette resolution fut prise, & quelle fut sçeüe, comme la nature fait de grands efforts, pour remedier aux grands maux, il accourut pour trauailler à ce saint ouurage, vne foule illustre de

Les persōnes illustres qui composent l'Assemblée.

personnes eminentes en qualité, & en toutes fortes de vertus; des Ducs & Pairs, des cordons bleus, des Lieutenans de Roy dans les Prouinces, des premiers officiers de la maison du Roy, des Marquis, des Presidens actuellement seruans, des Conseillers, des Aduocats mesme & des Procureurs, des Conseillers d'Estat, & des Maistres des Requestes & enfin des personnes eminentes qui ont esté Ambassadeurs & vn grand nombre de toute sorte d'autres personnes Charitables, leurs noms sont rapportés sur le registre de l'Assemblée.

Les Iuges ont promis d'appuyer le dessein. Monsieur le Bailly de S. Germain, qui est seul Iuge de ce Faux-bourg là, aussi grand qu'vne des plus grandes villes du Royaume, témoigna sa ioye, & fit offre de ses seruices, qu'il appuiroit & seconderoit ce bon dessein, toutes les fois qu'il en seroit requis; ce bon Iuge éclairé & animé de Charité, sçait qu'on ne perd rien pour assister les foibles, que les Magistrats ne tirent pas grand profit des Procez des pauures, qu'ils ne peuuent les poursuiure faute d'argent, qu'on se déchargera de leurs importunités, quand on les accommodera à l'amiable, & qu'enfin quand il y auroit quelque chose à perdre, que le Dieu de Charité est celuy des richesses, qu'il a dépoüillé Saül pour son auarice, & comblé Salomon de biens pour sa liberalité, & sa magnificence dans ce baftiment

baftiment fuperbe de fon Temple; à plus forte raifon ceux qui deffenderont les pauures qui font fes membres.

Si dans toutes les villes du Royaume il y auoit de ces Affemblées Charitables, voilà vn port affeu-ré, au foible, au miferable & à l'opprimé; il eft facile d'en eftablir fi N O S S E I G N E V R S les Euefques ont la bonté de s'en mefler, quafi par tout leur Charité a eftably des Affemblées de Par-roiffe, qui prennent foin des pauures honteux & des malades; les conuier d'imiter l'exemple de la Par-roiffe de S. Sulpice, nombre de perfonnes intelligen-tes fe ioindront à eux, conuier auffi Mrs les Curés de fuiure les traces de c'eft illuftre Curé de Paris, fi dans leur villes il n'y a point de ces Affemblées pour les pauures honteux, on ne laiffera pas d'y pou-uoir eftablir celles de ce Confeil Charitable, & dans les villes & dans les Parroiffes de la Cam-pagne, par tout il y a quelque perfonne bien in-tentionnée, toute prefte d'eftre Ambaffadeur de Paix, quand on l'aura inftruit; & qu'il fera fe-condé, il ne faut pas grande capacité pour cela comme nous auons dit, il ne faut qu'vn peu de bonne volonté, la charité eft fimple, & neant-moins fes termes font forts, & perfuadent; qui ne fera pas capable de iuger la difficulté, peut eftre Mediateur, il fera conuenir d'Arbitres, & l'a fera

Les Euef-ques peu-uent faire de fembla-bles Affem-blées dans leurs Dio-ceses.

Kk

decider par d'autres, & ainſi par tout on pourra
trouuer de ces Ouuriers de Paix, qui ſeconderont
dignement les bonnes intentions de NOSSEI-
GNEVRS les Eueſques & de Meſſieurs nos
Curez, iuſqu'à ce qu'il aye pleu à noſtre grand
Prince d'eſtablir ces Aſſemblées d'Aduocats & procureurs charitables de ſon Illuſtre Ayeul Henry IV.

●Ce ſera pour lors qu'on pourra dire de noſtre
inuincible Monarque, que ſa bonté aura eſleué
cette forphereſſe dans la maiſon d'Iſraël, pour la protection du foible, que toute la malice des hommes
ne pourra renuerſer.

CHAPITRE XVIII.

La Subſtance des Reglemens de ladite Aſſemblée.

IE ne mettray icy, que ce qui peut ſeruir pour
les Prouinces, pour n'eſtre pas long, & parce
que ſouuent, ce qui eſt bon à Paris, ne l'eſt pas
ailleurs, chacun doit faire ſes reglemens ſuiuant
l'humeur & la neceſſité des pays ou l'on eſt, ie
me contenteray donc de repreſenter l'eſprit de
celle de Paris.

1. Le deſſein eſt d'empeſcher tant que l'on

pourra, que le pauure ne perde pas son temps à plaider, afin qu'il puisse employer ce temps à gagner sa vie.

2. Pour y paruenir auant de luy donner aucune assistance, on luy demandera s'il consent de s'accommoder à l'amiable, au cas que sa Partie le veuille, s'il le refuse, on l'abandonnera.

3. Si le Procez n'est pas intenté, auant de le commencer, on priera sa Partie de vouloir s'accommoder, si elle y consent on nommera des Arbitres.

4. Si les Arbitres pris de l'Assemblée des pauures sont suspects au riche, le pauure en nommera d'autres.

5. On obligera le pauure à se tenir à vne Sentence Arbitrale, & iamais on ne l'assistera pour la suite de l'appel, si le grief n'estoit plus clair que le iour.

6. Si la Partie du pauure refuse l'accommodement, pour oster au riche tout pretexte de plainte, qu'on le vexe, qu'on le tourmente; le pauure luy fera notifier vne declaration par deuant Notaires, par laquelle il le priera d'auoir compassion de sa foiblesse, exposera comme il l'a déja fait prier de s'accommoder à l'amiable, qu'il l'en prie encore, & luy declarera, que quand il luy plaira,

dans tous les endroits du Procez, que luy pauure, sera touſiours preſt de venir à vn accommodement.

7. Le Procez du pauure s'il ſe trouue mauuais, & qu'il ſoit mis en Arbitrage, les Arbitres le condamneront ſans en auoir pitié, Dieu l'ordonne (*pauperis non miſereberis in iudicio*) leur Procez ſouuent ne ſont pas bons, des gens ſans biens, s'attachent à des eſperances, dont ils ont peine à démordre.

Exod. c. 13

8. Si au contraire leur Procez ſe trouuent bon, il ne faudra pas tirer tout à la rigueur, il ſera bon de ſe relâcher & faire remiſe d'vne partie, qui veut tout auoir, ſouuent n'a rien, & puis le pauure eſt bien heureux d'auoir la meilleure partie de ſon deu & qu'on luy procure la Paix, & du temps pour trauailler & gagner ſa vie, s'il n'eſtoit ſecouru d'ordinaire il n'en tireroit rien.

9. Outre cela ſi on vouloit tirer tout à la rigueur, on feroit peu d'accords; pour vn, ſe relâchant vn peu on en fera cent.

10. Les Procez qu'on n'aura peu accorder, auant de les pourſuiure, on les conſultera à 3. Aduocats des plus celebres des lieux, ſi on les trouue bons, on les addreſſera aux Aduocats & Procureurs de l'Aſſemblée, & on leur répondra des frais, pour que

que ladite Affemblée n'aye pas befoin de faire des auances.

11. On aura vn Procureur & vn Aduocat au fiege du lieu, & au Parlement du reffort, on les payera de leurs vacations tout du long, s'ils ne veulent volontairement faire quelque remife, l'épargne d'vne partie des frais n'eft pas confiderable au prix d'vne prompte expedition, & le payement y contribuë.

12. Les Procez des pauures qui feront bons, & bien inftruits, apparemment on n'en perdra guerre, pour ceux que l'on gagnera, le Procureur fera payé de fes frais & de fes auances par la partie du pauure, qui aura perdu.

13. Mais comme les meilleurs Procez fe perdent quelquefois, les frais fe pourront prendre fur ceux qu'on aura gagné, on alloüe en taxé des voyages ou diuertiffemens, que le pauure n'aura pas fait, qui aura efté affifté, le mieux feroit que l'Affemblée payant ces frais; mais dans les Prouinces, il y a nombre de perfonnes bien intentionnées, qui tous ne font pas riches, qui pourront auoir enuie de former ces faintes Affemblées, pour le fecours du pauure, & qui pourroient en eftre diuertis par la crainte de la dépenfe.

LI

14. Dans les grandes villes, il fera bon d'auoir vn Solliciteur à gages, & le payer graffement, l'affection & la diligence aide à terminer promptement les affaires, fur tout celles qu'on accommodera à l'amiable, dont le nombre fera grand, vn pauure qui meurt de faim, ou le foible qui fouffre oppreffion, ne voudroit il pas maintenant trouuer vn Solliciteur affectionné, à qui on ne donnera qu'vn petit payement apres l'affaire gagnée ?

15. Ces Affemblées auront vn Secretaire, qui tiendra regiftre des deliberations, les placets, que les pauures prefenteront, feront diftribués, & leurs affaires examinées auant d'en parler à l'Affemblée.

16. On s'affemblera de 15. iours en 15. iours chez le Curé du lieu, du moins en fa prefence, ou de quelque Ecclefiaftique commis de fa part, qui prefidera, & prendra les voyes de rang fans diftinction de qualités, la charité rend tout le monde égal, & les grands s'efleuent en s'abaiffans. Ces perfonnes illuftres de Paris, qui font des premiers de l'Eftat, le font dignement dans ces Affemblées de Charité.

17. NOSSEIGNEVRS les Euefques feront conuiés faifans leurs vifites, de faire la gra-

ce de visiter aussi ces Assemblées, pour réchauffer
& animer leur zele.

18. Enfin ces M^rs qui voudront assister les pauures, se souuiendront sur tout, qu'ils trauaillent
pour ce Dieu pacifique, qui est aussi *le Dieu doux
& humble*, que le bon seruiteur imite le Maistre,
& ainsi ils prendront bien garde de ne rien dire,
ny rien faire, qui puisse offencer les parties, ou
les Iuges des pauures.

19. Et pour conclusion, ces Ouuriers Charitables, doiuent se preparer à souffrir patiemment les
iniures, les reproches, & les ingratitudes des riches & des pauures; il y a long temps que l'Apostre nous a dit, qu'icy bas, Dieu ne promet que
persecution à ceux qui suiuent la pureté de l'Euan-   Math.
gile (*persecutionem patientur*, mais en reuange ce mes-   cap. 5.
me Apostre, promet dans les Cieux, cette recom-
pense dont la durée n'aura point de fin) *merces
vestra copiosa est in Cœlis.*

CHAPITRE. XXIV.

Que l'accord des Procez empéchera grand nombre
de Duels.

DAns les Prouinces quasi tous les Duels, viennent de ces querelles, de ces haines & animositès, que causent les Procez animés de la noblesse, pour ces droits honorifique de Fiefs, Iurisdictions, Préeminences, droits de chasse &c. entre voisins quand il y a Procez on est tousiours en guerre, on a son ennemy à la porte, quand les maistres seroient sages, les valets ne le seront pas, il y aura tousiours quelque démelé entre eux, ils se rencontrent à toute heure par les chemins, dans les Villages, & ailleurs, ils se battét, si on le dissimule, on craint d'attirer la persecution, & ainsi malgré soy il faut en venir aux mains; les amis prennent parti, d'vne querelle il s'en fait cent, & ces playes saignent long temps.

Cent exemples funestes de cela, par tout le Royaume, & pour comble de malheur, comme les Procez sont deuenus immortels en France, les haïnes & les querelles sont aussi deuenuës immortelles, il y a des familles ou les peres, grands

peres,

peres, & petits enfans, se sont battus en Duel, pour
le suiet d'vn mesme Procez, & qui n'est pas encore terminé.

Si donc on pouuoit accorder ces Procez à l'a-
miable, on empêcheroit ces querelles & ces Duels
malheureux qui les suiuent, si nos Curés & nos
Euesques ont la charité d'estre les Entremetteurs,
ils estoufferont ces monstres dans leur naissance,
toute la Noblesse le desire, les plus animés le souhaitent, & le demanderoient s'ils osoient, & si
on pouuoit sauuer les apparences.

C'est à nostre grand Roy d'acheuer son miracle, vn des plus grands de son Regne, c'est d'a-
uoir arresté le cours & la fureur de ces combats
singuliers, manie aussi vieille que la nation, qu'on
auoit succé auec le lait, & qu'on voyoit confir-
mée par l'exemple des plus vaillants; on se van-
toit d'estre descendu de ces Anciens Gaulois qui
passerent les Alpes, & qui allerent brauer les Romains iusques dans leur camp & les appeller en *Florus.*
Duel.

Et en effet à ne suiure que les mouuemens de
la nature, de tous les combats c'est le plus gene-
reux, & le plus digne de gloire; c'est pourquoy
l'Eglise & l'authorité du Prince, doiuent dautant
plus trauailler à en éloigner toutes les causes.

Iusques icy on n'a pas trouué de meilleur remede, que de faire signer à la Noblesse la Declaration du Roy contre ces combats; de mesme si

on luy faiſoit ſigner vne Declaration de n'auoir point de procez à l'auenir, que le demandeur n'offrit Arbitrage auant d'intenter ſon action, & qu'il y euſt vne amande contre le refuſant payable par prouiſion, tous ſigneroient cette Declaration auec ioye, parce que tous craignent le procez & l'apprehendent, & ainſi on les feroit ceſſer, & ces haines & ces querelles d'où naiſ-ſent les Duels.

Qu'il eſt facile d'é-pêcher ces Duels & pour ia-mais.

Ce moyen ſemble encore plus doux, & plus fa-cile dans l'execution, & deuoir eſtre de plus lon-gue durée; Car pluſieurs n'ont ſigné la Declara-tion du Roy qu'à regret, & ont peine à l'exe-cuter; & s'il arriuoit des guerres & des troubles, ou vn Prince moins ferme que le noſtre, il y auroit à craindre qu'on ne retombaſt dans l'ancienne er-reur, quand ce ne ſeroit que pour paſſer pour braue.

Mais la declaration contre le Procez, de n'en vouloir point auoir, qu'on ne termine à l'amia-ble, tous la ſigneront auec ioye, & l'executeront auec ioye, & eſtans vne fois acouſtumés à la dou-ceur de ce remede, il durera à iamais, & cette vnion, & ce bon exemple, ſeruira à empêcher les autres Duels & querelles, qui naiſſent d'autres cauſes. C'eſt pourquoy ceux qui ont l'honneur d'approcher du Souuerain, ſont priez de luy inſpi-rer ces ſentimens; le Marquis de la Motte Fenelon

Le Mar-quis de la Motte Fe-nelon, a

ſur tout y doit contribuer, luy qui a ſi dignement trauaillé, & ſi long temps, & auec vn ſuccez ſi

heureux, qu'il a perſuadé grand nombre des plus
braues de la Cour, & leurs a fait ſigner la con-
damnation de ces combats, auant que le Prince
l'euſt prononcée.

arreſté le
cours des
Duels, par
les bons
Conſeils
qu'il a
donné au
Roy.

CHAPITRE. XXV.

*Que les Prelats & grands Seigneurs qui approchent
du Prince, ſont priez de le conuier de contribuer
à l'execution des auis cy-deſſus, ſi on y
trouue quelque choſe de bon.*

CEux qui ont l'honneur d'approcher des Roys
& de ce (*Thrône de Puiſſance*) dont parle l'Eſcriture, qui fait les bonnes ou mauuaiſes deſtinées
des peuples, doiuent donner les bons Conſeils
aux Princes : Nous auons fait voir l'eſtat déplorable de la France deſolée par la chicane, par ces
longs Procez qui ruinent les familles, & ces haines & inimitiés malheureuſes qui deuorent les
Chreſtiens, nous auons fait voir que tous ſoûpi-
rent, & demandent au Ciel, & au Roy, la deſtru-
ction de ce monſtre de diuiſion & de diſcorde,
que tous ſouhaitent d'accorder leurs Procez à l'a-
miable, du moins de deux que l'vn le deſire, le plus
foible ou le plus ſage.

Nous auons fait voir encore que depuis la venalité des Charges, tous les Roys ont fait des
Edits pour abolir la chicane & abreger les Pro-

Que de-
puis la ve-
ralité des
Charges

tous les Rois ont fait des Edits pour abolir la chicane, qui n'ont pas esté executés, & pourquoy.

cez, qui n'ont point esté executés par les Iuges qui ont interrest d'y contreuenir, parce que profit leurs en vient, & qu'il y a à craindre qu'ils contreuiendront à l'auenir, par la difficulté qu'il y aura à punir les contreuenans, & à donner des fondemens si solides à la reformation, qu'ils ne puissent estre esbranlés par la negligence, l'auarice, ou la necessité des Roys qui succederont à nostre incomparable Monarque.

Que de toutes ces reformations exactes des Estats Generaux d'Orleans, de Blois &c. rien n'a esté executé que l'Edit des Iuges Consuls & pourquoy.

Enfin nous auons fait voir que de toutes ces grandes reformations de la chicane faite aux Estats Generaux d'Orleans, de Blois, Assemblées de Moulins, & depuis par Louis XIII. d'heureuse memoire, rien de tout cela n'a esté executé & n'est venu dans sa pureté iusqu'à nous, que l'establissement des Iuges Consuls (*Arbitres des Marchands*) parce que ce sont Iuges Electifs, qui iugent sans espices, sur le champ, sans Aduocats, sans Procureurs, comme font la pluspart de toutes les Nations, & quand on a voulu choquer ou supprimer les Consuls, les Marchands, les Villes les Communautés, & les Prouinces ou il y a des Estats, ont fait des supplications aux Roys & les ont maintenu, parce qu'ils y auoient interest.

Qu'il semble que si les Edits des Arbitrages estoient

De mesme, il semble & plusieurs croyent que si le Roy ordonnoit que les Edits des Roys ses Predecesseurs touchant les Arbitrages seroient executés, & qu'il ordonnast vne peine contre le
refusant

refufant, que tous les Procez quafi fe termineroient à l'amiable, dautant que la moitié des
plaideurs fouhaitent l'accord, comme nous
auons dit, & le demanderoient hardiment, & que
l'autre moitié n'oferoit le refufer à caufe de l'a-
mande qu'il faudroit payer comptant.

renouue-
lés auec
vne peine
contre le
refufant,
tous les
Procez
quafi s'ac-
corde-
roient à
l'amiable.

Par ce moyen tous ceux qui ont des Procez
indecis, s'entre-demanderoient-accord, comme les
Marchands autrefois demanderent leur renuoy deuant les Côfuls, dés que l'Edit fut publié, & qu'ainfi
en vn moment, on enuoyeroit par tout le Royaume, vne fufpenfion d'armes generale entre tous
les plaideurs, que les Palais & Tribunaux de-
uiendroient deferts, & qu'on y voiroit vn pro-
fond filence, & vne agreable folitude, & qu'enfin la malice des fiecles auenir ne pourroit rien
contre ce remede, car les peuples accouftumés à
la douceur de l'Arbitrage fi on vouloit le fuppri-
mer, feroient des fupplications aux Roys, pour
le maintenir comme les Marchands ont fait pour
le maintien de leurs Confuls : Mais ce n'eft pas à
moy d'aller fi auant, c'eft au Roy & à ces Mrs qui
trauaillent auec luy à cette glorieufe reformation
de l'Eftat, c'eft à eux à qui le Ciel diftribuë ces
viues lumieres qui font referuées à ceux (comme
dit l'Efcriture,) qui font *appellés dans le Sanctuaire.*

Ldits des
Confuls.

Neantmoins puis qu'on fouffre les fouhaits,
& les auis de ceux qui ont de bonnes intentions,

il femble que l'Arbitrage termineroit la plufpart des Procez, la nature nous l'infpire, le droit
des gens, & la pratique de tous ceux qui veulent
fuir les Palais & Tribunaux ; les petits & les
grands, les fçauans & les ignorans, fi vous auez
vn démelé vous difent, prenez vn amy qui vous
accommode.

Les Roys & les Princes conuiennent d'autres
Souuerains, qui terminent leurs guerres, qui font
les Procez des teftes Couronnées ; & enfin nos
loix, nos coûtumes, conſeillent & ordonnent
l'Arbitrage, & les focietés des Marchands par
toute la terre, l'article principal de leur maintien,
c'eſt en cas de differend que l'on conuiendra d'Arbitres.

Nous le voyons encore par experience, ce bon
Curé qui a trouué le fecret d'accorder les Procez
de fes Paroiffiens, ces bons Euefques qui accordent les leurs, & ceux de leur Dioceſe; ces grands
Seigneurs qui accommodent auffi & les leurs
& ceux de leurs voifins & vaffaux; & enfin ces
M^{rs} qui par la mefme voye accordent ceux des
pauures, témoin ce pere malheureux qui auoit
12. Arrefts inutiles, & fon fils ingrat s'eſt rendu
à vne feule parole d'vn Curé, parce qu'on a honte refufant l'accord de paffer pour vn méchant.

Si donc le Prince ordonnoit que les Edits des
Roys fes Predeceffeurs touchant les Arbitrages
feroient executés, auec vne peine contre le refufant, tout le monde coureroit ce remede, par

ce que comme nous auons dit, la moitié des
plaideurs voudroient eſtre d'accord, & l'autre
moitié ne l'auſeroit refuſer de crainte de la peine;
Ce ſeroit pour lors qu'on voiroit tout le monde
en Paix, l'Egliſe, la Nobleſſe, le Marchand, le
Payſant & Laboureur de terre, ce ſeroit lors que
la France pourroit dire, ce que Rome autrefois
diſoit d'Auguſte dans les tranſports d'eſtime quelle auoit pource Prince. *Deus nobis hæc otia fecit.* Virgil.
Il nous a donné vne PAIX profonde, il a fermé le
temple de la guerre de diuiſion & de diſcorde, Tacite
qui eſtoit le comble du bon heur parmi les Romains.

Et enfin on diroit de noſtre Roy, ce que l'Eſcriture dit d'vn grád prince, *fecit pacem super terram,*
& lætatus eſt Iſraël lætitia magna, & Seniores in ¹. Macab.
plateis ſedebant omnes, & loquebantur de bonis terræ, c. 14.
& Iuuenes induebant ſe gloriam, & ſtolas belli, &
ſedit vnus quiſque ſub ficulnea ſua & non erat qui
terreret eos; Il la fait la paix ſur la terre, dont
Iſraël s'eſt grandement rejoüie, les Viellards par-
loient du labourage & du commerce, & les Ieu-
nes le preparoient à la guerre, & vn chacun ſe
pouuoit aſſeoir en PAIX à l'ombre de ſon Figuier,
& n'y auoit perſonne qui troublât leur repos,
c'eſt à dire parmy nous, qu'il n'y auoit ny Huiſ-
ſier ny Sergent qui pût leur faire peur.

Il ne reſte donc qu'à conuier noſtre Prince de
vouloir acheuer ſon miracle, & pour y cótribuer re

noueler les Edits des Arbitrages, auec'vne peine contre le refufant qui en fera fommé; & pour les pauures vouloir eftablir ces Affemblées Charitables de fon Ayeul qui accorderont leurs Procez; on fupplie NOSSEIGNEVRS les Prelats qui ont l'honneur d'approcher de fa Maiefté de luy infpirer ces fentimens; on en fupplie M. l'Archeuefque de Paris, qui dans cette belle vie de Henry IV. a efté l'vn des premiers à dépeindre les malheurs de la chicane, & en faire efperer la guerifon; il fçait que dans cette Republique autrefois, fi bien reglée & policée, il eftoit deffendu de découurir les playes de l'Eftat, fi dans le mefme temps on ne propofoit le remede, & qu'on n'entreprit la guerifon.

M. l'Archeuefque de Paris.

On fupplie encore M. l'Euefque de Luçon de contribuer à vne fi fainte entreprife, luy qui a tant de pouuoir à la Cour, & qui trauaille auec tant de zele & de charitè, pour pacifier les Procez & differens de tous ceux de fon Diocefe: Enfin on en fupplie tous ces Prelats fages & vertueux qui approchent du Prince, qui doiuent trauailler pour faire immoler aux pieds des Autels, ces malheureufes victimes de Procez, de Duels, de haines & animofités, fi dignes d'eftre immolées, par les mains de ceux, qui offrent à Dieu tous les iours, des Sacrifices de Paix.

M. de Luçon.

FIN.

Façon du Compromis.

QVe ce bon Curé dont nous auons parlé, fait signer à ceux de sa Parroisse qui consentent de s'accommoder à l'amiable, il en porte tousiours d'imprimez auec luy, tel le signe sur le champ apres vne douce remonstrance, qui ne le signeroit apres, s'il y songeoit long temps.

· Au Compromis qui suit, & aux Sommations d'Arbitrages qui sont cy-apres, on pourra y adiouster ou diminuer ce que l'on iugera à propos suiuant l'vsage & le style du pays ou seront les parties.

Au reste le Compromis le plus court & le plus simple est le meilleur, souuent il y auroit plus de peine à dresser vn Compromis raisonné au gré des parties qui s'animent aisement, qu'à iuger l'affaire au fonds.

Compromis.

Les Soubs-signans sont demeurez d'accord de ce qui suit pour terminer à l'amiable les Procez meus ou à mouuoir entr'eux touchant l'execution de

& pour y paruenir le

sieur de   *à nommé pour*

Arbitre M^r de

& le sieur de   *à nommé*

pour Arbitre M^r de   *& pour*

... ont conuenu de M^r de

(mais s'ils n'en conuiennent pas signant le Compromis on pourra dire) *& d'vn tiers les Parties en
conuiendront cy. apres*, (& s'ils ont de la peine à conuenir d'vn, agreable aux deux Parties, le Curé, le
Mediateur ou les Arbitres le feront choisir, comme
il est dit au Chapitre xiv. du choix des Arbitres.

*Et lesd. Parties prendront assignation de Messieurs
leurs Arbitres dans*

*produiront deuant eux tous & chacuns leurs Actes, &
consigneront pour le dedit la somme de*

*pour estre baillée en cas d'appel à l'ac-
quiesçant, auec tout pouuoir qu'ils donnent ausd. sieurs
Arbitres de iuger & sententier, voulans que leur Sentence soit executée par prouision au terme de l'Ordonnance*, (si l'on a bien enuie de s'accommoder, on peut
adiouster) *voulans aussi lesd. Parties en cas d'appel, que
l'appellant ne pourra auoir ny pretendre aucuns dépens
&c. Fait par double &c.* Si l'on veut apres cela, ce
Compromis se pourra rapporter deuant Notaires,
& le mettre en forme.

Titu. ix.
des Arbitr.

Sommation d'Arbitrage.

Entre Esgaux
Il est bon quelle se fasse par des Notaires tant que
l'on pourra, & non par des Sergents pour les raisons
cy-deuant dites.
Deuant nous Notaires

a comparu en perſonne & deüement ſoubmis

qui nous a declaré que procez ſeroit meu entre luy & le
ſieur de   pour raiſon de

pour lequel Procez terminer promptement, facilement ſans peine & ſans frais, & nourrir paix, vnion &
amitié entre les Parties, comme elle doit eſtre entre des Chreſtiens, ledit ſieur declarant fait offre audit ſieur de
de conuenir d'Arbitres, & conſigner pour le dedit la
ſomme de   ſommant led. ſieur de
de declarer s'il conſent de nommer Arbitres de ſa part,
& le declarer par Acte Notarizé dans   iours, eliſant
à cette fin domicile chez   proteſ-
ſtant qu'au cas que led. ſieur refuſe l'accommodement, qu'il
ſera cauſe de tous les maux qui ſuiuent le procez, proteſtant en
outre de le rendre reſponſable de tous dommages intereſts & dépens ; de tout quoy led. ſieur declarant nous a demandé Acte,
& de vouloir nous tranſporter chez led. ſieur
(ou chez le ſieur de   ſon Procu-
reur en Cauſe) pour luy Notifier & deliurer coppie des pre-
ſentes declarations, offres & proteſtations, & a ſigné auec
nouſd. Notaires &c.
En conſequence nouſd. Notaires certifions nous eſtre tranſportés
chez led. ſieur de   ſur les   heures
de ce iour, ou y eſtant, parlant à
nous luy auons Notifié & deliuré coppie de ce que deſſus, le
ſommant d'y répondre &c.

Sommation d'vn grand à vn inferieur, adiouster à celle d'entre esgaux.

Et dautant que led. sieur   se pourroit plaindre qu'il a Procez contre plus puissant que luy, en biens, credit & amis, pour faire voir que led sieur declarant n'a pas dessein d'en tirer aduantage, & qu'on ne desire que conseruer le sien, led. sieur declarant fait offre de conuenir d'Arbitres &c.

Si c'est vn Fuesque, vn Curé, ou autre personne d'E-glise qui fait la sommation; il est bon d'y adiouster qu'on l'a fait en veuë du Ciel &c. i'en ay veu plusieurs touchez par là.

Sommation de l'inferieur à plus puissant que luy, adiouster à la Sommation d'entre esgaux.

Et dautant que la suite dud. Procez causera la ruine dud. & de sa pauure famille, qui n'a ny les biens, ny le credit, ny les amis dud. sieur led. declarant le prie & coniure pour terminer ledit procez promptement, sans peine & sans frais, d'auoir la charité de nommer des Arbitres &c.

i'ay veu ces sortes de Sommations reüssir souuent, mais il faut comme i'ay dit apres les auoir fait signifier au Procureur de l'homme puissant, les faire tenir au grand seigneur en main propre.

F I N.

TABLEAV

DES
MISERES
DV PLAIDEVR,
Pour persuader le menu Peuple.

La Robe de Cesar percée de coups , fit plus d'impression
sur le Peuple Romain , que l'Eloquence d'Antoine.

Socrate , le plus sage des Payens , crût pour persuader ;
que le chemin le plus court, estoit de plaire : Pour cela
Platon dans ses Dialogues le represente debitant ses
Maximes les plus éleuées , en riant & bouffonnant.

C'est pourquoy l'on a aussi, fait mettre icy,
la Figure qui suit.

BIBLIOGRAPHY

A

Aeschylus *Agamemnon* in Philip Vellacott *Aeschylus: the Oresteian Trilogy: Agamemnon, The Choephori, The Eumenides* Harmondsworth Penguin 1956

FRP Akehurst *The* Coutumes de Beauvaisis *of Philippe de Beaumanoir* Philadelphia University of Pennsylvania Press 1992

Michel Antoine and Yvonne Lanhers *Les Archives D'Ormesson* Paris Imprimerie Nationale 1960

Aristotle *The Art of Rhetoric* translated by Hugh Lawson-Tancred Harmondsworth Penguin 1992

B

KS Bader 'Arbiter, Arbitrator seu Amicabilis Compositor: zur Verbreitung einer Kanonistischen Formel in Gebieten Nördlich der Alpen' (1960) 46 *Zeitschrift der Savigny-Stiftung für Rechtsgeschichte: Kanonistische Abteilung* 239–76

JH Baker *An Introduction to English Legal History* 3rd edn London Butterworths 1990

Theodore Besterman ed *The Complete Works of Voltaire* Genève Institut et Musée Voltaire 1953–64; second edn by Besterman and others *Voltaire's Correspondence* Oxford Voltaire Foundation 1970–

François Billacois *Le Duel:* Paris Ecole des Hautes Etudes en Sciences Sociales 1986

—— *The Duel: Its Rise and Fall in Early Modern France* ed and tr Trista Selous New Haven Yale University Press 1990

Virginia Blain, Patricia Clements and Isobel Grundy eds *The Feminist Companion to English Literature* London Batsford 1990

André Blum *Abraham Bosse et la Société Française au XVIIe Siècle* Paris Albert Morancé 1924

Nicolas Boileau-Despréaux *Le Lutrin, Poëme Héroï-Comique de Boileaux* Paris Massin 1822 (Pt I 1674, Pt 2 1683)

PB Boucher *Manuel des Arbitres ou Traité Complet de l'Arbitrage* Paris
Arthus et Bertrand 1807
Susan Bradley ed *Archives Biographiques Françaises* London KG Saur
2nd edn 1999 microfiche
Jacques-Charles Brunet *Manuel du Libraire et de l'Amateur de Livres*
Paris Firmin Didot 5th edn 1860–65

C

*Catalogue Générale des Livres Imprimés de la Bibliothèque Nationale:
Auteurs* LXXXIX Paris Imprimerie Nationale 1926
*Catalogue des Livres Imprimés de la Bibliothèque des Avocats à la Cour
d'Appel de Paris* 2 vols Paris Durand et Pedone-Lauriel 1880–82
[Champlair] *L'Ami de la Concorde, ou Essai sur les Motifs d'Éviter les
Procès, sur les Moyens d'en Tarir la Source. Par un Avocat au Parlement*
London and Paris Monory 1779
A Charmolu *La Justice Gratuite et Rapide par l'Arbitrage Amiable*
volume 25 of *Petite Encyclopédie Sociale, Economique et Financière*
Paris 1898
Pierre Adolphe Chéruel *De l'Administration de Louis XIV (1661–1672)
d'Après les Mémoires Inédits d'Olivier D'Ormesson* Paris Joubert 1850
—— ed *Journal d'Olivier Lefèvre d'Ormesson et Extraits des Mémoires
d'André Lefèvre d'Ormesson publiés par de Chéruel* Paris 2 vols
Imprimerie Impériale 1860–61
Cicero *Pro Roscio Comoedo* in JH Freese *Cicero VI* Loeb Classical
Library Cambridge Mass Harvard University Press 1934
Pierre Clément ed *Lettres, Instructions et Mémoires de Colbert* 7 vols
Paris Didier 1861–82

D

Philippe de Beaumanoir, see Akehurst and Salmon
Armand de Conti *Mémoires de Monseigneur le Prince de Conty Touchant
les Obligations des Gouverneurs de Province et Ceux Servans à la
Conduite et Direction de sa Maison* Paris Denys Thierry 1667
—— *The Works of the Most Illustrious and Pious Armand de Bourbon,
Prince of Conti, with a Short Account of His Life &c* London W Bray
1711
De la Chenaye-Desbois et Badier *Dictionnaire de la Noblesse* Paris
Schlesinger 3rd edn 1872

GB Depping ed *Correspondance Administrative sous le Règne de Louis XIV* (Collection des Documents Inédits sur l'Histoire de France) 4 vols Paris Imprimerie Nationale 1850–55

Dictionnaire des Personnages Historiques Français Paris Bompiani 1962

Jean Domat *Les Loix Civiles dans leur Ordre Naturel* Paris Coignard 3 vols 1689–94

H Dörrie 'Leid und Erfahrung' *Abl AK Mainz Geister- und Sozialwissenschaft* Kl 1956/5

Joseph Drouet ed *L'Abbé de Saint-Pierre: Annales Politiques (1658–1740)* new edn Paris Champion 1912

E

François-Xavier Emmanuelli (ed Pierre Cardin Lebrest) *L'Intendance de Provence à la Fin du XVIIe Siècle* Paris Bibliothèque Nationale 1980

Theodore Evergates ed *Aristocratic Women in Medieval France* Philadelphia University of Pennsylvania Press 1999

F

M Fournel *Histoire des Avocats au Parlement et du Barreau de Paris depuis S Louis jusqu'au 15 Octobre 1790* Paris Maradan 2 vols 1813

G

PPB Gams *Series Episcoporum Ecclesiae Catholicae Quotquot Innotuerunt a Beato Petro Apostilo* Ratisbona Manz 1875

Charles Gavard *Versailles: Galeries Historiques* Paris Imprimerie Royale 5 vols 1838

Camilo Giardina 'I *Boni Homines* in Italia' (1932) 5 *Rivista di Storia del Diritto Italiano* 28–98, 313–94

VF Goldsmith *A Short Title Catalogue of French Books 1601–1700 in the Library of the British Museum* London Dawsons 1973

Jacques François Goubeau de la Bilennerie *Traité Générale de l'Arbitrage* Paris Renard 1827

JGT Graesse *Trésor de Livres Rares et Précieux ou Nouveau Dictionnaire Bibliographique* Milan Görlich 1950

H

AN Hamscher *The Parlement of Paris after the Fronde 1653–1673* Pittsburgh University of Pittsburgh Press 1976

Sarah Hanley *The* Lit de Justice *of the Kings of France: Constitutional Ideology in Legend, Ritual, and Discourse* Princeton Princeton University Press 1983

Lorna Hardwick *Translating Words, Translating Cultures* London Duckworth 2000

Hesiod *Works and Days* in HG Evelyn-White *Hesiod, Homeric Hymns, Epic Cycle, Homerica* Loeb Classical Library Cambridge Mass Harvard University Press revd edn1936

JCF Hoefer *Nouvelle Biographie Générale* Paris Firmin Didot 46 vols 1852–66

Horace *Epistles* in HR Fairclough *Horace: Satires, Epistles and Ars Poetica* Loeb Classical Library Cambridge Mass Harvard University Press 1955

J

GPR James *The Life and Times of Louis the Fourteenth* London Bohn 2 vols 1851

Charles Jarrosson *La Notion d'Arbitrage* Paris LGDJ 1987

Jourdan, Decrusy and Isambert eds *Recueil Général des Anciennes Lois Françaises depuis l'An 420 jusqu'à la Révolution de 1789, contenant la Notice des Principaux Monuments... et le Texte des Ordonnances etc* Paris De Plon 1822–33

Juvenal *Satire XV* in GG Ramsay *Juvenal and Persius* Loeb Classical Library Cambridge Mass Harvard University Press revd edn 1940

K

Thomas Kuehn *Law, Family and Women: Towards a Legal Anthropology of Renaissance Italy* Chicago University of Chicago Press 1991

L

Sieur de La Roche (pseud) *Lettre au Sieur Morin, Visionnaire Restaurateur de la Science Celeste; par le Sieur de la Roche* Paris Libraire de Montpellier 1655

Simeon de la Roche *Lois, Chartes et Coustumes du Chef-Lieu de la Ville de Mons* Mons L'Imprimerie de Simeon de la Roche 1663

Antoine de Laujorroys *Extraict des Principaux Points du Cinquiesme Livre de la Reformation de la Justice* Paris Vérac 1615

—— *Advis pour l'institution charitable des advocats et procureurs en faveur des vesfes, orphelins, pauvres gentilhommes, bourgeois, marchands, laboureurs et autres personnes misérables, qui, faute de conseil ou secours et assistance d'argent laissent perdre leur droicts … avec l'arrest du Conseil d'Estat, portant l'institution desdits advocats et procureurs des pauvres* Paris J Richer 1610

Arlette Lebigre *La Justice du Roi: la Vie Judiciaire dans l'Ancienne France* Paris Albin Michel 1988

Albin Lecky *A History of Greek Literature* London Duckworth 1996

NT Le Moyne des Essarts *Les Siècles Littéraires de la France ou Nouveau Dictionnaire Historique* Paris Le Moyne 1801–03

Charlotte Lennox *Memoirs of Maximilian de Bethune, Duke of Sully, Prime Minister to Henry the Great etc* 3 vols London Millar etc 1756

P de L'Estoile *Journal de Henri III, de Henri IV et de Louis XIII* new edn Paris Foucault 1826

Jean Longnon ed *Mémoires pour les Années 1661 et 1666* Paris Bossard (Collection des Chefs d'Oeuvres Méconnus) 1923

Georgius Lovetius *Notae ad Commentaria Caroli Molinari in Regulas Cancellariae Apostolicae* Paris Cramoisy 1656

Oeuvres de Charles Loyseau divisées en deux Tomes, desquels le Premier contient trois traités & le Second deux Paris Estienne Gamonet 1636 Tome I Du Droict des Offices, 3 'Des Offices Venaux', Chapter 1 'De la Vénalité des Offices' pp388-406

Charles Loyseau *Discours de l'Abus des Justices des Villages* Paris 1660 in *Oeuvres* Paris Jean Guignard 1701 repr Alibris 2001

M

NL Matthews *William Sheppard, Cromwell's Law Reformer* Cambridge Cambridge University Press 1984

Mémoires de Sully, Principal Ministre de Henri le Grand, Nouvelle Édition, plus Exacte et Correcte que les Précédents 6 vols Paris J-F Bastien 1788

M Merlin *Répertoire Universel et Raisonné de Jurisprudence. Troisième Édition, Corrigée, réduite aux objets dont la connaissance peut encore être utile, et augmentée, 1o. d'un grand nombre d'Articles, 2o. de Notes indicatives des changemens apportées aux Lois anciennes par les Lois nouvelles, 3o. de Dissertations, de Plaidoyers et de Réquisitoires de l'Éditeur sur les unes et les autres* Paris Bertin and Danel, and Garnery 1807

Roger Mettam *Government and Society in Louis XIV's France* London Macmillan 1977

LG Michaud *Biographie Universelle Ancienne et Moderne* new edn Paris Michaud 85 vols 1811–62 later edn Paris Desplaces, various dates

Jules Michelet *Histoire de France* Paris Lacroix 1874 Tome 13 'Louis XIV et la Révolution de l'Édit de Nantes'

Louis Moland ed *Oeuvres Complètes de Voltaire* Paris Garnier 1877–85

JBP Molière *The Plays of Molière in French with an English Translation and Notes by AR Waller* Edinburgh John Grant 8 vols 1926

Carolus Molinari, Georgius Louet and Antonius le Vaillant *Notae circa Rem Beneficiaram etc* Paris Cavelier 1723

Cecil Monro *Acta Cancellaria* London Benning 1847

R Mousnier *La Vénalité des Offices sous Henri IV et Louis XIII* 2nd edn Paris PUF 1971

N

National Union Catalogue Pre-1956 Imprints Mansell London 1974.

O

François Olivier-Martin *Les Lois du Roi* Paris LGDJ 1945–46 repr 1997

François Olivier-Martin *Histoire du Droit Français des Origines à la Révolution* Montchrestien Domat 1948

Bruno Oppetit *Théorie de l'Arbitrage* Paris PUF 1998

Paul Ourliac and Jean-Louis Gazzaniga *Histoire du Droit Privé Français de l'An Mil au Code Civil* Paris Albin Michel 1985

P

E Paringault 'Le Conseiller d'Etat Henri Pussort, Réhabilitation Historique' (1870) Series 4 Volume X *L'Investigateur: Journal de l'Institut Historique de France* 143–57, 167–75

Hardouin de Péréfixe *Histoire du Roi Henri-le-Grand* Paris Lecointe et Durey 1822

Jean Pierres *Commentaire sur l'Édit des Arbitres Composé par J Pierres, Lieutenant-Général de la Ville de La Rochelle* Rochelle B Berton 1564

Auguste Poirson *Histoire du Règne de Henri IV* Paris Didier 2nd edn 4 vols 1862

M Prevost and Roman d'Amat *Dictionnaire de Biographie Française* Paris Librairie Letouzey et Ané 1948

M Prevost, Roman D'Amat, H Tribout de Morembert and J-P Lobies *Dictionnaire de Biographie Française* new edn Librairie Letouzey Paris latest fascicle 1999 CXII Langumier-La Rochefoucauld April 2001

R

Orest Ranum *The Fronde: a French Revolution 1648–1652* New York Norton 1993

Recueil d'Édits et d'Ordonnances Royaux sur le Fait de la Justice et Autres Matières les Plus Importantes etc 2 vols Paris Montalant 1720

Derek Roebuck 'A Short History of Arbitration' in Kaplan, Spruce and Moser *Hong Kong and China Arbitration Cases and Materials* Hong Kong Butterworths 1994

—— 'Sources for the History of Arbitration: a Bibliographical Introduction' (1998) 14 *Arbitration International* 237–343

—— 'Captain Charles Elliot RN, Arbitrator: Dispute Resolution in China Waters 1834–1836' (1998) 14 *Arbitration International* 185–212

—— *A Miscellany of Disputes* Oxford Holo Books: the Arbitration Press 2000

—— *Ancient Greek Arbitration* Oxford Holo Books: the Arbitration Press 2001

Derek Roebuck and KK Sin 'The Ego and I and Ngo: Theoretical Problems in the Translation of the Common Law into Chinese' in Raymond Wacks ed *Hong Kong, China and 1997: Essays in Legal Theory* Hong Kong Hong Kong University Press 1993

S

Vita Sackville-West *Daughter of France: the Life of Anne Marie Louise d'Orléans Duchesse de Montpensier 1627–1693: La Grande Mademoiselle* London Michael Joseph 1959

Charles Irénée Castel de Saint-Pierre *Projet pour Rendre la Paix Perpetuelle en Europe* Utrecht Schouten 3 vols 1713–17

—— *Discours de la Polysynodie* London Tonsson 1718

—— *Mémoire pour Diminuer le Nombre des Procès* Paris Cavelier fils 1725

Amédée Salmon *Philippe de Beaumanoir: Coutumes de Beauvaisis* Paris Picard 2 vols 1899–1900 repr 1970

JH Shennan *The Parlement of Paris* 2nd edn Stroud Sutton 1998

William Sheppard *England's Balme; or Proposals by Way of Grievance & Remedy; Humbly Presented to His Highness and the Parliament: Towards the Regulation of the Law, and the better Administration of Justice. Tending to the Great Ease and Benefit of the Good People of the Nation* London William Sheppard 1656

KK Sin and Derek Roebuck 'Language Engineering for Legal Transplantation: Conceptual Problems in Creating Common Law Chinese' (1996) 16 *Journal of Language and Communication* 235–54

Paul Sonnino ed *Louis XIV King of France and Navarre: Mémoires for the Instruction of the Dauphin by Louis XIV* New York Free Press 1970

William Strahan *The Civil Law in its Natural Order together with the Publick Law, Written in French by Monsieur Domat etc* 2 vols London E Bell and others 1722

DJ Sturdy *The D'Aligres de la Rivière: Servants of the Bourbon State in the Seventeenth Century* Woodbridge Boydell Press for the Royal Historical Society 1986

—— *Louis XIV* London Macmillan 1998

T

J Techener *Bulletin du Bibliophile et Catalogue de Livres Rares et Curieux de Littérature, d'Histoire etc qui se trouvent en vente à la Librairie de J Techener* Paris Techener April 1857

Janet Todd ed *A Dictionary of British and American Women Writers 1600–1800* London Methuen 1987

—— ed *British Women Writers: a Critical Reference Guide* New York Continuum 1989

V

Pierre Varin *Archives Législatives de la Ville de Reims* Paris Crapelet 1848 Pt2 Statutes

Donald Veall *The Popular Movement for Law Reform 1640–1660* Oxford Oxford University Press 1970

Nicole Villa *Le XVIIe Siècle Vu par Abraham Bosse, Graveur du Roi* Paris Roger Dacosta 1967

CDRom *Voltaire Électronique* Oxford Voltaire Foundation and Chadwyck-Healey 1996

Index

This Glossary Index is intended to provide the reader not only with access to the text but also with a convenient alternative to looking up unfamiliar or technical words in a specialized dictionary. It also avoids the need for repetitive footnotes. Further elucidation may often be found in the larger histories of French law. The ones I have found most helpful are F Olivier-Martin *Histoire du Droit Français des Origines à la Révolution* (which has an excellent index); OF Robinson, TD Fergus and WM Gordon *European Legal History* and Jean Brissaud *A History of French Private Law*.

The index includes the introduction and the translation but not the French text. French words are in their modern forms. Words which appear on nearly every other page – arbitrator, arbitration, mediation, dispute, curé, bishop and so on – are excluded. Other terms, such as *arrest*, *avocat* and *procureur* are explained but are too frequent to be indexed.